PAUL, PHILOSOPHY, AND THE THEOPOLITICAL VISION

THEOPOLITICAL VISIONS

SERIES EDITORS:

Thomas Heilke
D. Stephen Long
and C. C. Pecknold

Theopolitical Visions seeks to open up new vistas on public life, hosting fresh conversations between theology and political theory. This series assembles writers who wish to revive theopolitical imagination for the sake of our common good.

Theopolitical Visions hopes to re-source modern imaginations with those ancient traditions in which political theorists were often also theologians. Whether it was Jeremiah's prophetic vision of exiles "seeking the peace of the city," Plato's illuminations on piety and the civic virtues in the Republic, St. Paul's call to "a common life worthy of the Gospel," St. Augustine's beatific vision of the City of God, or the gothic heights of medieval political theology, much of Western thought has found it necessary to think theologically about politics, and to think politically about theology. This series is founded in the hope that the renewal of such mutual illumination might make a genuine contribution to the peace of our cities.

RECENT VOLUMES:

The Fullness of Time in a Flat World
by Scott Waalkes

Christ, History and Apocalyptic
by Nathan R. Kerr

Redeeming the Broken Body
by Gabriel A. Santos

FORTHCOMING VOLUMES:

The Death of Secular Messianism
by Anthony Mansueto

Paul, Philosophy, and the
THEOPOLITICAL VISION

Critical

Engagements

with Agamben,

Badiou, Žižek

and Others

Edited by
DOUGLAS HARINK

CASCADE *Books* • Eugene, Oregon

PAUL, PHILOSOPHY, AND THE THEOPOLITICAL VISION
Critical Engagements with Agamben, Badiou, Žižek and Others

Theopolitical Visions 7

Cascade Books
An Imprint of Wipf and Stock Publishers
199 W. 8th Ave., Suite 3
Eugene, OR 97401

www.wipfandstock.com

ISBN 13: 978-1-60608-662-9

Cataloguing-in-Publication data:

Paul, philosophy, and the theopolitical vision : critical engagements with Agamben, Badiou, Žižek and others / edited by Douglas Harink

viii + 338 p. ; 23 cm. Includes bibliographical references and index.

Theopolitical Visions 7

ISBN 13: 978-1-60608-662-9

1. Paul, The Apostle, Saint. 2. Philosophy. 3. Agamben, Giorgio, 1942– 4. Badiou, Alain. 5. Žižek, Slavoj. I. Title. II. Series.

BS2650.52 P37 2010

Manufactured in the U.S.A.

Contents

List of Figures vii
Acknowledgments ix
List of Contributors xi

Introduction: From Apocalypse
to Philosophy—and Back · *by Douglas Harink* 1

PART I *From Apocalypse to Philosophy*

1 The Gospel Invades Philosophy · *by J. Louis Martyn* 13

PART II *Nietzsche, Heidegger, and Benjamin*

2 Living "As If Not": Messianic Becoming or the Practice
of Nihilism? · *by Travis Kroeker* 37

3 Heidegger's Paul and Radical Orthodoxy on the Structure
of Christian Hope · *by Justin D. Klassen* 64

4 The Messiah's Quiet Approach: Walter Benjamin's
Messianic Politics · *by Grant Poettcker* 90

PART III *Badiou and Žižek*

5 A Very Particular Universalism: Badiou
and Paul · *by Stephen Fowl* 119

6 Ideological Closure in the Christ-Event: A Marxist
Response to Alain Badiou's Paul · *by Neil Elliott* 135

7   Subjects between Death and Resurrection:
    Badiou, Žižek, and St. Paul · *by Geoffrey Holsclaw* 155

PART IV   *Agamben*

8   The Cross as the Fulcrum of Politics:
    Expropriating Agamben on Paul · *by Paul J. Griffiths* 179

9   Messianic or Apocalyptic? Engaging Agamben on Paul
    and Politics · *by Ryan L. Hansen* 198

PART V   *Hermeneutics, Ecclesia, Time*

10   Hermeneutics of Unbelief: Philosophical Readings
     of Paul · *by Jens Zimmermann* 227

11   On the Exigency of a Messianic Ecclesia: An Engagement
     with Philosophical Readers of Paul · *by Gordon Zerbe* 254

12   Time and Politics in Four Commentaries
     on Romans · *by Douglas Harink* 282

Bibliography 313
Index of Names 327
Index of Subject Keywords 330

Figures

1: "Paul on Mars Hill." Stained glass, Tiffany Studios,   135
19th century. Courtesy of St. Paul's on the Hill.
Photograph by Cathy Carpenter, used with permission.

2: Abu Ghraib. Online: http://commons.wikimedia.org/   142
wiki/File:Abu_Ghraib_17a.jpg.

3: Matthais Grünewald, "The Mocking of Christ" (1503).   143
Online: http://commons.wikimedia.org/wiki/
File:Gr%C3%BCnewald_Christ_Carrying_the_Cross.jpg.

Acknowledgments

This volume is the final product of a project begun in 2005 with a grant from the Council of Christian Colleges and Universities. I am grateful to the CCCU and Harold Heie for their generous support. That grant enabled me to gather a group of scholars to study the growth of interest in the apostle Paul among some recent Continental philosophers. Besides myself, the scholars in our seminar included Jeff Dudiak (The King's University College), Chris Huebner (Canadian Mennonite University), Travis Kroeker (McMaster University), Mark Reasoner (Bethel University), and Gordon Zerbe (Canadian Mennonite University). I am grateful to these marvellous colleagues for their enthusiasm and their intellectual commitment to this project. We met once a year for three years at McMaster University, where Travis Kroeker and a number of his very talented graduate and doctoral students (two of whom have essays in this volume) hosted our discussions. I am grateful to them, and to the McMaster University Department of Religious Studies, for their hospitality and generosity. I am also thankful to my own institution, The King's University College, for supporting this work in a variety of ways, not least with a series of travel grants.

Our seminars culminated in a conference, "Saint Paul's Journeys into Philosophy," held in Vancouver, British Columbia in June 2008. The essays in this volume are a selection from the many marvellous presentations at that conference. I only regret that more of those essays could not be included here. My thanks to all who presented at the conference, and to the two institutions that hosted it, Carey Theological College and Vancouver School of Theology. I am also very grateful to Steve Martin, my colleague at The King's University College, for all the work he did in creating and maintaining the Web site for that conference. Thank you to Nicole Brandsma for skilfully preparing the indexes for this volume, and to Jens Zimmermann who generously offered to fund the indexing work through his Canada Research Chair grant.

Travis Kroeker and Mark Reasoner contributed their own time and extraordinary talents to help me make the final selection of essays for this volume. They have also supported me with their encouragement and friendship. My thanks to them.

Contributors

Neil Elliott teaches biblical studies at Metropolitan State University and United Theological Seminary in the Twin Cities. Acquiring Editor in biblical studies at Fortress Press, he is the author of *Liberating Paul: The Justice of God and the Politics of Paul* (1994) and *The Arrogance of Nations: Reading Romans in the Shadow of Empire* (2008).

Stephen Fowl is Professor of Theology at Loyola College in Maryland. He has written widely about the relationships between biblical studies and theology. His recent works include a theological commentary on Philippians and the Cascade Companion to the *Theological Interpretation of Scripture* (2009).

Paul Griffiths is Warren Chair of Catholic Theology at Duke Divinity School. Among his recent publications are *Intellectual Appetite: A Theological Grammar* (2009) and "The Quietus of Political Interest" (*Common Knowledge* 15/1 [2009] 7–22).

Ryan Hansen is a PhD candidate in biblical theology at Garrett-Evangelical Theological Seminary, Evanston, Illinois, and associate pastor at Grace Fellowship Church of the Nazarene in Chicago.

Douglas Harink is Professor of Theology at The King's University College in Edmonton, Alberta. He is the author of *Paul among the Postliberals: Pauline Theology beyond Christendom and Modernity* (2003) and *1 and 2 Peter* (2009) in the Brazos Theological Commentary on the Bible.

Geoffrey Holsclaw is a PhD candidate at Marquette University, Milwaukee, Wisconson, and co-pastor of Life on the Vine Christian Community in Chicago. He is co-author, with D. Stephen Long, of "Martyrdom as Exteriority: Politics after Bare Life," in *Witness of the Body: The Past, Present and Future of Christian Martyrdom* (edited by Michael L. Budde and Karen Scott, 2009).

Justin D. Klassen is Visiting Assistant Professor of Religious Studies at Austin College in Sherman, Texas. He is co-editing a forthcoming volume of essays on the work of Charles Taylor, and revising for publication his (McMaster University) dissertation on Kierkegaard and Radical Orthodoxy. He recently published the article "Truth as a 'Living Bond': A Dialectical Response to Recent Rhetorical Theology" (*International Journal of Systematic Theology* 10/4 [2008] 431–46).

Travis Kroeker is Professor in the Department of Religious Studies, McMaster University, Hamilton, Ontario. He is co-author, with Bruce Ward, of *Remembering the End: Dostoevsky as Prophet to Modernity* (2001) and has published numerous articles on philosophy, theological ethics, and political theory.

J. Louis Martyn is Edward Robinson Professor Emeritus of Biblical Theology, Union Theological Seminary, New York. He is the author of *Galatians* (1997) in the Anchor Bible commentary series, *Theological Issues in the Letters of Paul* (1997), and *History and Theology in the Fourth Gospel* (3rd ed. 2003), as well as numerous articles on Paul and other New Testament themes.

Grant Poettcker is a PhD candidate in religious studies at McMaster University. In addition to his interest in Walter Benjamin, he is preparing a dissertation on Girard and von Balthasar.

Gordon Zerbe is Professor of New Testament at Canadian Mennonite University, Winnipeg, Manitoba. He is co-author, with Muriel Orevillo-Montenegro, of "The Letter to the Colossians," in *A Postcolonial Commentary on the New Testament Writings* (edited by R. Sugirtharajah and F. Segovia, 2007), and has published several articles on Paul's political theology.

Jens Zimmermann holds the Canada Research Chair for Interpretation, Religion and Culture at Trinity Western University, Langley, British Columbia. His recent publications are *Theologische Hermeneutik* (2008) and the edited volume *Dietrich Bonhoeffer and Continental Thought: Cruciform Philosophy* (2009).

Introduction: From Apocalypse to Philosophy—and Back

by Douglas Harink

What Paul has joined together, let no one put asunder. "God," "Messiah," "Holy Spirit," "philosophy," "apocalyptic," "political"—these terms which have so often occupied separate intellectual spaces are everywhere being thought together in the essays in this volume. And they are being thought together here because, according to most of the authors of these essays as well as the philosophers about whom they are writing—Heidegger, Benjamin, Taubes, Badiou, Žižek, Agamben—they are from the beginning intimately bound together in Paul's thought.

Except, perhaps, "philosophy." J. Louis Martyn concludes his essay in this volume with these words: "There is [for Paul] no route from any segment of philosophy to the gospel, no philosophical route to the word of the cross as God's active power." But on this, too, most of our authors and philosophers would agree. For example, Alain Badiou characterizes Paul as an "antiphilosopher" of the event; by which he means that what makes Paul of such foundational importance for philosophy is precisely that Paul's *euangelion* has no origin or foundation in philosophy. "Paul's faith is that from which he begins as a subject, and nothing leads up to it."[1] For our philosophers the unconditioned, inexplicable interruption—the messianic event—constitutes the beginning of philosophy and the very possibility of a critical political theory. "Christ is *a coming* [*une venue*]; he is what interrupts the previous regime of discourses."[2] The messianic event, as the interruption, qualification, and

---

1. Badiou, *Saint Paul*, 17.
2. Badiou, *Saint Paul*, 48 (emphasis original).

1

transfiguration of all discourses, marks the common theme of the essays of this volume. It is what our philosophers have detected as the singular contribution of Paul to philosophy and political thought, whether that event is characterized primarily in terms of resurrection (Badiou), crucifixion (Žižek), or "the messianic" (Benjamin, Agamben).

Put theologically (which is the primary discourse of most of the essays here), what creates Paul as a subject and interrupts the "previous regime of discourses" is an *apokalypsis*. Interpretations of Paul by Ernst Käsemann, J. Christiaan Beker, J. Louis Martyn, and Martinus de Boer (see the bibliography) present Paul as an apocalyptic thinker through and through. His thought revolves completely around the singular *apokalypsis Theou*, the act *of God*, who, in the crucifixion, resurrection, and exaltation of Jesus Messiah, frees humans from bondage to the enslaving powers of Sin and Death, and sends the Holy Spirit who creates the messianic community as the sociopolitical anticipation of the coming new creation. The *apokalypsis Theou* in Jesus of Nazareth and the Spirit creates and conditions all experience, thought, and action that may claim to be messianic. Most of the authors of the essays in this volume—indebted especially to J. Louis Martyn—therefore use the term "apocalyptic" to describe Paul's messianism. If Paul becomes important for philosophy and political theory, therefore, he does so through a *messianic apocalypse*, and because of it. A shocking thought! For we might consider the entire project of modern philosophy to be to render a "messianic apocalypse" absolutely unnecessary to reason: whatever such an "apocalypse" might be, it is the work of modern philosophy to restrain, contain, and explain it in terms of what comes before and conditions it, experientially, rationally, historically. But the philosophers studied here have found in Paul's apocalyptic messianism a point of departure for a fundamental criticism of modern philosophy.

I must make it clear, however, that the likes of Badiou, Žižek, and Agamben are all wary of the term "apocalyptic," taking it to signify end-time scenarios, varieties of millenarianism, perhaps even theocratic political orders, and therefore (rightly) avoiding its use with reference to Paul. Further, *apokalypsis/apokalyptō* in Paul always signifies an irreducibly *divine* act; but our philosophers (at least *qua* philosophers—although Badiou and Žižek are also explicitly and militantly atheist) studiously refrain from making any theological claims. Indeed, guided by Walter Benjamin's parable of the puppet and the dwarf, the first of his "Theses on the Philosophy of History," our philosophers are intent to keep theology out of sight. "The puppet called 'historical materialism' is to win all the time. It can easily be a match for anyone if it enlists the services of theology [the dwarf], which today, as we know, is wizened and has to keep out of sight."[3] For Agamben, for example, while Paul's explicitly *theological* writings are considered to be of crucial importance, they are thoroughly absorbed into a philosophy and political theory of the *profane* order as witnesses of "the messianic," which is itself a completely profane concept for Agamben.

> Asked in an interview why he so frequently returns to religious or theological motifs in his work, Agamben answered, "I think that it is only through metaphysical, religious, and theological paradigms that one can truly approach the contemporary—the political—situation" (PWP, 22). Agamben's interviewer then asked, "And how close does one thereby come to the doctrine of a Divinity?" to which Agamben replied:
>
>> My books . . . are confrontations with theology. Walter Benjamin once wrote: my relation to theology is like that of blotting paper to ink. The paper absorbs the ink, but if it were up to the blotting paper, not a single drop would remain. This is exactly how things stand with theology. I am completely steeped in theology, and so then there is no more; all the ink is gone. [PWP, 22][4]

Our philosophers absorb Paul's apocalyptic ink. The authors of our essays—most of them theologians in some sense—are invariably respectful of that philosophical move. Nevertheless, in various ways they also attempt in some measure to recover the ink; or rather, to show that the ink is infinitely more than the blotter can absorb. They aim to let Paul speak also in his messianic apocalyptic—that is, his distinctly theological—voice. In their own renderings of "the messianic" they seek to discern and set forth the fundamental difference between divine action and human action, without setting them against each other in a competitive relationship; in other words, to show how divine and

3. Benjamin, "Theses," Thesis I, 253. One of the key texts by Žižek bears the title *The Puppet and the Dwarf*.

4. De la Durantaye, *Giorgio Agamben*, 369. The internal references are to "Der Papist ist ein weltlicher Priester," an interview with Abu Bakr Rieger in *Literaturen* (Berlin), June 2005, 21–25.

human action are constituted and revealed, "apocalypsed," in their fundamental difference and communion precisely in the singular Messiah Jesus of Paul's gospel. Bringing theology back into view for the sake of messianic witness, each essay in some way attempts to critique, sublate, and transfigure the crucial import of our philosophers by the Pauline apocalyptic gospel—not in order to mute, but rather to amplify the philosophers' voices through Paul, even as these philosophers have enabled us to hear Paul's voice again in new and world-altering ways. The *apokalypsis Theou* here generates philosophical and political thought, yet always draws us back to itself as beginning, context, and end.

We begin with an essay by J. Louis Martyn, who, as already noted, is a seminal figure in understanding Paul as an apocalyptic theologian. Martyn takes us immediately to the heart of the issue of the relation of apocalyptic and philosophy by examining the relation of divine and human action in Paul against the background of popular Greek philosophy and its variation in Hellenistic Judaism. Against the idea of the human being as an autonomous moral agent deciding between "two ways," life and death, set before us by God, who nevertheless remains "off the scene," Martyn describes the Pauline "three-actor moral drama" in which human beings are not autonomous moral agents, but enslaved to anti-God powers (Sin and Death), which set them against God and the Messiah. There is no philosophical way out of that enslavement; indeed, philosophy itself is enslaved. Rather, God apocalyptically invades the enslaved cosmos in the Messiah's crucifixion and resurrection and frees humans from their bondage. Through the gift of the Spirit, God recreates human moral agency (and reason itself) in the messianic community. That apocalyptic event is the all-encompassing context within which philosophy itself must be judged and transfigured.

With the stage set by Martyn, the essays in the second part turn to some of the earlier figures in the modern philosophical engagement with Paul: Nietzsche, Heidegger, and Benjamin. Travis Kroeker launches into a wide-ranging discussion of the nature of sovereignty, engaging in particular Nietzsche's radical and derisive criticism of Paul's celebration of messianic "weakness." Drawing in particular on Benjamin and Kierkegaard, Kroeker shows how "Paul's messianism will not accommodate conventional discourses of human mastery—which is to say, all conventional political discourses." Paul presents instead a discourse of "weak messianic power" (Benjamin), revealed in the crucifixion, which institutes a "counter-sovereignty" in the messianic community that puts into question the sovereignty claimed by conventional political discourses. "For Paul the *logos* of the *stauros* (the word of the cross, 1 Cor 1:18) is the very power of God; precisely the scandal of the cross disrupts the humanist appeals of the wise and the strong." The messianic community enacts its witness to God's power revealed in the Messiah Jesus by living dispossessively, living "as if not."

In an effort to unseat Radical Orthodoxy's "powerful" rhetorical theology, based on the assumption "that only a direct, 'aestheticized' appeal to *caritas* [comparable to Badiou's direct appeal to the resurrection, apart from the cross] can give rise to Christian faith as a distinct way of being," Justin Klassen turns to Heidegger's early lectures on 1 and 2 Thessalonians. On the one hand Klassen argues that Radical Orthodoxy's dismissal of Heidegger as a necrophiliac nihilist is wide of the mark; that Heidegger, via Paul, is actually in accord with Radical Orthodoxy's conviction that "true life is a *way* and not a thing." On the other hand, "Heidegger's reading of Paul is . . . striking for theology . . . because it suggests that theological rhetoric, like the 'cognitive treatment' of the Parousia, misses how the possibility of life in the truth calls one away from the 'peace and security' of any public language." By contrast, Paul and Heidegger encourage living in hope, which more appropriately comports itself in the "silence of religious anxiety." According to Klassen, then, Heidegger too grasps the Pauline way of dispossession, which is not to be confused with nihilism.

As already noted, Walter Benjamin is a fount from which our philosophers (particularly Agamben) regularly draw. Grant Poettcker provides a clear account of Benjamin's messianic politics by examining the relationship between "the profane/mythical/political order and the divine/messianic order" as Benjamin develops it several key texts, including the "Theses on the Philosophy of History." Poettcker shows how Benjamin's messianic politics "accords strikingly with that found in Paul's letters." At the heart of Benjamin's messianic politics is a radical critique of historicism along with the progressivist politics (whether conservative, liberal, or Marxist) and "mythic violence" that are invariably associated with it. In messianic politics the human agent does not strive for "progress" towards "creating a better future"; rather, in solidarity with the victims of "progress" the messianic agent acts in the present moment, in the "now-time," always in expectation of the "decisive interruption," the "quiet" arrival from beyond of the messianic kingdom.

In the third part the essays engage the work of Alain Badiou and Slavoj Žižek. Stephen Fowl notes that "[Paul] scholars and Christians have a tendency to domesticate Paul and his writings, gathering supposed conceptual and religious antecedents to central Pauline terminology so that he appears to be little more than a small tremor on the theological terrain, something you can feel, but which does not bring down any buildings." In contrast, following a summary of Badiou's presentation of Paul, Fowl concludes that, like the apocalyptic interpretations of Paul by Martyn and others, "Badiou's Paul is certainly not domesticated. Badiou has grasped the urgent compulsion inherent in Paul's activity." For Paul "there is a new creation." Nevertheless, Fowl argues, against Badiou's drive toward an undifferentiated universalism, Paul seeks within the revolutionary apocalyptic interruption to "establish new lines of continuity [with the histories of Israel and the nations] in the aftermath of Christ event." There is indeed no historical or narrative "development" from Abraham and Israel to Christ, from cross to resurrection, or from Christ to the church to the nations. The arrival of the Messiah, the resurrection, the church, and the coming messianic kingdom are the new-creation act of God through the power of the Spirit; but *in Christ* Israel, the church, and the nations *in their difference and distinction* are taken up into the new creation, reconciled, and given their place together in the life of the triune God.

Neil Elliott takes Badiou in another direction, conscripting the apocalyptic Paul and the Marxist Badiou together into a critique of empire, whether that be the ancient Roman Empire or the contemporary capitalist order. Following from Badiou, Elliott argues that Paul's announcement of resurrection, of the arrival of a new political order, of a new creation, of the redemption of "all Israel," is an "ideological gesture of defiance," a declaration of "what is *real*," over against the appearances created by the dominant order. A rupture, a disorientation, in that order is created for those who believe Paul's message, which is itself a "moment in the *struggle* against the ideological hegemony of the imperial order." Elliott himself is inclined, however, to let Paul's theological ink be more or less fully absorbed into political theory.

Geoffrey Holsclaw asks what kind of political subject is created through the readings of Paul (in particular of Romans 7) by Badiou and

Žižek. Badiou's focus on resurrection in Paul is aimed toward creating a subject "subtracted from every figure of the law and suspended by a truth-event" and thereby able to act within a situation to proclaim its truth. "This proclamation is presented as the generation of the universal beyond all differences." Žižek on the other hand focuses on the crucifixion in Paul, in which the political subject dies (and kills oneself) with respect to the reigning symbolic order (the Law), thereby suspending it, in order that the subject might be newly created as an agent of love. Holsclaw concludes that both Badiou and Žižek attempt "a plundering of Paul and Christianity, on the way back to the politics and the philosophy of Athens." Holsclaw himself turns from Romans 7 to Romans 6 to articulate the Pauline political subject as "suspended between death and resurrection." In Romans 6 Paul presents baptism as incorporation into *both* the death and the resurrection of Jesus Christ. "Anchored in Christ" through baptismal incorporation, the Pauline political subject is enabled to resist "political realism," to engage in political action which is "deeply personal, integrating both the person acting and that towards which one acts," and in a discerning manner ("neither statist nor sectarian") to both protest and collaborate with "the current political regime."

The essays in the fourth part focus on Giorgio Agamben. As Agamben despoils the treasures of "the Christian archive"—notably Paul's writings—in order to think through current problems in political theory, so Paul Griffith's aims in his essay to "begin the process of despoiling him [Agamben] for the benefit of the church." To do this, Griffith's provides us first with a lucid account of Agamben's despoiling of Paul, a kind of short introduction to Agamben's political theory. Then, building on Agamben and invoking Pascal, Griffiths develops his own description of the Christian political agent. This agent is "quietist," one who "playfully uses politics without the law, as Agamben would have it, [and] does so with political interest crucified, with a deep skepticism about her capacity to predict the results of enacting a political proposal, and with a refusal to be discouraged by predictions of failure, or of success with undesirable results." That is the kind of political agent the apocalyptic gospel creates

Ryan Hansen is less intent to "despoil" Agamben for Christian purposes and more intent to show the difference between Agamben's messianic politics and Pauline apocalyptic politics. "Agamben's messianic politics are immanentized, assuming a metaphysics of univocity" that "emphasizes a 'determinate sameness' to all political existence, where opposition or resistance is trapped within the same plane as that which it opposes." In contrast, Hansen proposes, with the help of philosopher William Desmond, "an apocalyptic Pauline politics and metaphysics [that] is capable of a truly new politics because only it provides a politics and citizenship that is not captured by the immanent flow of history. The apocalyptic is truly another politics because it arrives not in opposing itself to anything else [cf. Griffith's "quietist" politics], but in arriving fills up the whole." In a variety of exegetical forays into Paul's writings, Hansen displays clearly the "logic of porosity between immanent and transcendent"—the "metaxological" (Desmond)—in Paul, which is exactly what is missing in Agamben's (still modern) philosophy of pure immanence.

The essays in the final group draw out several other themes in Paul and our philosophers. Jens Zimmermann employs Gadamer's philosophical hermeneutic to analyze the basic philosophical assumptions that guide the likes of Taubes, Badiou, and Agamben in their readings of Paul. Zimmermann identifies in them a "hermeneutics of unbelief," a commitment to pure immanence that in the end requires them to overlook "the central christological elements of incarnation and participation in Paul's writings," which in turn "deprives Continental philosophy of important insights concerning philosophy's own quest for a subject defined by transcendence." Zimmermann beckons philosophy to attend to the challenge of Paul's *theological* convictions. Thus, when Zimmermann himself turns to "grasp the complex combination of beliefs that actually motivates Christian dissent in politics," he looks to Dietrich Bonhoeffer rather than the philosophers for guidance, finding in Bonhoeffer a clearer reflection of the Pauline grounding of the political subject in Christ's incarnation and our participation in Christ.

Gordon Zerbe raises the important question, where is the ecclesia in our philosophers' accounts of Paul? He sets forth a "three-fold typology" of their ecclesial proposals. Agamben's ecclesia is "an abstract aggregate of [anarchist-ethical] messianic callings"; Taubes's messianic ecclesia is "an apparently socially identifiable entity," which delegitimates the empire while serving a "representational function"; Badiou and Žižek construe the ecclesia as an "activist-vanguard" movement rooted in "fundamental fidelity" with a "more transformational vocation relative to the whole of society." Zerbe explicates each of these ecclesial forms in a careful reading of the texts of the philosophers, and critically assesses each in light of crucial texts from the Pauline writings. While each of the three forms is problematic in some measure, Zerbe's final word is that the philosophers enable the Christian church not to forget "that it ultimately has identity only in the universal, eschatological economy of salvation when God will be all in all." The church cannot secure itself *against* the world; it can only seek the world's messianic transfiguration, and itself be a witness to that.

Time and history under the impact of the messianic event are crucial themes in all of the philosophers discussed in these essays. In the final essay I take up the matter of time and history in the light of the messianic apocalypse in Jesus Christ, and ask what difference the basic concepts of time and history assumed by commentators make in how they write their commentaries on Romans. I examine commentaries that assume a historicist notion of time (Robert Jewett), a salvation-historical notion (N. T. Wright), a time-and-eternity dialectical notion (Karl Barth), and a "messianic" notion (Agamben). I conclude that "the commentary that comes to be written . . . displays in the very character of its production and writing a particular understanding of time and human agency." In that sense the kind of commentary least capable of enabling us to hear Paul in his own voice is the historical-critical, insofar as it locates itself in a temporal world completely other than Paul's, which is constituted by the *apokalypsis Theou* in Jesus Christ. A salvation-historical commentary misconstrues Paul's sense of time as divinely directed linear progression, and fails to grasp the fundamental interruption, relativization, and contextualization of time and history by the messianic apocalypse in Jesus Christ. By contrast, the commentaries by Barth and Agamben not only display a much greater sensitivity and affinity to Paul's apocalyptic-messianic sense of time, but also attempt to participate in and communicate that sense of time in the very form of the commentaries that they write.

It is our hope that each of these essays illuminates in some way the connections between Paul's apocalyptic theology and recent philosophy and political theory. We hope further that in tracing and critically evaluating those connections this collection will, on the one hand, reveal the theological significance of the philosophers in question, and, on the other, make an important contribution to strengthening the witness of the messianic community, in its thought and action, to the Messiah Jesus who has called and created it.

PART I

From Apocalypse to Philosophy

The Gospel Invades Philosophy

by J. Louis Martyn

GOSPEL AND PHILOSOPHY, INITIAL SKETCH

How shall we approach the issues that arise when, before turning to modern philosophical interpreters of Paul such as Alain Badiou and Giorgio Agamben, we ask about the apostle's own journey into what a number of his Greek-speaking contemporaries—pagan and Jewish—called *philosophia*? We begin with four observations.

(a) *Philosophia*. Several Hellenistic witnesses—notably Stoics—tell us that the established philosophical curriculum of the time was made up of three major parts, each a human endeavor: *to physikon* is our investigation of the cosmos; *to ethikon* is our engagement with human behavior, actions right and wrong, wise and foolish; *to logikon* is the cerebral work in which we concern ourselves with *logos*, understood to include our ways of knowing things, epistemology.[1] A man of great mental agility, indeed of considerable sophistication, Paul could surely have written a brief treatise relating a part of his "scripture" to one or another of these three philosophical divisions, producing an essay in some regards similar perhaps to the work of Philo.

In his own ways he does in fact refer numerous times to the cosmos, the subject of *to physikon*. A person who had achieved wisdom in that philosophical division—one affirming, for example, the Epicurean notion of cosmic conservation—would certainly have found a topic for sharp debate in Paul's statement that "the form of this world" is passing away (1 Cor 7:31). Indeed, Paul's apocalyptic uses of the term *kosmos*

---

1. Long and Sedley, *Hellenistic Philosophers*, ¶ 26.

would have raised both Greek and Jewish eyebrows.[2] And what of Paul and *to logikon*? We can be sure that lively philosophical discussion was in fact elicited by several of the passages in which Paul ventures into epistemological issues. One thinks, for example, of 1 Cor 2:6–16 and of the link he draws between epistemology and apocalyptic theology in 2 Cor 5:16–17.[3]

(b) *Euangelion*. The apostle wrote, however, no philosophical treatise. He was no philosopher. As he made his literal journey from one part of the Aegean to another, he did not carry to his hearers what he called a *philosophia*. On the contrary, he conveyed *to euangelion*, a joyous announcement focused not on human endeavors of any kind, but rather on an act of God that had just now occurred, that was still occurring, that would occur climactically in the near future. Specifically, with the term *euangelion* he referred to and expanded upon what he identified in the first instance as God's new, militant act in the invasive sending of his Son Jesus Christ.

(c) *An Invasive Meeting*. This gospel, then, was literally the new invader as Paul traveled from one place to another; and with regard to primary subject matter, it was focused on the new invasion of God in the person of his Son. In city after city, in one market place (*agora*) and workshop (*ergasterion*) after another, Paul's joyous announcement plunged headlong into the established philosophies of the setting, announcing that divine advent. And here we pause over an epistemological issue that arose immediately.

(d) *Contextualization: Philosophy and Gospel or Gospel and Philosophy?* We take a moment to enter imaginatively into the mind of one of Paul's hearers, an auditor who can be a paradigm for us as we ourselves seek genuinely to listen to the apostle. Being a typical human being, this hearer will have assumed that Paul's *euangelion* could be assessed on the basis of the philosophy that had already won that hearer's assent, whether Epicurean, Stoic, Skeptic, or some homemade and unsophisticated form of popular wisdom. That is always the first

2. Regarding the word "apocalyptic" in the present essay see notes 13 and 24 below. By "apocalyptic uses of the term *kosmos*" I mean primarily (a) the expression "this world" and (b) instances in which we see that for Paul *kosmos* and *aion* are to some degree interchangeable.

3. See my essay "Epistemology at the Turn of the Ages," in which I speak of "the turn of the ages" as an apocalyptic matter.

human assumption, the scarcely examined one that is evident in one of our modern, commonplace uses of the term "sense." We assume, that is, that "having sense," we can use this sense as a yardstick to measure anything new that comes along. Upon hearing a new statement, we often say, "Yes, indeed, that makes sense" or "That cannot be true; it makes no sense at all."

To speak about the meeting of Paul's message with philosophy in the Greek *agora*, we can employ a somewhat more sophisticated locution. We can follow Walter Lowe and Douglas Harink in their illuminating use of the verb "to contextualize."[4] To say that A contextualizes B is to say two things, both implying that A is the senior partner. First, when A contextualizes B, A functions as the master map on which B is located. Furnishing the basic criteria of perception, A is the context in which B is discerned and interpreted.[5]

Second, when A contextualizes B, A is the point of departure for thinking about the relationship between A and B. A does not get all of the words, but it does get the first word and that first word is basic.

Thinking of Paul in the *agora*, we can say, then, that his typical auditor would have taken for granted that *philosophia* contextualizes *euangelion*. Listening to Paul's preaching, one assesses the gospel in the context of *philosophia*, the latter serving as the master map, the senior partner, the basic frame of reference.

Will that have been Paul's assumption as well? Here we have a question of considerable import for the present essay, for while our formal focus will lie for the most part on the gospel and *to ethikon*—with a brief glance in the direction of *to physikon*—the epistemological dimensions of *to logikon* also come into play. Specifically, in epistemological terms how did Paul understand the gospel's invasion? Did the established philosophies—especially some of their common assumptions—function as the stable context in which the invasive good-news announcement necessarily found its place? And, finding its place in

---

4. See Lowe, *Theology and Difference*, 19–22, 138–39; note also Douglas Harink's reference to the "contextualizing power of the gospel" in his essay in this volume.

5. One thinks, for example, of interpretations of God's commandments that "explain" them on the basis of a frame of reference that is external to them and that is considered—consciously or unconsciously—in some regard senior to them. See Halivni, *Midrash, Mishnah, and Gemara.*

this philosophical context, was it subject to criteria of perception that were already basic in that context?

With those questions playing their strong roles in the background, we come now to our formal subject, the gospel's invasive meeting with *to ethikon*, the latter being represented by an established philosophical drama of morality.

AN ORTHODOX, PHILOSOPHICAL DRAMA OF MORALITY: THE TWO WAYS AND THE TWO STEPS

The Two Ways in Pagan Moral Literature

Even a modest survey of moral literature composed by polytheistic pagans in the Hellenistic period leads one to sense a coherent ethical portrait of the human being that was so widely presupposed as to warrant our referring to it as one of the era's orthodox philosophical constructs. In its numerous and various forms from Hesiod to Seneca and beyond, it had as its focal figure the human being who as traveler stands center stage before a road fork at which two ways open out before him, each being a viable option. He is *homo viator in bivio*.

There was also more to this established philosophical construct than the two ways. With variations and some qualifications, it was made up, in fact, of five major elements:

(1)   Frequently so fundamental as to be linked to cosmic, universal pairs of opposites, the two ways are either taken for granted—they simply exist as, for example, life and death, virtue and vice—or they are *presented* to the human being, often by an older and wiser person, or even—in poetic form—by personifications of virtue and vice.

(2)   Accompanying the presentation, there is explicitly or implicitly a strong *hortatory element designed to persuade* the human agent to take the way that is identified as the better of the two. Explicit or implicit exhortation and the effort to persuade are hallmarks in a massive amount of Hellenistic moral instruction, so much so that even when they stand alone, they very frequently indicate that just below the surface lies intact the whole of the two ways.

(3) Exhortation and the effort to persuade also presuppose a certain anthropological given: *moral competence in the precise sense of the ability to choose.* Even in emphatically theistic authors such as Epictetus, the two ways is a fundamentally anthropological construct focused on volitional action of which the human agent is capable. He is able to see the two ways—often, to be sure, with instruction—and he is able—often after deliberation—to decide between them. In short, the human being is morally competent to make his own choice.

(4) Faced with the two ways, often identified, as I have said, as a pair of opposites, the human being does in fact choose one or the other; he exercises his moral competence by making an *all-determining decision.* In the happy scenario he chooses to follow the way that is "choiceworthy" (*haireton*), achieving moral progress (*prokopē*) by repeatedly choosing virtue in preference to vice.[6]

(5) His choice has momentous *consequences*; it determines his future.

One hardly needs to say that the part of Hellenistic philosophy denominated *to ethikon* was both large and complex, being so partly because the Stoics focused the good and the bad almost altogether on ethics. Amidst that complexity one is struck, then, by the relative simplicity and the near ubiquity of the two-ways portrait of the human being.

The simplicity is evident, for example, in pagan traditions in which the two-ways pattern is assumed—as noted above—more or less as a natural, cosmic given, no personal presenter being mentioned. The near ubiquity is attested by many passages in which the popular philosophers speak in an ethical, paraenetic manner that presupposes some form of the two ways.[7] Notably impressive and pertinent witnesses also include two pieces of widely influential ethical instruction, the Heracles legend of Prodicus and the *Tablet of Cebes.*[8]

6. On the force of the preposition *pro* in the term *prohairesis* as used by Epictetus, see the recent argument for the comparative meaning in Asmis, "Choice in Epictetus' Philosophy." A person chooses something *in preference to something else*, a clear reflection of the tradition of the two ways.

7. See esp. Malherbe, "Hellenistic Moralists and the New Testament"; and idem, *Paul and the Popular Philosophers.*

8. For the Prodicus legend see Xenophon *Memorabilia* 2.1.21–34. On Pseudo

Sirach Representing the Jewish Sages:
The Two Ways Acquire a Highly Influential Addition

The two-ways portrait of the human being is also common among the Jewish wise men of the Hellenistic era, where it is basically formed from classic Israelite theology dramatically portrayed in Deuteronomy.

The Canonical Picture. Here there is indeed a presenter, the single God of Israel, the two ways being emphatically determined by him as the essence of his gracious gift of life to his people Israel via the Sinaitic Law. As the giver of the Law and as the presenter of the nomistic two ways, he is Yahweh, the Lord of heaven and earth; and one of the two ways is even identified as his own way—his way, that is, *for Israel*. According to Deut 11:22, the way of "the Lord your God" is to be the way of Israel, consisting, as it does, of the commandments issued by God. From that divine way Israel is not to turn aside to another way (Deut 11:28; 30:19).

As the divine presenter, God is possessed of awesome gravitas in the classic scene in which, speaking through Moses, he explicitly lays out before corporate Israel the two ways, defining them by a specific pair of opposites: life-giving observance of the Law of Sinai and death-dealing non-observance of that Law.

> I call heaven and earth to witness against you this day, that I have set before you life and death, blessing and curse; therefore choose life that you and your descendants may live, loving the Lord your God, obeying his voice, and cleaving to him . . . (Deut 30:19–20)[9]

It is a scene firmly inscribed in Israel's memory, as we see numerous times in the writings of the Hellenistic sages. The identity of this divine presenter is made fully known to the Israelites, however, only when, with the guidance of their historians and prophets, they take into account his deeds prior to this dramatic scene. He is the God who

---

Cebes see Fitzgerald and White, *Tabula of Cebes.*

9. The plural verbs and pronouns in this and similar passages tell us something important about exhortation in ancient Israel. Having been chosen by God, *corpus Israel* is the entity that is exhortable. For Paul the same is true of the *corpus Christi*, leading in his letters to a linguistic pattern of hortatory plural verbs and pronouns that is without true parallel in Hellenistic *paraenesis* in general. On the latter, see Starr and Engberg-Pedersen, *Early Christian Paraenesis.*

earlier made an indelible promise to Abraham, the God who brought about the corporate liberation of Israel from bondage in Egypt, the God who then graciously gave the Law to Israel on Mount Sinai, the Law being God's instrument for granting life.

The Highly Influential Addition of Human Autonomy: the Two Separate Steps. Sirach 15 can represent numerous instances in which Hellenistic Jews drew, explicitly or implicitly, on the Deuteronomic two ways. Sirach is also one of our clearest witnesses to an influential—Paul might have said fateful—Hellenistic tendency notably evident in some of the Jewish sages, and no less palpable in pagan sources: what we may call "the two separate steps" is added to the classic two ways.

No ancient Israelite theologian entertained the thought that, when God exhorted Israel to "choose life," he meant them to act independently of himself, to carry out their obedience removed from his presence, to keep his statutes as their own act strictly separated from the power of his word. Far from it. Israel is to *love* the Lord, her God, consistently *cleaving* to him in dependent and sustained affection.

The Hellenistic period saw a new development of great consequences. We now reckon with the emergence of several strains of philosophical determinism, notably the Stoic assertion of the universal, ruling hand of Fate, understood to be God.[10] To many—not least many among the Jewish sages—that assertion of divine Fate seemed to bring the threat of rank ethical irresponsibility, moral chaos. On the whole the Stoics were very far from the simplistic statement that vice is as fated as virtue, but some other philosophers thought that to be at least partially implied in their philosophy of divine Fate.[11]

Returning to the Jewish sages, we note that the threat of theological determinism and consequent moral irresponsibility lies behind a famous and influential passage in Sirach. And here the antidote to such irresponsibility involves the influential addition of the two separate steps:

> Do not say it was he [God] who led me astray [into transgression] . . . From the beginning he [God] created the human being, and he left him in the power of his own decision. If it is

10. In this brief essay I leave aside the motif of determinism in Qumran. See, e.g., Alexander, "Predestination and Free Will."

11. See above all Bobzien, *Determinism and Freedom*.

> your will to do so, you will keep the commandments, and to act
> faithfully is a matter of your own choice. (15:12–15)

Here the Deuteronomist's exhortation "choose life" has become
a reference to "*your own choice*," reflecting a moral drama that now
contained two distinct steps.

First, God presents the two ways, emphasizing that the way of life
is an offer that can be chosen or rejected. *Second* comes the all-determining step, the one taken by the human agent *in the power of his own
decision*. For Sirach, as for countless of his philosophical confreres, that
decision falls emphatically under the heading of "the things that are up
to us" (*ta eph' hēmin*).[12] It is as though, having created the human being
with the autonomous power to make his own choice, having left that
human agent in the power of his own decision, and having explicitly
offered the way of life, the divine agent steps off stage, in order *not* to
play a role in the human agent's choice.

The second step is, then, more than second. As the human agent's
act of decision, it is also emphatically *separate from* the offering act of
God. In the *decisive* moment that follows the presentation of the two
ways, the human agent stands alone center stage at the parting of those
ways, clothed emphatically and solely with his own autonomy.

THE LETTERS OF PAUL: THE TWO WAYS AND THE TWO STEPS REPLACED BY THE CONFLICT BETWEEN TWO POWERS[13]

Paul's Gospel Meets to ethikon Encapsulated in the Drama of the Two Ways/Two Steps

Countless passages in the letters show us that the Pharisee named Paul
was himself one of the Jewish sages mentioned above. He was, that is, a
disciplined and sophisticated Israelite thinker well acquainted with the
two-ways drama in its canonical Deuteronomic form (e.g., Rom 10:5).
Thinking first of Paul as the highly intelligent Jewish youth, we can eas-

12. The matters referred to by the expression *ta eph' hēmin* are numerous and complex. See ibid.

13. Foundational studies that are highly illuminating for what follows here are
those of de Boer, especially "Paul and Apocalyptic Eschatology" and "Paul and Jewish
Apocalyptic Theology."

ily imagine a scene in his School of Scriptural Study that had a lasting effect. At the head of his class, he was surely more than once involved with his fellow students in an exegetical discussion of Deuteronomy 30 itself.[14]

Chiefly we know, however, of later scenes in which Paul encountered our orthodox philosophical construct in the course of his apostolic labors. Two different settings hosted these encounters of gospel with the two-ways drama as a topic in *to ethikon*. And in those settings two different groups of "wise persons" served as Paul's critical interlocutors.

The Gospel in the Greek Market Place. There was first the scene in the pagan market place (*agora*) of one Greek city after another.[15] There Paul found thoughtful persons devoted to their own growth in wisdom and virtue, their advancement not least in matters of *to ethikon*. Given the character of our sources, we can speak here especially of the gospel's encounters with philosophy in Corinth, events that were highly influential on Paul and that are numerous times reflected in his Corinthian letters.[16]

The Gospel in the Church. There was also the scene that emerged when a given church became a Christian House of Scriptural Study, a scene, then, in which Paul's chief interlocutors were Jewish sages who had become followers of Jesus Christ without losing their devotion to our orthodox moral drama. Five instances of this inner-church scene prove to be of major import.

(1)   The earliest known to us was the conference in which the Jerusalem church hosted the church of Antioch for deliberations focused on the circumcision-free evangelical labors carried out among Gentiles by Paul and Barnabas (Gal 2:1–10). In these deliberations Paul met and had sharp exchanges with certain Christian-Jewish sages who were influential in the Jerusalem church and to whom he refers as "false brothers." What made them "false"? They attempted to use their power in the Jerusalem church—and in that of Antioch as well—to compel the circumcision of the Gentile

14. Cf. Watson, *Paul and the Hermeneutics of Faith.* See also my review of this work in the *Scottish Journal of Theology.*

15. As noted earlier, there were similar scenes in Paul's work places.

16. See first Adams and Horrell, *Christianity at Corinth.*

converts. Was not Abrahamic, Sinaitic circumcision the *true context* into which the newly arrived gospel of Christ had come, and to which it was the junior partner?

(2) Proceeding chronologically, we have next the scene in the Antioch church in which, as Paul saw it, the issue was again the contextualizing of the gospel by the Sinaitic form of *to ethikon*. As the church of Antioch was of mixed ethnic background, the Jewish food laws were regularly ignored there in the celebration of the Lord's Supper. When, however, during a visit from Peter, a delegation came from the Jerusalem church to the church in Antioch, the food laws were suddenly enforced with Peter's support, Sinai being again seen as the senior context into which the gospel had come (Gal 2:11–14). The long hand of the "circumcision party" in the Jerusalem church (Gal 2:12) was now reaching north into the church of Antioch, subsuming the gospel under the senior context of Sinai. Here Paul saw not only hypocrisy but also an instance of contextualization that brought infidelity to "the truth of the gospel."

(3) We have next the meeting of gospel with philosophy that constituted Paul's letter to his Galatian churches. Virtually from the letter's beginning to its end Paul brought his gospel face to face with the two-ways orthodox moral drama in its Sinaitic form, thus taking another step in his journey into philosophy.

(4) A second epistolary meeting of the gospel and the orthodox moral drama was fashioned by Paul as he composed the sophisticated arguments of Romans. Numerous accents he addressed in Galatians were continued and enriched in this intricately crafted epistle. Paul addressed it to the house churches in the capital, but virtually packing his bags for a trip to Jerusalem, he found that with part of his mind he was thinking anxiously of yet another encounter with the "circumcision party" in the Jerusalem congregation (Rom 15:25–33).

(5) Finally we can be confident that the relationship between Paul's gospel and the Sinaitic form of our orthodox moral drama played a decisive role in the Jerusalem church's discussions when Paul arrived with the collection he had gathered from his congregations,

ethnically almost totally uncircumcised Gentiles. In Jerusalem Paul had necessarily to deal again with the "circumcision party," indeed with those he considered "false brothers"; and, to judge from the final chapters of Acts, the earlier polarity was climactically deepened with awesome consequences.

Full treatment would lead us to attend in detail to the pagan marketplace meetings of gospel and *to ethikon*—exegetical exercises especially in 1 Corinthians—and to all five of the inner-church discussions. In the present essay we make a beginning by focusing our attention on the third of the latter, Paul's letter to his churches in Galatia.

Galatians. Paul wrote this letter to the churches he had founded among pagans in ethnic Galatia. Should we detect in it a reflection of our orthodox moral drama, we could expect that reflection to be seasoned by pagan accents designed by Paul to make contact with the letter's Gentile recipients.

What we find, however, is emphatically and distinctly Jewish-Christian, and the reason is not difficult to detect. After Paul left his Galatian churches in order to carry his gospel into cities of the Aegean, certain Jewish-Christian evangelists—I will call them "the Teachers"—came into those Christian communities, declaring themselves to be sponsored by powerful elements in the mother church of Jerusalem.[17] Noting tensions and mutually destructive fights in the Galatian churches, and finding also that Paul had left those communities without the guidance of the Sinaitic Law, these Teachers identified the former as the inevitable result of the latter. As Paul had failed to convey to his churches what the Teachers considered the only adequate moral anchorage, God's signal gift, the Law of Sinai, these evangelists were not surprised to find that the communities had become unruly and chaotic.

Giving daily thanks, then, to God for the Law of Sinai, and having a mission to carry that life-giving Law to Gentiles, the Teachers undertook to bring to Paul's Gentile churches in Galatia the Law's orthodox moral drama. The first step was doubtless a presentation of the Sinaitic two-ways, combined with a hortatory call to choose the way of Law observance. As a second step, many men in the Galatian churches made

---

17. See especially Gal 4:21—5:1 and the interpretation proposed in my *Galatians* commentary; and cf. now de Boer, "New Preachers in Galatia."

their decision. They brought their families into compliance by assenting to circumcision, thus choosing the path of Law observance.[18]

Given these developments, Paul composed a highly emotional and sharply worded letter designed to be read aloud to his Galatian churches, the Teachers being yet present and more than ready to give their interpretation. He necessarily included numerous references to the two-ways drama focused on the Sinaitic Law precisely as it is volitionally accepted in the human agent's act of assenting to circumcision. Galatians presents to us, then, a significant segment of Paul's journey into a Jewish-Christian form of *to ethikon*, the philosophical, two-ways/two-steps drama. We consider briefly a single text, Gal 5:13–25.

Here, beginning to bring his letter to a close, Paul shows that in one respect he agrees with the Teachers. Community tensions and fights are an altogether serious matter. He joins those evangelists, then, in warning his churches about the community-destroying capacity of a certain entity; and to name that entity he employs a Jewish expression, "the Impulsive Desire of the Flesh" (Gal 5:16; he sometimes abbreviates, referring simply to "the Flesh"). It is an expression with which he became well acquainted in his school days (Hebrew *yeser basar*; Greek *epithymia tēs sarkos*).[19]

It is also one which the Teachers are already using in their Sinaitic moral instruction of the Galatians. For them "the Impulsive Desire of the Flesh" names the inclination that, internal to the human agent, leads that agent to walk in the path of transgression, violating God's commandments. The Teachers also speak at length of what they identify as the salutary antidote. The corrective opposite of that path, they say, is the path of righteousness, volitional observance of the Sinaitic Law.

And here the *pagan* setting in Galatia is significant. As the Galatian Gentiles had not been born in the Abrahamic/Sinaitic covenant, the Teachers undertook first to present it, placing these Gentiles before the two ways of life and death, the two ways of Law-observance and non-Law-observance. Having placed them there, the Teachers

18. The Teachers' message also included as a constituent part of that orthodox drama, the good news of Jesus in a form that largely eclipsed the cross. Cf. Matt 5:17–19.

19. The Greek locution *epithymia tēs sarkos* renders the Hebrew *yeser basar*, both referring to what is called in many Jewish traditions "the evil inclination." On this matter see the seminal studies of the evil inclination by Joel Marcus listed in the bibliography of my *Galatians* commentary.

doubtless exhorted them to use their own power of decision (cf. Sir 15:14), choosing the path of observance. The Teachers also threatened the Galatians with the way of death, telling them that they would be excluded from God's gift of life if they failed to take their own step, choosing to commence Law-observance in the rite of circumcision (Gal 4:17). In their threat, as in their exhortation, the Teachers took for granted the Galatians' moral competence, their inborn ability to choose the path of Law observance.

In this reasonable two-ways instance of *to ethikon* Paul sees an infidelity to the truth of the gospel that required immediate, concerted, and uncompromising opposition, accompanied by a re-proclamation of "the truth of the gospel" as it powerfully confronts the Teachers' form of *to ethikon*. Much of the confrontation and re-proclamation is what we find in Gal 5:13–25:[20]

> (13) You were indeed called to freedom, brothers and sisters; only do not allow freedom to be turned into a military base of operations for [the Impulsive Desire of] the Flesh . . . (16) In contradiction to the Teachers [specifically in contradiction to their view of the moral drama], I, Paul, say to you: Lead your daily life guided by the Spirit [of Christ, sent into your hearts by God], and in this way you will not end up carrying out the Impulsive Desire of the Flesh. (17) For the Flesh is actively inclined against the Spirit, and the Spirit is actively inclined against the Flesh. Indeed these two powers constitute a pair of opposites at war with one another, the result being that you do not actually do the very things you wish to do. (18) If, however, in the daily life of your communities you are consistently led by the Spirit, then you are not under the authority of the Law.
>
> (19) The [community-destroying] effects of the Flesh are indeed clear, and those effects are: fornication, vicious immorality . . . belief in magic, instances of irreconcilable hatred . . . mercenary ambition . . . separation into divisive cliques . . . (21) . . . In this regard I warn you now, just as I warned you before: those who—not being puppets—practice things of this sort will not inherit the Kingdom of God.
>
> (22) By contrast, the [community-building] fruit borne by the Spirit [of the crucified one] is love, joy, peace, patience, kindness, generosity, faith, gentleness, self control . . . (25) If,

20. I use the translation offered and explicated in my *Galatians* commentary.

then, we live by the Spirit—and we do—let us carry out our
daily lives under the guidance of the Spirit.

A great deal is at stake in this paragraph, all of it pertinent to Paul's
own journey into philosophy, for given the developments in Galatia, he
now brings face to face with one another *two radically different portraits
of the moral drama*: the old orthodox one belonging to the two-ways
Sinaitic tradition as a topic in *to ethikon*, and a new one parented by the
graciously powerful and invasive word of the gospel.

Numerous instances of difference between the two could claim
our attention. Here we turn to the one signaled by the carefully paired
locutions in Gal 5:19 and 22, *ta erga tēs sarkos* (the effects produced by
the Flesh) and *ho karpos tou pneumatos* (the fruit borne by the Spirit).

The Effects of the Flesh and the Fruit of the Spirit: Supra-Human Powers and Their Acts as Signs of the Militant, Apocalyptic Moral Drama

To some extent Paul specifies those two expressions by listing secular
pairs of opposites that remind us of Hellenistic lists of vices and virtues
that contain, in fact, a number of the same terms.[21] When, therefore, we
take Paul to list in this passage what he himself considers general vices
and virtues universally practiced by human beings who, being morally
competent, make straightforward, independent choices, we surely find
in his own words an edition of the two ways and the two steps. Does
he not refer in essence, that is, to "the *way* of the Flesh" and "the *way* of
the Spirit"? And does he not exhort the Galatians to choose the way of
the Spirit, the way of virtue? In effect a number of modern interpreters
have understandably thought so.[22]

Reading Paul in His Own Time and Place. Here, however, we pause
in order to pose a historical question that can lead us, I think, to Paul's
intention. What are we to say about interpreters *of his own time and
culture*, Hellenistic readers/hearers of at least rudimentary philosophi-

21. Fitzgerald, "Virtue/Vice Lists."

22. See especially Meeks, *Origins of Christian Morality*, 69, a book from which I
have learned much.

cal sophistication? There were such in the Galatian churches. What did they find in this text? What did Paul intend them to find?[23]

At least some of these early interpreters will have noticed something easily overlooked by modern readers: Paul uses here the terms "the Flesh" and "the Spirit," doubtless contrasting the one with the other. But he does not bring *these two terms* into a two-ways, hortatory, two-steps, volitional relationship with the human agent. Indeed, reading with care, we see that he does not speak simply of the Flesh and the Spirit. His pair of opposites consists of *ta erga tēs sarkos, the effects* of the Flesh, and *ho karpos tou pneumatos, the fruit* borne by the Spirit of Christ.

Instead, then, of speaking in the orthodox and expected mode of the two ways, either of which might be elected by the essentially autonomous human agent, the Galatians, Paul refers descriptively to the Flesh and the Spirit of the crucified Christ as *two active powers*, each of which flexes its muscles in such a manner as to produce certain effects. In short, these two powers are themselves *two supra-human, cosmic actors* who, being in combat with one another (5:17), do opposite things in what Paul identifies as the *real* moral drama, the one inaugurated by the militant coming of Christ and his Spirit, the one that actually exists in the *real world* and thus in the Galatian communities.

The Three-actor Moral Drama. We have noted that in theological texts the orthodox moral drama has two actors, the divine agent and the human agent. As we see in Galatians 5, the gospel's moral drama—an instance of Martinus de Boer's "cosmological apocalyptic eschatology"—is fundamentally different in that it has three actors: (1) the divine agent (here the Spirit of Christ), (2) the human agent (the Galatian communities), and (3) anti-God powers (represented here by the Impulsive Desire of the Flesh, the power which Paul elsewhere calls Sin in the singular).[24]

The matter of supra-human powers could claim our close attention at length, being a firm clue to what we can denominate *the apocalyptic moral drama embraced in its Christian form by Paul.* Here it suffices to note that he refers *descriptively* to the effects of the Flesh and the fruit

23. See the reference to a hermeneutical rule of Walter Bauer in my book *Theological Issues in the Letters of Paul,* 209.

24. See again the studies of de Boer mentioned in note 13 above. In the present essay I use the term "apocalyptic" to refer to the *three-actor* drama.

borne by the Spirit precisely where our Hellenistic interpreters would have expected him to engage in simple, voluntaristic exhortation drawn from the tradition of the two ways.

In the broad context beginning at Gal 5:1 and continuing through 6:10 he does indeed use a number of imperative and hortatory verbs. It is no accident that major parts of the passage are consistently classified as *paraenesis*. But what kind of exhortation is it that coheres with descriptions of the *activities* of supra-human powers, the Flesh and the Spirit of the crucified Christ? In a scene focused on powers and their activities rather than on the two ways and the simple volitional choice of the human agent, what happens to the hortatory dimension of moral instruction?

Given the massive role played in Paul's philosophical culture by such *paraenetic* instruction, that is a question of obvious importance. It is also one that demands separate treatment elsewhere. Here we simply take further note of Paul's references to God's sending of the Spirit of Christ into the Galatians' hearts (Gal 4:6). For in that earthshaking, invasive event, God has commenced *his own participation in human morality*, and that participation has clearly brought radical changes to the whole of the human moral drama.

Dual Agency and Love.[25] Centrally it has changed the moral scene by inaugurating what we do well to call a *dual agency*—a startling cosmic *novum*, to be sure, but also one that can be brought into sharp focus by asking a simple question.[26] Rereading Gal 5:22–23, we are led to ask: Who is it who loves, rejoices, lives at peace, and is patient? Clearly members of the Galatian congregations; for love, patience, and peaceful behavior are human acts carried out by human beings. But, carrying his gospel's three-actor moral drama as he journeys into philosophy, Paul speaks in terms clearly apocalyptic. He says that when the Galatian churches do these things, they do them as a new moral agent.

25. In speaking of "dual agency," I draw on George Hunsinger's reference to "double agency" in *How to Read Karl Barth*, 185–224. See also Webster, *Barth's Ethics of Reconciliation*, 107.

26. I refer to the dual agency in Gal 5:22–23 as a cosmic *novum* because we can be sure Paul saw it as such. In fact Stoic traditions included numerous forms of compatibilism that could be compared with Paul's dual agency. Indeed we have here a desideratum, for we do not yet possess a detailed and full-dress study focused on such a comparison and worthy of standing beside the sterling work of Bobzien, *Determinism and Freedom*.

They act, but they act precisely in the *three-actor, apocalyptic drama* in which *their deeds* of love, joy, and peace prove to be—in the first instance and corporately—fruit borne in their communities by the Spirit of God's Son, *the actor* sent by God into their hearts.

The New Moral Agent. The essence of this new (human) moral agent does not lie, then, in something it has itself done—achieving autonomous, moral progress, for example, by strenuous philosophical endeavor. Its essence lies in something that was and is done *to* it by God. To be sure—this is a crucial point—this new moral agent is by no means God's marionette. On the contrary, it is radically free, liberated from the nefarious and lethal power of Sin, liberated to love, to rejoice, to be patient, to have faith, to be gentle, to have self-control, and to bear the other's burdens, thus fulfilling the Law of *Christ*, thus *truly* obeying the God whose demand of fidelity to himself remains absolute (Gal 5:21).[27] But far from being free in its own autonomy, it is liberated precisely and only in the dual agency created by God's act of invasion in the Spirit of his Son.

Dual Agency and the Cross. The new moral agent is also free only in its dual agency with the Spirit of the *crucified Christ*, the figure who in Paul's preaching is hanging on the bloody cross in what the Roman world knew to be abject weakness, ultimate punishment, and deserved defeat, the hideous death largely reserved for disobedient slaves (Gal 3:1). The newly created dual agency has, then, two aspects.

First, in his war against the power of Sin God has established the christological dual agency by bringing light into darkness, by sending the Spirit of his Son, that is, into the hearts of the Galatians, calling them into being as cohesive groups empowered to love, to rejoice with those who rejoice and weep with those who weep, to make peace. Second, the same dual agency has another face, a decidedly dark one. It brings to Paul and to all of his churches participation in the horror of Christ's death, his crucifixion itself. What is to be said here about this second aspect?

We begin to understand it when we attend to another Galatians text, one in which Paul declares that the crucifixion of "our Lord Jesus Christ" was and is a *cosmic* event: "As for me, God forbid that I should boast in anything except the cross of our Lord Jesus Christ, by which

27. Cf. Vollenweider, *Freiheit als neue Schöpfung.*

the cosmos has been crucified to me and I to the cosmos. For neither is circumcision anything nor is uncircumcision anything. What is something is the new creation" (Gal 6:14–15; cf. Phil 3:4–11). Interpreters are right to accent the last sentence, but we also note that Paul comes to it only through the others. Before referring to God's glorious new creation marked by communal love, joy, and peace, Paul speaks of the *death by crucifixion of the cosmos, and of himself.* To what cosmos and to what self does he refer?

The cosmos that suffered crucifixion was the world of the Sinaitic, orthodox, two-ways moral drama, the world of circumcision and uncircumcision, the world that the Teachers were seeking to impress on the Galatian Gentiles. It was also the world in which Paul himself previously lived. And here we see the indelible link between God's newly effected dual agency and what we may call Paul's cosmic death. Earlier in the letter Paul said that he was crucified with Christ (2:19). Here, near the end, he provides explication, saying that Christ's crucifixion became and remained the deadly crucifixion of the Paul who had been a highly successful, perfectly moral human being according to the orthodox, two-ways, Sinaitic drama (Phil 3:4–6). Christ's crucifixion was Paul's death because it was the death of his cosmos, the moral drama that constituted the stable ground below his feet. One sees him being hurled by the cross through and into the unfriendly space of chaos, deprived of familiar markers, the dependable standards of the two ways. The cross of God's Son was thus the loss of morally orthodox, cosmic, oppositional pairs. It marked the death of moral instruction drawn in simple form from the Law's commandments *as those commandments had been made to serve the two-ways drama.*[28] Specifically, Paul's participation in Christ's crucifixion brought the eclipse of the Sinaitic oppositional pair, discrete sins and nomistic righteousness.

But beyond Israel, the cross was the *cosmic* event in that its lethal reach was universal, extending also into the whole of the pagan world. It brought the demise of the oppositional pair universally called vice and virtue, the pair called moral weakness (*akrasia*) and the strong capacity to make autonomous decisions.[29]

---

28. See the uncommonly perceptive study of Lindemann, "Die biblische Toragebote."

29. See my essay "Apocalyptic Antinomies."

In Galatians 5 and 6 we see the new moral agent who is characterized both by love and by suffering the crucifixion of the familiar, orthodox moral drama. And it is in this cosmic crucifixion that Paul discerns the *life* of the new creation (cf. 2 Cor 4:11)!

Dual Agency of the Community. Where is God establishing the new creation by causatively participating in the human morality of love, joy, and peace, *and* by bringing about the painful and horrifying termination of the orthodox moral drama (1 Cor 1:19)? Unless these acts of God are to have no substance beyond the mists of a disembodied mysticism, there must be a locus. Where concretely can Paul find and portray the new creation that is marked by the complex dual agency?

Not in the timeless and universal individual who was in *to ethikon* the consistent subject of philosophical inquiry, the individual who was also the consistent addressee of the philosophers' moral instruction. We notice and ponder the simple linguistic fact that Paul puts his hortatory and imperative verbs often and characteristically in the plural, a locution that sets him apart from the traditions of popular philosophy, and sets him apart from those of the Hellenistic Jewish sages as well. Characteristically he exhorts the church community *as community*, and that simple linguistic fact tells us that God has elected to participate in the *corporate morality of a community as community.* The newly competent agent is, then, a corporate entity, the *community* that Paul will later identify as "the body of Christ," the *sōma Christou*, the *corpus Christi* (1 Corinthians 12).

Community Genesis. We come to the end of the present essay by asking about the genesis of the community that is itself God's new moral agent. Earlier, reading Gal 5:22–23, we considered the daily life of this community, its sustained moral life characterized by God's gift of dual agency with the Spirit. Now we ask whether that gift is in effect a reward God grants to those who have earlier made an autonomous decision to believe the gospel. Or does God's gift of dual agency go all the way back to the community's genesis, all the way back to the point at which the gospel is believed and the community born?

Those questions in mind, we find it instructive for our basic topic to consider briefly one of the numerous ways in which Paul could have understood the birth of the new community in a philosophical frame of reference, one in which human decision is a second and separate act, one of "the things that are up to us" (*ta eph' hēmin*).

Leaving Sinai behind and giving a brief nod in the direction of Chrysippean tradition, Paul could have employed such terms as "impression" (*phantasia*) and "assent" (*sunkatathesis*), in order to construct a reasonable bridge from philosophy to the birth of the new-creation community. He could have understood his task as that of presenting his gospel as an impression that stamped the hearer's mind with two possible courses of action. Second, he could have counted on a brief period of deliberation, after which the hearer would take his own step vis-à-vis the gospel. The hearer, that is, would grant the assent Paul calls faith (*sunkatathesis = pistis*). Or, alternatively, he would withhold assent, refuse to believe the gospel.

In fact, however, Paul builds no such reasonable bridge. Instead, he speaks of the generative power of the gospel itself. He concentrates his attention in the brevity of four little words he derives from the prophet Isaiah: *hē pistis ex akoēs*, "faith is *ignited* by the gospel message itself" (Rom 10:17; Isa 53:1).

The gospel is not one *phantasia* among others. The gospel is the *dynamis theou*, the present, powerful, intrusive *act* of the God who raised his crucified Son from the grave. The gospel is *the* specific apocalypse of Christ as God's own end-time act. And acting in the gospel, God recreates agency itself, as we have seen. There is, then, no route from any segment of philosophy to the gospel, no philosophical route to the word of the cross as God's active power.

Because God himself is acting in the gospel as the fundamental instance of dual agency, the gospel calls neither for deliberation nor for an autonomous decision. Precisely as the word of the cross it is the dynamic power of God, the revelatory message in which God himself steps on the scene. On the one hand, God destroys the philosophy of the two ways when it is mistakenly taken to be the context for the gospel (1 Cor 1:19). On the other hand, precisely in his dual agency *he acts in the word of the cross, inciting faith* and empowering his apostle to take every philosophical thought captive to obey Christ (2 Cor 10:5).[30]

30. In the terms of the three-actor, apocalyptic drama, God's granting to the gospel the power to incite faith is not immediately invincible vis-à-vis "the god of this world," for the struggle continues: that god has blinded the minds of the unbelievers (2 Cor 4:4). And in the same apocalyptic terms the ultimate victory will come not because of an inborn faculty of the human agent to have faith, but because God's mercy is more powerful than the human capacity to be disobedient (Rom 11:32). The gospel story begins and ends with the grace of divine agency for the sake of the human agent.

The Father of Jesus Christ is emphatically not a god who, after offering two ways, withdraws off stage in order to assure an autonomous decision on the part of the human agent. Precisely the opposite. This God *comes* invasively and causatively, inciting faith where there was none. We may take the apostle quite literally when we hear him speak of the genesis of the newly moral community, *identifying it from its inception forward as God's new creation*, for as God's new creation this community owes both its birth and its sustained life to God's powerful act in the gospel and to nothing else.

PART II

Nietzsche, Heidegger, and Benjamin

Living "As If Not": Messianic Becoming
or the Practice of Nihilism?

by Travis Kroeker

> Where is the wise? Where is the scribe? Where is the debater of
> this age? Hath not God made foolish the wisdom of the world?
> . . . But God has chosen what is foolish in the world to con-
> found the wise; God has chosen what is weak in the world to
> confound the things which are mighty. And base things and
> things which are despised in the world hath God chosen, yea,
> and things that are not, to bring to nought things that are . . . (1
> Cor 1:20, 27–28)

What might this confounding messianic wisdom have to say to contemporary political philosophy? In *The Anti-Christ* Nietzsche cites this
passage at length to show how completely out of touch with reality the
dysangelist Paul really was. He calls Paul the greatest of all apostles of
revenge, an insolent windbag who tries to confound worldly wisdom—
but to no effect, says Nietzsche.[1] Nietzsche notwithstanding, certain
recent Continental philosophers have been reading Paul the Apostle's
confounding letters to great effect, allowing his messianic message to
disrupt certain modern conventions, political ontologies, and habits
of mind; to challenge the technological globalizing wisdom and rulers
of this age and to suggest a hidden messianic counter-sovereignty not
conceived in any human heart. Modern political theory has often re-
garded messianic political theology in particular as a dangerous threat
to secular liberal democracy—and not without reason. Yet it is also the
case that the first theory of the *saeculum* in the West, Augustine's *City*

1. Nietzsche, *Anti-Christ*, section 46.

of God, was developed precisely within a Pauline apocalyptic messianic understanding of history and the political. It is also the case that notions of neutral technology and juridical state sovereignty that underlie current conceptions and embodiments of the secular are themselves dangerously totalitarian, exclusivist, and violent, though often hidden beneath the veneer of progressivist liberal assumptions.

This is the position articulated in the apocalyptic messianism of Walter Benjamin, whose position is closely related to the Paul of the New Testament on the question of sovereignty, which is the central focus of this essay. The political theological concept at the heart of modern secular politics and political theory was given its classical formulation by Carl Schmitt. "Sovereign is he who decides on the exception," says Schmitt, which requires that sovereignty be seen not in strictly juridical terms but as a limit concept in which there is an agential power behind the law who decides on the "state of emergency" that suspends the normal rule of law.[2] This founding notion of sovereignty must be read together with Schmitt's founding definition of the political, namely, the distinction between friend and enemy.[3] For Schmitt the ultimate challenge to this basic political principle is found in the words of Jesus: "Love your enemies" (Matt 5:44)—which Schmitt, in keeping with conventional Christendom ethics, regards as a private, spiritual and individual, not a public political ethic. Surely former President George W. Bush would agree. So also would ultraliberal Canadian Prime Minister Pierre Trudeau have agreed when he invoked the War Measures Act in Canada during the FLQ crisis of 1970, thus deciding the exception that suspended "normal law" in the face of an "emergency situation."

Walter Benjamin had precisely this definition of sovereignty in mind when he wrote his Thesis VIII on the philosophy of history:

> The tradition of the oppressed teaches us that the "state of emergency" in which we live . . . is the rule. We must attain to a conception of history that is in keeping with this insight. Then we shall clearly realize that it is our task to bring about a real state of emergency, and this will improve our position in the struggle against Fascism. One reason why Fascism has a chance is that in the name of progress its opponents treat it as a historical norm. The current amazement that the things we are

2. Schmitt, *Political Theology*, 15.
3. Schmitt, *Concept of the Political*, 26f.

experiencing are "still" possible in the twentieth century is *not* philosophical. This amazement is not the beginning of knowledge . . . (§VIII; emphasis original)[4]

Benjamin clearly sets himself against the secular progressivist politics to which all seeming political options are conformed, and he does so in the name of a "*weak* Messianic power," in which each day is lived as the day of judgment on which the Messiah comes, "not only as the redeemer" but also "as the overcomer of Antichrist" (§II and VI). Such a "Messianic time" may not be thought within the categories of historicism but only from the perspective of a "*Jetztzeit*" (§XVIII), a "real state of emergency" that calls into fundamental question the normal state of emergency—i.e., the politics of modern secular state sovereignty—in which we live. It will bring into view the violent and destructive foundation of this sovereignty with its homogeneous and totalitarian order by remembering another sovereignty, a messianic counter-sovereignty that reorders the secular on completely different terms—terms compatible, argue certain recent Continental philosophers, with Paul's gospel.[5]

The apostle Paul stands in the messianic tradition of biblical political theology, where the central overriding claim is "Yahweh is sovereign," a claim that subverts any merely human claim to sovereignty and political authority. This includes, as Jacob Taubes points out, any claims for the sovereignty of law—whether that law be the Torah mediated by Moses or the Nomos mediated by Greco-Roman philosophy, or (we might add) the Christendom tradition of secular juridical state sovereignty and its many modern liberal copies. "We preach Messiah crucified," says Paul, "to the Jews a stumbling block and to the Greeks foolishness" (1 Cor 1:23)—and to triumphalist globalizing Christians, one might add, a foolish scandal. Paul's messianism will not accommodate conventional discourses of human mastery—which is to say, all conventional political discourses. As Alain Badiou puts it, for Paul the "becoming subject" founded by the messianic event "is a-cosmic and

---

4. Here and following, in parenthetic citations as well as footnotes, the symbol § with a Roman numeral denotes an individual Thesis in Benjamin's "Theses on the Philosophy of History."

5. See especially, Taubes, *Political Theology of Paul*; Agamben, *Time that Remains*; Agamben, "Messiah and the Sovereign."

illegal, refusing integration into any totality and signalling nothing."[6] For Badiou, Paul's relevance for the contemporary political situation is precisely to counter the relativism of postmodern identity politics, the multicultural consensus of neoliberal progressivism that has become conscripted to the globalized logic of capital. Here the only common currency is the abstract imperialist count of commercial and economic homogeneity—an empty universality that cashes out all communitarianisms. The beneficence of contemporary French cosmopolitanism that gets worked up at the sight of a young veiled woman nicely displays this problem.[7]

Into this political context Badiou proposes the radical disruption of Paul's messianic proclamation concerning the conditions for a "universal singularity" that defies the globalizing logic of the count, and its prevailing juridical and economic abstractions. It does so by an appeal to what Badiou calls an "eventual truth" that reconfigures the universal messianically with reference to the resurrection, as a human "becoming subject" in relation to a truth that is universal but not abstract.[8] For Badiou Paul is a "poet-thinker of the event" that neither constitutes nor claims authority from an identity or a law. It cannot therefore be a logic of mastery. Rather it is a discourse of rupture, a discourse of the sending of the Son that is detached from every particularism and every form of mastery. Paul's apostolic calling is characterized by "militant

---

6. Badiou, *Saint Paul*, 42.

7. Ibid., 9–11.

8. In using this language of "becoming subject," Badiou recalls Martin Heidegger's phenomenology of the religious life in which Heidegger meditates on the meaning of Paul's "having become" language in 1 Thess 1–2, which Heidegger relates to the "coming" of Messiah (Heidegger, *Phenomenology of Religious Life*, part I, 65f.). That is, for Heidegger as for Badiou, Paul's central concern is with the *how* of subjective enactment, not the *what* of a theoretical teaching, and is therefore characterized by proclamation and not the theorization of objective content (see ibid., 83f.)—which is what Badiou means when he calls Paul "*an antiphilosophical theoretician of universality*" (Badiou, *Saint Paul*, 108; emphasis original) that must not conceptualize but rather must subjectively enact the universal. Behind Heidegger, of course, lies Kierkegaard's Pauline emphasis on subjective enactment, though Kierkegaard will radically integrate and not divide the christic "how" and "what" of messianic becoming. That is, Heidegger's (and Badiou's) reading is influenced on this point more by Nietzsche than by Kierkegaard. I hope my essay will help to show why this is significant.

peregrinations,"[9] a "nomad leadership,"[10] that is equally out of place everywhere, a "nomadism of gratuitousness"[11] that exceeds every law and therefore disrupts every established identity and difference. Evental grace has a particular site of course, but the "becoming subject" that it founds is one that must "displace the experience historically, geographically, ontologically": it can do that not by escaping the embodied particularity of customs and differences, but rather by "passing through them, within them."[12] As Paul puts it in 1 Cor 9:19–22, "For though I am free from all . . . I have become all things to all people."

For Badiou, then, Paul's messianic logic offers a critique of all onto-theologies, all discourses of mastery rooted in appeals to wisdom and power as divine attributes. It does this by making possible an advent of subjectivity as "becoming son," a process of messianic filiation rooted in the foolish and scandalous power of weakness (1 Cor 1:17–29). This means that, contra Nietzsche, such a messianic becoming may not become a subject discourse of glorification that builds a new economy of power and wisdom on the strength of the ineffable. Paul will not glory in his mystical visions or try to tell "things that cannot be told"; he will glory only in his weakness, "for when I am weak, then I am strong" (2 Cor 12:1–10). But what is the "real content" of this "naked declaration" that is borne in militant weakness by messianic earthen vessels?[13]

Here the Continental clouds of fabulation begin to obscure the figure of the real, of the truth procedure that is in question. Badiou is deeply suspicious of any messianic appeal to the way of the cross. While he wants to insist on a Pauline "subjectivity of refuse," of abasement (cf. 1 Cor 4:13), this subjectivity must be detached from any historical particularity that would make of Christ a "master" or an "example."[14] The truth that founds the Christian subject is not a matter of historical content; it is a birth, a filiation in which subjects are founded equally and universally as "sons" insofar as they take up the work of filiation. For Badiou's Paul, the law organizes life according to the dictates of death,

9. Badiou, *Saint Paul*, 19.

10. Ibid., 67.

11. Ibid., 78.

12. Ibid., 99.

13. Ibid., 54.

14. Ibid., 60.

whereas messianic filiation dwells only in life; this is the meaning of resurrection.[15] Paul himself, however, would have refused Badiou's account of the messianic event. This new gnostic politics of fabulation divides what Paul's messianism unites: the cross and resurrection. Like any good worldly philosopher Badiou too is finally scandalized by both the cross and a resurrection that testifies to a Messiah raised up by divine agency, the Holy Spirit. That is, like Nietzsche and possibly also Heidegger (to whom Badiou is finally indebted for the "becoming son" language), Badiou is scandalized by Paul's messianic appeals to *pneuma* and the pneumatic. Here I want to turn to Jacob Taubes and his claim that "Nietzsche has been my best teacher about Paul,"[16] precisely because Nietzsche sees Paul correctly as the greatest enemy of his philosophy. Nietzsche discerned what is at issue between a "decadent" nihilistic Christianity (founded by Paul) and his own Dionysian higher humanity: the meaning of martyrdom and suffering.[17] Nietzsche's claim is that Paul's invention of the great lie of the messianic "redeemer" trades on the false currency of spiritual causality, a counterfeit transcendence ("*Jenseits*") most evident in the nihilistic doctrine of resurrection—a denigration of the "wisdom of this world" that is in fact a slanderous negation of the natural suffering endemic to the realm of human becoming.[18] I shall here examine this central engagement of the question of nihilism and messianic "becoming" in Paul—which in my view is of crucial importance to the current philosophical interest in Paul's political theology, especially on the question of messianic sovereignty.

At the heart of the conflict between Paul's messianic political theology and Nietzsche's Dionysian *Übermensch*, argues Taubes, lies the question of *pneuma* or spirit.[19] The importance of *pneuma* for Paul is displayed in two crucial distinctions developed in 1 Corinthians 2:

1. between the *pneuma tou kosmou* (spirit of the world) and the *pneuma ek tou theou* (spirit from God) (2:11–12), and

---

15. Ibid., 62.
16. Taubes, *Political Theology*, 79.
17. See Nietzsche, *Writings from the Late Notebooks*, 250.
18. See Nietzsche, *Anti-Christ*, sections 38–43.
19. Taubes, *Political Theology*, 43f.

2. between the *pneumatikos* (spiritual human being) and the *psychikos* (sometimes translated "natural human being," who judges not according to the spirit of God but according to the flesh, the immanent spiritual measure of worldly wisdom attuned to the spirit of the world) (2:14–15).

Paul suggests that only those who discern according to the "spirit from God" are able to see in the crucifixion a mysterious and hidden divine wisdom "not conceived in any human heart" (1 Cor 2:6f.: Kierkegaard's refrain in *Philosophical Fragments*) that counters all human sovereignties, which Paul says "are doomed to pass away" (*katargoumenon*, 1 Cor 2:6)—the key word here being one of Paul's favorite apocalyptic verbs, *katargeō/katargēsis*.[20] Before looking more closely at this verb, however, I want to note that Paul's appeal to the messianic mind or *nous* (1 Cor 2:16; 1:10) closely relates this spiritual judgment to the mysterious "mind" of the Lord (*kyrios*, sovereign). In 1 Corinthians 2, as in Romans 11:34, Paul is quoting Isaiah 40: "For who has known the mind [*nous*] of the Sovereign?" The Greek *nous* is used in the LXX to translate the Hebrew *ruah* or spirit, so closely linked to understanding in the Torah. The pneumatic messianic mind is therefore an apocalyptic discernment given by the divine Spirit, and it is this that scandalizes a natural human wisdom attuned to the spirit of the world, Nietzsche's warrior wisdom which more clearly than Badiou sees what it is up against.

In *Daybreak* Nietzsche gives us an early indication of his assessment of Paul: Paul's appeals to the "Holy Spirit" and the messianic *katargēsis* of the law through the crucifixion reveal "a mind as superstitious as it was cunning."[21] It is closely related to Christian philology and the "art of reading badly,"[22] which is to say, the art of spiritual or figural reading.[23] By the time he writes *Der Antichrist*, Nietzsche is much more

20. See the excellent discussion in Agamben, *Time that Remains*, 95f.

21. Nietzsche, *Daybreak*, 68f.

22. Ibid., 84.

23. See the illuminating accounts of Paul's typological hermeneutics as spiritual or figural, not allegorical, reading in Breton, *Saint Paul*, ch. 2; Taubes, *Political Theology*, 38–54; Agamben, *Time that Remains*, 62–87. Erich Auerbach has provided an important account of "figural interpretation" as the connection between two historical events in their spiritual relation to divine providence—a relation that therefore cannot be reduced either to historical causality or semiotic representations of meaning. Figural

bitter: "A religion like Christianity, which is completely out of touch with reality, which immediately falls apart if any concession is made to reality, would of course be mortally opposed to the 'wisdom of this world,' which is to say *science* [*Wissenschaft*]."[24] More specifically, this anti-realist Christianity is Paul's invention, of a god who ruins the wisdom of the world in its specific forms of philology and physiology, the two great adversaries of all superstition. "Indeed," says Nietzsche, "one cannot be a philologist or a physician without at the same time being *anti-Christian*."

This we must try to understand before we turn to Paul, for it represents the common sense of our age, as it did the age of Paul. Let us not forget Nietzsche's comment that there is only a single figure who commands respect in the New Testament, and that is Pilate, the Roman governor: "The noble scorn of a Roman, confronted with an impudent abuse of the word 'truth,' has enriched the New Testament with the only saying that *has value*—one which is its criticism, even its *annihilation* [*Vernichtung*]: 'What is truth?'"[25] The greatest crime against humanity committed by Pauline Christianity is the destruction of natural causality by spiritual causality, the replacement of truly philosophical knowledge (human, worldly wisdom) by religious superstition (hidden, "divine" wisdom)—a decadence represented above all by the Pauline teaching on the spiritual resurrection of the body, thus turning away from the natural nobility of this world in favor of a weaker spiritual one. "Once more I recall the inestimable words of Paul: 'The *weak* things of the

---

interpretation relies on a mimetic discernment understood as a spiritual act that deals with historical events experientially rather than in conceptual abstraction. The temporal participates in and points toward the eternal for its meaning, which therefore requires spiritual attentiveness and imitation if it is to be apprehended—as an enactment. See Auerbach, *Mimesis*. We are reminded here of Benjamin's description of the messianic *Jetztzeit* as coinciding precisely with "the" *Figur* that human history has in the universe: "*Die Jetztzeit, die als Modell der messianischen in einer ungeheueren Abbreviatur die Geschichte der ganzen Menschheit zusammenfasst, faellt haarschaft mit der Figure zusammen, die die Geschichte der Menschheit im Universum macht*" and again "*der Jetztzeit, in welcher Splitter der messianischen eingesprengt sind*" (§XVIII, p. 261 in Benjamin, "Ueber den Begriff der Geschichte"). This description established for Benjamin the manner in which Jews experience their liturgical "remembrance" (*Eingedenken*) of the past: "Every second of time was the narrow gate through which the Messiah might enter" (my translation).

24. Nietzsche, *Anti-Christ*, section 47.

25. Ibid., section 46.

world, the *foolish* things of the world, the *base* and *despised* things of the world hath God chosen.' This was the formula; *in hoc signo* decadence triumphed."[26] The teaching of the resurrection, of course, puts the scandal of miracle at the heart of reality: God creates the world *ex nihilo* at each moment; the world is not an immanent becoming according to causal laws of nature. Nietzsche's use of "*in hoc signo*" is an ironic reference to the "*in hoc signos vinces*" of the Constantinian slogan in which the sign of contradiction and weakness, the cross, becomes attached to triumphalistic state religion, the cross and the sword, Christian sovereignty religion—a development for which Nietzsche holds Paul responsible.

In *Twilight of the Idols* Nietzsche clarifies his alternative to Pauline spiritual causality when he states flatly that there are no spiritual causes, only instinctive ones.[27] While he agrees with the Pauline displacement of the human ego (i.e., "will" for Nietzsche is not rooted in spiritual consciousness or subjective ego),[28] he argues for the primacy of instinctual drives or the will to power. His argument against Pauline Christianity is that it privileges weak and decadent instincts by cultivating a divinely willed pity, which "makes suffering contagious"[29] and persuades human beings to *nothingness*, the practice of nihilism. As such Christian culture loses its natural, noble instincts, its rootedness in "life itself" as "the instinct for growth, for durability, for an accumulation of forces, for *power*: where the will to power is lacking there is decline,"[30] there is decadence.[31] In keeping with this analysis, Nietzsche argues for the revaluation of all Pauline values by posing the problem of what type of higher human being may be bred and willed that is worthier of life, more attuned to strong natural instincts. This is his Dionysian *Übermensch*, to which I shall return later.

---

26. Ibid., section 51.

27. Nietzsche, *Twighlight of the Idols*, 495.

28. Nietzsche, *Writings*, 59: "All deeper men—Luther, Augustine, Paul come to mind—agree that our morality and its events do not correspond with our *conscious will*—in short, that an explanation in terms of having goals [teleological causality] is *insufficient.*"

29. Nietzsche, *Anti-Christ*, section 7.

30. Ibid., section 6.

31. Ibid., section 17.

First let us now consider more carefully Paul's apocalyptic verb, *katargesis*, rooted as it is in a *mē*-ontology that so offends Nietzsche. I wish to show that Paul might be considered not so much a nihilist as a messianic *ex nihilo*-ist who at every moment seeks to dwell in the power of divine life, a power displayed above all in the crucifixion, that emblem of worldly weakness and failure (Constantine and triumphalist Christendom notwithstanding). *Katargēsis* is the verb Paul uses in 1 Cor 1:28 with reference to the cross: God chooses the things without being (*ta mē onta*) in order to bring to nothing (*katargēse*) the things with being (*ta onta*). The same verb is used also in 1 Cor 15:24 where Paul with reference to resurrection says Messiah will *katargēse* every earthly rule and authority and power, including death. Nietzsche is right to detect here Paul's understanding of sovereign divine freedom as a power realized in weakness—that is, as Stanislas Breton puts it, "it is nothing of what we would like it to be."[32] God does not inhabit our human dwellings, and to discern the passage of God in a world that is passing away requires a mortification of natural inclination—the sort of inclination described by Paul in Romans 1 (the desire to worship the creature rather than the Creator), but also the sort aroused or "energized" by the law (Romans 7). While Nietzsche admires the sovereign divine freedom here, he despises and suspects Paul's tying this to the mortification of the flesh as another worldly power play, despicably hypocritical because it uses the crucified Christ to establish a new, anti-natural and therefore decadent law. Nietzsche of course *has* to take this line since he refuses the realism of faith in the miracle of pneumatic divine creation *ex nihilo* as expressed, for Paul, in the Messiah Jesus.

In Romans 7 Paul talks about "dying to the law through the body of Messiah" in order to live in the life of the Spirit. His argument is that the law goes to the heart of desire, and indeed Paul quotes the summing commandment in Exod 20:17, "you shall not desire [LXX, *epithumēseis*]," which echoes Eve's response to the prohibition pertaining to the tree of knowledge of good and evil: "the tree was to be desired to make one wise" (Gen 3:6). The law thus addresses the root of sin, violence, and death: my desire to possess for myself, my "ego," my flesh, all the goods belonging not only to my neighbor in the socio-mimetic cult of desire, but also all the goods belonging to God in the ethico- and

32. Breton, *Word and the Cross*, 50.

religio-mimetic cult of judicial, moral, and spiritual desire for sovereign divine perfection/wisdom/authority. For Paul there is no escape from the fallen desire of the human condition, which is held captive and might indeed find expression in Zarathustra's "Yes and Amen Song" (itself a parody of 2 Cor 1:20): *"Doch alle Lust will Ewigkeit—will tiefe, tiefe Ewigkeit."*[33] For Nietzsche's Dionysian higher humanity, facing up nobly to this tragic ring of recurrence is all-important, and he correctly discerns in Pauline messianism a mortification of this erotic will to power.

Paul says in Rom 7:6, "Now we are *katērgēthēmen* from the law, dead to that which held us captive." The law's energy to arouse sinful desire is rendered inoperative (see Agamben[34]) or transfigured messianically away from juridical codes to the service of love in the new life of *pneuma*. The apocalyptic messianic meaning of this is explored by Paul in 2 Cor 3:12–18, where the veil of the written law is removed, and we are transfigured by the divine *pneuma* of freedom into the *eikōn* of God, which is the created human destiny. Mimesis is now shaped not by the *psychikos* of fallen desire but by the messianic *pneumatikos* that takes the form of the cross—i.e., the kenotic form that is also the human becoming which relinquishes divine power in order to take the form of the servant as a suffering passage in the world that is passing away. This unveiling is not an external matter, though it is also the case that messianic becoming (the *parousia* of Messiah in 1 and 2 Thessalonians) forces a decisive choice between messianic becoming as a relational enactment of the messianic way of life that entails waiting and suffering, and satanic power that is revealed in terms of external worldly signs and wonders. Even the restraint (*katechōn*, 2 Thess 2:7) of this latter power, however, is not a messianic task, contrary to conventional Christendom political theology. The messianic enactment, the *parousia*, is not the creation of a better world (it is not a "what" or a "when") but bearing witness to the world's passing away and transfiguration through divine love (it is a "how") which builds up not external edifices, but only (as Kierkegaard emphasized in *Works of Love*) builds up love—and thus fulfills the law![35]

33. Nietzsche, *Thus Spoke Zarathustra*, part III.

34. Agamben, *Time that Remains*, 95.

35. Kierkegaard also notes the connection between *katargēsis* of the law and messianic enactment in *Works of Love*, 97; the connection is the kenosis of Christ, a love

Nietzsche, as I said, also seeks a trans-juridical sovereignty beyond good and evil, but he will posit this in an anti-messianic human becoming, a sovereignty of instinct in the value-positing creative will, Paul's *pneuma tou kosmou*. Nietzsche's analysis of an ethic of reactivity and *ressentiment* in Christendom political theology is astute precisely to the extent that he follows the messianic, but his flawed reading of Paul as a priestly moralist is rooted in something deeper than historical or philological error. It is rooted in his attunement to what is at stake and entailed in the claims to a divinely revealed sovereignty of the slain Lamb—hence Nietzsche's declaration of war in *Ecce Homo*: "Dionysus *versus* the Crucified."[36] The only spirit Nietzsche can finally accept is the human *psychikos* attuned to the *pneuma tou kosmou*, the spirit of the world. No less than the crucified Messiah is the Dionysian *Übermensch* given to suffering and martyrdom; the difference, as Nietzsche says, lies in the meaning of it: whether a messianic meaning or a tragic meaning. "The tragic man says Yes to even the bitterest suffering: he is strong, full, deifying enough to do so. The Christian says No to even the happiest earthly lot: he is weak, poor, disinherited enough to suffer from life in whatever form."[37]

Kierkegaard rightly points out the difference between Paul and Nietzsche in his short piece "Of the Difference between a Genius and an Apostle," when he suggests that only if one may reintroduce the distinction between the sphere of immanence and the sphere of transcendence will one be able to discern Paul's apostolic message—it is a revelation, not a philosophical teaching; it is rooted in a divine, not a human authority; it cannot be rationally penetrated, only spiritually discerned in a complete submission to the *logos* of the *stauros*.[38] Attuned, that is to say, not to a human-to-human "pathos of distance,"[39] as between a noble warrior and a slave, but to a divine-human pathos of distance that Kierkegaard calls the "passion of faith"—a passion intensified when the divine becomes a slave. Here we have the difference between the Dionysian tragic hero and the messianic knight of faith. By

---

that gives up heavenly perfections in order to come down and love changeable, mortal persons in all their changeable imperfection (ibid., 173).

36. It is the final sentence of Nietzsche's *Ecce Homo*, 151; cf. *Writings*, 249–50.

37. Nietzsche, *Writings*, 250.

38. Kierkegaard, "Difference between Genius and Apostle," 174f.

39. Nietzsche, *Anti-Christ*, section 43.

faith in the miracle of divine passage the knight of faith performs the movement not only of relinquishment in the face of suffering (and does so without noetic or ontic protection of any kind from tragic reality); he or she performs the added movement, a movement given as a breathing room[40] from beyond the immanent sphere, of conforming the self to a messianic becoming that dwells in a love that exceeds death. This is what Paul struggles to express in 1 Corinthians 13 and 15.

In order to pursue this I want to turn to a concluding comparison of Walter Benjamin's "weak messianic power" (which both Taubes and Agamben, rightly, in my view, call Pauline) and Nietzsche's will to power on the question of redemption. We could also discuss this contrast in terms of the different "*Untergangen*": Dionysian abundance or messianic emptying? I begin with Nietzsche's Zarathustra, the *Fürsprecher*, the advocate or forerunner who prepares the way of the Dionysian "overman" who alone can overcome the nihilistic becoming of the Platonic Christian division between immanence and transcendence in order, as Heidegger tellingly puts it, to "let becoming *be* a becoming."[41] Nietzsche thus creates poetically the thinker of the most burdensome thought, the tragedy of time, who is able to say "Yes" to the supreme "No"; and here again Heidegger helpfully shows us that Zarathustra's teaching of the eternal recurrence in keeping with a Dionysian anthropology is not a "what" or a "when" but a "how," a "how to become"—no less than Paul's discussion of the *parousia* of Messiah in 1 Thessalonians, in which it is a shared form of becoming and not an abstract doctrine that is communicated. This becoming is above all an agonistic struggle in keeping with the agonistic becoming of all things. Though Zarathustra's *Untergang* is described in the prologue as a *kenosis* in a parodying reference to Philippians 2;[42] what he seeks is not to empty himself of divine attributes in order to lovingly serve human beings, but rather he seeks to bring human beings the gift of Dionysian superabundance.[43] As he puts it in the section "On

40. Kierkegaard, *Sickness unto Death*, 28.

41. Heidegger, *Nietzsche*, 1:218.

42. Nietzsche, *Zarathustra*, 122; see also the kenosis of love, 196, and the descent of power into beauty, 230. On kenosis as parody, see Gooding-Williams, *Zarathustra's Dionysian Modernism*, 55f.

43. Nietzsche, *Zarathustra*, 123; cf. 334f.

the Higher Man," "All great love does not *want* love: it wants more."[44] In contrast to the messianic *Fürsprecher* of and for "the little people" who had to die because of the "overpitying" nature of his self-emptying love,[45] Zarathustra seeks the overcoming of such a love (an overrated "neighbour love"[46]) in order that we may become divine earthly creators once again—higher, stronger, more worthy human beings. Let us not forget that Zarathustra's animals are the craftiest serpent and the proudest eagle, and that he counters "neighbour love" with "love of the farthest" in overflowing (not self-emptying), creative, warring (not other serving) friendship.

In order to overcome the nihilistic becoming of the slavish, spiritual messianic revaluation of natural noble values, so as to make possible an affirming, creative, earthly becoming humanly possible once again, Zarathustra faces a self-overcoming represented in his "most abysmal" thought. This thought is the very heart of the tragic condition found in the "passing away" of earthly life and all the "no-sayers" who deny the temporality of human becoming (and with this, the highest earthly values) with their theological appeals to eternity. This thought is "the vision of the loneliest,"[47] and it is a vision of self-redemption through creative willing that accepts its suffering, above all the suffering of time, impermanence.[48] The greatest challenge here, the only pathway to the creative, yes-saying will, is to overcome the spirit of revenge: "the will's ill will against time and its 'it was.'"[49] This is not a reconciliation between time and eternity (that would be to go beyond tragedy via superstition), but something higher than reconciliation: the meeting of time running backward (the past) and time running forward (future) in the *Augenblick* of the eternal "now."[50] This, for Nietzsche, can only

44. Ibid., 405.

45. Ibid., 378.

46. Ibid., 172f.

47. Ibid., 268, 271; cf. Nietzsche, *Gay Science*, section 341.

48. Nietzsche, "On Redemption," in *Zarathustra*, 249f.

49. Nietzsche, *Zarathustra*, 252.

50. Ibid., 270. It bears noting that Kierkegaard too understands the gateway of human willing as a "Moment," which he calls *"ojeblikket"* in *Concept of Anxiety*, 87, but unlike Nietzsche and like Benjamin, the paradoxical face of this moment is for Kierkegaard messianic.

be understood parabolically:[51] the doorway called *Augenblick* has two faces that contradict each other and "offend each other face to face."[52] The challenge for the *Übermensch* is to face the "spirit of gravity" that proclaims all truth to be crooked and all time a circle,[53] and wills nevertheless to affirm the human creativity and uniqueness of one's life in a joyful, innocent forgetting of the "all is vanity" of eternal return. The redemption here is not penitential; it is not received as a messianic reconciliation. It is a decision to become a warrior self who engages the *agon* of saying "Yes" to all suffering and all destruction, life in all its chaotic contradictions. This parabolic becoming stands opposed to the messianic: "The god on the cross is a curse on life, a signpost to seek redemption from life; Dionysus cut to pieces is a *promise* of life: it will be eternally reborn and return again from destruction."[54]

Benjamin's messianic *Untergang*, by contrast, pays attention to the implications of the cruciform curse for the tragic abundance of Dionysian becoming that is motivated by the desire to transform humanity but not through the love of particular humans. Like Paul, Benjamin does not see weakness or the kingdom of God as a curse on life, but rather as a scandal for those seeking ontological strength. This is because, as Benjamin puts it in his "Theologico-Political Fragment," only the Messiah consummates (*vollendet*) all historical becoming "in the sense that he alone redeems, completes, creates its relation to the Messianic," something that nothing historical can do "*von sich, aus sich.*"[55] Historically speaking, the kingdom of God is not a *telos* of historical becoming—Benjamin is very clear that the messianic can have nothing to do with a humanist progressivism—but is rather the transfigured "end" of history. Messianic becoming is apocalyptic, an interruption of the natural that suspends its immanent laws ("flourish-

51. "It is of time and becoming that the best parables should speak: let them be a praise and a justification of all impermanence [*Verganglichkeit*]" (Nietzsche, *Zarathustra*, 198–99).

52. Nietzsche, *Zarathustra*, 269f.

53. This spirit of gravity ("all is vanity") articulated by the dwarf, is the message of *Qoheleth*: "What is crooked cannot be made straight" (Eccl 1:15; cf. 7:13); and the circular nature of time in Eccl 3. These slogans pervade *Zarathustra* (e.g., 198, 245, 270, 316, 330).

54. Nietzsche, *Writings*, 250.

55. Benjamin, "Theologico-Political Fragment," 312.

ing of the fittest") so as to point to its hidden divine passage through it, its truest becoming and indeed its truest, eternal "happiness." The messianic parable, in Benjamin as in Kierkegaard and in Paul, is not that of the poetic thinker making up an entertaining fable; rather, the Messiah is the second Adam, the man from heaven who became in the flesh a life-giving spirit (1 Cor 15:45–49), and did so in self-emptying servanthood. It is a divine enactment in time, and this is only possible if history is not reducible to the endless repetition of natural causality— or, as in the "Fragment," "nature is Messianic by reason of its eternal and total passing away."[56]

And yet this becoming is not somehow happening behind the back of history or the order of the profane; it is happening within it as a mysterious redemption for those with eyes to see. The "eyes to see" are attuned to a messianic intensity marked not by a "No" to this world but by a "Yes and Amen" happiness in which the earthly seeks its *Untergang* and indeed its transfiguring "*zu Grunde gehen.*" Like Kierkegaard, Benjamin stresses the paradoxical character of this becoming: in immediacy, this messianic "intensity of the heart" of the single one passes through an unhappiness, as "suffering." It is a complete giving away of itself in nihilistic, loving service to what is passing away. And yet in this spiritual service it experiences a worldly restitution of the true form of the world—its passing away as a becoming not unlike Paul's portrayal of *agapē* in 1 Corinthians 13: while all human actions and words, even the highest and most noble, will pass away (again the verb is *katargēsis*), *agapē*, the divine passage in the world never ends. There is a close, transfiguring connection between worldly *katargēsis* and divine agapic agency. Indeed, in contrast to human *gnosis* which "puffs up," divine *agapē* "builds up" (*oikodomei*, 1 Cor 8:1–2); the difference is that *agapē* is divine, not human knowing, and what is built up is the relation to divine completion of "all things" (*ta panta*, 1 Cor 15:28; Rom 11:36).

This agapic messianic movement, as Benjamin shows in his "Theses on the Philosophy of History," is rooted in the power of weakness, both spiritual and material, that will not conform to the triumphalist progressivist politics of the world. "The Messiah," says Benjamin, "comes not only as the redeemer, he comes as the overcomer of Antichrist" (§VI). Here there can be no historicist siding with the victors; a messi-

56. Ibid.

anic historical materialist must "brush history against the grain" (§VII) on the side of oppressed victims: the weak, the foolish, the lowly and despised (Benjamin, like Paul, imitates Messiah in being a *Fürsprecher* for the weak, "*die kleine Leute*").[57] This goes against the triumphalist politics of social democracy and Marxist belief in the technological mastery of nature no less than against Fascism, insofar as these are rooted in anti-messianic conceptions of human sovereignty that do not recognize that the form of the world is "passing away." Benjamin identifies anti-messianic triumphalism with an immanent natural causality, the concept of a progression through homogeneous time (§XIII). To this must be counterposed a messianic time as apocalypse, "time filled by the presence of the now [*Jetztzeit*]" (§XIV). Such a time can only be understood and lived figurally, in which one's own time is lived in relation to the whole of time, namely eternity, in such a manner that I comprehend myself and my time in critical relation to a spiritually discerned past and future. As Paul puts it in 1 Corinthians 10, where he complicates the position of the so-called strong by appealing to the Exodus in the kind of figural interpretation that drove Nietzsche crazy, "all our fathers were under the cloud, and all passed through the sea, and all were baptized into Moses, . . . and all ate the same spiritual food and all drank the same spiritual drink. For they drank from the spiritual Rock which followed them, and the Rock was Messiah. . . . Now these things happened to them as a warning, but they were written down for our instruction, upon whom the ends of the ages has come. Therefore let any one who thinks that he stands take heed lest he fall" (1 Cor 10:1–4, 11–12). That is, any particular historical event or time is passing away and points for its completion in the *Figur* of history as a whole, which both Paul and Benjamin identify as messianic. But it can only be lived in such a relation to the messianic figure, both past and future, in the kairotic "now"—the *Jetztzeit* (§XVIII). Why? Because, as Benjamin quoting the rabbis puts it, "every second of time [is] the small gateway through which the Messiah might enter" (§XVIII, B). In such an enactment, in which my life and time becomes a spiritual attentiveness to and mimesis of messianic becoming, the actual meaning of the deed remains mysterious—it "passes away" as do all human deeds. And yet it becomes, in a material and worldly way, a "building up" of the

---

57. Cf. Nietzsche, *Zarathustra*, 378.

messianic passage of God in the world. In this way is the lived deed both retained in a remembering and, as Benjamin puts it (§XVII), "*aufgehoben*"—using Luther's German translation for Paul's apocalyptic verb "*katargēsis*"[58]—into the movement of all things to their "end." I note in passing that for both Paul and Benjamin this figural messianic becoming is closely tied to liturgical and sacramental participation. This is not accidental insofar as the liturgical and sacramental are emblematic precisely of the parabolic, figural, trans-immanent character of all reality.

But precisely here we face the daunting challenge identified by Taubes, for the liturgical and sacramental heart of the messianic emblem of redemption for Paul is the crucifixion: "Messiah redeemed us from the curse of the law, having become a curse for us" (Gal 3:13). This is what so scandalizes Nietzsche: the earthly parabolic symbolism of mantic Jesus (the "Jesus Seminar" Jesus) is turned by Paul into a messianic cosmic mystery, a divine "*sacrifice*" of atonement[59] that undergirds a vast priestly power structure called "Christendom" used to tyrannize the masses and form moralistic herds via the painful, life-denying creation of conscience.[60] Let us hear Taubes on Nietzsche's view of this:

> . . . Christianity hypostatizes sacrifice rather than abolishing it, and thus perpetuates it. Let someone come and really theologically challenge this! This is in Nietzsche a deeply humane impulse against the entanglement of guilt and atonement, on which the entire Pauline dialectic—but even already that of the Old Testament—is based. This continually self-perpetuating cycle of guilt, sacrifice, and atonement needs to be broken in order finally to yield an innocence of becoming (this is Nietzsche's expression). A becoming, even a being, that is not guilty. Whereas Paul really does believe that humanity and the cosmos are guilty [Rom 7:7–25]. A guilt that can be redeemed by means of sacrifice and atonement. Justified. But what a terrible price is paid in this entanglement! What terrible cruelty, from which there is no escape![61]

58. See Agamben, *Time that Remains*, 99f.

59. Nietzsche, *Anti-Christ*, section 41.

60. This is the story of Nietzsche's *Genealogy of Morals*.

61. Taubes, *Political Theology*, 87–88.

At this point Taubes breaks off the engagement with a fizzling excursus on Freud rather than taking up the parabolic pattern of messianic atonement and martyrdom in Paul. And as far as I can tell, the current Continental philosophical interpretations of Paul want to remain indirect about this as well. Of course I'm going to fizzle here too, but let me gesture to Kierkegaard and Dostoevsky as nineteenth-century thinkers who engaged this Nietzschean critique, albeit indirectly, before ending with some reflections from the recent literature on the implications of this for political sovereignty. Nietzsche proposes the abolition of Christendom atonement theory by abolishing Pauline messianism with its spiritual causality and divine passage. In his parable of "The Madman" in *The Gay Science*, Nietzsche's solution to this whole idolatry of the "holy lie" is to proclaim unabashedly the murder of God, a recognition that God is already dead as a result of the collective murder in which all of us moderns are implicated:

> God is dead. God remains dead. And we have killed him. How shall we, the murderers of all murderers, comfort ourselves? What was holiest and most powerful of all that the world has yet owned has bled to death under our knives. Who will wipe this blood off us? What water is there for us to clean ourselves? What festivals of atonement, what sacred games shall we have to invent? Is not the greatness of this deed too great for us? Must not we ourselves become gods simply to seem worthy of it? There has never been a greater deed; and whoever will be born after us—for the sake of this deed he will be part of a higher history than all history hitherto.[62]

Nietzsche thus violently reverses Christendom atonement theory with yet another murderous sacrifice. By contrast, Kierkegaard and Dostoevsky draw a crucial distinction between the sinful violence of Christendom atonement theory and practice, to which Nietzsche rightly objects but then imitates, and the penitential movement away from this violence (moral, political, religious) in the messianic becoming witnessed to by Paul. That is, they will not seek to become worthy of the divine creativity after which Nietzsche sovereignly grasps. Indeed, for Pauline messianism, that is precisely the sinful heart of the human unlikeness to God that leads invariably to further violence, from which

---

62. Nietzsche, *Gay Science*, 95.

those who seek to participate in a truly human becoming must repent. It is a repentance that is provoked paradoxically in the messianic apocalypse in which God joins human beings in this unlikeness in order to nullify it. To understand this requires the downfall of worldly human understanding, a reshaping of desire that is so radical it can only be described as a "rebirth" or a "new creation," a *metabasis eis allo geno*" (transition to a different becoming, as Kierkegaard puts it[63]). No less than for Nietzsche does this entail an act of willing in time, in the "moment" in which time and eternity touch each other. But here Kierkegaard makes reference to the spiritual causality displayed in the resurrection and to Paul's language in 1 Cor 15:52, in which Paul speaks of the "moment" as the "twinkling of an eye" in which the perishability of mortal nature puts on the imperishability of the immortal.[64] No naturalization of this miraculous paradox is possible by which the scandal may be removed:[65] it remains foolish to worldly wisdom precisely insofar as worldly wisdom seeks its own sovereignty.[66]

In conclusion let me return to where we began. Badiou is faithful to Paul's messianic logic when he says it critiques all onto-theologies, all discourses of mastery rooted in human appeals to wisdom and power as divine attributes. A messianic identity or movement may not become a discourse of glorification that builds a new economy of power and wisdom on the strength of the ineffable. Paul will glory only in his weakness, in a subjectivity of abasement that continually goes outside itself in loving service. Badiou is very nervous about Christian triumphalism that "glories in the cross," coercively trading in the political capital of sacrificial victimhood. This is an understandable worry, but for Paul one cannot address it simply by doing away with scandalous messianic content. "Jesus the crucified Messiah is cosmic sovereign" is Paul's claim, one that Badiou doesn't really engage. Badiou's portrait of Paul is indebted to that of another French philosopher, Stanislas Breton, a Catholic,[67] who argues that for Paul the messianic call to dispossession

63. Kierkegaard, *Philosophical Fragments*, 73.

64. Kierkegaard, *Concept of Anxiety*, 87–88.

65. Kierkegaard, *Philosophical Fragments*, 95f.

66. And thus, as Benjamin puts it, must perpetuate the violence both mythically and juridically; see Benjamin, "Critique of Violence."

67. And therefore perhaps of all philosophers these days most to be despised. Most conventional philosophers are tempted, following Kant, to join the company

and critical detachment from prevailing orders of human sovereignty cannot bypass the path of the cross as Badiou does. For Paul the *logos* of the *stauros* (the word of the cross, 1 Cor 1:18) is the very power of God; precisely the scandal of the cross disrupts the humanist appeals of the wise and the strong. In Jesus the crucified Messiah the sovereignty of history and all creation is disclosed in the form of the suffering servant, and only those willing to empty themselves of possessive desires that cling graspingly to the eternal form (whether it be a teaching, an ethic, or an identity), only those who take the kenotic form of the servant may journey messianically with the eternal in time. Here we may be reminded of Badiou's worry about a morbid and *ressentiment*-laden glorying in the suffering of the cross. Does not this "path of the cross" simply constitute a reversal of worldly values in which obedient Christians build up heavenly treasures by trading on a divine spiritual economy that denigrates this world only to gain pre-eminence in the other world? Breton is fully aware of this danger; he says, "The God of the Cross is not the God of desire, and that is why this God does not know how to be a God of the superlative."[68] What is scandalously revealed in the resurrection event is precisely that the superlative God has died on the cross; the power of the cross thus confounds every "what is" that may be desired by the weakness of "what is not," and this "meontological mission" is the focus of Paul's gospel. The power of the cross is therefore a performative act, a mission that continually moves outside itself in unseen, quotidian service to the least, the lowly, the despised, even those who are not—and thus becomes a foolish spectacle, the refuse of the world, the offscouring of all things. Such a dispossessive, exilic love serves "what is not" not out of resentment or impotence but because God creatively acts *ex nihilo* in a love that is endlessly kenotic and dispossessive rather than acquisitive and accumulative.

Of course, we may ask, what has all this got to do with politics and sovereignty? Is this but a story of the exodus of the soul or the

---

of liberal Protestant scholars who domesticate Paul's messianism by (a) controlling it through scholarly contextualization that gets rid of its political incorrectness, its scandal factor, and (b) aligning it with the most progressivist of modern humanisms— liberal democracy and all its colonizing works carried out in the name of sacrificial victims and human rights. In which case, who needs Paul? He really is only finally an embarrassment—and it is the embarrassment factor by which the unconventional philosophers I am interpreting are intrigued.

68. Breton, *Word and the Cross*, 9.

postmodern diaspora self? Breton is clear that the *logos* of the *stauros* may not be so understood—it is very much related to an *ekklēsia*, those called out to a body politic that cannot be reduced to an experience of the individual soul nor to a church that lives unto itself (whether in a liturgy of adoration or in a separatist isolationist sect). The dispossession displayed in Acts, represented in the sharing of the fractured Eucharistic body, must be continued in the diasporic messianic body: "instead of persisting as establishment," Breton writes, "the church must in the final analysis be forgotten in the service of the poor, that is to say, in Paul's very language, in unconditional devotion to 'those who do not exist.'"[69] Whatever else this might mean, it cannot mean anything like a Christian nation or any other self-enclosed political entity. Breton suggests that it will be a politics of "*hōs mē*"—making use of the world "as if not" (*hōs mē*) using it (1 Cor 7:29–31).

This *hōs mē* political theology is further developed in the interpretations of Paul by the German Jewish philosopher Jacob Taubes and the Italian philosopher Giorgio Agamben.[70] Of course it is fashionable these days to reclaim the Jewish Paul, but Taubes and Agamben, like Walter Benjamin, are not interested in what is fashionable. At the center of Paul's messianic logic is his declaration of faith in the crucified Messiah as the divine act of atonement by which "all Israel" shall be saved. For Taubes this is neither a noetic universalism nor a liberal *nomos* universalism: "Sure, Paul is also universal," says Taubes, "but by virtue of the 'eye of the needle' of the crucified one, which means: transvaluation of all the values of this world . . . This is why it carries a political charge."[71] The death of the Messiah as a scapegoat, a criminal, signals for Paul nothing less than the end of righteousness based upon law. "Outbidding Moses," Paul's political theology believes the Messiah, condemned according to the Law, accomplishes what the Law cannot, namely, the healing of the nations. Hence the place of Moses and the Law is transfigured messianically in the direction of "all Israel," an Israel whose definition can no longer be restricted only to Jews.

---

69. Ibid., 56.

70. I develop a fuller account of this in my essay "Whither Messianic Ethics?" and, in relation to the political theology of John Howard Yoder, in "Is a Messianic Political Ethic Possible?"

71. Taubes, *Political Theology*, 24.

This transfiguration, moreover, takes the election of Israel seriously in a manner that is perhaps all the more embarrassing for modern
Christianity. The Messiah redeems Israel by extending divine mercy to
the unrighteous enemy, even calling "my people" those who were not
a people and "beloved" those who were not beloved. In Romans 9–11
this is linked to a mysterious "drama of jealousy" that is paradoxical:
"all" will be saved but only by the messianic "remnant" who proclaims
mercy to the enemy and to those who are *not* a people. Hence the central importance of enemy love in Paul's political theology, in a (contra
Nietzsche) completely non-moralistic way. The sovereign Messiah, by
suffering death, bears witness to the breakdown of every human moral
claim to self-sufficiency or righteousness. It is *God* who elects a people
for the sake of redeeming all, in a politics of messianic suffering and
martyrdom where, in the "time that remains," the "called" live *hōs mē*,
as if they have not. Only such a messianic politics will be able to discern
that the "state of emergency" in which we live is the norm, and that its
task is to bring into view the "real state of emergency" in which divine
sovereign action proclaims the messianic exception.

Giorgio Agamben helps us pursue this further. Like Taubes, he
emphasizes that Paul is a diaspora Jew whose Greek is neither properly
Jewish (Hebrew) nor Greek. He cites Taubes's wonderful story of his
student days in Zurich when his teacher in classical Greek, Emil Staiger,
confided: "You know, Taubes, yesterday I was reading the Letters of the
Apostle Paul. To which he added, with great bitterness: But that isn't
Greek, it's Yiddish! Upon which I said: Yes, Professor, and that's why I
understand it!"[72]

Paul speaks the language of Jews in exile in a manner that works
over the host language from within and confounds its identity. The
messianic is precisely related to this diaspora linguistic situation. In
order to understand how this relates to the politics of a messianic community, Agamben reflects first on what he calls the structure of messianic time, expressed in 1 Cor 7:29: "the *kairos* has been contracted;
in what remains, let those who have . . . live *hōs mē* as though they
have not . . ." This is Benjamin's "*Jetztzeit*"—the time of the "now" in
which the accumulative flow of *chronos* is interrupted, burst open or

72. Ibid., 3–4.

"contracted" by a messianic event that coincides with the very *"Figur"* that reveals human history.

For example, Paul refers to himself frequently as *doulos*, slave of the Messiah (the term that so offends Nietzsche). This is a juridical term that Paul now confounds from within, since the sovereign Lord whom the *doulos* serves is a crucified Messiah. As such the condition of *doulos* is itself transformed, and it stands for a general transformation of worldly-political-social conditions here blasted out of the continuum of history. This also has everything to do with the language of "calling"— Paul's calling as *doulos* of the Messiah but also the calling (*klēsis*) of the *ekklēsia* (further described in 1 Cor 7:17f.) in confounding the relation to worldly "callings"—"remain with God in the calling in which you have been called"—including that of a slave. Contrary to Weber's secularization thesis (influenced by Nietzsche) in which "calling" indicates an eschatological indifference to the worldly, Agamben shows that for Paul "calling" is the language of messianic transformation.[73] Above all, it stands for the nullification and revocation of every vocation.[74] The nullification of every worldly vocation here is not abandoning the world for an "elsewhere" but is a dwelling within it in dispossession, thus confounding its identity from within and allowing the power of God to transform it in keeping with its true condition or "figure," that is, its "passing away" toward an end that lies beyond it. In other words, the messianic is not a new identity with its own set of rights; it is rather the power to use without possessing. In this way worldly vocations and identities are never "replaced" by something new; there is rather a "making new" that occurs within them that transfigures and opens them up to their true use in keeping with their true condition.[75] In effect, this is a slavery liberated from juridical bondage to worldly possession for free creaturely action in a world that is passing away.

For Benjamin this weak messianic power accomplishes what Marx's proletariat revolution cannot. It hollows out the progressivist, abstracting grip of the capitalist count from within, and yet with reference to the very sovereign power of creation, i.e., redeeming love.[76] For

73. Agamben, *Time that Remains*, 19f.

74. Ibid., 23f.

75. Ibid., 26.

76. I realize this claim with regard to Benjamin is controversial, yet it is how I read his "Theses"—not as advocating a cheap, empathic love rooted in an "indolent heart"

Paul the *ekklēsia* is precisely this classless society where all are freed by becoming slaves of the Messiah. They become free not by possessing rights nor by taking over the instruments of power for their own superior Christian control, but precisely by using the world "as if not," in a dispossessive manner that assesses the value of each particular thing or relation with reference to the passage of God in the world. This "as if not" messianic ethic thus also stands in opposition to Kant's "as if" (*als ob*) moral universal that strives to possess an ideal (Kant says: act *as if* God, immortality, and freedom exist as regulative ideals). Paul's position is rooted in a kenotic movement of dispossession that cannot become yet another act of (self-) legislation; it relinquishes its moral striving and its hold—whether of the technological means of progressive liberation from the decay of nature, or the political means of liberating particular identities from the burdens of oppression. The point is rather to open up all worldly callings to the transfiguring passage of God—through slavery to the sovereign crucified Messiah. Here it is necessary to get beyond possessive identities and aspirations altogether via messianic healing. With Karl Barth and Franz Kafka, the Pauline messianic subject "knows that in messianic time, the saved world coincides exactly with the lost world"[77]—there is no path to salvation except via self-losing service to what cannot be saved. This is why both Kafka and Barth emphasized the secular language of the parable as the proper discourse for ethics: the parabolic reversal of conventional criteria by which we measure strength and weakness, success and failure.[78] It does

---

(§VII) but as a love that is referred to "redemption" (§II), a happiness beyond either envy or conformity to a history defined by "victors." That is, it is love as a struggle for a redeemed humanity in the apocalyptic "fullness" of each historical moment (§III), which brushes history "against the grain" of its violent progressivist myth (§VIIf.) in which past victims are expendable.

77. Agamben, *Time that Remains*, 42.

78. For Barth the language of parable, in the section of the *Römerbrief* called "The Problem of Ethics," is tied explicitly to 1 Cor 7:31: "the form of the world passes away," and therefore the only ethical form that bears testimony to divine action is one that is "offered up" sacrificially in self-dissolution or worldly failure or brokenness (see Barth, *Epistle*, 433f., 445, 462f.). Kafka's discussion of parables, of course, is parabolically mediated in his inimitable "On Parables," 158; "Many complain that the words of the wise are always merely parables and of no use in daily life, which is the only life we have. When the sage says: 'Go over,' he does not mean that we should cross to some actual place, which we could do anyhow if the labor were worth it; he means some fabulous yonder, something unknown to us, something that he cannot designate

this by discerning the passing action of God, not from above in world-historical dominance, but from below—in exile. Only thus is the world hollowed out (and hallowed out) for its reconciliation in the divine passage through it.

In the secular present, all knowledge and prophecy is "in part," but the messianic body looks forward in hope to the "all in all." The only way to relate "in part" to the all, in Paul's view, is through self-sacrificing love. It is the patient, non-possessive "waiting" of love that constitutes the messianic time in which the messianic body is called to live. The remnant therefore is not the possessive object of salvation so much as its instrument in the ministry of reconciliation, and it is precisely the kenotic movement toward the "unsavable" that effects salvation. In the time that remains, then, the messianic ethic of the *hōs mē* is the time in which time and eternity coincide transformatively—as the caesura of *chronos*, but not yet eternity. It is therefore a time of judgement, "the time that time takes to make an end,"[79] the only time we have as creatures to exercise our calling as (in Breton's words, borrowed from Meister Eckhart[80]) "adverbs of the Verb," the divine speech that is the hidden life of each created being. And so Paul urges, "make the most of the time [*kairos*]"(Gal 6:10; Eph 5:16; Col 4:5), seizing it not as a proprietary possession but as a loving "bringing to fulfillment" (the "fullness [*plērōma*] of time," Eph 1:9–10) in keeping with the messianic agency of the *hōs mē*. It is also here that the ethical importance of Paul's typological approach to Scripture becomes clear as figural rather than allegorical. There is a relation between the ages that is messianically configured for Paul—a parabolic configuration, not a noetic one. Paul insists, "If anyone imagines that he knows something, he does not yet know as he ought to know. But if one loves God one is known by him" (1 Cor 8:2–3). To be known by God is to participate in the messianic

---

more precisely either, and therefore cannot help us here in the very least. All these parables really set out to say merely that the incomprehensible is incomprehensible, and we know that already. But the cares we have to struggle with every day: that is a different matter. Concerning this a man once said: Why such reluctance? If you only followed the parables you yourselves would become parables and with that rid of all your daily cares. Another said: I bet that is also a parable. The first said: You have won. The second said: But unfortunately only in parable. The first said: No, in reality: in parable you have lost."

79. Agamben, *Time that Remains*, 67.

80. Breton, *Saint Paul*, 29f.

motion of kenotic love, a "fullness of time" that unites, literally "recapit-ulates," all things in heaven and on earth (Eph 1:10; cf. Col 1:17f.). Such a process is not a hermeneutics that seeks to "replace" one meaning with another in a movement from particular to universal possession of meaning. It is rather the dispossessive process of "becoming para-bolic" in a manner that allows the redemptive aim of the law to come to fulfillment in a world that is passing away; for Paul, above all, each commandment is recapitulated in "love your neighbour as yourself" (Rom 13:8–10).

CHAPTER 3

Heidegger's Paul and Radical Orthodoxy on the Structure of
Christian Hope

by Justin D. Klassen

> Now concerning the times and the seasons, brothers and sis-
> ters, you do not need to have anything written to you. For you
> know very well that the day of the Lord will come like a thief in
> the night. (1 Thess 5:1–2)

Introduction: Contemporary Theology
and the "New" Paul

A recent wave of philosophical interest in the letters of Paul has generated numerous book-length treatments, many of which have posed
fundamental and sometimes insurmountable questions to a wide
range of prevailing discourses. For example, Alain Badiou has recently
articulated a Pauline rejoinder to contemporary liberal-democratic
assumptions about subjectivity, belonging, and truth—assumptions
that for decades have determined the nature of social theory and discourse, both academic and public, in the West.[1] The interruptive or
revolutionary character of Badiou's Paul is best illustrated by a brief
comparison with the conclusions of Daniel Boyarin, who some years
earlier developed an assessment of Paul as a "radical Jew."[2] Drawing
chiefly upon Galatians, Boyarin extracts from Paul's letters what he
takes to be a universalizing counter to the "ethnic particularism" of

1. Badiou, *Saint Paul.*
2. Boyarin, *Radical Jew.*

contemporary Israeli state politics. Yet he concludes in the end that "the Pauline option," while avoiding the dangers of political exclusivity, can unfortunately be recognized today in "the coercive universalism of a France."[3] On Boyarin's reading, therefore, what is "radical" about Paul is just his surprising alignment with modern liberal social theory. Such a treatment stops short of allowing Paul to speak in excess of prevailing political discourse, or to call it radically into question. Alain Badiou's reading of Paul, by contrast, suggests in various ways that Paul is not only relevant but *original*, and that the true bearing of his letters on contemporary social theory is utterly shattering.[4] Let us begin with a brief consideration of this interruption.

While Badiou admits to caring "nothing for the Good News [Paul] declares,"[5] Paul remains for him, nonetheless, "a founder, in that he is one of the very first theoreticians of the universal."[6] Whereas the Jewish and Greek discourses that Paul combats maintain that truth appears only as "sign," or only according to a totalized system of "wisdom," Paul's own discourse *begins from the Christ-event itself*, refusing to subject that event to any preconceived framework in order to proclaim its truth. For Badiou, moreover, this particular occurrence in Paul signifies evental primacy as such, which he claims enables us to extract from it "a formal, wholly secularized conception of grace."[7] That is, the "purely fabular" nature of Christ's resurrection makes it so much more than "sign" or "cause" that it alerts us to the excess of every event, and thus to the folly of all mastery. This possibility of a secularized grace in turn has radical implications for how we are to understand and participate in the process of becoming subjects. Consider, on the one hand, that a primary subjective fidelity to the logic of a preconceived discourse entails a kind of "slavery," a relation to occurrences that can see them only as movements "already known" by the discourse, which itself really "institutes" or delimits the real. On the other hand, a subject who is faithful to life as event, in excess of any discourse, escapes mastery

3. Ibid., 260.

4. The following also come to mind in this regard: Taubes, *Political Theology*; Agamben, *Time that Remains*; Breton, *Word and the Cross*; Žižek, *Puppet and the Dwarf*; and Heidegger, *Phenomenology of Religious Life*.

5. Badiou, *Saint Paul*, 1.

6. Ibid., 108.

7. Ibid., 66.

and finds freedom in the "excessive multiplicity" of the universally human as such.[8] Against the backdrop of the social debates that characterize Badiou's native France, then—which oscillate between appeals to an abstract universality and a "barbaric" identitarianism—this Paul throws up an irreducibly *revolutionary* figure.

In contrast to liberal social theory, contemporary Christian theology—and perhaps especially Radical Orthodoxy—seems able in certain ways to evade its own shattering or silencing confrontation with Paul. This evasion appears likely first of all because Paul seems obviously to "belong" to theology, and second because Radical Orthodox social theory already casts its own revolutionary shadow. Indeed, just as Badiou's reading of Paul argues that the resurrection sets up an "immanentization of the spirit" in every singular event—thus overcoming the dualism of abstract universal and exclusivist particular—so too does Radical Orthodoxy seek to overcome the binaries of "secular reason" by appealing to the incarnate Christ as the archetype of a continuing spiritual revolution—a true "*Sittlichkeit.*"[9] Moreover, just as Badiou suggests that a genuine relation to truth demands an attunement to the primacy of occurrences, Milbank too claims his approach is "radically realist," meaning "there are no prior criteria for truth, since in that case truth would be governed by something other than the truth, which would therefore have to be false."[10] Milbank does not add, of course, that this implies a "wholly secular conception of grace," but claims instead that his understanding is derived from a specifically Trinitarian ontology. Such an ontology suggests that there is no irrevocably "secular" truth at all, since all *knowing* happens through one's participation in "occurrences" whose mysterious arrival is analogous to the infinite differentiation of the Trinity itself. Thus, far from secularizing Christianity, Milbank's perspective on truth turns all knowing into a relation to divine revelation. Accordingly, he writes that "the sort of considerations that Karl Barth applied to revelation apply to knowledge as such."[11]

Yet it would be misleading to conclude too hastily that Radical Orthodoxy's refusal of "secularization" implies a real dissonance with

---

8. Ibid., 78.

9. For the prototypical expression of this Radical Orthodox argument, see Milbank, *Theology and Social Theory*, esp. chs. 6–8.

10. Milbank, "Invocation of Clio," 4.

11. Ibid., 7.

Badiou, since Radical Orthodoxy has something quite specific in mind when it refers to the "secular." As we shall explore in greater detail below, for Radical Orthodoxy all forms of "secular reason" rely upon a division between transcendence and immanence, spirit and flesh, universal and particular, a division whose supposed "metaphysical justification" can be exposed as an unnecessary pretension to mastery. Once this exposure is realized, the subjective posture that gives rise to such a "boundary" can be countered by the rhetorical offer of another, equally "unjustified" wager—that of faith in the reconciliation of spirit and nature effected by Christ, or what Badiou calls the "immanentization of the spirit" that Christ "sets up."[12] For Radical Orthodoxy and Badiou both, in other words, all "secular" wagers (or wagers of "mastery"), in contrast to that of Pauline faith, are stymied by the "objective" differences between universal and particular truth, and thus remain unable to conclude that truth is not a thing but a "*way*" of living—or again as Badiou puts it, a "process" that is both "singular" and "diagonal relative to every communitarian subset."[13] The question of contemporary theology's relationship to the "new" philosophical Paul is hereby resolved, in some measure, in virtue of Radical Orthodoxy's comfortable symmetry with Badiou.

Something about this symmetry itself, however, might raise further and more difficult questions. In particular, it seems important in the context of our discussion that among recent philosophical interpreters of Paul, Badiou especially emphasizes the absence in Paul of any "path of the Cross."[14] To name just one counterexample, Stanislas Breton argues that the spiritual reconciliation of the human being figured in Paul's discourse beckons precisely from the "null point of the cross"[15]—indeed, beckons one to become "nothing." The possibility of such an alternative reading at least raises the question of whether Badiou's *direct* appeal to the resurrection—or indeed, whether any "rhetorical" appeal whatsoever to the New Testament promise of spiritual life—implies an evasion of the subjective "death" to which Paul also refers. Radical Orthodoxy, for its part, has clearly settled on the unique

---

12. Badiou, *Saint Paul*, 69.

13. Ibid., 14.

14. Ibid., 67.

15. Breton, *Word and the Cross*, 95.

capacity of rhetoric to evade, if not death as such, then surely nihilism. That is, Radical Orthodoxy's critique of nihilism gives rise to a *necessarily* rhetorical form of theological communication, by means of which theology accomplishes the charitable reconciliation of aesthetic form with mysterious spiritual presence. My own argument begins with the suggestion that at precisely this point we are offered a fruitful entry-point for a less "symmetrical" confrontation between Paul and contemporary theology. Thus I shall argue below that a certain Heideggerian construal of the anguish of Christian hope in Paul eviscerates Radical Orthodoxy's assumption that only a direct, "aestheticized" appeal to *caritas* can give rise to Christian faith as a distinct way of being. Instead, as I will try to show, an insistence upon an indirect form of theological communication does not bespeak the nihilism of secular reason so much as it maintains Christian life as an inexorable task of temporal enactment. These claims will be unpacked more clearly as we proceed.

Given the nature of our stated entry-point, the importance for our purposes of Martin Heidegger's early lectures on 1 and 2 Thessalonians should be obvious, since Heidegger comes across in Radical Orthodox theology as the worst sort of nihilist one could imagine, not least for his ostensible "necrophilia" in *Being and Time*. In what remains of this essay I shall therefore attempt to carry out the following three tasks: (1) to show why Heidegger is singled out as a nihilist, especially by Radical Orthodoxy; (2) to mine Heidegger's reading of Paul for his actual view of "annihilation"; and (3) to discover what Heidegger's ruminations on the "structure of Christian hope" can tell us about his offensive claim in *Being and Time* that death is Dasein's "ownmost possibility." Ultimately we shall find that death in Heidegger is no means of abstraction from the temporal site of human life, but represents the possibility of "turning around," in a Pauline sense, from an idolatrous "peace and security" to the real temporal situation of Dasein, which above all requires a courage for anxiety. Thus shall we discover, over the course of the paper, both an obscured resonance of Heidegger's Paulinism with many of Radical Orthodoxy's authentic concerns, and a possible Pauline critique of the viability of Radical Orthodoxy's rhetorical "going further."

SECULAR REASON AND HEIDEGGER'S ESPECIAL NIHILISM

Theological "Meta-Suspicion"

John Milbank's landmark *Theology and Social Theory* opens with an uncharacteristically concise statement: "Once, there was no 'secular.'"[16] The rest of the book is concerned with explicating and persuading us of this claim, as well as developing its implications for how theology must respond to the prevailing metadiscourse. Milbank thus addresses "both social theorists and theologians,"[17] and in particular those theologians who assume that "a sensibly critical faith is supposed to admit fully the critical claims of sociology."[18] In response to such approaches, which stand ready to reduce the presence of religion in the world to transparently immanent "social" factors, Milbank's primary aim is to persuade us to adopt a theological "'meta-suspicion' which casts doubt on the possibility of suspicion [of religion] itself."[19] Milbank's principal adversary in this regard is the metanarrative of modern and especially Protestant theology, which tells of the "providential" emancipation of true religion from the authoritarian grasp of institutional order. Such a story comes to justify an evisceration from public discourse of any "theological" concern with all of the ways in which our lives are organized socially and enacted historically. Modern theology's hope, of course, is that such a concession of territory will be a "propaedeutic to the explication of a more genuine religious remainder," but Milbank is quick to remind us that if this remainder "concerns some realm of 'private experience,' then we have every reason to believe that this does not really escape social mediation."[20] At this point, where religion stands on the brink of being excised from the realm of human possibility altogether, the "acquiescent" Protestant trajectory culminates in "neo-orthodoxy," which according to Milbank responds to sociology with an *equal* suspicion of religion, insisting "on the absolute contrast between the revealed word of God and human 'religion,' which as a mere historical product can safely be handed over to any reductive analyses

---

16. Milbank, *Theology and Social Theory*, 1.

17. Ibid., 1.

18. Ibid., 101.

19. Ibid., 102.

20. Ibid., 101.

whatsoever."[21] Such neo-orthodoxy aims to undermine *all* pretensions to religiosity from the "immanent side," be they those of ecclesiology or even of the individual's "personal experience" of faith. Milbank's own "meta-suspicion," by contrast, seeks to cast "doubt on the very idea of there being something 'social' (in a specific, technical sense) to which religious behavior *could be* in any sense referred."[22]

The characteristic of modern sociology that most directly justifies its "hypostasization" of the secular is its putative ability to read history in entirely objective terms. According to Milbank, Max Weber perfected such a historical science by claiming that even religion, while itself inexplicably transcendent, can only have an enduring impact on the world via its total assimilation to the rationally traceable processes by which that world operates. As distinctly "religious," its impact is but a momentary interruption, which only really "registers" in history through an immediate incorporation into a reified temporal economy. This much is evident in the irreconcilability of Weber's categories of "charisma," on the one hand, and "routinization" on the other.[23] Milbank's counter-suggestion is not that theology can make history *more* transparent. Instead he points out that any assumption that historical routinization is metaphysically inevitable must ignore the equally tenable suggestion that even in the most "routinized" of series, "one can never fully 'account for' what comes after in terms of what precedes," since "preceding conditions are only causally adequate at the point where they have already

21. Ibid. Despite Milbank's suggestions in this direction, Karl Barth, for example, is anything but confident of the transparency of the immanent, and in fact allows the "sciences of man" their own integrity *only insofar as they do not become "dogmatic,"* or, we might say in Radical Orthodox terms, only insofar as they do not try, scientifically, to justify any suspicion of religion: "The exact science of man cannot be the enemy of the Christian confession. It becomes this only when it dogmatizes on the basis of its formulae and hypotheses, becoming the exponent of a philosophy and world-view, *and thus ceasing to be exact science.* As long as it maintains restraint and openness in face of the reality of man [i.e., a finally irreducibly spiritual reality], it belongs, like eating, drinking, sleeping and all other human activities, techniques and achievements, to the range of human actions which in themselves do not prejudice in any way the hearing or non-hearing of the Word of God, which become acts of obedience or disobedience only in so far as they belong to individuals with their special tendencies and purposes. . . . To the extent that it remains within its limits, and does not attempt to be more or less than exact science, it is a good work. . . . Opposition is only required if it becomes axiomatic, dogmatic, and speculative" (CD III/2:24–25; emphasis added).

22. Milbank, *Theology and Social Theory*, 102.

23. Ibid., 85.

been superseded by the new circumstances."[24] Thus, for Milbank, the notion of an objective history, which is required if sociology is to have a legitimate "domain," is, at most, one conjecture among others. Power, even "charismatic" power, can be operative in the world in more subtle ways than the "formal regularity" of Weberian history can allow. This means, by extension, that historical transitions may be better (though not more "transparently") approached via "narration," a practice that remains embedded in the series it describes. Such a "historiographical" rather than "explanatory" approach to history retains in historical transitions something more mysterious than "formal regularity," and thereby shatters the supposed "necessity" of sociology's separation of religion from the social, charisma from routine.[25] It may turn out, then, that even a nominally secular society only operates by virtue of an ever-recurring irruption into social life of "transcendent" factors, which an objective historical science cannot pretend to master.

Milbank's proposed "historiographical" engagement with the human bears a distinct resemblance to the Nietzschean turn to a "genealogical" method, which implies that postmodern historicism's suspicion of religion will be more germane to theology itself. Interestingly, rather than shoring up theology's defenses *against* such historicism, Milbank tries to "outhistoricize" it, by showing that the utterly *relativizing* character of postmodern thought reveals where it is not historicist *enough*. That is, a characteristically postmodern genealogy maintains that every historical enactment, every human commitment to a particular tradition, is an equally *arbitrary* wager of the will-to-power, which means that temporal differentiation as such is "coded" so as to exclude from the outset any possibility of a harmonious or even consistent repetition.[26]

24. Ibid., 83. Note the parallel between this claim and that of Kierkegaard's Johannes Climacus in *Philosophical Fragments*, esp. 72–88.

25. Milbank will also suggest that some non-Western societies put sociology into question in this regard. As he says, "the more it is the case that the social order is totally 'inside' a religion, then the more the idea of a 'social factor' dissolves away into nothingness," and the more it becomes "impossible to give explanatory 'priority' to social causation over religious organization." In an Islamic society, for example, the near-identity of the "religious" and the "social" will make it difficult to separate out "charisma" from "routine," revelation from "social effect." The existence of such societies indicates that it may be quite possible to understand the "social" as already inherently "charismatic," so to speak (Milbank, *Theology and Social Theory*, 89).

26. Ibid., 261.

As Milbank puts it, for postmodernism, "the obvious implication of 'many truths,' or rather, 'many incommensurable truths,' is that every truth is arbitrary, every truth is the will-to-power."[27] The distinction of theology is its suggestion that this "code" itself is just a subjective wager, and one that is possibly refused—by reference to a tradition animated by a different wager.[28] The peculiarity of Christianity, in other words, resides in its faith in a form of life that is "coded" by an ontology of peace, itself justified not metaphysically but only through a *living participation* in the tradition or series such a faith deploys. Thus Christian theology counters the postmodern genealogy of violence by posing a self-referential question: "Why should the natural, active, creative will not be understood . . . as essentially the charitable will, the will whose exercise of power is not a will to dominate . . . but rather to endorse . . . the human other?"[29]

Heidegger's "False" Historicism

This theological counter to postmodernism's false historicism becomes especially forceful in Milbank's discussion of Heidegger. "According to Heidegger," he writes, "an 'authentic' human existence . . . takes responsibility for its own mortal life and exhibits a 'care' for the distinctive possibilities handed down to it."[30] The problem, however, is that we do not *live* authentically; we tend toward a mode of relating to other beings and even to ourselves as "things" we can understand fully, and whose destinies we can command. This "forgets" the opening of Being in beings, or more specifically, it forgets the "irreducible questionableness of the relation of beings to Being."[31] For Heidegger, as Milbank notes, authenticity requires that we "remain with this questionableness, and not seek in any way to reduce the mystery of the ontological difference."[32] This requires us to remain radically *disinterested* in the possibility of qualitatively ranking the relationships of various finite

27. Ibid.

28. Milbank notes that the unique character of Christianity's ontological "wager" may make it the only "tradition" as such (ibid., 430).

29. Ibid., 288.

30. Ibid., 297.

31. Ibid., 298.

32. Ibid.

constellations to the opening of Being in time. To be "interested" in this mystery always reduces authentic living to mere "using." Yet precisely at this point, where Heidegger seems to suggest that *any* interest is "inevitably" a forgetting, Milbank argues that he remains faithful not to questionableness and mystery, but to an *a priori* determination of Being's temporalization *as falling*. That is, Heidegger's suggestion that we "remain with this questionableness" is here shown to be rooted in a metaphysician's confidence that the temporalization of Being is nowhere "more" or "less" transparent, because the ontological difference is everywhere absolute. Hereby inauthenticity or sin as forgetting ceases to be an existential qualification and becomes a sort of "objective" state—not a way of living that can be opposed by another way, but the essential and inescapable structure of "ontical" life as such.

For Milbank, by contrast, a true meta-critique cannot rule out the possibility of advocating a robust "interestedness" in some traditions over others, not with reference to a metaphysical vantage point, but through an appeal whose "force" itself is always already "inscribed" in the series from which it originates.[33] For him, then, and for the Radical Orthodoxy that follows from his imperatives, theology remains uniquely opposed to nihilism only when it explicitly transgresses secular reason's "boundary" between transcendence and immanence. Thus Heidegger's refusal to recommend any particular historical commitments—his refusal to think about historical interestedness as anything but a "falling"—remains nihilistic because it tends toward a relentless "objectification" of the subject, via the implication that authenticity can only hold at an objective remove from the ontic as such.

Catherine Pickstock develops a somewhat different account of nihilism from that of Milbank, though one in which the condemnation of Heidegger comes across with still greater clarity.[34] For Pickstock, the nihilism of all non-theological thought resides in its determination of language as fundamentally *written*. Right from Phaedrus's preference for the word-for-word transcription of Lysias's speech over Socrates' proposed oral performance,[35] the history of philosophy has fallen prey to the sophistic inclination to reify truth apart from its temporal per-

33. See ibid., 305.
34. Pickstock, *After Writing*.
35. See Plato's *Phaedrus*, 228a–e.

formance, in what really amounts to a subjective "gesture of security" against the void of time's passing. At first glance it would seem that postmodernism's overturning of the modern prioritization of epistemology offers a helpful critique of the confidence in the written that one might attribute to Phaedrus. Derrida's emphasis on writing, for example, presupposes the deathliness of every "sign," and thereby seems to indicate a refusal of the sophistic "gesture of security."[36] For Pickstock, however, the supposed shift from modernity's necrophobia to postmodernism's utter renunciation of a "life" secured against death fails to express a genuinely new gesture. This is because the postmodern disavowal of confidence in the written retains the modern presupposition of an abyss between temporal flux and self-present being, just as for Milbank postmodern historicism relies upon the old modern assumption of the irreconcilability of time and eternity—which assumes by extension the impossibility of a genuinely *incarnate* Spirit. Postmodern philosophy therefore ends up recommending necrophilia rather than countenance any surrender to a continually and mysteriously donated selfhood. And this, Pickstock suggests, is most explicit in Heidegger:

> Heidegger wrote that by facing up to one's own death, "one is liberated from one's lostness in those possibilities which may accidentally thrust themselves upon me," thus seeming to prioritize an *essence* of ourselves, according to a metaphysical distinction between substance and accident. It would also seem, from this quotation, that being resolute in the face of death is not a *disinterested* stance, as Heidegger claims, but rather a defiant strategy of security against the arrival of the unknown.[37]

On Pickstock's reading of Heidegger, therefore, death *as my own* becomes the last resort of sophistry, the paradoxically self-present tranquility through which I can finally secure myself against the flux of time. Hereby "life" remains, as it was for Phaedrus, synonymous with

---

36. In his essay, "Signature Event Context," Derrida argues that "to write is to produce a mark that will constitute a kind of machine that is in turn productive, that my future disappearance in principle will not prevent from functioning. . . . For the written to be the written, it must continue to 'act' and to be legible even if what is called the author of the writing no longer answers for what he has written, for what he seems to have signed, whether he is provisionally absent, or if he is dead" (in Derrida, *Margins of Philosophy*, 316).

37. Pickstock, *After Writing*, 111.

the refusal of any temporal living. Thus does Pickstock conclude that Heidegger's "necrophiliac urge" is no advance, but "just a cover for an all too modern necrophobic desire to get to death before it gets to you."[38]

A Note on the Sublime and the Beautiful

The vehemence of such theological condemnations of Heidegger is ultimately rooted in the Radical Orthodox postulate that "the thought of God as infinite Being, as difference in harmony . . . *ends and subsumes all philosophy*, just as the Christian counter-ethics ends and subsumes all politics."[39] This "end" of philosophy is only realized, however, when theology refuses to stop with its own moment of skepticism about the possibility of temporal repetition, the possibility, in short, of a temporal enactment of the religious life. To stop with skepticism, as Heidegger's advocacy of "disinterest" seems to do, is to capitulate to secular reason's reification of the "distance" of temporal differentiation as an irrevocable "abyss." The more thoroughgoing historicism proper to theology enables it to "go further" than philosophy here, and construe temporal transitions not as the inevitably repeated treachery of beings against Being, but as the compelling possibility of harmony through the dispossessive enactment of charity. In a provocative essay on Kierkegaard, Milbank explains that the possible responses to human anxiety over the unpredictable impendence of the future include fear (with all of its concomitant possessive results), and faith, which Milbank says is action toward a future still construed as distance, but a distance that is "beguiling," even erotic.[40] The Christian task is therefore to "build" upon Jesus's action, which for Milbank means to continue the tradition he initiates and sustains—a tradition that does not reduce the contingency and uncertainty of temporal repetition, but lives toward that contingency with a faith in love's capacity to be the "interval" between present moments.

The theological imperative, by extension, enjoins a rhetoric that "beguiles" the reader toward the sublime as an opening rather than a

---

38. Ibid.
39. Milbank, *Theology and Social Theory*, 430 (emphasis added).
40. Milbank, "Sublime in Kierkegaard," 73.

dead end, which is precisely what Milbank's criticisms of the stultifying objectifications of secular reason are meant to accomplish. The differing intrinsic to temporality itself can indeed be known objectively only as the "sublime," which accosts all knowing. Yet one can possibly "see" this sublime differing as time's suspension by a beguiling "beauty," or in other words, by a measure that makes objective uncertainty compelling as an opening onto infinite being, rather than a final closure against the possibility of repetition. Ultimately, therefore, any theology that goes as far as "objective uncertainty," or Kierkegaardian skepticism, without going further and "wooing" us toward a particularly beautiful *traversal* of uncertainty, remains precariously and even damnably close to secular reason's fearful relationship to the sublime. A truly Christian theology must instead champion the objectively uncertain yet rhetorically persuasive "beauty" of *caritas*.

In order to respond to such a conclusion, our guiding concern as we proceed with Heidegger must be whether or not his refusal to "rhetorize" a particular way of being in time really means that for him all temporal ways of life are commensurate with annihilation, while death itself is held up as true life. Does Heidegger's opposition to historical "interest" really indicate a "Gnostic" fidelity to a metaphysical *a priori*? Or might it be the case that only an "anti-rhetorical" construal of "the structure of Christian hope" is capable of maintaining the religious life as inexorable enactment? Let us keep such questions in mind as we turn, first, to Heidegger's lectures on Paul, and then to *Being and Time* on death.

HEIDEGGER ON THE STRUCTURE OF CHRISTIAN HOPE

Paul's "Situation"

Martin Heidegger's early lectures on Paul's letters to the Thessalonians make for difficult, albeit provocative reading.[41] In general terms, Heidegger offers a phenomenological approach to the letters that is meant to contrast with prevailing approaches, both historical-critical and doctrinal. Unlike the historical-critical approach, Heidegger is not concerned with what he calls "the object-historical situation of Paul as

41. See Heidegger, *Phenomenology of Religious Life*, chs. 3–4.

he wrote the letter."[42] At the same time, however, a phenomenology of religious life cannot disregard Paul's *situation*. That is, one must avoid the temptation to abstract the theological content of the letter from the need to read *with* Paul as he writes. This view of empathy differs from the historical-critical orientation primarily because it assumes that "what is crucial is *not* the material character of Paul's environment, but rather only his own situation."[43] In striving for an attunement to Paul's situation, then, the phenomenological approach aims not to abstract from history as such, but it does intentionally distance itself from history *as objective*. Heidegger hereby avoids any dichotomizing of historical (i.e., materially concerned) and philosophical (i.e., doctrinally concerned) approaches, and affirms philosophy as "return to the original-historical."[44]

The original-historical situation is not materially defined, as we have seen, but rather is "something that belongs to understanding in the manner of an enactment," something that is "like an I."[45] The "like an I" is to be distinguished from everything else by the fact that it *is* in its relations or comportment: "That which is 'like an I' *is* and *has* the not-I, the not-I merely *is* and does not *have*."[46] In turning around methodologically to the "enactment-historical" we therefore "return" to history insofar as true history can be said to inhere in "the having-relation of that which is 'like an I.'"[47] For Heidegger the methodological question of empathy is therefore never a question about who Paul is and who the Thessalonians are, if by "who" we mean "what." Rather, the question about Paul's situation concerns *how he has* the Thessalonians. On this score Heidegger concludes that "for Paul the Thessalonians are there because he and they are linked to each other in their having-become."[48] Here "having-become" means acceptance of the proclamation through which one "treads upon an effective connection with God."[49] What is accepted is not a truth abstracted from the temporal flow of factical life,

42. Ibid., 61.
43. Ibid., 62 (emphasis added).
44. Ibid., 63.
45. Ibid.
46. Ibid., 64.
47. Ibid.
48. Ibid., 65.
49. Ibid., 66.

but rather something that relates to "the how of self-conduct"—more specifically, it means "a turning-*toward* God and a turning-*away* from idol-images."[50] Acceptance of the proclamation therefore means entering into life (becoming) as a "how," and the how itself *is* this "turning around."

Heidegger goes on to argue that such a turn does not yield a new peace and security, as if true becoming were structurally akin to the tranquil comfort of idolatrous being. Rather it consists "in entering oneself into the anguish of life. A joy is bound up therewith, [but] one which comes from the Holy Spirit and is incomprehensible to life . . . The acceptance is in itself a transformation before God."[51] Thus we can say that for Heidegger the Thessalonians only "have" God insofar as they are in the anguished situation of transformation, of turning away from that which once "secured" them. God is not "had," in other words, in the manner of an epistemological relation to a doctrine, nor of an "attitudinal" relation to matter, both of which characterize idolatry; instead, God "is" for the believer who "treads upon" the effective connection, who is transformed in factical life by his acceptance of the proclamation and his entering into anguish. The "proclamation" itself concerns the coming again of Christ, and the anguish refers to the unique character of hope in relation to this return: "The experience [of hope] is an absolute distress which belongs to the life of the Christian himself."[52] Heidegger concludes that upon arrival at this hope, which is at the same time absolute distress, "we are introduced into the self-world of Paul."[53]

Hope as Distress and Life

Is Christian waiting distressful in the same sense that all waiting means being put in suspension? If so, does cognitive anticipation of the fulfillment of this waiting mitigate the distress of the suspension? Or by extension, is there a beguiling measure through which one can embark upon this suspension? Is such beguiling anticipation what Paul means

50. Ibid.; see 1 Thess 1:9.
51. Ibid.; see 1 Thess 1:5.
52. Ibid., 67.
53. Ibid.

by the "joy" of the Spirit? Heidegger argues that Paul is quick to dash such hopes, by answering the question of the When of the Parousia with "a total distance from a cognitive treatment."[54] What remains decisive, then, is not my ability to make an accurate future prediction (which might have brought me some comfort), but only "how I comport myself to it in actual life."[55] For Paul, in other words, one enters into a "knowing" relation to the Parousia not through persuasion by a beguiling hope, but by venturing all known security in the "how" of anguish. It is of critical importance to Heidegger, moreover, that even this is no reference to the esoteric knowledge of a religious elite, since for Paul, "the extraordinary [i.e., the mystical experience] in his life plays no role for him. Only when he is weak, when he withstands the anguish of his life, can he enter into a close connection with God."[56] If the extraordinary were to play a role, the "having-become" that characterizes Christian life experience would be no different from historical-critical or exclusively "philosophical" suppositions about human life, which is to say that having-become would concern "what" one is, in virtue of objectifying material-historical or abstract doctrinal considerations. For Heidegger, the religious life is more authentically characterized by anguished perseverance in weakness than by the attainment of objective distinction, because only when anguish is primary does life remain "situated" in the enactment-complex of the "like an I"; only such anguish wards off the falling tendency to identify oneself as a "what." Having-God Christianly, then, through its requirement of a peculiar kind of expectancy, "is the opposite of all bad mysticism. Not mystical absorption and the special exertion; rather withstanding the weakness of life is decisive."[57]

Life for Paul is therefore contingent on a "having-become" that determines life itself *as comportment to the factical*, instead of as a particular factical situation. Thus Paul never answers the question of the When with a prediction, but always "refers the Thessalonians back to themselves and to the knowledge that they have as those who

---

54. Ibid., 70.
55. Ibid.
56. Ibid.; see 2 Cor 12:1–10.
57. Ibid.

have become."[58] Precisely in its "total distance" from cognitive or direct communication, then, Paul's letter seeks to maintain his hearers in the *how* of their distressing comportment, a comportment that forgoes rejoicing in security in the worldly sense. Those who do so rejoice will be "surprised" by ruin, for their expectation "is absorbed by what life brings to them," and thus "the ruin hits them in such a way that they cannot flee from it."[59] Here we see that expectation in the manner of an absorption with the "what" of life is insufficient because it cannot effect an *obstinate enough* waiting, since in this case a factical situation of loss and weakness is allowed to disconfirm the expectancy. By contrast, the anguish of living in the factical while turning away from life as a what—the anguish of "losing" the factical—cannot possibly refute Christian expectancy, for such hope is *constituted by venturing the factical* as religiously determinative. To want to be *what one has*, instead of being in the *how* of one's having, is not to want to be "like an I"; it is not, in other words, to want to be a "self." Those who conceive of the When as an event that is objectively graspable therefore "cannot save themselves, because they do not have themselves, because they have forgotten their own self, because they do not have themselves in the clarity of authentic knowledge."[60] Paul brings the question of the When "back to my comportment"[61] because this alone sustains an authentic expectancy, a hope in which alone I *have* a life. Thus "there is no security for Christian life," which for Heidegger is no declaration of despair, but "an urging to awaken and be sober."[62]

Antichrist and Annihilation

The imminence of the Parousia and thus the urgency of the expectant comportment is seemingly reduced or delayed in Paul's second letter to the Thessalonians, in virtue of its prediction of the Antichrist's intervening appearance.[63] Biblical scholars take this to imply that whoever

58. Ibid., 72.
59. Ibid.; see 1 Thess 5:3.
60. Ibid.
61. Ibid., 73.
62. Ibid., 73, 74.
63. See 2 Thess 2:3ff.

wrote the second letter obviously had to deal with the disappointment of imminent expectations, and devised a strategy for maintaining the authority of the Parousia in the lives of the Thessalonians without the need to produce immediate "results." For Heidegger, by contrast, the apparent difference between the two letters is more properly understood as a heightening, not a reduction, of the very same and original existential tension. On this account, the problem that faces the writer of the second letter is not that of how to "revise" the object-historical claims of the first, but rather of how to address the *misunderstanding* on which some took the first letter to contain such claims in the first place. The author of the second letter therefore does not mean to warn about Antichrist as a new objective fact; rather, the apparently shifting objective emphasis must be understood as a refocusing on the *how* of Christian life. In this refocusing, Heidegger claims, the "meaning of the proclamation of the Antichrist is the following: one must take Antichrist for Antichrist."[64]

Heidegger further explicates this injunction as the need to guard oneself against the inclination to read the end or fulfillment of religious expectancy in any object-historical situation, lest the enactment complex be reduced to something that is not "like an I." The supposed "delay" does not then oppose idling because it gives us more time to work on "other things." No, Paul does not oppose idleness with busywork at all, but identifies the two, thus correlating the real "work" to which he implores the Thessalonians with that very anguish mentioned in the first letter.[65] As Heidegger puts it, the tone of the second letter emphasizes even more strongly that "the 'obstinate waiting' is not some ideational 'expectation,' rather a serving God."[66] Understandings that disown Paul of the second letter because of a difference at the "ideational" level therefore risk what Catherine Pickstock calls the "spatialization" of the real, the abstraction of life from the *how* of its temporality. On Heidegger's reading of Paul, similarly, one must give up one's identity as objective and possibly "written" timelessly, in order to remain alive to life as enactment. Real annihilation, real nihilism, resides in the desire, at the height of object-historical greatness, to want to *be* one's facticity,

---

64. Heidegger, *Phenomenology of Religious Life*, 78.
65. See 2 Thess 3:11.
66. Heidegger, *Phenomenology of Religious Life*, 79.

or in the unwillingness to give up despair and acquire hope in the situation of weakness. Those who succumb to Antichrist are thus "deceived precisely in their highest bustling activity with the 'sensation' of the Parousia, and fall from their original concern for the divine. For this reason, they will be *absolutely annihilated*."[67]

Here we come to see that in Heidegger's reading of Paul, there is no connection between true life and a refusal of temporal enactment—which is the Radical Orthodox accusation—whereas a connection *is* drawn between "sensation," or an aestheticized hope, and soporific abstraction. In addition, one begins to feel a resonance here between what Heidegger takes Paul to be saying about the challenge posed by Antichrist to the religious life, and what he himself will later say about the human tendency to fall from an authentic comportment to the mystery of Being's opening in time, into inauthentic publicity. To resist this fall is not easy, and the effort must be made repeatedly. Antichrist will *not* scare you off: "the appearance of the Antichrist in godly robes facilitates the falling-tendency of life; in order not to fall prey to it, one must stand ever ready for it."[68] Standing ever ready implies a kind of earnestness to anguish persistently in the expectancy that maintains the "like an I" in its enactment-complex. Such persistence must also recall that those who are rejected do not lack their own sort of earnestness: "they are not indifferent; they are highly busy. . . . They do not neglect what is Christian as irrelevant, but rather show a peculiar increase, which fulfills their blindness and completes the fall to the anti-godly."[69] The more properly Christian earnestness must therefore concern itself especially with warding off any fascination with the extraordinary that could tempt one to believe in the possibility of an object-historical fulfillment of expectancy, and by extension a reification of the religious life itself.

Above all, then, we can say that Heidegger's phenomenological approach derives from Paul's letters an antithesis to the objectification of human life; his Paul stops at nothing in the form and content of his communication to ensure that what remains in focus is life as irreducible enactment in facticity—he provides no "satisfaction" that

67. Ibid., 80.
68. Ibid.
69. Ibid.

would resolve the anguish of being as a *how* and not a *what*. Yet far from abstracting the authentic being of the self from the temporal site of its enactment, Heidegger ultimately claims that from the Christian "complex of enactment with God arises something like temporality to begin with."[70] Keeping this reading of Paul in mind, we turn now to Heidegger's *Being and Time*, where I suggest we shall find that his reflections on death are concerned with the "ownmost possibility" of Dasein as a call to living that always shatters the self as objective, in either of its abstract or present-to-hand modes.

DEATH'S CALL OUT OF TRANQUILIZATION

The Idle "They"

To begin here we may recall for a moment that according to Pickstock, Heidegger's emphasis on the importance of facing up to one's death seems "to prioritize an *essence* of ourselves, according to a metaphysical distinction between substance and accident," which means resoluteness in the face of death can be read as "a defiant strategy of security against the arrival of the unknown."[71] For Pickstock's Heidegger, in other words, my death is "essential" because according to its determination I can "be" at an abstract remove from the unpredictability of temporal flux. Death as Dasein's ownmost possibility hereby comes to mean the reification of the self as the most sublime "what," the result of an ultimately despairing assessment of every "how." On this reading, Heidegger comes to the "ruin" of what he earlier called a "bad mysticism," unable to maintain the Pauline sense of life as *in* the enactment-complex of that which is like an I. I shall oppose this suggestion by arguing that Heidegger's Pauline polemic against peace and security allows us to read death in *Being and Time* as "essential" to Dasein not because it frees Dasein from a temporality conceived as "accidental," but because an "existential conception" of death frees Dasein *for* what it really "is"—"the entity which *exists*."[72] That is, the existential conception of death frees Dasein *for* existing, in time.

---

70. Ibid., 81.
71. Pickstock, *After Writing*, 111.
72. Heidegger, *Being and Time*, 286.

In *Being and Time*, Heidegger suggests that death is Dasein's "ownmost" possibility because it effects "a freedom which has been released from the illusions of the 'they.'"[73] By this he means freedom from a certain, untruthful *way of living*, a freedom "essential" to Dasein as the possibility of existing authentically. This is not meant to suggest the freedom of tranquil possession of unchanging "attributes," but freedom *from* all identifications with objective attributes. At the same time, however, facing up to death does not mean becoming an abstractly pristine "essence," but becoming *essentially* Dasein, which means essentially *existing* and therefore "anxious"[74] rather than tranquil. Indeed, the temptation of the language of the "they" is precisely the temptation to "be" securely in the face of death, *to "be" Dasein without heeding the call to live.* Let us examine this language more closely.

In the everyday public language of the "they," death is prevented from becoming a possibility that actually belongs *to me* as an entity that exists: "in Dasein's public way of interpreting, it is said that 'one dies,' because everyone else and oneself can talk himself into saying that 'in no case is it I myself,' for this 'one' is the 'nobody.'"[75] Such alienation from the possibility of *my own death*, for which "no one can be my representative,"[76] is the "consoling solicitude" intrinsic to the everyday understanding of existence. To buy into it is to attain security against the putatively morbid notion that true living means existing in the anxiety provoked by the "non-relational" character of death's impendence. In the language of the "they," life means freedom from the challenge of any non-relational possibilities; it means living toward possibilities that are *actualizable* in the sense of coming under my control. Such living propels itself forward by constantly aestheticizing the "gap" inherent in temporal differentiation, by constantly reducing the distance of futurity to a "sensible" measure. And thus it is "a matter of public acceptance that 'thinking about death' is a cowardly fear, a sign of insecurity on the part of Dasein, and a somber way of fleeing from the world. *The 'they' does not permit us the courage for anxiety in the face of death.*"[77]

73. Ibid., 311.
74. Ibid.
75. Ibid., 297.
76. Ibid.
77. Ibid., 298 (emphasis original).

What Heidegger opposes in the "they" is therefore precisely its "gesture of security" against anxiety, for anxiety is "essential" to Dasein insofar as Dasein is the "non-relational potentiality-for-Being."[78] "The 'they' concerns itself with transforming this anxiety into fear in the face of an oncoming event,"[79] which means that to be "freed" from the illusions of the "they" is to be released from the "falling" tendency to protect life from the intrusion of the non-relationality intrinsic to Dasein's true existence *in the temporal*. In the language of Heidegger's reading of Paul, it is to be freed from the aestheticized "sensation" of one's success in traversing the distance of temporal differentiation, and instead to become "awake and sober."

Death as the Shattering of Understanding

Thus it is not the putative deathliness of the temporal as such that functions in Heidegger as the catalyst of inauthenticity, as on Pickstock's reading, but the temptation of the public "gesture": "When Dasein, tranquilized, and 'understanding' everything, thus compares itself with everything, it drifts along towards an alienation in which its ownmost potentiality-for-Being is hidden from it."[80] We can now recognize the ways in which this claim is derived from Heidegger's reading of Paul, in that Paul's communication, too, refuses to cater to the "understanding" on the question of the When of the Parousia. For Paul, this is because those who are related to this question cognitively are comported in factical life in such a way that they have "lost themselves." Thus when one "understands" everything in the language of the "they," as Heidegger puts it, one corresponds to those Thessalonians who have not heard Paul correctly, those who are now "idle" even in their busywork, who are busy only because they understand everything, not because they labor authentically under the anguish of life. They are alienated from their ownmost potentiality-for-Being because in their "understanding" of the When—and by extension, of everything—they have fallen into an identification with the factical, and so have fallen out of the situation of that which is "like an I." Facing up to one's death therefore cannot

78. Ibid.
79. Ibid.
80. Ibid., 222.

proffer security against temporality as the empty sign, but instead effects a breaking open of the spatialized "understanding" that prevents genuine living.

Anxiety is provoked by facing up to one's death because here it is seen that what is essential to Dasein is its potentiality-for-Being; here one hears the call to live without any definiteness in regard to one's possibilities, to *be* without *being defined* in any written schema. Facing death as one's ownmost possibility thus configures the "sublime" as a provocation to live, not as the object of fear that begets "secular reason." To face up to your death means not to be secured "against the arrival of the unknown," as Pickstock claims, but to be dispossessed of yourself as "written" in the public language of the "they." Inauthenticity, therefore, is not the necessary "structure" of the ontic, but a particular way of being that can be resisted and refused. As Heidegger claims explicitly, "inauthenticity characterizes a kind of Being into which Dasein can divert itself and has for the most part always diverted itself; *but Dasein does not necessarily and constantly have to divert itself into this kind of Being.*"[81] To be resolute in the situation of dispossession brought about by facing up to your death means to have your potentiality-for-Being before you as the genuinely temporal possibility of living all of your relations "non-relationally"—e.g., "charitably," or through a surrender of the grasping of self-control to the mystery of temporal differentiation.

Remaining with Kierkegaardian skepticism thus does not mean denying the possibility of charitable temporal repetition; instead it ensures that such a possibility remains an inexorable human *task*, without ever becoming the mere intellectual "sensation" of activity and hope. This, finally, is how death brings Dasein face to face with its "essence" and "totality"—not as an object, but *as the possibility of living*. Heidegger concludes that "*anticipation*," in which we should now discern a resonance with what he some years earlier called the structure of Christian hope, "turns out to be the possibility of understanding one's *ownmost* and uttermost potentiality-for-Being—that is to say, the possibility of *authentic existence.*"[82] Like Radical Orthodoxy, then, Heidegger seeks to expose the apparent objectivity of secular reason as mere subjective despair (i.e., "inauthenticity"); but in recognizing that existential de-

81. Ibid., 303 (emphasis added).
82. Ibid., 307 (emphasis added).

spair is only "refuted" when the contrasting possibility of faith is taken up *in a life*, Heidegger understandably stops short of furnishing us with a merely rhetorical refutation of such despair. In this, I have argued, he has surely learned something from Paul's sense that the faithful Thessalonians "do not need to have anything written" to them.

Conclusion: The Shattering of Theological Rhetoric

My primary aim in this essay has been to reveal the dubiousness of contemporary theology's dismissal of Heidegger as a nihilist, and to show, with recourse to Paul, where Heidegger's concerns in fact align with those of Radical Orthodoxy. In the first section we saw that for Radical Orthodoxy, secular reason is nihilistic because it makes a "wager" against the possibility of authentic living as *Sittlichkeit*. That is, secular reason characteristically reduces infinite and finite being to "things" whose objective qualities render them irreconcilable, whereas according to Christianity, to quote Milbank, "the created world of time participates in the God who differentiates," which implies that "there are no substances in creation, no underlying matter, and no discrete and inviolable 'things.'"[83] For theology, therefore, the opposites of secular reason can be traversed by a *way* that cuts across their division.

By now we have seen much in Heidegger that resonates with this account. In his reading of Paul, the Christian life is characterized by an anguished "turning-around," where "anguish" refers to suffering the loss of oneself as a "what," in order to be released from the annihilation of forgetting one's true self in the enactment-complex of that which is "like an I." Thus the When of the Parousia is for Heidegger's Paul not a written objective truth to which one assents intellectually, but a provocation and a return to one's authentic having-become. Paul's "religious" response to the question of the When takes the form of an injunction to "take Antichrist for Antichrist," which means to live the continual venture of one's security in the objective. Similarly for Heidegger himself, in *Being and Time*, facing death as Dasein's ownmost possibility means being dispossessed of one's stultifying "understanding" of all of life's possibilities. Resoluteness therefore does not abandon the temporal as such, but rather from it, as from Pauline religiousness, "arises some-

---

83. Milbank, *Theology and Social Theory*, 424.

thing like temporality to begin with."[84] All of this is to suggest, much like Radical Orthodoxy's counter to secular reason, that true life is a *way* and not a thing.

The secondary but no less crucial aim of the essay has been to suggest that the genuine remaining difference between Heidegger and Radical Orthodoxy speaks to a possibly shattering confrontation between Paul and theology itself, specifically on the question of rhetoric. We saw first how Radical Orthodoxy construes secular reason's "hypostasization" of the immanent and the transcendent as based upon a particular response to existential anxiety. That is, in the case of modernity, it is fear of the sublime "leap" determining our relation to the future that leads to a reification of time as giving rise to a predictable, objective history (cf. Weber's "routinization"). In the case of postmodern nihilism, a less deluded attunement to the genuine unpredictability of temporal transitions gives way to fear once again, in the conclusion that such transitions cannot be traversed whatsoever. In the first case, fear of death gives rise to self-protection; in the second case, fear of surrendering the self to a spiritual traversal gives rise to necrophilia. Christian theology, in its Radical Orthodox vein, is meant to counteract these subjective gestures through its "allegorical" depiction of temporality as itself the differentiating movement of divine love. This we can see in Milbank's characteristic suggestion that a properly rhetorical theology can offer a reading of history as "a true concrete representation of the analogical blending of difference."[85] Herein Milbank suggests that theology can persuasively narrate historical transitions as occurring according to the measure of *caritas*, and thereby persuade us into living according to this measure. Such a rhetorical narration is moreover a *necessary* way in which theology "goes further" than such as Heidegger, continuing past Kierkegaardian skepticism in order to "suspend" its hearers out over the sublime distance of the future, via the beguiling form of beauty. To refuse to go further in this way is ultimately to discredit Christianity's proclaimed reconciliation of skepticism with faith.

For Heidegger, on the contrary, such a theological rhetoric "synthesizes" skepticism and faith, joy and anguish, rather than safeguarding their *living* reconciliation by emphasizing its character as irreducibly

---

84. Heidegger, *Phenomenology of Religious Life*, 81.
85. Milbank, *Theology and Social Theory*, 279.

paradoxical, rather than *aesthetic*. Heidegger's reading of Paul is therefore striking for theology, as I hope I have shown, because it suggests that theological rhetoric, like "the cognitive treatment" of the Parousia, misses how the possibility of life in the truth calls one away from the "peace and security" of any public language. On a Heideggerian understanding, then, to rhetorize is to shout over the more appropriate silence of religious anxiety. Such theological silence Heidegger derives from his reading of 1 and 2 Thessalonians, in that the Pauline shattering of peace and security, to the end of situating human beings in the "nowhere" of the enactment-complex of that which is "like-an-I," is also, for Heidegger, the "end" of theology, or at least of theology as a "consummating" discourse. The no-place of the "effective connection with God" must remain characterized by the persistent and anguished working of one who *expects* according to the structure of Christian hope, a hope whose obstinacy would only be diluted by the attainment of a persuasive synthesis with the aesthetic. By insistently using "discourse" only to bring me "back to my comportment," to situate me, without written recourse, before my own possibility of living, both Heidegger and Paul will therefore remain, by the measure of contemporary rhetorical theology, markedly silent: "*Now concerning the times and the seasons, brothers and sisters, you do not need to have anything written to you. For you yourselves know very well that the day of the Lord will come like a thief in the night.*"[86]

---

86. 1 Thess 5:1–2.

CHAPTER 4

The Messiah's Quiet Approach:
Walter Benjamin's Messianic Politics

by Grant Poettcker

INTRODUCTION

The philosophy of Walter Benjamin has often been interpreted as leading to political quietism, as his politics is decidedly non-universaliz-
able, or to a kind of Gnosticism, as his apocalyptic vision of history
seems to consign the world of messianic actuality and fulfillment to an
unapproachable beyond. This makes the recent recovery of Benjamin's
thought for political philosophy and theology all the more remarkable,
for this "unclassifiable"[1] writer cannot help but be a scandal both to
political philosophers for whom the requisite is *radical* action for the
good of all, and to political theologians whose question remains that of
life within the *saeculum*. To make sense of this recovery, I will follow up
Giorgio Agamben's suggestion that Benjamin's thought becomes newly
legible when it is made to form a constellation with the thought of the
Apostle Paul.[2] In coming to form what Benjamin calls a "dialectical
image"[3] with one another, both Benjamin and Paul are rescued from

1. Löwy, *Fire Alarm*, 2.

2. Agamben, *Time that Remains.*

3. Benjamin describes a dialectical image thus in *The Arcades Project* (Convolute
N, 2a, 3): "Image is that wherein what has been comes together in a flash with the now
to form a constellation. In other words, image is dialectics at a standstill. For while the
relation of the present to the past is purely a temporal, continuous one, the relation of
what-has-been to the now is dialectical . . . only dialectical images are genuine images

90

historicist domestication and from the ineluctable decay of memory that comes with the passage of time; indeed, in this constellation both become our contemporaries.

In this paper, I will attempt to undercut both the quietist and the Gnostic interpretations of Benjamin's thought by showing how Benjamin's messianic politics, which is indeed the politics of a remnant, calls into question, both discursively and practically, the attempts that universalizing or progressivist politics make at realizing justice in the current age. In order to do so, I will thematize the relationship between the profane/mythical/political order and the divine/messianic order as Benjamin develops it in the "Theses on the Philosophy of History," "Critique of Violence," and "Theological-Political Fragment." This thematization will display the way in which Benjamin articulates a critique of law that accords strikingly with that found in Paul's letters. By highlighting the sense in which Benjamin's politics is mediated by a messianic apocalyptic, I will show that Benjamin's seemingly resolute insistence on the Pauline *not yet* allows, at all points, vision of the revolutionary Pauline *already*—though, of course, in a hidden way, a way in keeping with the Messiah's quiet approach.

Benjamin on the Messiah's Advent for the Proletariat

Considering the fact that Benjamin's "Theses on the Philosophy of History" are clearly directed at delineating the proper mode of engagement for the proletariat, it seems rather remarkable that neither the term "justice," nor "right," nor any of their cognates appears in this text. One may attempt to explain their absence by arguing that Benjamin, following Carl Schmitt, acknowledged that the use of these terms would make theological resonances unavoidable. Since Benjamin claims in the "Theses" that "theology . . . is wizened and has to keep out of sight" (§II),[4] it would follow that "justice" and "right," with their

---

(that is, not archaic)."

4. Here and following in parenthetic citations the symbol § and a Roman numeral denotes an individual Thesis in Benjamin's "Theses on the Philosophy of History." Unless noted, I make use of Harry Zohn's translation as it appears in Benjamin, *Illuminations*, 253–64. The "Theses" can be found in their original German in Benjamin's *Gesammelte Schriften*, 1:691–706. Page references to the *Gesammelte Schriften* will be marked by the abbreviation GS.

theological resonances, would likewise need to remain out of sight. But the import of this explanation is limited, for Benjamin claims to write the "Theses" because the revolutionary politics of the proletariat itself has an interest in the restoration of "a genuinely messianic face . . . to the concept of classless society."[5] So justice and proletarian politics should coincide—but they do not, in the "Theses." Why does Benjamin deny historical materialism the ability to initiate a just relation between the classes? And given that this denial abrogates the messianic efficacy of proletarian politics—even as Benjamin nonetheless grants to proletarian politics an unavoidable relation to the messianic and is himself engaged in this politics in the writing of the "Theses"—in what sense may the proletariat's activity be messianic?

We have received our initial answer to these questions in Benjamin's insistence that the theological dwarf must play the guiding role in its relationship with the historical materialist puppet (§I). Benjamin's diagnosis of the party's problem is two-fold: First, any proletarian politics that could become integrated into state machinery in the way the Social Democrats had would be problematic in that this integration precludes the necessary gestures of withdrawal from and critique of the dominant politics. So, for reasons of political form, proletarian politics is the politics of a minority. Second, the fact that the party has developed this problem of political form displays, for Benjamin, that the proletariat must "enlist the services of theology" if it hopes to "win all the time" (§I). For only theology offers resources for a genuine critique of profane politics[6]—i.e., the politics of universalist progressivism.

Progressivism presupposes a concept of progress. And the concept of progress presupposes, in most cases, (1) a subject that progresses, and (2) some index against which that subject's progress is measurable. When human progress is in view and the index is one of success,

---

5. Benjamin, "Paralipomena to 'On the Concept of History,'" 4:403.

6. It is because theology offers these resources that Žižek suggests that the time has come for the theological dwarf to emerge from the automaton described by Benjamin in the first Thesis. The irony of Žižek's suggestion is, however, that the moment of theology's emergence from the automaton would coincide with its "melting into thin air," as Žižek's *Puppet and the Dwarf* makes clear. In a Benjaminian light, then, Žižek's work appears as anti-messianic precisely because it refuses (or claims for itself) an apocalyptic moment that is other to an immanent temporality. Žižek effectively strips proletarian politics of the resources it would need for its reorientation to the messianic.

progress brings happiness. But what is the quality of this happiness? Benjamin writes,

> reflection shows us that our image of happiness is thoroughly colored by the time to which the course of our existence has assigned us. The kind of happiness that could arouse envy in us exists only in the air we have breathed, among people we could have talked to, women who could have given themselves to us. (§II)

The examples of envy-arousing happiness that Benjamin offers are examples of happiness that is temporally bound; this is a form of happiness that is *for us, now*. And they are also uniquely *unsharable* forms of happiness; no man whose woman gives herself to another is a happy man. These two attributes—finitude and privacy—condition all forms of profane desire.

The very consistency of the modalities of desire throughout history makes Benjamin ask whether such an immanentist picture of desire is adequate. He asks, "Doesn't a breath of the air that pervaded earlier days caress us as well? In the voices we hear, isn't there an echo of now silent ones? Don't the women we court have sisters they no longer recognize?" (§II).[7] Benjamin therefore argues, "our image of happiness is indissolubly bound up with the image of redemption" (§II). Because it insists that redemption must figure in the index by which human life is judged, theological analysis is able to display the fallacy that underpins progressivist politics, which is its understanding of progress. The theological question of redemption puts our relations to other generations on the table in a unique and valuable way. Any account of human desire that portrays desire and the goods that desire will pursue as strictly immanent will be inadequate. Accordingly, any politics that understands the pursuit and attainment of temporally-limited and unsharable goods as amounting to progress will be inadequate. In Benjaminian style we may say, theologically guided historical materialists are aware of this.

This is not to suggest, however, that Benjamin would say there are simply two indexes—one immanent, one transcendent—two kinds of progress, one profane, one redemptive. This sort of thinking leads one

---

7. These three sentences do not appear in the translation of the "Theses" that appears in *Illuminations*. I here quote Harry Zohn's newer translation of the "Theses" as it appears in *Selected Writings*, 4:390.

to accept too easily that there may be a straightforward institutional mediation of the good life, say, the proletariat's mediation of certain Marxist virtues, and the church's mediation of others. On the contrary, Benjamin's criticism attempts to discern the messianic movement that needs to animate engagement in either tradition in order that those virtues most highly prized may be developed and displayed. To put it another way, Benjamin's concern for the proletariat of his day is not directly for their status in the class struggle—whether they are "winning" or "losing"—because both of those "statuses" assume that "winning" or "losing" is a matter of quantitative stuff rather than qualitative attributes. His concern for the proletariat's health works itself out in the *how* of the proletariat's engagement in the struggle. His concern is for the extent to which the "spoils" that fall to them in the course of the class struggle "have a retroactive force [that] constantly call[s] into question every victory" (§IV)—including their own. For Marxist politics may come to conform to the rule of mere life[8] precisely by losing its relation to the messianic.

But what is this rule of mere life? Where is it given display? And why is it such a threat for the proletariat? Benjamin argues that the rule of life is given display in history. It is by way of the philosophy of history—that is, by way of the analysis of the coming to be and passing away of political orders—that one may discern the operation of the rule of mere life. In the "Theological-Political Fragment"[9] Benjamin writes, "The order of the profane should be erected on the idea of happiness." The category of the profane traverses all (post-lapsarian and pre-apocalyptic) political orders, as it is only to the extent that the goods around which a political order organizes itself lead to happiness that that political order has stability. The fact that different societies organize themselves around different goods bears witness to the multiple possible forms of happiness. It also bears witness to the extent to which a subject's happiness admits of political management.

The state has an interest in constructing forms of happiness that are reliably able to motivate political subjects, for the form of happi-

8. This term "mere life" (*blosses Leben*) derives strictly from Benjamin and is not to be confused with Agamben's much more fully developed "bare life." See Benjamin's "Critique of Violence," 299 (*GS*, II/1:201; and compare Agamben's *Homo Sacer*).

9. Benjamin, "Theologico-Political Fragment." I will hereafter cite this text parenthetically as TPF.

ness that a political subject enjoys may just as easily undermine state power as buttress it. To that end, the state will organize society around goods that political subjects are likely to recognize as goods. Physical well-being is one such easily recognizable and motivating good, as are safety from threats to property and access to forms of pleasure. It is the task of any historical materialist to take note of these different forms of happiness and of their historical alterations and adaptations. For all forms of profane happiness serve to underwrite the political powers. It is only thus that happiness can serve as the order on which the profane can be erected.

One might therefore read Michel Foucault's major works as an extended description of precisely this political transaction; state power is maintained through the enactment of social conditions and through the promulgation of knowledges that define and enable the pursuit of a certain form of human happiness. Foucault may thus be taken to have carried out the kind of pre-theological historical materialist analysis that Benjamin had in mind.

What Foucauldian analysis fails to see is that its own immanentist picture only ever describes the operation of the rule of mere life; there is indeed infinite movement within this picture, but this movement is only ever within the single field of power. Foucauldian analysis is characterized by a refusal of apocalypticism; it refuses to entertain the possibility that finitude of goods, temporally and spatially, only *came to be* with the end of the paradisical state. To put it another way, the good historical materialist will be able to describe in rich detail the way one regime manages political goods differently than another. But it does not follow from the fact that he possesses this ability that he will also grasp what is for Benjamin the more crucial disjunction, which is between the happiness of those who inhabit the former, paradisical state, and those who inhabit profane political orders. For this disjunction lies not *within* the field of profane politics, but beyond it, in theology.

As a result, the historical materialist could find *for himself* an easily-recognizable and motivating good in the kind of glory that accrues to one who exercises dominion in space and over time. And thus the politics of the proletariat could become a politics that obeys the rule of mere life. In a fragment called "World and Time"[10] Benjamin

10. Benjamin, "World and Time," 1:226–27. I will hereafter cite this text parenthetically as W&T.

offers an analogous analysis of Catholicism; here, too, one finds the degeneration of a potentially radical politics. Benjamin writes, "the problem of Catholicism is that of . . . (false, secular) theocracy." Although Catholicism claims divine power as its basis, it in fact has "domination as its supreme principle." Divine power cannot serve as the basis for a worldly politics because the latter makes the happiness of the earthly subjects who constitute it into its primary concern. Catholicism's version of theocracy drifts toward a hypocritical and ultimately secular form of political order because the nature of its so-called divine rule is ultimately determined by the character of the happiness of the subjects who are served by this enactment.

Divine power would demand a mortification of profane desire. Divine power will therefore be at odds with worldly politics, for despite the fact that abiding by God's command would lead to humanity's improvement, worldly politics demands, above all else, stability and endurance. The precarious, occasionalistic way in which divine power manifests itself in the world puts it at odds with worldly politics. Benjamin writes, "where divine power enters into the secular [*irdische*] world, it breathes destruction" (W&T). Basing one's political platform on such a power would therefore be misguided at best, for the sovereign who would attempt to monopolize and impose such a power on a political subject would find that divine power breathes destruction on whomever it pleases. This is not to say that divine power is capricious. On the contrary, it has its own order. This is only to say, rather, that the success of any human attempt to enact theocratic rule within profane history hinges on its having access to a form of grace unmediated by God's will and election. Theologically considered, this attempt would fail because such grace would be unworthy of the name, for grace is extended precisely in order that God's will would be all in all. Anthropologically considered, this attempt would fail because profane humanity, in its relation to the Divine, continues to be characterized by the rebellion that is crucial in the Fall narrative—and this extends equally to those members of humanity that are sovereigns.

Benjamin further analyzes the dynamics of profane desire in a fragment entitled "Even the Sacramental Migrates into Myth,"[11] though here on an ethical level. Benjamin considers the relationship between

11. Benjamin, "Even the Sacramental Migrates into Myth," 1:402–3.

profane desire and the grace that is extended through the sacrament (Benjamin's term) of marriage, which ought, according to Benjamin, to discipline erotic desire such that it would lead up to the divine. Benjamin considers the following (quite likely autobiographical) situation:[12]

> Two couples become acquainted; the bonds uniting them are loosened. Two of them . . . are mutually attracted to each other. Very soon the other two also enter into the most intimate relationship . . . To the best of their ability the former spouses promote the new relationship of the couple now turning away from them.

In such a situation, the divine, sacramental power of marriage is "exposed within itself," as the new relation of the mutually attracted couple—which is precisely that of a married couple, i.e., that of love—relates parasitically to the sacrament of marriage. "The spirit of the Black Mass lives here again: the sacrament takes the place of love; love replaces the sacrament." The revealed sacrament of love, namely marriage, is inverted into its opposite by the power of the "mythical, natural forces" according to which the couple that turns away from their former spouses act.

Myth is that order that prevails in the natural, pre-theological world.[13] The couple that turns away acts according to the forces at work in this order, in that by acting—indeed, by acting *naturally*—their actions appear as those which nature demanded of them. Their happiness does not derive from their innocence, but from their having satisfied nature's demand. The fact that they do the latter unconsciously, however,

12. This situation is significantly similar to the one described in Goethe's *Elective Affinities*. In the narrative, an aristocrat named Eduard is married to his first love Charlotte. When they are joined at their country estate by his friend, the Captain, and Charlotte's niece, Ottilie, Eduard and Charlotte each find themselves attracted to the houseguest of the opposite gender. Much of the substance of this fragment appears in a preparatory note for Benjamin's essay "Goethe's 'Elective Affinities'" (*GS*, 1:838). The full version of this essay appears in *Selected Writings*, 1:297–360 (*GS*, 1:123–202).

13. It is important that "pre" not be understood as designating a strictly temporalized (which would be what Benjamin would call an historicist understanding of this) relation between the order of myth and the theological order. Indeed, Benjamin uses the category of myth to describe a *present* possibility, one whose key features may be characteristic of political orders that come to be long after the *historical* "age of myth" has come and gone. Richard Wolin therefore misses the mark when he charges that "Benjamin runs the risk of de-historicizing the usage of [the] category [of myth]" in "Goethe's 'Elective Affinities'" (Wolin, *Walter Benjamin*, 56).

tempts them to commit "the most grievous offense, *hubris*."[14] Their action therefore threatens to enmesh them in a network of guilt; the gods declare guilty those who rail against their integration into the natural order of causes by claiming, in such a case, that their love is its own ground, and that it will withstand fortune's withering force. The gods therefore strike at that in the subject which can exist within the order of myth, namely the mere life that is in him. Within myth's economy, guilt serves to inculpate and death serves to expiate; this mechanism maintains the order of nature, with its rhythms of coming to be and passing away.

The mechanism that operates within this order does indeed have the capacity to structure human desiring in a way that leads to the development of virtues like temperance and prudence, as *hubristic* desire is indeed restrained by the mythic threat. Moreover, this order also has its own kind of temporality in that guilt passes down from one generation to the next; guilt could be described as a substance that continues to accrue (thereby introducing a certain linearity to the order of myth)[15] despite the total passing away of natural life. This temporality is not structured by "an autonomous time, but [by one which] is parasitically dependent on the time of a higher, less natural life."[16] Likewise, the moral order of myth—i.e., that order of human things that attempts to conform to the rhythms of nature—stops short of giving display to that which transcends the immanent, natural order, and for that reason it is incapable of structuring human desire in a way that accords with the transcendent in human desiring.

The relations between the immanent and transcendent in human desiring may be thematized by putting them in the terms of the example just considered. The lover's desire for his beloved ought to consummate in the sacramental relation of marriage, for this would accord with both the transcendent in human desiring and the authentic mode of temporality, which is fateless (*schicksallos*).[17] Here, however, the sac-

14. Benjamin, "Fate and Character," 306. A fuller thematization of the mythic and of its network of guilt appears in Hamacher, "Guilt History."

15. See the section of this essay titled "Benjamin and the Pauline *Already* and *Not Yet*" for a discussion of the mythic character of historicism.

16. Benjamin, "Fate and Character," 308.

17. Ibid., 307 (*GS*, II/1:174). This term, and the themes of guilt and fate and freedom are given extended treatment in Jacobson, *Metaphysics of the Profane*, esp. 42–45.

ramental relationship stands in the way of the consummation of a new love relationship, which, ostensibly, would lead to the lover's happiness. If the prior sacramental relationship were to dissolve, however, the profanity of the subsequent relation would likewise manifest itself, as the advent of the sacrament in the subsequent relation would effectively put an end to the happy love relationship that is its occasion.

To sum both of these examples up, in obeying the dictates of the order of mythical nature, the couple that turns away from their spouses seeks a happiness outlined in the rule of mere life. And in receiving what they will recognize as good and will reliably desire, Catholic political subjects receive just that which Benjamin offers as his "definition of politics: the fulfillment of an unimproved humanity" (W&T). The ironic or even sarcastic tone of Benjamin's usage of "fulfillment" here is echoed in the "Theological-Political Fragment" when Benjamin writes, "in happiness all that is earthly seeks its downfall, and only in good fortune is it destined to find it." The "good fortune" in view here is only good by immanent standards. It would be better if all that is earthly were frustrated—that it would only find bad fortune. Why? Not in order that the couple would be prevented from enjoying a merely immanent happiness; it is callous indeed to wish misfortune upon another simply because their finding happiness would threaten to integrate them into the moral and temporal economy of myth. Rather, it would be better if their earthly desire were frustrated in order that their desiring would not find its downfall but its transfiguration.[18] For this might expose the

---

In my judgment, Jacobson erroneously makes Benjamin's intention with *schicksallos* line up with Scholem's. This, in turn, leads to Jacobson's failure to distinguish, in the interpretation of "Fate and Character" that follows in *Metaphysics of the Profane*, between the sphere of fate and that of messianic responsibility.

18. This argument stands in opposition to that advanced by Wolin in *Walter Benjamin*, 52: "According to Benjamin, the sphere of natural life where mythical forces hold sway can be surmounted *only through death*. Death represents the overcoming of man's 'natural' earthbound life, and his elevation to a state of communion with divine life." This interpretation only holds if "Fate and Character" is understood as being written in Benjamin's own voice rather than as an immanent critique of the concepts of fate and character. Numerous textual points within "Fate and Character" would suggest otherwise, chief among them being the "autonomous time" to which Benjamin makes reference. More decisive against Wolin's argument, however, is the dissonance to which his position leads when "Fate and Character" and "Critique of Violence" are read together. Perhaps Wolin realizes this, as the latter text is one of the few by Benjamin upon which Wolin does not comment in his magisterial study. This point is one of crucial contention for this paper because Wolin's interpretation (which

sense in which the lovers *already* participate in the order of myth—and in order that they might escape this order. For the lovers' desire here is not disciplined by a sacrament, but by a custom, which is part of the mythico-natural order to which all political orders give display. Similarly, the mortification of the Catholic political subject's desire would expose the sense in which Catholic "theocracy" is buttressed by a profane attachment to the glory of holding sway. While political orders may shape the forms of happiness that are characteristic of their subjects, it by no means follows that this shaping will amount to or result in an improvement of the latter. It is in this sense that profane politics is "the fulfillment of an unimproved humanity" (W&T).

The proletariat is threatened with a degeneration similar to that of Catholicism[19] precisely because it is that discourse that both serves and shapes the happiness of the proletariat. If historical materialist analysis were to claim that the party's happiness consisted in its ex-acting vengeance on the masters on behalf of the current generation's enslaved ancestors, in this it would simply be obeying the rule of mere life. In such a case, the victory the proletariat wins is neither properly its own, nor that of those who have gone before; the melodies sung at a victory parade attended only by the living ring hollow. Thus temporal succession jeopardizes any claim that profane happiness coincides with redemption. When the Messiah sits in the judgment seat, by contrast, all humanity attends his victory. It is in this sense that Benjamin intends the following remark in the "Theological-Political Fragment": "If one arrow points to the goal toward which the profane dynamic acts, and another marks the direction of Messianic intensity, then certainly the quest to free humanity for happiness runs counter to the Messianic

---

is the dominant one in Benjaminian scholarship) *does* consign the world of messianic actuality to an unapproachable beyond, and it is precisely "Critique of Violence" and the underappreciated aspects of "Fate and Character" that point to the sense in which the messianic apocalypse *is now*. If, as Wolin claims, man's "natural" earthbound life needs to be overcome in order for communion with divine life to be possible, the reading that characterizes Benjamin's "soteriology" as Gnostic would be quite accurate.

19. In using this example I am not suggesting that Protestant politics somehow avoids what Benjamin calls "the problem of Catholicism." On the contrary, Protestant politics may be even more gravely threatened by this problem to the extent that it fails to acknowledge the analogous role that their own ecclesial hierarchy plays. This rather illustrates the way the messianic cuts through the life of institutions irruptively, and for the sake of the preservation of a faithful remnant.

direction." The happiness that profane politics attempts to liberate humanity *for* is a happiness that is fully intelligible by immanent standards; it is unsharable, and it is temporally bound.

But Benjamin continues:

> just as a force can, through acting, increase another that is acting in the opposite direction, so the order of the profane assists, through being profane, the coming of the Messianic Kingdom. The profane, therefore, although not itself a category of this Kingdom, is a decisive category of its quietest approach.

How does this seemingly paradoxical relation work? The success an order has in sustaining itself and extending its reach only serves, ironically, to point more directly to its profane aspect. It will serve us well here to spin out the image Benjamin offers in Thesis VII. The victor carries the spoils of war among the people, and celebrates the new era that has dawned, in which he and his subjects may enjoy possession of the cultural treasures that have been captured. The victor's glory is inseparable from his having taken possession. But in order for the victor to be celebrated, the people must desire that which he bears, whether that be the victory itself or its spoils. Such a victor *cannot* bear a new economy of desire, for if he were to do so, he would be rejected and humiliated rather than celebrated. The Messiah therefore stands in opposition to the victor in bearing a victory that interrupts possession and glory in mastery, one which does not satisfy desire, but which transfigures it.

This messianic and transfigurative possibility may be illustrated by considering a modality of desire that Benjamin does not develop in "Even the Sacramental Migrates into Myth," but which remains true to the terms laid out in the fragment. The problem of a happy, *sacramentally ordered* love relationship depends on the realization not of a profane love, but of a happiness that has been re-formed and re-ordered by the sacrament such that it remains immediate to the sacrament. In such a case, the sacrament will continue to manifest itself destructively in the residual profanity of that love relationship by calling the subject's natural desire into question. The sacrament functions here in mediating what Benjamin calls "divine violence." Happiness will nonetheless arrive, but only, as it were, through the back door—and now only in a way purified by this violence. The profane, by being profane, therefore assists the coming of the messianic kingdom by giving display to the messianic despite itself. "The profane . . . although not itself a category of the Kingdom, is a decisive category of its quietest approach" (TPF) precisely because in falling away from the messianic and in seeking its own downfall through its realization, the profane displays its own inner nature in contradistinction to that of the messianic.

We may thus imagine the corresponding possibility for the proletariat of Benjamin's "Theses." The Messiah's advent for the proletariat would enable the proletariat to become the class envisioned by Marx, a class that attains universality by having its *partisan* interests coincide perfectly with the interest of all classes, a party whose very mode of activity dissolves the condition sustaining the currently operating oppressive social order as well as the condition of its own social being. Benjamin argues that the nature of those partisan interests requires examination, lest the party's desire remain profane and its activity become that of an interest group rather than a radically dispossessive, self-dissolving class-beyond-all-classes. Benjamin's conclusion that temporal succession jeopardizes the proletariat's hold on its claimed victory leads Benjamin to insist that class struggle cannot merely be a matter of what—i.e., of material forces and relations of production—but of how—i.e., of the qualities of those engaged in the struggle. The Messiah's advent, which is, in Pauline fashion, always now and always yet to come, provokes the re-examination of the party's partisan interests—the necessity of which was made evident for Benjamin by Social Democracy's capitulation—such that the party's revolutionary fervor does not slacken due to the satisfaction engendered by material "successes." Permanent revolution is, then, not conditional upon knowledge of the laws of history, but on the cultivation of messianic awareness. Given this, Benjamin's insistence that the theological dwarf ought to pull the strings of the historical materialist puppet becomes newly intelligible.

Benjamin's Pauline Critique of Law

But the question remains: How is the profane economy of desire overcome, and how does the profane economy of desire unwittingly bear witness to the possibility of participation in a messianic economy of desire? Simply put, the answer to both of these questions is, through violence. As Milbank might say, violence requires discernment,[20] so we must ask the following questions: What kinds of violence are in view here? How do they differ in character? And what historical agents bear these different kinds of violence?

In "Critique of Violence"[21] Benjamin offers a critique of law that displays the character of profane politics and of its violence, while also delineating a mode of political engagement that is attentive to the re-ordering force borne by an alternative, divine power. Benjamin could have written, with Paul, "do not be conformed to this world, but be transformed by the renewing of your minds" (Rom 12:2). For just as Paul is concerned that the Galatians are returning to "enslave[ment] to [powers] that by nature are not gods" (Gal 4:8) because they fail to recognize that the law to which they are returning does not offer freedom from profane (fleshly) power (Gal 5:1–21), so Benjamin is concerned that the proletariat's inability to maintain its revolutionary fervor stems from its inability to see the inner nature of the mechanism by which profane politics always operates. Paul and Benjamin both argue that renewal comes through a proper relation to a law that is spiritual in origin, and they each offer critiques of law that are designed to wrest specifically the Mosaic law from the profane political forces that threaten its reference to its divine origin.

In order to see how Benjamin develops his critique of law, it will be helpful to recall Benjamin's assessment of Catholicism: for Benjamin, the problem of Catholicism is "that of . . . (false, secular) theocracy" (W&T). The principle upon which Benjamin bases this judgment is this: "authentic divine power can manifest itself *other than destructively* only in the world to come (the world of fulfillment)" (W&T; emphasis original). This is so because "in its present state, the social is a manifestation of spectral and demonic powers, often . . . in their greatest tension to God, their efforts to transcend themselves" (W&T). By means of such self-transcendence the powers attempt to secure their own position against what Benjamin calls "divine violence."

Law, as that political institution which aims at providing a mechanism whereby the competing private and temporally bound interests of citizens can be reconciled with one another, is chief among the efforts

---

20. Milbank, *Being Reconciled*, 27.

21. Benjamin, "Critique of Violence" (*GS*, II/1:179–203). I will hereafter cite this text parenthetically as CoV.

at self-transcendence undertaken by the "spectral and demonic powers" that characterize the social. It is law that binds a "social organization" (W&T)[22] together, and one's status before the law that determines
whether one belongs at the center or on the margin. But how does the
law borne by profane political power initiate its political subject into a
profane economy of desire?

In "Critique of Violence" Benjamin argues that both positive and
natural law understand violence's relation to justice as one of means to
ends. Natural law safeguards access to natural ends—which are inherently just. Violence can therefore be used legitimately as long as one
only seeks natural ends through its use. Positive law underwrites its
claim to legitimacy through its ability to ensure that the use of means
is always already governed by the distinction between sanctioned and
unsanctioned violence. It claims that if this distinction is maintained
(through its own violence), it can guarantee the justness of ends. Both
natural and positive law view extra-legal violence as a threat. Benjamin
asks, however, whether law insists on its own monopoly on violence
for the sake of the ends it protects, or for the sake of *its own role* in
protecting those ends.

Benjamin suggests that this tendency in fact evinces profane
law's tendency toward self-protection. In order to make his point in
"Critique of Violence," he contrasts law's relation to the revolutionary
general strike and to the political strike, since the reason why law fears
extra-legal violence "must be especially evident where its application,
even in the present legal system, is still permissible" (281). The right
to the political strike is legally guaranteed, and it is characterized by
the strikers' willingness to return to work should certain conditions be
met. This type of strike remains violent, however, in that it is a form
of extortion. The revolutionary general strike, by contrast, "[sets] itself
the sole task of destroying state power . . . for it takes place . . . in the
determination to resume only a wholly transformed work, no longer
enforced by the state" (CoV, 291–92). When the state "takes emergency

22. Benjamin distinguishes between "community" and "social organization" in
"World and Time." The former is distinguished by its active openness to divine power's
operation in its midst. The "spectral and demonic forces" just mentioned have free
reign in "social organizations," however, and for this reason, Benjamin argues, "the
divine manifests itself in them only in revolutionary force."

measures ... since the right to strike was not 'so intended'" (CoV, 282), the violence of profane law itself becomes evident.

Law must take such measures because extra-legal violence, like legal violence, has a lawmaking function. Through the strike, the revolutionary proletariat threatens to enact an end—a "wholly transformed work"—that is heterogeneous to that "work" protected by the legal order. The revolutionary general strike therefore threatens not only the current form of work—an end that is maintained by the political strike—but also law's own relation to that end. Even if law is successful in quelling the proletarian uprising, however, this victory will only affirm that "violence crowned by fate . . . is the origin of law" (CoV, 286). Benjamin means by this that only fate decides whether the violence of the currently prevailing legal order will prevail over that of the proletarian uprising. As Benjamin puts it, "from the point of view of violence, which alone can guarantee law, there is no equality, but at the most equally great violence" (CoV, 296). The nature of law's guarantee therefore ensures law's downfall, since "all law-preserving violence, in its duration, indirectly weakens the lawmaking violence represented by it, through the suppression of hostile counter-violence" (CoV, 300). Put differently, the force required to maintain law comes more and more to resemble the threat (lawlessness, say) in the name of which the prevailing system of law was itself enacted. This guarantees that one regime will replace another; here temporal succession raises its profane head yet again. We may read this as another illustration of the way the profane assists, by being profane, the coming of the messianic kingdom.

Profane law assists the coming of the messianic kingdom precisely because in exercising its power it ensures its own downfall; it thereby displays its own inner nature in contradistinction to the messianic. In its establishment, by contrast, profane law displays its fundamental *identity* with the order of myth. In "Critique of Violence," Benjamin illustrates this by making reference to the legend of Niobe. Niobe declared herself the happiest of mothers, and too strong even for fortune to subdue; her "arrogance . . . challenges fate—to a fight in which fate must triumph, and bring to light a law only in its triumph" (294). The anteriority of violence to law is crucial here; the so-called punishment of Niobe by Artemis and Apollo conforms to no law. On the contrary, Benjamin writes, "their violence establishes a law far more than it punishes for the infringement of one already existing" (294). In just the same way, a military force conquers and establishes law that *retroactively* declares the conquered rulers guilty. Thus, "at the very moment of law-making, [mythical violence] establishes as law not an end unalloyed by violence, but one necessarily and intimately bound to it, under the title of power" (295).

Benjamin therefore asks, "How would it be . . . if all the violence imposed by fate, using justified means, were of itself in irreconcilable conflict with just ends, and if at the same time a different kind of violence came into view?" (CoV, 293). Awareness of this irreconcilability with just ends would arise from the fact that legal ends are the expression not of legitimate force but of pure power. If such a divine mode of end-making were possible—a mode of end-making that would issue from the "different kind of violence" Benjamin has in mind—a new relation to the category of justice would be initiated. This justice would *not* be that which is secured by the mechanisms of profane law. That is to say, it is not a justice authenticated by juridical standards that find their ultimate ground in what profane political subjects can be relied on and/or motivated to desire. Rather, it would be a mode of justice that would "call a halt to mythical violence" (CoV, 297). It would do this by opposing the violence that prevails within the immanent with a violence that issues from the transcendent, and it would thereby revoke the claims to ultimacy that mythical violence makes for itself.

Benjamin offers this account of the way divine violence confronts and opposes its antithesis:

> If mythical violence is lawmaking, divine violence is law-destroying; if the former sets boundaries, the latter boundlessly destroys them; if mythical violence brings at once guilt and retribution, divine power only expiates; if the former threatens, the latter strikes; if the former is bloody, the latter is lethal without spilling blood. (CoV, 297)

Divine violence is indeed violent, and it irrupts within the profane order destructively. But whereas mythical violence secures itself through sacrifice, divine violence merely accepts sacrifice in order to reorder the living through it (CoV, 297). This means that divine violence is capable of re-ordering the ethical subject in a way that registers as a critique of profane politics despite the fact that it is not politically universalizable.

This is paradigmatically true of the Mosaic law, which meets the question "May I kill?" with the irreducible commandment "Thou shalt not kill" (CoV, 298). This revealed law, however, does not confront its subject in a way identical to that in which profane law confronts its subject. With Mosaic law, Benjamin writes, "the commandment precedes the deed . . . but . . . the injunction becomes inapplicable, incommensurable once the deed is accomplished" (CoV, 298).[23] Profane law, by contrast, is constructed to deal with cases fully commensurable with it. This law preserves itself through its exercise of violence and justifies this by making reference to what the deed does to the victim, or perhaps to some doctrine of "sanctity of life" (CoV, 298). Profane law reorders the legal subject's desire by threatening the life of the transgressor. Profane law's use of this mechanism, however, precludes it from raising the subject from mere life to moral life, for in striking at the life of the transgressor, it only redoubles the transgressor's attachment to that which is passing away in him.

Because existence is the precondition for the enjoyment of the other goods that lead to profane happiness, this mechanism often succeeds. When it does so, it leads to the development of virtues like temperance and prudence. At the same time, however, the use of this mechanism arouses a rebellious passion in the transgressor, who comes to desire that which is forbidden precisely because it is forbidden. The fact that the transgressor may happen to escape law's violence, or may bear violence in himself that may be victorious over that borne by law, furnishes the transgressor with grounds for rebellion, precarious though they may be. This is precisely the inner truth captured by natural law theory (though the Leviathan would make the grounds for such rebellion precarious indeed). The subjects of such a law, however, will be characterized by willful arrogance that glories even in being overcome by law's power (we could call this the *Spartacus* modality), or by fearful servility (we could call this the *1984* modality); in either case, the subject obeys the rule of mere life.

23. If the commandment "becomes inapplicable . . . once the deed is accomplished" it is impossible, properly speaking, for one to become "righteous before the law." For the law forms the heart—or, in Pauline terms, the "conscience" (*syneidēsin* in 1 Cor 10:25–29, for example)—of the one who relates to it in its "spiritual" (Rom 7:5) aspect. In such a case, "the very commandment that promised life" would not "prov[e] to be death" as the Mosaic Law did for Paul (Rom 7:10).

Not so with divine law. Divine law does not provide a juridical criterion that would enable the kind of decision rendered by a human judge—whose judgment, it bears noting, is ultimately granted its legitimacy by way of its reference to the profane desire of the political subjects he represents. Rather, divine law always remains heterogeneous to the transgression. "The injunction becomes inapplicable, incommensurable once the deed is accomplished" (CoV, 298). With divine law, "neither divine judgment, nor the grounds for this judgment can be known in advance." Furthermore, "no judgment of the deed can be derived from the commandment" (298). Divine law must therefore reorder the subject in a different way.[24] Divine law's judgment on the transgressor—i.e., God's wrath on the transgressor—manifests itself in the transgressing subject through that subject's own recognition that, by transgressing, he has descended from moral existence—an existence ordered by the command—to one of mere life. "The reason for the commandment [is to be sought] no longer in what the deed does to the victim, but in what it does to God and the doer" (CoV, 298–99). Just as justice is its own reward, so here transgression is its own punishment.

The commandment therefore unmasks the fallacy of profane law, which holds existence higher than a just existence and expresses this fallacy by striking at the life of the transgressor. Divine law remains autonomous, offering not a juridical criterion, but a "guideline for the actions of persons or communities who have to wrestle with it in solitude and, in exceptional cases, to take on themselves the responsibility of ignoring it" (CoV, 298). Revealed law sweeps away the rule of myth, and the Mosaic law is to be understood precisely as revelation, for only as revelation can it exercise this function. By cultivating an awareness of revelation's account of the order that prevails between the divine and the subjects of divine law, the subject attains freedom from the order constructed by myth and profane politics. The subject thereby attains the freedom that can only be had through obedience to the command, which manifests itself in the divinely ruled subject by destroying the base motivations that otherwise hold sway within the human subject in its profanity.

24. Paul reaches the same conclusion in Romans; neither the perverted Mosaic law (Rom 7) nor the law borne by public authority (Rom 13) suffices to lead one to righteousness.

This initiates a new relation to the category of justice in the subject of divine law, for "justice is the principle of all divine end-making." Divine law determines its subject only to those ends that are in accord with this principle, and unallied with "power" which is "the principle of all mythical lawmaking" (CoV, 295). The subject may thus participate in God's opposition to myth and its violence by participating in the messianic economy of desire that is initiated by divine law. Participation in this economy is at all points dependent on the eventual irruption of divine violence within the historical, for it is only thus that the relation of the historical to the messianic can be created.

Benjamin and the Pauline *Already* and *Not Yet*

Throughout his letters, Paul is to be found in a paradoxical situation: he has become a witness to the messianic apocalypse in the life, death, and resurrection of Jesus, but still awaits the *parousia*, the fulfillment of the promise held out by this apocalypse. It is this apocalypse that exposes sin's deceptive profanation of the law and the subject's need of rescue from a flesh enslaved to sin, and it is this apocalypse that provides the needed rescue. This gives rise to the well-known distinction between the *already* and the *not yet* in Paul. It would either be bald metonymy or extravagant esotericism to claim that the Jewish Benjamin understands the life of Jesus to have the same import as it did for Paul. Nonetheless, Benjamin's messianism is mediated by an apocalyptic that bears striking similarity to Paul's.

The account of "Critique of Violence" that has been developed above demonstrates the way in which the Mosaic law functions apocalyptically in the life of the Jew (or in the life of the Jew after the Spirit, in Paul's language) and in the life of the Jews (Rom 11:5). The apocalypse that is the law creates a people by reconstituting their inner nature, and it creates the subject in the same way; it enacts the inner circumcision of which physical circumcision is a sign (Gen 17:11). Indeed, in light of the above discussion, circumcision may be read as a form not of mythical, but of divine violence—a violence that orders its subject toward ends unallied with mythic power. Although Benjamin is careful to note that "only mythical violence, not divine, will be recognizable as such with certainty" (CoV, 300), circumcision seems a particularly appropriate example of divine violence; one can see, in circumcision as with the incident at Korah (see Numbers 16),[25] "the deep connection between the lack of bloodshed and the expiatory character of this violence" (CoV, 297).

The violence of circumcision does not grant the circumcised, first of all, a new identity that can be claimed or, in Pauline language, boasted about. This is clearly not a point lost on Paul, as he spends much of Romans 2:25—4:12 exploring the value of circumcision in light of its hidden mode of signification. For Benjamin, rather than serving as an identity marker, circumcision initiates the one circumcised into a new practice of existence, a new way of relating to the Mosaic law. The one circumcised thereby comes to relate to the law as the hypothetical happy lovers cited above relate to the sacrament of marriage—that is, immediately, such that the law can continue to manifest itself destructively in the subject's residual profanity. In similar fashion, the law will continue to mediate divine violence for the community[26] in order that the myth-making tendencies of its social organization may come to naught. Benjamin offers an illustration of how tradition may function authentically in the *Anhang* to the "Theses": "We know that the Jews were prohibited from investigating the future. The Torah and prayers instruct them in remembrance, however. This stripped the future of its magic, to which all those succumb who turn to soothsayers for enlightenment" (§B). Rather than becoming part of Jewish "heritage," the Torah's prohibition on soothsaying provided the Jews with instruction in remembrance. In functioning thus, the prohibition mediates divine violence. In order to function thus, those who promulgate the prohibition (the privileged Levites, originally) must understand that the prohibition can never become the monopoly of a human institution.

In the "Theses," Benjamin proposes the partnership between historical materialism and theology precisely in order that this sort of enactment could come to characterize the revolutionary activity of the proletariat. For, as mentioned above, Benjamin writes the "Theses" because "a genuinely messianic face must be restored to the concept of

25. This is one of the few concrete examples Benjamin gives of divine violence; see CoV, 297.

26. That the law *does* mediate divine violence is clear in "World and Time": "the divine manifests itself . . . only in the community, nowhere in 'social organizations.' Such manifestations are to be sought, not in the sphere of the social but in perception oriented toward revelation and, first and last, in language, sacred language above all."

classless society and, to be sure, in the interest of furthering the revolutionary politics of the proletariat itself."[27] The classless society must
come to function, for the proletariat, in an way analogous to that in
which Torah functions for the Jews—that is, not as a Kantian "infinite
task"[28] (as the Social Democrats claimed), nor as a directly enactable
material condition (as would have been counseled by Marx's conception of revolution). Rather, the classless society is a condition that is perpetually coming to be in the moment of the proletariat's revolutionary
interruption of the victors' politics. For it is only as the tensions of the
revolutionary moment resolve themselves and new institutions form
and come to replace old ones that the mythic order returns to cover
over the caesura—that opening to the transcendent in the immanent
which has opened in the revolutionary moment. If the revolutionary
party could attain to a proper perception of what is demanded by the
idea of a classless society, they would recognize that "there is not a moment that [does] not carry with it *its* revolutionary chance—provided
only that it is defined in a specific way, namely as the chance for a completely new resolution of a completely new problem [*Aufgabe*]."[29] The
"Theses" articulate a conception of messianic enactment that situates
the subject in the present moment, which is the very moment in which
the messianic kingdom is coming to be.

It is for this reason that the tension between Paul's *already* and *not
yet* proves so fruitful for Benjamin. Divine violence clearly operates in
the Pauline *already*. Paul says that "God . . . was pleased to reveal his
Son to me" not in order that Paul could boast in being so graced as
to receive this revelation, but "in order that I [Paul] might proclaim
[Christ] among the Gentiles" (Gal 1:15–16). The apocalypse of Christ
sets Paul a task in the here and now. Similarly, Benjamin suggests that
in the break with "mythical forms of law" (and we may extend his logic
to include, in Paul's case, the break from a Jewish law that had adopted
mythical form) "a new historical epoch is founded" (CoV, 300), for this
constitutes a break in the rule of myth within the historical.

This "new historical epoch" is not an epoch on the order of those
of the historicist historians whom Benjamin relentlessly attacks in the

---

27. Benjamin, "Paralipomena," 4:403 (*GS*, I:1232).

28. See also the remark from ibid., 4:401–2 (*GS*, I:1231).

29. Ibid., 4:402 (*GS*, I:1231).

"Theses." That is to say that this epoch cannot be arranged neatly in a sequence with other historical epochs. Rather, it is an epoch that, in messianic fashion, ruptures the continuity of that which is otherwise considered history. This epoch cannot be archaically represented—which is why, in the *Anhang*, Benjamin deftly avoids locating the Jews who were "instructed in remembrance" (§B) on any historical timeline. For to say in historicist fashion that the prohibition mediated divine violence "once upon a time" (§XVII) obscures the messianic aspect of the activity of those who were thus instructed. For the historical materialist's awareness of this messianic aspect of the Jews' activity is one of great benefit for the historical materialist's becoming aware of the messianic aspect of his own.

Benjamin's vehement opposition to historicism in the "Theses" therefore arises from his concern that the proletariat was losing a sense for the temporality that ought to characterize messianic agency. This had a negative effect on its engagement in both of the tasks that make up its praxis: the fomentation of revolution and historical materialist analysis. The proletariat's engagement in the latter task ought to have supported its engagement in the former. But because historical materialism had succumbed to historicism, which attempts to assimilate historiography to natural science by formulating a causal account of the sweep of history and/or through the attempt to formulate "laws" for the course of historical events,[30] historical materialism had lost precisely what is distinctive in its mode of historiography.[31] A historiography modeled on natural science performs a function directly analogous to that of myth; it depicts the human as fully circumscribed by an order of causality over which he has no control, and out of which it is impossible to break. Like myth, science presents the human being in his imma-

30. Benjamin explicitly mentions his concern with this historicist technique in ibid., 4:401 (*GS*, I:1231).

31. Agamben is certainly right when he warns, in his essay "Benjamin and the Demonic," against "the temptation to bend Benjamin's categories in the direction of a historiographical practice," which domesticates Benjamin's conception of a "unique experience of the past" and makes it resemble "the recuperation of alternative heredities" (Agamben, *Potentialities*, 152). Nonetheless, Hanssen's study of the category of history in Benjamin (*Walter Benjamin's Other History*) does crucial work in tracking the disjunctions between Benjamin's historiography and his contemporaries' (Heidegger, particularly), and in drawing the connections between historiography and the philosophy of language in Benjamin's work.

nence, according to the mere life that is in him; scientific and mythical narrations of human existence both culminate in the claim that freedom is impossible. It follows that historicism's documentation of history is only historical in a degenerate sense; mythic time and homogeneous, empty time are both "parasitically dependent on the time of a higher, less natural life."[32] Historical materialist historiography is, by contrast, designed to highlight the sense in which the subject is more than the mere life that is in him (the subject eludes science's framing), and the present moment is fraught with revolutionary possibilities (historicism cannot monopolize the past).

Historical materialism does so by subordinating historicism's homogeneous, empty time to the "now-time" (*Jetztzeit*), that is, the time that is "filled by the presence of the now" (§XIV). In the now-time the temporal distance that historicists claim separates the present moment from the moment in the past is collapsed, such that the past moment is brought to fulfillment in the present. In this way, the historian "grasps the constellation which his own era has formed with a definite earlier one. Thus he establishes a conception of the present as the 'time of the now' which is shot through with chips of Messianic time" (§A). Benjamin performs precisely this form of historiography in Thesis B when he appropriately discerns in the activity of the Jews that were instructed in remembrance through the prohibition on soothsaying a messianic aspect that becomes informative for the proletariat. One could say that Benjamin's historical materialists become contemporary with these Jews—for in appropriating a messianic mode of activity both come to live and move within the newly dawning messianic epoch. In this dawning the past is brought to fulfillment, and the present moment becomes shot through with fragments of all previous moments of messianic time. Benjamin's "redemptive criticism" (*rettende Kritik*)[33] is not, then, a form of analysis that encourages esotericism or withdrawal. Rather, in redeeming the phenomena of history by charting the relationship they bear to the messianic, Benjamin is making of them the raw materials necessary for a new form of proletarian revolution. This revolution issues from the present generation's "weak Messianic

32. Benjamin, "Fate and Character," 308.

33. Jürgen Habermas is one of the scholars who has done the most to popularize the use of this term, as it figures prominently in his essay "Walter Benjamin: Consciousness or Rescuing Critique" ("Rescuing Critique" translates "*rettende Kritik*").

power." And in pursuing it, the present generation has cause to hope that it may make good on the claim the previous generation makes on it (§II).

In "Critique of Violence," Benjamin goes so far as to suggest that one might see the coming age arriving even in the gesture made by the revolutionary activity of the proletariat. Indeed, Benjamin writes, "If the rule of myth is broken occasionally in the present age, the coming age is not so unimaginably remote that an attack on law is altogether futile" (CoV, 300). An attack on profane law may participate in the coming of the new age, for in catalyzing the overcoming of the currently prevailing order, revolutionary force may participate with divine violence in laying bare the mythical foundations of that order. One might surmise that Paul's anti-nomianism may register according to Benjaminian criteria as one form of this revolutionary attack on law.

It would, of course, be an egregious miscalculation to claim that the revolutionary force borne by the proletariat arises directly from a divine agency, for this would fail to reckon with the character of human action within the historical, which, while being constructed within the immanent, aims at the transcendent—often despite itself. We therefore must say that, like all forces that arise from human agency, revolutionary force has a dual aspect.

The profane aspect of revolutionary force is on display in its intention to instantiate a new set of conditions which are more conducive to the pursuit of a profane happiness. Here the element of the Pauline *not yet* that appears in Benjamin takes shape. One must hold a certain eschatological reserve when assessing human action (perhaps particularly revolutionary force) because of the non-identity of happiness—the desire for which alone can motivate human action, though the character of this happiness may differ—and redemption. Nonetheless, insofar as the revolutionary attack on law may serve to unmask the goals defined by profane politics as deceptive, even a revolutionary violence that arises from profane motives may serve to mediate divine violence.

Benjamin wrote the "Theses" in order that the profane aspect of the revolutionary force borne by the proletariat could be mitigated to the greatest extent possible. It is the unavoidability of this aspect that makes an insistence on the *not yet* necessary. The fact that he develops the theologically guided historical materialist hermeneutic by which the proletariat could become oriented to the messianic suggests that for Benjamin, as for Paul, the boundary between the current, profane age and that of messianic fulfillment is permeable. For Benjamin, this permeability manifests itself in the way the principles of immanence, namely myth and mythic violence, open—often despite themselves—to the transcendent. This does not mean that those who reject profane law as an ordering principle—Benjamin's proletariat or Paul's messianists—will not be subject to its violence. Indeed, the opposite may be true. It does, however, revoke the ultimate significance mythic violence has for them, such that they groan not for the preservation of their flesh—or not for its preservation for its own sake. Rather they groan with all of creation (Rom 8:23) for the decisive interruption of this law's operation even while continuing to dwell in the calling to which they have been called (Eph 4). This interruption is, for both Paul and Benjamin, in one sense *not yet*, but in another, it is *already*. It is already in that the withdrawal from the profane economy of desire—which alone gives mythic violence its power—is possible to the extent that the subject can participate in the economy of desire borne by the Messiah through membership in the messianic community. It is this community that affirms, with Paul, that "the present [profane] form of this world is passing away" (1 Cor 7:31), and, with Benjamin, that the profane is nevertheless "a decisive category of [the kingdom's] quietest approach" (TPF).

PART III

Badiou and Žižek

A Very Particular Universalism: Badiou and Paul

by Stephen Fowl

PRESENTING BADIOU

For some time, and from a distance, biblical scholars have witnessed a growing body of literature written on Paul by philosophers and others who stand well outside the guild of biblical scholars and theologians. When I point out this work to colleagues, I am struck by the variety of their reactions to having philosophers and other unauthorized types romp in our playground.

As a group, Paulinists are pretty insular and not much interested in contemporary philosophy. Anthony Thiselton and, in very different ways, Troels Engberg-Pedersen are some of the notable exceptions. As a result, a lot of the conversations I have had tend to reflect a rather indignant attitude. There is a voluminous secondary literature on Paul. Thus, to presume to write on Paul without seriously engaging this literature seems a bit presumptuous. I do not share this view, but I understand it.

The great counterexample to this is Daniel Boyarin's, *A Radical Jew: Paul and the Politics of Identity* (1994). In the relatively few years he took to write this book Boyarin made himself into a Pauline scholar. He mastered the secondary literature and was able to engage in complex exegetical discussions. Many, myself included, may disagree with his views, but there is no doubt that Boyarin would be counted as a full member of the guild of Pauline scholars. This may be a dubious distinction, but it is not easy to attain.

The works of scholars such as Alain Badiou, Giorgio Agamben, Slavoj Žižek and so forth, are not like Boyarin in this respect. Rather, they have appropriated a version of the longstanding Christian practice of plundering the Egyptians. Instead of Christians engaging pagan philosophers to advance a theological agenda, we find philosophers engaging Paul in serious but ad hoc ways to advance their own particular projects.[1] In such a situation it seems to me that one Christian way of responding to such would-be plunderers is to welcome them and try to be hospitable.

That is what I aim to do in this essay with regard to the work of Alain Badiou. I want to engage closely and hospitably with his work on Paul in order to show that appropriating Paul in the ways that he does comes at some cost. Moreover, I hope to indicate that a more rigorously theological reading of Paul may found a politics that provides a way to advance some of the political aims Badiou wants to achieve without some of the attendant side effects.

Although I believe I can do some justice to Badiou's treatment of Paul in *Saint Paul: The Foundation of Universalism*,[2] I make no claims to have any insight into the astonishing breadth of Badiou's work. Indeed, one might lay at my door the same sort of criticism my colleagues might lay at Badiou's. That is, I have not really done justice to the breadth of Badiou's work, not to mention the secondary literature. I cannot hope to dodge this criticism fully. I have engaged secondary works on Badiou and Paul and I feel confident that my understanding is compatible with those works. Moreover, my aim here is not so much to comment on Badiou's work as a whole, but simply his brief book on Paul. Thus, I hope my aims are suitably limited.

As I understand him, Badiou is primarily interested in constructing a notion of subjectivity that can assert universal truth or a universal truth procedure. Badiou seeks a third way between the universalizing claims of freely circulating capital across open markets (9), on the one hand, and the isolating fragmentation of identity politics, on the other hand (11). Although these two ways may seem opposed to each other,

---

1. If Paul Griffiths is correct, this practice is not the work of a victor plundering a defeated foe. Rather it reflects the paucity of resources left to philosophy with the demise of modernity. See, Griffiths, "Christ and Critical Theory."

2. Throughout this essay citations to Badiou's *Saint Paul* are in the form of parenthetic page references to the English translation listed in the bibliography.

they are also parasitic upon each other, as the universalizing movement of capitalism seeks ever more specially defined niche markets.

Badiou pursues this third way with a Pauline type of urgency. This is because his concerns are particularly relevant to current French politics, where "there exists a despicable complicity between the globalized logic of capital and French identitarian fanaticism" (9). Given this set of concerns, it is clear why a text like Gal 3:28 would captivate Badiou. He sees it as a proclamation of a difference-transcending "*indifference that tolerates differences*" (99, emphasis original).[3] I will need to say more about this later.

For Badiou, such a result requires a subjective truth that is not constituted by law-like universal generalities or axioms.[4] Instead, truth lies in an event subjectively encountered. This event constitutes a subject as the subject both proclaims the event and seeks to be faithful to that proclamation (14). Two consequences follow from this:

> First, since truth is evental, or of the order of what occurs, it is singular . . . No available generality can account for it, nor structure the subject who claims to follow in its wake. Consequently, there cannot be a law of truth. Second, truth being inscribed on the basis of a declaration that is in essence subjective, no preconstituted subset can support it; nothing communitarian or historically established can lend its substance to the process of truth . . . It is offered to all, or addressed to everyone, without a condition of belonging being able to limit this offer, or this address (14).[5]

In this light, it becomes more evident why Paul might become a figure of interest for Badiou. To be fair, Badiou is quite clear that he has no interest in the Christian particularities that, one might argue, comprise the heart of Paul's subjectivity. Paul will have to be demythologized if he is to be of any real use to Badiou. What emerges is a Paul

---

3. Daniel Bell argues that Badiou's dogmatic atheism ultimately traps him within the communitarianism he seeks to escape. See "Badiou's Faith and Paul's Gospel," 100.

4. "Truth is entirely subjective (it is of the order of a declaration that testified to a conviction relative to the event)" (Badiou, *Saint Paul*, 14).

5. Paul Griffiths notes that for Badiou the "evental site" is "a place in which something radically other occurs, something that cannot be accommodated by the ordinary categories of its site and that makes a universal demand" ("Christ and Critical Theory," 51).

constituted by the event of Jesus's resurrection. Badiou even claims that Paul reduces Christianity to a single statement, "Jesus is resurrected" (4). I think this reduction is not true to the apostle. I will try to explore later why this choice of words is crucial to Badiou rather than the much more obvious proclamation, "Jesus Christ is Lord." For now, let this claim stand.

The resurrection is an event that ruptures reality with a message of life. It could neither be anticipated nor accounted for by the discourses of Jew or Greek. It is this evental truth which can provide a third way between what Badiou characterizes as Jewish and Greek discourse. For Badiou, "Greek discourse is essentially the discourse of totality, insofar as it upholds the *sophia* (wisdom as internal state) of a knowledge of *phusis* (nature as ordered and accomplished deployment of being)" (41). Alternatively, Jewish discourse is marked by the figure of the prophet. "But a prophet is one who abides in the requisition of signs, one who signals, testifying to transcendence by exposing the obscure to its deciphering. Thus Jewish discourse will be held to be, above all, the discourse of the sign" (41).

Neither of these two discourses can achieve the universality that Badiou desires because, like capitalism and communitarianism, they "presuppose the persistence of the other" (42). Their competitive inter-dependence blocks the universal announcement that constitutes Paul. "Paul's project is to show that a universal logic of salvation cannot be reconciled with any law, be it one that ties thought to the cosmos, or one that fixes the effects of a special election" (42).

Both Jewish and Greek discourses are, according to Badiou, dis-courses of the Father. Paul's proclamation is a discourse of the Son, universal, detached from any particularity. Badiou repeatedly asserts that Paul has no interest in Trinitarian relations or doctrine. Indeed, Badiou's Son cannot in any serious sense be the Son of the Father with-out jeopardizing the universality of the discourse of the Son.

This discourse must be proclaimed and not proven. "For Paul, the event has not come to prove something; it is pure beginning. Christ's resurrection is neither an argument nor an accomplishment" (49).[6] This allows Paul to be an anti-philosopher whose credo is most aptly summarized in 1 Cor 1:17–29. Paul's gospel is one that does not rely

---

6. Rom 1:3 comes immediately to mind as the counter to this claim.

on wisdom, power or even being; "this event is of such a character as to render the philosophical logos incapable of declaring it" (46). Paul's proclamation is marked by a newness that could not be anticipated or contained by Jewish or Greek discourse. The Christ-event interrupts all prior discourses, and is sundered from all prior places of thought. "For Paul, the Christ-event is heterogeneous to the law, pure excess over every prescription, grace without concept or appropriate rite. The real can no more be what in elective exception becomes literalized in stone as timeless law (Jewish discourse), than it is what comes or returns to its place (Greek discourse)" (57).

As Badiou understands it, the Christ-event allows Paul to render all cultural and ethnic differences as *adiaphora,* insignificant. This is the universalist thrust of Paul's proclamation (57). Indeed, on this scheme, the Christ-event can constitute all subjects to the extent it remains a truth-procedure that resists being tied to any cultural or ethnic particularities and resists becoming a tradition or a set of teachings. This seems to call for a constant or, at least, repetitive state of encounter with the Christ-event as it interrupts and breaks through every established routine (66). This repeated or ever renewed event seems to be what Badiou means by the working of grace: "it is incumbent upon us to found a materialism of grace through the strong simple idea that every existence can one day be seized by what happens to it and subsequently devote itself to that which is valid for all, or as Paul magnificently puts it, 'become all things to all men'" (66).

Recall that, according to Badiou, Christ's resurrection enables Paul to proclaim an indifference to differences. How does Christ's resurrection have the power to suspend differences? Certainly it is not by defeating death in any sort of systematic or comprehensive way. Christ's death is completely disjoined from the resurrection. Death is merely the immanent and contingent site of the resurrection. For Badiou, the cross and its reconciling power bears only a negative and limited relationship to salvation, "which is the evental power of the resurrection" (70).[7]

Of course, in this light the law will also be a hindrance to the gracious and evental character of salvation. The law, for Badiou, exhib-

---

7. Daniel Bell offers a theologically substantive account of the death of Jesus that renders it much more amenable to Badiou's overall concerns with the crucifixion in "Politics of Fear," 446–49.

its an unrelentingly "statist" character. "By 'statist' I mean that which enumerates, names and controls the parts of a situation" (76). Further, if truth is to have a universal address it must be "nondenumerable, impredicable, uncontrollable" (76). Grace is all of these things, law is none of them. The salvation that results from such grace is liberation from sin. Sin in this case is a sort of infection. "Sin is nothing but the permutation of the places of life and death under the effect of the law, which is precisely why Paul, dispensing with the need for a sophisticated doctrine of original sin, can simply say: we *are* in sin" (84).

Liberation from sin, understood in this way, subjects one to a new, non-literal law named love. "Love names a non-literal law, one that gives to the faithful subject his consistency, and effectuates the postevental truth in the world" (87). Hence, the subject captivated by the universal evental truth seeks to be faithful to a continuing truth procedure, maintaining the universal truth of the event through love. "It is incumbent upon love to become law so that truth's postevental universality can continuously inscribe itself in the world, rallying subjects to the path of life" (88).

Love and the pursuit of life over death seem to be practices of Paul's universal truth procedure. On the one hand, these seem to be consistent with Paul's own views. On the other hand, who really is opposed to love and the pursuit of life? For Paul, the character of love, which is the fulfilling of the law (Rom 13:10), is inseparably bound to the other-regarding, self-offering death of Christ, who is the *telos* of the law (Rom 10:4). As Douglas Harink has noted in his own accounting of Badiou,[8] this is precisely that element of Paul's thought with which Badiou wants to have no part.[9]

Instead, it would seem that for Badiou the practice of love and the pursuit of life manifest themselves most clearly both in recognizing and transcending differences. Love renders all particularities into *adiaphora*. "Differences can be transcended only if benevolence with regard to customs and opinions presents itself as *an indifference that tolerates differences*" (99, emphasis original). "What matters, man or woman, Jew or Greek, slave or free man, is that differences *carry the universal which happens to them like grace*. Inversely, only by recognizing in dif-

8. See Harink, "False Universal?"

9. See esp. Badiou, *Saint Paul*, 102.

ferences their capacity for carrying the universal that comes upon them can the universal itself verify its own reality" (106, emphasis original). Thus, what Paul urges is a constant awareness of particularity and a persistent struggle to render particularity inconsequential. Indeed, for Badiou this is what Paul means by not being conformed to the world but being transformed by the renewing of one's mind (Rom 12:2) (110). In this way, "Differences, like instrumental tones, provide us with the recognizable univocity that makes up the melody of the True" (106).

PROBING BADIOU

Badiou presents a Pauline scholar with a bracing slap in the face. His Paul is unlike anything else on offer in places such as the Society of Biblical Literature. Although one might want to contest almost every single interpretive claim Badiou offers, I don't think that would really prove to be a productive way forward. Instead, I want to probe Badiou on three or four central points regarding his picture of Paul, his use of Paul, and his understanding of differences. In the light of those probes I will conclude by offering a counter, and I think more Pauline, account of differences.

Douglas Harink encourages us to see Badiou's Paul in apocalyptic terms. Although I do not think that Badiou's Paul and the Paul of a scholar such as J. Louis Martyn share much in common, I do think that this is probably the closest analogy.[10] This apocalyptic view of Paul emphasizes that "Paul's good news is that in the cross and resurrection of Jesus Christ and the sending of the Holy Spirit God has *apocalypsed* himself, that is, God has decisively and conclusively invaded the cosmos, enslaved under the hostile powers, to conquer those powers and to bring about deliverance from the condition of enslavement to them."[11] In Jesus, God invades the cosmos in a manner that is unanticipated, shocking, and utterly destabilizing for Paul as he encounters it on the road to Damascus.[12] This apocalyptic view matches up in numerous

10. In addition to Harink's essay, see Martyn, "Epistemology at the Turn of the Ages."

11. Harink, "False Universal?" 12.

12. This apocalyptic view stands in contrast to those history-of-religions approaches to Paul that tend to reduce Paul to a set of cultural and religious antecedents, whether Jewish or Greek.

respects with Badiou's understanding of the resurrection as the event which captivates and animates Paul's militant proclamation.

These apocalyptic accounts of Paul are a persistent reminder that both scholars and Christians have a tendency to domesticate Paul and his writings, gathering supposed conceptual and religious antecedents to central Pauline terminology so that he appears to be little more than a small tremor on the theological terrain, something you can feel, but which does not bring down any buildings. Badiou's Paul is certainly not domesticated. Badiou has grasped the urgent compulsion inherent in Paul's activity.

In emphasizing the apocalyptic power behind Paul's work in the ways that he does, Badiou would have us think that the Christ-event leaves Paul as a subject without an identity. Strangely, however, he ignores one of the passages that would have helped him make this case best: Phil 1:12–18. Here Paul offers to the Philippians an account of his situation in prison. In the course of this discussion, Paul's subjectivity, his dispositions, his hopes, and his expectations, become inseparable from the progress of the gospel. If there were any place where Paul's subjectivity were to become simply identical to his proclamation it is here. Even in this case, however, it is clear that Paul's subjectivity is constituted by the new and unanticipated place he has come to occupy in the drama of God's salvation. Because he is so firmly rooted in this drama he is able to tie God's providential supervision of the gospel to his own situation in prison. Apart from this standpoint, this subjective location, Paul could not envision and narrate his circumstances in the way that he does.

This specific example leads to a more general set of comments about Badiou's Paul. One of Paul's primary activities is thinking theologically about God's invasion of the world in Christ. He does not abandon the discourse of Judaism in the light of the Christ-event. Instead, the Christ-event compels him to rethink both his own life in Judaism and the narrative of God's election and sustaining of Israel that had directed his life prior to Christ. He is not a subject without an identity. He is a subject who has had to reconstitute his identity under the guidance of the Spirit in the light of God's activity in Christ. We see this on a personal level in both Galatians 1 and in Philippians 3, and more generally throughout Romans.

Paul does not reconstitute his subjectivity primarily for the sake of his own sanity. Rather, he seeks to establish lines of continuity between God's call of Abraham and promises to Israel, on the one hand, and God's redemption of the world through the life, death, and resurrection of Jesus, on the other hand, in order to show that God's invasion of the world in Jesus Christ does not fundamentally undermine God's righteousness.

Badiou's assertion that Paul reduces Christianity to the statement "Jesus is resurrected" allows him to obviate this need to establish new lines of continuity in the aftermath of the Christ-event. This comes, however, at some expense to an understanding of Paul. If Paul were to reduce Christianity to a sentence, I think we can be confident that the sentence would be, "Jesus Christ is Lord." Such a sentence both invites and summarizes the narrative and theological expansion that Paul offers in his various writings, and which Badiou largely ignores. Only at the end of his book does Badiou make a limited gesture toward this. He claims, "The task Paul sets for himself is obviously not that of abolishing Jewish particularity, which he constantly acknowledges as the event's principle of historicity, but that of animating it internally by everything of which it is capable relative to the new discourse and hence the new subject. For Paul, being Jewish in general, and the Book in particular, *can and must be resubjectivated*" (103). This interesting but undeveloped assertion leaves one wondering how Badiou would have understood Paul's struggle to "resubjectivate" Judaism and the Book apart from the sort of engagement with the crucifixion that Badiou eschews.

It seems both possible and necessary to keep the apocalyptic and generative element of Paul's proclamation together with Paul's subsequent and more systematic theological reflection on God's invasion of the world in Christ. Indeed, as I will try to show at the conclusion of the essay, any genuinely Pauline politics must seek to hold both of these elements together, allowing the truly apocalyptic force of God's work in Christ to shine forth, while also thinking theologically about this event's connections to God's previous dealings with Israel and the world at large.

Earlier I compared Badiou's approach to Paul and Pauline scholarship with that of Daniel Boyarin. I want to return to this comparison briefly in order to probe a different aspect of Badiou's interest in Paul.

In some respects Boyarin and Badiou are working on a similar problem. Boyarin posits that Paul is attempting to work out the relationship between his messianic universalism, which comes to Paul from Hellenism (particularly Hellenistic Jews such as Philo), and his particular identity as a Jew. According to Boyarin, Paul achieves this by allegorizing Judaism. That is, Paul takes the concrete practices, beliefs, and texts of Judaism and treats them as ciphers for a deeper, spiritualized, universal community in which "there is neither Jew nor Greek, neither slave nor free, neither man nor woman." This same text from Galatians is crucial for Badiou as well. For Boyarin's Paul, once this more perfect form is revealed in Christ, there is little use for the fleshly, material cipher. In short, Paul's spiritualizing of Judaism effectively dissolves the concrete people of Israel.

Although fascinating and insightful in many respects, I think Boyarin is ultimately incorrect about Paul and about allegorical interpretation. I do, however, think Boyarin's criticism of Paul is instructive for understanding something of Badiou's approach to Paul. That is, if Boyarin claims that Paul allegorizes Judaism in ways that dissolve the concrete people of Israel, then along similar lines one can also argue that Badiou allegorizes Paul in ways that dissolve the concrete apostle and his writings. For Badiou, Paul is simply a cipher for an apocalyptic or evental notion of truth and its attendant procedures. Once that notion has been developed and displayed, there is very little need to retain the figure that provoked or generated the allegory in the first place.

This is not necessarily to be taken as a criticism of Badiou. Indeed, I see no reason for him to reject the notion that he is allegorizing Paul in this way. This observation did lead me to ask in a new way a question that often plagued me as I read Badiou: "Why Paul?" There seem to be numerous others who have been captivated by an event, who might also display the evental character of truth. Abraham comes immediately to mind. Although Badiou briefly discusses Abraham's importance for Paul he does not treat Abraham as a proclaimer of evental truth. This is all the more intriguing in the light of the tremendous importance Badiou places on Gal 3:28. Remember that the supposed elision of differences in Christ that Paul proclaims here is ultimately a way of indicating that all believers, both Jew and Gentile, are filiated with Abraham and the promises made to him.

Regina Schwartz suggests that Moses also fits the bill here, though I suspect that Moses's intimate connection with the law and literalism would make him problematic for Badiou.[13] Of course, the Bible is not the only place where one might find characters who are both captivated by an event and display an unwavering devotion to the proclamation of that event and to living in some sort of fidelity to that event. Robespierre, Mao, and Pol Pot come immediately to mind.[14] Of course, just as quickly one can see that they would ultimately be unsuitable for Badiou's political project.[15] That project is the advancement of difference-transcending benevolence that "presents itself as an *indifference that tolerates differences*" (99, emphasis original). In this respect it becomes clear why Paul should be the cipher on which Badiou relies. Paul, as interpreted by Badiou, is the most straightforward path to the political arrangements Badiou advocates. Ultimately Badiou's passion for a universal subjectivity that is evental in nature is tied to his concern with French society and the various forces that tear at it. As noted above, these forces are organized by the free circulation of capital on the one hand, and the fragmentation of identity politics on the other hand (11).

It is here, with regard to this benevolence that is indifferent to differences, that I want to make my final probe of Badiou. I wish to raise two questions. The first concerns whether indifference to differences is really a sufficient understanding of what Paul (or most others) means by love. The second question concerns whether or not Badiou is able to conceive of differences existing in a non-competitive relationship.

As Badiou sees it, love is the outworking of fidelity to the event (90). "It us [*sic*] incumbent upon love to become law so that the truth's

13. See Schwartz, "Revelation and Revolution," 376–82.

14. In a partial response to this sort of claim Badiou writes in the preface to the English edition of *Ethics*, that the event on its own does not determine its own outcome: "I was then obliged to admit that the event opens a subjective space in which not only the progressive and truthful subjective figure of fidelity but also other figures every bit as innovative, albeit negative . . . take their place" (lvii).

15. See Griffiths, "Christ and Critical Theory," who notes, "The sense of loss from which Badiou reads Paul is palpable. He needs 'a new militant figure . . . to succeed the one installed by Lenin and the Bolsheviks'. That figure (Badiou does not say but implies) is lost, frozen in the Gulag, crushed under the tracks of Soviet tanks as they rolled into Prague, withered by the increasing willingness of China to accept capital's blandishments, and dismembered by the breakup of the Soviet empire" (51).

postevental universality can continuously inscribe itself in the world, rallying subjects to the path of life" (88). For Badiou, the key Pauline text here is Rom 13:10 (also 13:8) where Paul claims that love is the fulfilling of the law. The beginning of that verse notes that "love does no wrong to a neighbor." This on its own sounds very much like the benevolent indifference to differences that Badiou advocates.

Of course, this is only a very partial picture of a Pauline account of love, and Badiou himself hints that he is aware of this when he briefly asserts that "Paul is in no way a theoretician of oblatory love, through which one would forget oneself in devotion to the Other" (90). That is, by seeking to short-circuit this account of love, Badiou must be aware that there are a large number of Pauline texts that speak of love in terms of regard for others, at least for one's brothers and sisters in Christ. Indeed, in Phil 2:12–18 Paul speaks of joyfully being poured out as an oblation upon the altar of the Philippians' faith. Ostensibly, Badiou is concerned that such other-regarding love is a recipe for self-anni-hilation, thus making it impossible to love one's neighbor as oneself (89–91).[16] Although Paul has no notion of an other-regarding love that annihilates the self, it is indisputable that *agape* is, at least in part, con-stituted by an outward looking, other-regarding disposition. Nowhere is this clearer than in Philippians, especially in 2:1–4. Throughout the epistle Paul urges the Philippians to display patterns of thinking, feel-ing, and acting that are directed towards the benefit of others, towards the formation of a common life in Christ that is characterized by true humility and deep joy, as they participate both materially and spiritually with Paul in a friendship that is founded upon and sustained by the life, death, and resurrection of Christ, particularly as narrated in 2:6–11. Moreover, Paul is confident that in living this way the Philippians will strengthen rather than obliterate their true selves, even if such a way of life would lead the authorities to kill them.

16. In chapter 2 of *Ethics*, "Does the Other Exist?," one can posit that Badiou's clearly false claims about Paul may be driven by his desire to oppose Levinas and an ethic of "otherness," which Badiou takes to be the dominant form of moral reasoning among philosophers today. Such an ethic according to Badiou elevates difference to the supreme moral category over "the same" and requires some sort of belief in God, "the Altogether-Other." This begins to make more sense of his indifference to differ-ences that he attributes to Paul. As I will argue below, however, it still requires Badiou to think of differences as fundamentally competitive.

Philippians may be the most striking example of other-regarding love in Paul's corpus, but it is by no means an isolated or idiosyncratic example. Recognizing this, however, would have serious consequences for Badiou's account in two important respects. First, it would require him to recognize that the death of Christ has a significance for Paul that goes well beyond serving as the contingent point at which resurrection can take place. Paul places a great deal of "post-evental" importance on the character of Christ's death and its central role in the narrative of God's invasion of the world.[17]

Second, a fully Pauline account of *agape* will not be satisfied with indifference to differences. *Agape* recognizes differences, seeks to extend hospitality to them and to bring differences into communion with each other, a communion which reconciles but does not erase differences. Of course, this requires communal negotiation, conversation, and, presumably, admonition, all of which demand a form of love that cannot afford to be indifferent. When Paul uses the image of a body comprised of many parts to describe the church in 1 Corinthians 12 it is clear that the various parts of the body must both recognize their differences and recognize their interdependence. Indeed, when the Corinthian Christians actually display indifference towards one another and leave in place the real social and material differences between them, it leads Paul to deny that their common meal manifests the character of the Lord's Supper (1 Cor 11:17–34).

If the political alternatives are either various forms of civil strife or indifference to differences, then one must recognize both the appeal of Badiou's option and its similarity to political liberalism. At the same time, one must acknowledge the great distance that lies between Badiou's alternative and the forms of common life Paul advocates for his brothers and sisters in Christ.

I think the basis of the divergence of Badiou's position from Paul's lies in the ways they understand differences. For Badiou, differences are fundamentally competitive and agonistic until they come under the power of grace that comes through an encounter with an evental truth. At that point, differences become vehicles for carrying the universal and univocal proclamation of the True. "Differences, like instrumental

---

17. As Bell in "Politics of Fear" (444–46) reminds us, however, the importance of Christ's death is not primarily to pay some sort of debt to God created by human sin.

tones, provide us with the recognizable univocity that makes up the melody of the True" (106). The True transforms differences from being the basis of competition and struggle to being *adiaphora*, matters of indifference. As long as the "melody of the True" is played, it matters not whether one plays string, brass, or woodwind. At the end of the day, differences either remain competitive or are erased under the univocity of the True.

Badiou understands his account of indifference to differences to have its basis in Paul's claims in Gal 3:28 that there is neither Jew nor Greek, slave nor free, man nor woman. Badiou's is probably not the best account of Paul's views here. Moreover, it is a distinctly problematic account from a theological point of view. If Paul imagines that in Christ all differences are rendered insignificant or matters of indifference, then he is left with a very difficult task of explaining how God remains faithful to Israel and to God's covenants. Although one would not want to reduce Jewish identity to a set of social, material, and religious particularities, it is very difficult to imagine Jewish identity without any of these. If God's fidelity to the covenants is secured only through rendering all Jewish particularities insignificant for either Jews or Gentiles, then this is a very strange sort of fidelity. Paul's assertion that all Israel will be saved in Rom 11:25–36 is, as Paul recognizes, a great mystery. That is, Paul is convinced that God will save all Israel, but he is not very clear about how this will happen. Nevertheless, it would not be very satisfactory if all Israel is saved precisely to the extent her members stop being Jewish, or treat their Jewishness as a matter of indifference.[18]

Moreover, the pairs of Jew and Greek, slave and free, man and woman, do not simply nominate specific differences. Rather, they are loci of alienation and sin between humans. Ephesians is especially articulate about the alienation between Gentile and Jew, and both groups' alienation from God. Although Paul has particular prescriptions for slaves and masters in 1 Corinthians 7, these appear as ad hoc advice for how best to live faithfully in the time that remains until Christ's return. Paul is equally clear that all believers are slaves of Christ. Finally, as any Jew would, Paul recognizes that the creation of man and woman

18. As part of his argument that Badiou's universalism is anti-Jewish, Bell remarks that Badiou's Jews are Jews just like "a food court taco is a taco" ("Badiou's Faith," 102).

together is part of God's will. At the same time, Genesis 3 makes it clear that human sin not only results in alienation from God, but ruptures relations between the first humans. Thus when Paul asserts in Gal 3:27–28 that, "As many of you as were baptized into Christ have clothed yourselves with Christ. There is no longer Jew nor Greek, slave nor free, man nor woman for you are all one in Christ Jesus," he must presume that this oneness is achieved through reconciliation accomplished in and through Christ. Badiou is wary of notions of reconciliation. He calls reconciliation the "operation of death" and seeks to distinguish it sharply from "salvation," which is enabled by the event of resurrection (70). Badiou seems to understand that thinking of differences in terms of reconciliation will inevitably tie Christ's resurrection into a larger narrative, one in which the death of Christ as well as the earthly Jesus's practice of forgiveness will need to play significant roles.

Reconciliation cannot occur and is not strictly necessary if one merely cultivates indifference to differences. On Badiou's account, whatever alienation may have occurred through and in the midst of human differences, they are insignificant in the light of the event. It is thus conceivable that victim and victimizer may equally become filiated to the Truth. It is, however, difficult to see what sort of future they have together apart from some sort of reconciliation—reconciliation that would have to treat their differences seriously even as it worked to ensure that their sin was not the final word on their relationship to each other and to God. There seem to be no resources for this in Badiou's scheme. Victim and victimizer each simply take up their instruments and begin to play the melody of the True in unison.

A Pauline Politics of Difference

It is at this point that I wish to posit a Pauline and Christian alternative account of differences. Space considerations will limit me here to comments that are all too understated. Nevertheless, I hope it will be sufficiently suggestive to pose a real alternative.

From Paul's explicit comments it is clear that regardless of whatever he thought prior to God's invasion of the cosmos in Christ, his vision of the church is animated by God's promise to Abraham in Genesis 12 that through him and his seed all the nations of the earth would be blessed. This universal blessing, as Paul now recognizes, is accomplished in and through the life, death, and resurrection of Christ, the seed of Abraham. Paul is convinced that through Christ, the Messiah, Israel's redemption has been manifested to the world in an astonishing way. The promises to Abraham are fulfilled in Christ in ways Paul could never have imagined apart from being grabbed by the resurrected Christ on the road to Damascus.

Moreover, the blessing of all nations through the seed of Abraham is brought about in and through the life and witness of the church, a church in which Jew and Gentile, slave and free, man and woman are reconciled to God and to each other in Christ. As an alienated and unreconciled world perceives God's work through the peaceable reconciled life and witness of the church, they will be fascinated and compelled to join in. Thus, all the nations will be drawn to God. Although he does not quote Isa 2:1–4 directly, some account very much like this one must have played a significant role in Paul's thinking. Moreover, theologians as diverse as Justin Martyr, Origen, and Tertullian make explicit connections between the life and witness of the church and the fulfillment of Isaiah 2.

In the church differences are reconciled without being erased. In Christ, differences are understood in the light of the shalom that characterized both the garden in Genesis 1–2 and the new Jerusalem in Revelation 21. As intended by God, differences serve to reflect the superabundance of love that generated creation in the first place. They need not be competitive or matters of indifference. Rather than being rendered insignificant in playing the melody of the True in unison, Christians imagine that differences in the church of the reconciled combine harmoniously to praise the one God, Father, Son, and Holy Spirit.

CHAPTER 6

Ideological Closure in the Christ-Event: A Marxist Response to
Alain Badiou's Paul

by Neil Elliott

A PARADOX

At the church I serve as part-time
priest, St. Paul's on the Hill, a great
stained-glass window looms over
the altar rail depicting St. Paul "on
the Hill" of Mars, the Areopagus in
Athens (Acts 17). The Parthenon
in the background identifies the
location, the gorgeous hues of
sunset indicate evening is at hand.
The philosophers have departed,
laughing derisively at Paul's notion
of the "resurrection of the dead,"
gone to seek better entertainment
elsewhere. As one approaches the
altar rail, one is left in the small
company of enlightened souls who
remain, bowing reverentially in
prayer.

The contemporary scene in
Paul studies offers a peculiar reversal of that biblical tableau. Those
Christians today who haven't given
up on Paul as the arrogant homo-

Figure 1: *Paul on Mars Hill.*
Stained glass. Tiffany Studios, 1903.
Photo: Cathy Carpenter, 2007.

phobe, the patriarchal male chauvinist, the authoritarian apostate Jew, the apostle of the status quo—even those who style themselves Paul's loyal sympathizers—often seem hard-pressed to make the case that the apostle's apocalyptic theology has anything meaningful to say to our time until it has been thoroughly demythologized. It has proven much easier for theologically oriented Paul scholars to focus on the inclusion of "Gentiles" and the legitimization of the "Gentile mission" as the core of Paul's gospel and thus to read him as the champion of those good liberal ideals of universalism, inclusiveness, and multicultural tolerance (as opposed to narrow ethnocentrism and tribalism).[1] Much of contemporary discussion around the "New Perspective" turns on the question whether we can proclaim Paul's gospel of inclusion without indulging in that ancient Christian habit of attributing its opposite, "exclusivism" or "ethnocentrism," to Paul's own people, the Jews of the Roman world. The best critical voices in the New Testament guild, prominent among them the late Lloyd Gaston, have called on us to renounce that habit.[2] It nevertheless remains sorely tempting for "multicultural" and "postcolonial" readings to enthuse about Paul's distance from the narrowly tribal thinking of his Jewish contemporaries. That temptation indicates that we have not yet thought seriously enough about the political and ideological context of Paul's thought and praxis.[3]

But now a new crowd has resolutely taken their stand beside Paul. They are precisely those philosophers (or self-styled "antiphilosophers")—distant descendants of the Areopagus crowd?—who

1. The late Krister Stendahl set the agenda for decades of Paul scholarship when he argued that the purpose of Romans was to argue for the legitimacy of the Gentile mission; see his *Paul among Jews and Gentiles*, 23–40; and *Final Account*, ix.

2. Gaston, *Paul and the Torah*. Gaston modeled for the guild of Pauline scholarship the restless intellectual curiosity and moral gravitas that refuses to be placated by conventional wisdom, not least in his insistence on the principle that "it makes a difference" whether Paul's audience was "Gentiles or Jews." I therefore find all the more ironic his presumption, without argument, that "Paul's major theological concern" was "the justification of the legitimacy of the Gentile mission" (6).

3. The voluminous literature on the "New Perspective" seems to increase daily, as documented by the invaluable Web site The Paul Page (www.thepaulpage.com). The fountainhead of the New Perspective is the essay by James D. G. Dunn, "New Perspective on Paul"; see also Dunn's magisterial *Theology of Paul the Apostle*. Critiques include Hodge and Buell, "Politics of Interpretation"; Hodge, "Apostle to the Gentiles"; Eisenbaum, "Paul, Polemics, and the Problem of Essentialism"; Liew, "Margins and (Cutting-) Edges." I offer my own alternative to the New Perspective in *The Arrogance of Nations*.

have no interest at all in what Alain Badiou calls the "fable" of the resurrection of the dead.[4] To some theologians this new crowd of enthusiasts, including Badiou, Jacob Taubes, Giorgio Agamben, and Slavoj Žižek, appear as impertinent interlopers, poaching on the rightful territory of theology and exegesis as practiced within the Christian church.[5] On these terms, the philosophers are criticized for doing theology poorly. For Paul J. Griffiths, for example, they are objects of "Christian pity and concern" because, despite their erudition, they stubbornly and irrationally resist the only true answer to their questions, which is to be found in "the peace given by explicit knowledge of the God of Abraham," and communion with the church catholic. It is "the Church here below," Griffiths declares, that most fully embodies the community free of political and economic domination that philosophers like Žižek seek.[6] Similarly, theologian Daniel M. Bell protests that Badiou fails to grasp a central truth at the heart of Christianity: that the salvation he seeks is possible only through "ontological union" with Israel's messiah, which makes possible "humanity's being taken up into the divine life of the Trinity." According to Bell, it is not philosophical analysis but the church's works of mercy that offer the fullest resistance to capitalism's depradations.[7]

At just this point an interested onlooker might well wonder whether these theologians are looking at the same church "here below," a church that is—at least in the United States—so integrated into capitalist society that Žižek is hardly alone in finding it quite irrelevant to the radical project. In a post-Soviet world, it may be tempting to compare the *achievements* of what were once actually existing Marxist

4. Badiou, *Saint* Paul, 4–5. Badiou, styling himself an "anti-philosopher," takes his own place rhetorically alongside Paul at the Areopagus, over against contemporary philosophical projects (ibid., 58). Other radical thinkers showing recent interest in Paul include Taubes, *Political Theology* (German original 1993, compiled from lectures given in 1987); Agamben, *Time that Remains*; Žižek, *Fragile Absolute*; and Jennings, *Reading Derrida/Thinking Paul*.

5. Gignac employs the metaphor playfully in "Taubes, Badiou, Agamben," 156. Jennings describes how the reading of Romans in particular "has largely been restricted to a confessional/ecclesiastical ghetto of doctrinal interest" and pleads for engagement with philosophical readings (*Reading Derrida/Thinking Paul*, 1). Robbins ("Politics of Paul") also discusses the dynamics of a certain territoriality within New Testament and theological "guilds" when confronted by keenly interested outsiders.

6. Griffiths, "Christ and Critical Theory," 46, 50, 54–55.

7. Bell, "Badiou's Faith," 108.

states with Christian *theory*; on the other hand, comparing Marxist *theory* with the *achievements* of actually existing ecclesiastical institutions offers considerably less room for Christian self-congratulation.[8] Ward Blanton makes the point from the perspective of Christian theology when he writes, with genuine respect, of the "unexpected hodge podge of neo-Paulinists" who, quite outside of the boundaries of any religious community, have been

> able to do what mainline Protestantism in the U.S. has not been able to do, namely, to contest in a committed, clear, and thoughtfully aggressive way the hegemony of an American Christendom that has become little more than a crutch for the sometimes faltering conscience of U.S. imperialism abroad. . . . Christianity risks today being the false conscience of an imperial system of staggering proportions.[9]

I take that assessment to be accurate precisely as a *theological* summation of what Blanton calls the "difficult Pauline *krisis*" confronting churches in the United States today. Caught up in currents of self-delusion, churches may believe they are doing their own thing faithfully and independently of the powers that be. But, Blanton protests, it is precisely the Pauline "demand for actuality" that indicts the ineffective hand-wringing of a complacent church: "it is precisely that moment when Christendom laments the unfortunate war, the unfortunate policy, the unfortunate dead—known and unknown—that one must be haunted by this shocking Paulinist motif: to say, to feel, even to speak the liberating word is *not* the same thing as doing it."[10]

Blanton insists that it is precisely the "atheistic fighting neo-Paulinists" who are "doing it"—that is, opening up a space where "genuine lines of contestation" with imperialistic powers may be drawn.[11] The greater offense that these radical philosophers present to mainstream liberal theology is that they are not just "unbelievers," adamantly uninterested in the abstractions of Christian doctrine. They are resolute

---

8. Years ago, an economist colleague at the College of St. Catherine made the point with regard to Haiti: "If the saturation of Christian missionaries per square mile were going to make any difference to actual living conditions under capitalism, anywhere in the world, we should see it first in Haiti."

9. Blanton, "Disturbing Politics," 5.

10. Ibid., 5.

11. Ibid.

leftists, implacable advocates of what Badiou calls "the Communist hypothesis," opposed to the capitalist world order in which so many Christians in the West are relatively comfortable, if not entirely content. And the radicals now claim that Paul is one of *them*, a "militant figure," an "activist" committed to "large-scale struggle," busy organizing little enclaves of those who will serve as "vectors of a new humanity."[12] In his name, they call us not to an intensified religiosity but to a political militancy with which U.S. churches are in general acutely uncomfortable. Suddenly, theological liberals who thought they were Paul's last, truest friends are put in the unfamiliar position of being offended by a scandalous Pauline gospel!

PAUL "OUR CONTEMPORARY"

Why are these less-than-religious thinkers interested in Paul, of all people?

The "Present Evil Age"

It is important to recognize the context in which the appeal to the figure of Paul is made: namely, the particular crisis that recent decades have presented *for adherents of dialectical materialism*. However convincing Marx's analysis of capitalism, history has not turned out the way his theories suggested. Socialist revolutions have taken place in the wrong places, generated by the wrong classes, and ushering in centralized states that have shown not the least tendency toward "withering away." History has presented committed Marxists with a conundrum as powerful as any cognitive dissonance faced by the first believers in the risen Christ's imminent return. In this "time of radical reaction,"[13] characterized by disorientation on the Left and the collapse of any sense of alternative to the existing capitalist order, the "communist hypothesis"—that "the logic of class . . . is not inevitable"—seems chimerical, vanquished by the cold hard facts of history. Badiou is by no means the only Marxist to point out the consequences:

---

12. Badiou, *Saint Paul*, 2, 20, 21.
13. Peter Hallward uses the phrase to situate Badiou's work in *Badiou*, xxxi.

What is at stake in these circumstances is the eventual opening of a new sequence of the communist hypothesis. But it is clear that this will not be—cannot be—the continuation of the second one. Marxism, the workers' movement, mass democracy, Leninism, the party of the proletariat, the socialist state—all the inventions of the 20th century—are not really useful to us anymore. At the theoretical level they certainly deserve further study and consideration; but at the level of practical politics they have become unworkable.[14]

The proposed explanations (from a Marxist point of view) are as familiar as the question itself. The proletariat failed to mobilize because of the success of "ideological state apparatus" (Louis Althusser), or more subtly, the cultural hegemony of the ruling class (Antonio Gramsci); and capitalist culture itself has proven almost infinitely adaptable to new challenges, chameleon-like (Fredric Jameson).[15] Badiou observes that in the new order in the West, "the left no longer frightens anyone"; rather the slogan of the day is "*Vivent les riches,* and to hell with the poor."[16] But the promises of capitalism are empty: the collapse of the Berlin wall has not ushered in "a single world of freedom and democracy"; rather, "the world's wall has simply shifted: instead of separating East and West it now divides the rich capitalist North from the poor and devastated South. New walls are being constructed all over the world . . . the 'unified world' of globalization is a sham."[17]

The "empty universality" of capital means that the enemy of a true and vital human particularity is not a single homogeneous culture, as the liberal vision of multicultural diversity would have it. Instead, the wide range of human particularities are themselves rendered commodities to be trafficked in one niche market after another. The commodification or "communitarization of the public sphere" means that in place of "the law's transcendent neutrality"[18] or any unifying vision of a common good shared by all—a true *political* universal—the capitalist

---

14. Badiou, "Communist Hypothesis," 37.

15. See Terry Eagleton's lucid discussion in *Ideology*; and Jameson, *Postmodernism*.

16. Badiou, *Saint Paul*, 7; on our current situation see 6–13. See also Badiou, "Communist Hypothesis," 29.

17. Badiou, "Communist Hypothesis," 38.

18. Badiou, *Saint Paul*, 9.

ideological order offers only a cockpit wherein the voices of various marginalized groups may compete against one another for momentary attention. Capitalism's universalism is hollow because it enfranchises only those who submit themselves to the inexorable logic of the market. Law becomes a device for distinguishing those to whom material resources may be allocated, for a price, from those who must be excluded.[19] Human well-being is not the measure of economic health; rather it is the free flow of *capital,* which requires increasing restriction on the movements of human beings.

Against this false universality, Badiou seeks a true universality, one that can be *collectively* affirmed as a universal truth, such as the declaration, "There is only one world." But such an affirmation flies in the face of the evidence around us. It "is not an objective conclusion. It is performative: we are deciding that this is how it is for us." For me to decide "that all belong to the same world as myself" requires, is nothing else than, an absolute *political commitment.*[20]

Giorgio Agamben similarly exposes the fraud of the capitalist claim to universalism. In *Homo Sacer* he argues (taking up Michel Foucault's discussion of biopolitics, but revising it) that the sign of sovereign power is always "the production of a biopolitical body," by which he means a body for which the very conditions of life have become the object of political demarcation and boundary making. While Aristotle declared that the human is a "political animal," Agamben argues that sovereign power consists in the power to decide not only what is the proper sphere of political activity, but also what is excluded from politics and law. In the modern state, the decision to *include* as a political object what had previously been excluded as "natural"—to render the very condition of life a matter of political contest—is "the original activity of sovereign power." Inverting Aristotle, for whom the proper distinctiveness of the human animal was its *logos,* its power to communicate, Agamben declares that modern sovereign power is manifest in the production of life forms incapable of communication. The Nazi death camps are for Agamben the inevitable end of this "biopolitics," representing the sheer

19. Badiou has the French situation particularly in mind, where the popular slogan "France for the French" requires "the persecution of those people arbitrarily designated as the non-French" (*Saint Paul,* 8). Here I find invaluable the analysis provided in Mike Davis's magisterial study *Planet of Slums.*

20. Badiou, "Communist Hypothesis," 38–39.

and arbitrary determination of which objects shall be included and which excluded from the conditions for life. They are "the space where the exception begins to become the rule," where the production of non-living beings—the walking dead, the mute "*Musselmänner*"—is the inevitable outcome.[21]

Figure 2: A prisoner under U.S. military custody at Abu Ghraib, Iraq.

In our own day, the language of "extraordinary rendition," in which a sovereign state reserves the sovereign authority to declare a permanent state of exception to its own laws, in this case regarding torture, shows the relevance of Agamben's analysis.[22] And it begs an Agambenesque question: what is the *ordinary* rendition of human beings, if not the creation of mute objects of capital's sovereign power? If, for Agamben, the work of "biopower" in the Nazi death camps was to create the lifeless walking form of the *Musselman*,[23] we may ask whether the industrial-scale transformation of Muslims into "*Musselmänner*" in prisons like Abu Ghraib is the signal characteristic of sovereign power in our own day. And theologically, we must ask what relation can exist between such production of *Musselmänner* and the embodiment of Christ in our world.[24]

---

21. Agamben, *Homo Sacer.*

22. As used in the United States, "extraordinary rendition" refers to the state's exercise of sovereign authority to remove human beings to other nations where they are subjected to torture that remains illegal in the rendering state (the U.S.)—though the latter has proven to be a quite malleable category. Agamben helps us to understand the significance of a previously secret 2003 executive finding by the U.S. president that while no legal constraint barred the executive branch from authorizing torture, he "declined" to provide such authorization "at this time." See Hersh, *Chain of Command*, 5.

23. See Agamben, *Homo Sacer*, ch. 7.

24. Though it is beyond the scope of this essay, important resources for such discernment are Cavanaugh, *Torture and Eucharist*; and Ellacuría, "Crucified People."

The Body of Christ

Figure 3: Matthias Grünewald,
The Mocking of Christ, 1503.

When Badiou declares that Paul is "our contemporary," it is in part because he finds a precise parallel between Paul's situation and ours. But it is also because he finds in Paul the ideological gesture, the performance, of a "universal truth" that militates against the ideological constraints of Paul's situation and our own.

Both Paul's situation and ours are characterized, Badiou declares, by "the destruction of all politics," evident then in the legal usurpation by the principate of the political structures of the Republic, and in our own day by a parliamentary-democratic system that carefully insulates the economic order from popular will, that is, from politics.[25] (He is speaking of Europe; the constitutional crisis in the United States is arguably more severe.) Though Badiou does not expand on the comparison, a number of valuable recent studies of the economic, military, and ideological aspects of Roman Empire confirm its aptness.[26] We may go further, however, in light of Agamben's insistence that biopower is the characteristic of sovereignty not only in the modern age but in the age of the Roman Empire as well. But if the homology between

25. Badiou, *Saint Paul*, 7; idem, "Communist Hypothesis," 31–32.

26. See Garnsey and Whittaker, *Imperialism in the Ancient World*; De Ste. Croix, *Class Struggle in the Ancient Greek World*, esp. chs. 6–7; Garnsey and Saller, *Roman Empire*; Price, *Rituals and Power*; Zanker, *Power of Images*; and Galinsky, *Augustan Culture*. Richard Horsley brought these insights together with applications by New Testament scholars to Paul and his letters in *Paul and Empire*. I have relied on these and other studies in my own effort to situate Paul's thought and practice in the context of Roman imperialism (see *Liberating Paul* and *Arrogance of Nations*).

an anti-politics (Badiou), or the sovereign exercise of biopower against bare life (Agamben), in Paul's day and our own is important for our appropriation of Paul today, it is even more important for us to recognize that the fundamental ideological requirements of Roman imperialism are directly opposed in Paul's representation of the body of the crucified and risen Christ in the world.

In Marxist terms, we may identify the "cultural dominant" of the Roman Empire in terms of a transition from an agrarian, tributary mode of production to a reliance on slave labor.[27] If "religion" and the prerogatives of (divine and human) monarchy were the indispensable ideological apparatus of the tributary state (what Marx called the "Asiatic" mode of production), a society expanding to include more and more territory (and thus more and more agrarian production) in an economy increasingly reliant on slave labor faced a more complex ideological challenge. A slavery society depends upon the careful maintenance of a symbolic system of difference: citizens must be distinguished from noncitizens, free persons from slaves—and conquerors from conquered. In the Roman era, the distinction was represented visually through iconography and rehearsed "ritually" through sites as distinct as the civic arena and extra-urban sites of crucifixion. A specific symbolic code distinguished those who could not be tortured or crucified from those who could. But in our own day as well, the ritualized distinction between powerful captor and powerless captive, the production of mute biopolitical bodies as a gesture of sovereign power, is just as important as in a slave-based economy. This is true whether or not the distinction is publicly displayed—but of course it *is*, as in the photos from Abu Ghraib, where the abject misery, humiliation, and injury of the prisoners stands in the sharpest possible relief to the consistently relaxed postures and smiling, smug comportment of the captors.

---

27. See Roland Boer's excellent discussion of "the question of mode of production" in *Marxist Criticism of the Bible*, 229–46. Norman Gottwald applies the Marxist understanding of modes of production to ancient Israel's history in *The Hebrew Bible*. Fredric Jameson, in *Political Unconscious*, 89–102, points out that Marx's presentation of a "sequence" of modes of production must be adapted to recognize the possible simultaneity of incompatible modes of production, some ascendant, some vestigial, and others only anticipated. Boer's and Jameson's discussions inform my own proposals regarding the ideological constraints in Paul's day (see Elliott, *Arrogance of Nations*, 29–30, 156–59).

My point is not to draw a sentimental equivalence between the crucified Christ and contemporary prisoners at Abu Ghraib, although theologically the comparison bears sustained reflection. My point is to compare in both situations, ancient Rome and our own, the dynamics of sovereign power to generate "necessary" exclusions from its own laws, and the ideological apparatus that justified these exclusions.

In the Roman Empire, the careful distinction of bodies that could and could not be tortured went hand in hand with an elaborate ideological representation of the emperor as benevolent monarch, a supreme patron, father, and priest; that is, the symbolization dominant in an *agrarian* mode of production overlapped with and in part was used to routinize and legitimize the symbolization dominant in a *slave* mode of production.

This is the necessary ideological context in which alone we can fully understand Paul's proclamation of a crucified and risen Christ. Paul insists (and scholars agree this is his own contribution to whatever preexisting Christian traditions he inherited) that Christ took "the form of a slave" and "became obedient to the point of death—even death on a cross" (Phil 2:7–8).[28] That phrase has traditionally been taken to refer generically to Christ's appearance *as a human being*, but surely refers more pointedly to the manner of his death, the shameful subjection to a *slave's* death by crucifixion. Such a death publicly reinscribed on certain bodies the status of slave/conquered and thus reinforced the routinization of the symbolic cultural dominant. For Paul to proclaim that just such a body, inscribed in death as slave by the power (Agamben might stipulate, the *biopower*) of the Empire, had been raised from the dead by God, and that this divine act established the true filiation of a free people regardless of their ascribed status in the Roman symbolic economy—this was inherently and irreducibly subversive.[29] So, for that matter, was what we must assume was Paul's defiant practice of *performing* the "dying of Jesus" as crucified, whatever form that performance took,

---

28. See Dunn, *Theology of Paul*, 244–52.

29. The characterization of Paul's proclamation as "subversive" has recently found potent substantiation in the arguments of Lopez, *Apostle to the Conquered*; and Kahl, *Galatians Re-Imagined*. Both studies focus attention on the ideological character of Roman iconography, which displayed the power of Rome in part through the representation of subjected and defeated bodies.

for it repeatedly embodied a counter-representation of status.[30] As Paul puts it in 2 Cor 2:14–16 (NRSV):

> But thanks be to God, who in Christ always leads us in triumphal procession, and through us spreads in every place the fragrance that comes from knowing him. For we are the aroma of Christ to God among those who are being saved and among those who are perishing; to the one a fragrance from death to death, to the other a fragrance from life to life.[31]

These contours of Paul's proclamation, which indicate its direct and inescapably antagonistic engagement with aspects of Roman imperial ideology, are surely important to understanding what he means by affirming Christ's resurrection. They are ideological dimensions that Badiou unfortunately fails to address because of his general dismissal of the resurrection as "fable."[32] Just this dismissal brings down on Badiou the criticism of Christian theologians who consider that he has thrown out the Pauline baby with the bathwater (and betrayed his own inconsistency regarding the "truth-event").[33] This is an apt criticism, but not because Christian theologians possess some additional datum that Badiou refuses to acknowledge, as though resurrection were a discrete episode given to us in history. The proclamation of resurrection, the *concept* of resurrection, makes sense—it has meaning—only within a symbolic context, what many of us would call a *mythological* context, that points inexorably forward to a consummation of history that Paul, for one, considered absolutely *real*.[34] Badiou dismisses the reality of the resurrection-as-discrete-episode apparently without recognizing its

---

30. Paul's initial proclamation was an "exhibition" of Christ crucified (Gal 3:1 NRSV); his apostolic presence was a "carrying in the body the death of Jesus" (2 Cor 4:10); the Eucharistic assembly was a proclamation of "the Lord's death until he comes" (1 Cor 11:26).

31. The metaphor implies that Paul is a *conquered prisoner* of Christ. See Duff, "Metaphor, Motif, and Meaning"; and Elliott, "Apostle Paul's Self-Presentation."

32. A point Badiou repeats, for example when he emphasizes that "the event that [Paul] takes to identify the real *is not* real" (*Saint Paul*, 58).

33. So Griffiths rightly points to "a persistent lack of clarity in Badiou's understanding of truth," if "Paul's proclamation of Christ resurrected can be true even if Christ was not in fact resurrected . . . There is a conundrum here that Badiou does not resolve" ("Christ and Critical Theory," 52).

34. Here of course I am guided by the force of J. Christiaan Beker's argument in *Paul the Apostle*.

place in that larger apocalyptic understanding of the real. Of course, this observation hardly gives Christian theologians an upper hand, since they can no more point to the *evidentness* of history's consummation than can Badiou. Indeed, given the apocalyptic coordinates of Paul's affirmation of a risen Christ, any theological appropriation of Paul should accept as a theological-critical axiom—in the most *materialist* terms—Paul's own exclamation in 1 Corinthians: if Christ has not been raised, "if for this life only we have hoped in Christ," if, that is, the resurrection does *not* point inexorably to a *real* consummation of history, then "we are of all people most to be pitied" (1 Cor 15:19). If Badiou's Paul is the "master of the gesture,"[35] so at last, so far as the course of history to date would indicate, is the Christian's Paul.

What does that gesture mean? Read in apocalyptic terms, Paul's proclamation of Jesus's resurrection means, inevitably I think, that the biopower of the state is *not* sovereign, that its totalizing claims can be resisted (for, indeed, the proclamation is itself such resistance). The formation of a community whose collective subjectivity depends upon the failure of the state's totalizing claims over their allegiance is inherently subversive. For such a community to practice an economic mutualism that crossed, and thus annulled, the distinctions of *slave vs. free* or, implicitly, *conqueror vs. conquered*, would have constituted the performance of a genuine collective universalism such as Badiou describes.[36]

The Body of Christ and Jewish Bodies

Badiou goes a different way. Rather than exploring the inherent political significance of Jesus's death and resurrection in opposition to the very totalizing ideology that used crucifixion as an indispensable signification,[37] Badiou focuses—as so much of Protestant theological

35. Griffiths, "Christ and Critical Theory," 52.

36. On the significance of the practice of mutualism as a survival strategy among the poor, see Meggitt, *Paul, Poverty and Survival*; on the collection see Wan, "Collection for the Saints," 206–10. I use the qualifier "implicitly" above because we can speak only with some ambivalence of the distinction "conqueror vs. conquered" being overcome in the Pauline churches: in Corinth, for example, there is evidence of members of the Roman elite joining with much lower-status believers in the congregation, but the resulting tensions make Corinth the test case. Welborn addresses precisely this test case in *That There May Be Equality*.

37. Jennings, in "Paul and (Post-modern) Political Thought," criticizes Badiou on just this point for missing the unmistakable political aspects of crucifixion and there-

interpretation has focused—on the dichotomy of Jew/Gentile and the supposed exclusion inherent in Jewish law. What Paul sought, Badiou muses, was "to drag the Good News . . . out from the rigid enclosure within which its restriction to the Jewish community would confine it."[38] (He goes on to insist that Paul sought to free the gospel from the constraints of Roman law, too, but this rather theoretical assertion is not pursued, and remains incidental to his project.) More important for him is the assertion that "Paul emphasizes rupture rather than continuity *with Judaism*."[39] Rather paradoxically, Badiou seeks to distance himself from the anti-Semitic and supersessionist aspects of the Christian theological tradition, but for him, as for much of Christian theological scholarship, especially the liberal Protestant scholarship aligned with the "New Perspective" on Paul, Pauline universalism is fundamentally and inevitably opposed to Jewish "exclusivism." "Jewish discourse is a discourse of exception" over against "Greek discourse," which is the discourse of a natural (or naturalizing) totality.[40] These two discourses are bound up with each other, indeed they "are the two aspects of the same figure of mastery": "In the eyes of Paul the Jew, the weakness of Jewish discourse is that its logic of the exceptional sign is only valid *for* the Greek cosmic totality. The Jew is in exception to the Greek."[41] In the place of this relationship of totality and exception Paul affirms a universalism based in the event. The central problem of Paul's thought is, for Badiou, the question, "What is it in this resurrection, this 'out from the dead,' that has the power to suspend differences? Why, if a man is resurrected, does it follow that there is neither Greek nor Jew, neither male nor female, neither slave nor free man?" (referring to Gal 3:28).[42]

The direction in which I pointed above answers the last part of this question: it follows quite clearly within an apocalyptic logic that if a *crucified* man is resurrected, there is neither slave nor free person, since resurrection *means* a divine intervention that ruptures the very system of significations that oppose slave and free, man and woman. Badiou

---

fore of resurrection as well.

38. Badoiu, *Saint Paul*, 13.
39. Ibid., 35 (emphasis added).
40. Ibid., 41–42.
41. Ibid., 42.
42. Ibid., 73.

restricts himself to the first opposition, Greek/Jew, because he takes it to be homologous with the opposition in contemporary French politics between the false universalism of a totalizing nationalistic identity and the identity politics of minority groups;[43] also because he considers it central to Paul's thought.

Here Badiou follows what some of us regard as a flawed tradition of Protestant scholarship going back at least to F. C. Baur. He reads Paul in opposition to a "Jewish Christian faction" in the early church and declares it "*impossible to overestimate* the importance of the incident at Antioch" (Gal 2:11–14).[44] To the contrary, however, such "overestimation" happens all the time; indeed it has long been a mainstay of Protestant dogmatics. "Paul *never stops telling us*," Badiou writes, "that the Jews are looking for signs and 'demanding miracles,' that the Greeks are 'looking for wisdom' and asking questions, that the Christians declare Christ crucified."[45] To the contrary, however, Paul makes the statement *only once*, at 1 Cor 1:22–25; he first opposes Jews not to "Greeks" but to *ethnē*, those from among the nations ("Gentiles" in the NRSV); and in the context of that rhetorically freighted argument it is clear that it is the Greek/"ethnic" clamoring for wisdom, rather than a Jewish proclivity for signs (let alone a Jewish "exclusivism," which Paul does not name here), that is his target in the Corinthian assembly.

My point is simply that Badiou, like so much of Protestant scholarship, wrongly places a supposed opposition to Judaism, Jewish identity, and the "exceptionalism" of Jewish law as such at the center of Paul's thought. He consequently overemphasizes the significance of passages where Protestant scholarship is accustomed, rightly or wrongly, to read the traces of that opposition.[46] Against these well-worn habits, pioneering scholars like Lloyd Gaston have insisted that we must read Paul's letters, and what he says about the law in them, first in terms of their intended effect among *non-Jewish* audiences who are tempted to

---

43. Ibid., 12–13.

44. Ibid., 22–26 (emphasis added).

45. Ibid., 58 (emphasis added).

46. Characteristic is Günther Bornkamm's insistence that in all of his letters "Paul's opponent is not this or that section in a particular church, but the Jews and their understanding of salvation" (*Paul*, 11–12). It is no surprise that Badiou (*Saint Paul*, 3) selects Bornkamm's book as one of two books on Paul that he recommends to his readers, the other being *Saint Paul* by Stanislas Breton.

misinterpret or to misuse that law for their own *non-Jewish* purposes.[47] Jewish scholars have insisted that Christian interpreters of Paul renounce the morally unacceptable practice of trading on historically inaccurate stereotypes about Jewish boasting, works righteousness, exclusivism, and so on.[48] And attention to the political context of the Roman Empire and Roman imperial ideology has allowed us to see the oppositions of "Jew and Greek," "Greek and barbarian," *Ioudaioi* and *ethnē*, not as a single ethnic or religious binary but as positions within a more complex configuration of identities in Roman imperial culture.[49]

PAUL AND THE IDEOLOGICAL GESTURE

These criticisms are meant not to disqualify Badiou's deployment of Paul but to suggest ways in which that deployment might be set on different grounds, grounds both more historically defensible and more congenial to Badiou's own political purposes.

I have already suggested that Paul's proclamation of the resurrection of a *crucified* messiah was irreducibly political in its implications, reversing and neutralizing the significations on which the slave mode of production (and the Roman imperial order based upon it) relied. Badiou moves in this direction when he discusses, with reference to 1 Cor 1:18–29, the cross for Paul as the event that renders "the philosophical logos incapable of declaring it."

> The most radical statement in the text we are commenting on is in effect the following: "God has chosen the things that are not [*ta mē onta*] in order to bring to nought those that are [*ta onta*]." That the Christ-event causes nonbeings rather than beings to arise as attesting to God; that it consists in the abolition of what all previous discourses held as existing, or being, gives a measure of the ontological subversion to which Paul's antiphilosophy invites the declarant or militant.[50]

47. Gaston, *Paul and the Torah*.

48. Fundamental here are Fredriksen, *From Jesus to Christ*; Boyarin, *Radical Jew*; and Nanos, *Mystery of Romans*.

49. Here the decisive works are Lopez, *Apostle to the Conquered*; and Kahl, *Galatians Re-Imagined*. See also my *Arrogance of Nations*, ch. 1.

50. Badiou, *Saint Paul*, 46–47.

Badiou is concerned here to oppose Paul to efforts to domesticate or accommodate the event into a positive *philosophical* logos. But the same point can be made over against a *political* logos, that is, against a totalizing ideology such as that of the Roman Empire (or of contemporary capitalism, or for that matter of contemporary Christianity's accommodation to the capitalist order). Badiou's philosophical-political universal truth—that "there is only one world"—can indeed be drawn from Paul, and *has* been drawn from this specific Pauline text, though without reference to Badiou. Expounding upon the thought of martyred Jesuit theologian Ignacio Ellacuría, Jon Sobrino has distilled Paul's claim regarding God's creation of a new community out of "things that are not"—a political *creatio ex nihilo*—into a single theological axiom: *ex pauperes nulla salus,* "no salvation outside [or apart from] the poor." Sobrino's seminal work makes clear that the universal truth at the heart of the Pauline gospel is no philosophical abstraction but is realized in an alternative politics, the civilization of human solidarity that is the civilization of poverty.[51]

The civilization of poverty can of course be perceived and analyzed, from structuralist or functionalist perspectives, as one segment—even a necessary or inevitable segment—of society ordered according to the regime of capitalism. To declare, as Sobrino does, that the civilization of poverty is a sign of the world's future, a *utopian* sign, will seem, from within the thought-world of capitalist ideology, nonsensical, fantastic, *merely* utopian. It will seem as much an empty, formal "gesture" as Badiou's appeal to a resurrection without a risen body.

But Badiou and Sobrino alike have a precedent in these seemingly utopian gestures: Paul himself. A Marxist understanding of the ways ideological forces constrain cultural expression—and the ways a countervailing force opposes and resists those ideological forces—allows us to see the ideological gesture in Paul's thought and praxis.

Quoting Karl Marx, Fredric Jameson describes the ultimate horizon of interpretation as "the collective struggle [in history] to wrest a realm of Freedom from a realm of Necessity." The consequence is that it is "something worse than an error" to distinguish "political" texts from non-political—for example, "religious" ones. Such a categorical distinction is symptomatic of the pervasive logic of capitalism, which relegates to the private sphere what would otherwise be collective visions and

---

51. Sobrino, *No Salvation outside the Poor.*

imaginings of an alternative future ("utopia") as it usurps for itself the public arena of political action. Because (according to Jameson's Marxist cultural theory) the ideological forces arising in any social order act to constrain collective imagination, including what may be thought or imagined in the production of texts (like Paul's letters), the interpreter's task is to identify the ways in which a text has been constrained by ideology. But because the ultimate horizon of interpretation is not the static operation of ideological necessity but the *struggle* between the dominant ideological forces and the human strivings and imaginings that those forces operate to limit and channel, the interpreter's task is also to trace and tease out the impulses at work in the text that seek to work against ideological closure, impulses that "remain unrealized in the surface of the text." Those impulses, Jameson argues, arise from what may be described as a collective "political unconscious."[52]

That Paul's thought is constrained by the ideological forces prevailing in the early Roman Empire is evident in his assertion of a coming "lord" (*kyrios*) who "rises to rule the nations" (Rom 15:12). Of course, that *kyrios* is the messiah, consequently a lord other than Caesar—a fact that has led some interpreters to conclude that Paul's gospel is at least implicitly opposed to the claims of Roman imperial propaganda.[53] But the alternative that Paul imagines to Rome's evil rule—to a "bad kyriarchy," we might say, doomed to destruction (1 Cor 2:8; 15:24–25)—is not a completely different social configuration, but a "good kyriarchy," the rule of a *benevolent* lord. That Roman kyriarchy might come to an end without the ascendancy of a new and better kyriarchy, and that the world might be configured in a way completely free of the rule of a monarch—these notions were for Paul, and, we may presume, for countless others of his time, apparently unthinkable.[54]

But there is better evidence for ideological constraint on Paul's thought. He declares in Romans that the world has been "subjected to futility" and "bondage to decay," meaning that *God* has subjected it (Rom 8:20–21). Yet God's Spirit also militates *against* that subjection through the "groaning," as of a woman in labor, of a creation yearning for liberation, and agitates among those who wait for "the glorious liberation of the children of God" and "the redemption of our bodies"

---

52. Jameson, "On Interpretation."

53. For example N. T. Wright, "Paul's Gospel and Caesar's Empire."

54. See on this point my *Arrogance of Nations*, 50–57.

(8:22–23). Thus, for Paul God is simultaneously the source of the world's coming liberation, and the one who has imposed the present subjection (8:20). The tension between these statements—a tension Paul does not mitigate, indeed a tension of which he actually seems unaware—is, following Jameson, an expression of the deeper, unconscious tension generated by the "restless" energy of a collective unconscious militating against the ideological constraints of the environment (Roman imperial ideology). Paul's apocalyptic assertion that "the appointed time has grown short" (*ho kairos synestalmenos estin*, 1 Cor 7:29) may be typical of an apocalyptic way of thinking (cf. Mark 13:20, "if the Lord had not cut short those days . . ."); but it is the nature of the assertion *as ideological gesture* that bears attention.

The apocalyptic assertion is an attempt to achieve a standing place over against the ideological force of Roman realized eschatology, which declares constantly that history has reached its decisive climax in the supremacy of Rome and the triumph of "the Roman people." Against this ubiquitous claim Paul can only announce a "mystery" (Rom 11:25): that God has—inscrutably, invisibly—intervened in history, interrupted its progress. God has subjected the world to a "futility" that renders any attempt to read the future from present circumstances not only futile, but counter to the *real* future that God alone will bring about. Present circumstances (meaning the *apparent* triumph of Rome and the *apparent* relegation of Israel to the vanquished peoples of the earth) can only deceive the senses; only the one who perceives according to reason (*logos, logismos*)—meaning, reason *shaped by divine event*—can perceive that real future. The argument in Romans 9–11—I would argue, the argument of the whole letter—is an example of what the "New Rhetoricians" call an argument by *dissociation of concepts,* here the dissociation of what *appears* true, given present circumstances, from what is *real.*[55]

That rhetorical trope-as-ideological-gesture was a commonplace among Paul's Jewish contemporaries, to judge from Philo of Alexandria and the author of 4 Maccabees.[56] But it is also a rough ancient analogue

55. See Perelman and Olbrechts-Tyteca, *New Rhetoric,* 411–59; and Elliott, *Arrogance of Nations,* 83–85; 50–57.

56. In 4 Maccabees the Greek tyrant appeals to the defiant Jews to listen to reason (*logos*). They reply that they *are* listening to reason; the tyrant is being *alogos.* Their minds are informed by the law, that is, the Torah. Philo similarly challenges his reader

for the truth procedure Badiou describes, the truth procedure for which Badiou appeals in a contemporary world in which capitalist ideology claims to have reached "the end of history."[57] That claim causes a profound "disorientation" in the present to men and women "imprisoned within the temporality assigned us by the dominant order"; the words are Badiou's, but they might be Paul's. "What takes courage is to operate in terms of a different *durée* to that imposed by the law of the world," says Badiou. "You know what time it is . . . The night is far gone, the day is near," says Paul.[58]

A Christian posture that claims to hold the truth of resurrection as a discrete possession fails to recognize the character of Paul's proclamation as ideological assertion, as one moment in a *struggle* against the ideological hegemony of the imperial order. For Paul, that struggle was couched in the language available to him, that of Jewish apocalypticism. In our own time, many of us are unused to thinking according to the cosmological and kyriarchal fabric of apocalypticism. Those who often claim to have recovered the *terms* of Paul's response in a literal way have often advocated a theistic determinism that legitimates political quietism and acquiescence—postures we can scarce afford, given "the impending crisis" (*tēn enestēsan anankēn*, 1 Cor 7:26). We need instead to recover the character of Paul's proclamation (and of the practices of which it was a part, including the economic mutualism of his assemblies) precisely as ideological gestures of defiance—or in theological terms, as signs of a heavenly citizenship (Phil 3:20). Toward that end, Alain Badiou may be an indispensable guide.

---

to perceive not with the bodily senses, that "discern [only] what is manifest and close at hand," but to perceive with *logismos* which will reveal the divine providence in human history (*Embassy* 1–3). See my *Arrogance of Nations*, 146–50.

57. So Fukuyama, *End of History*.

58. Badiou, "Communist Hypothesis," 41; Rom 13:11–12.

CHAPTER 7

Subjects between Death and Resurrection:
Badiou, Žižek, and St. Paul

by Geoffrey Holsclaw

Alain Badiou and Slavoj Žižek have emerged among a vanguard of
European philosophers reengaging religion, specifically Christianity, in
the hopes of rescuing politics from the malaise of liberalism's capture
by parliamentary capitalism. To do this both Badiou and Žižek have
attempted to rearticulate a theory of the subject beyond postmodern
dismissals that the subject has little if any role to play in contemporary
philosophy or politics. For strategic and philosophical reasons, this
rearticulation has led both Badiou and Žižek to mine the texts of Saint
Paul with the hope of illuminating a revolutionary subjectivity beyond
those produced by global capitalism and its inverse communitarian
impulse. This subjectivity takes on a distinct dimension for Badiou and
Žižek in relation to their own fidelity to Jacques Lacan. Badiou seeks
to move beyond Lacan's theory of the subject and articulates a Pauline
theology in line with this project, while Žižek follows Lacan and hears
in Paul a consonant echo. In relation to Paul, this places a clear emphasis on resurrection for Badiou, and an emphasis on death for Žižek,
each coordinated to their respective political projects.

   This essay begins with Badiou and then moves to Žižek's reading of
Paul, ending with a counter reading. This will be accomplished through
a brief explication of their political thought and their appropriation of
Paul, centered on their reading of the law in Romans 7. Following this,
instead of offering a counter reading of Romans 7, I will shift to Romans
6 to show that Paul's concerns lie not so much with how one relates to

the law, but in and through whom one is related to the law. It will be shown that baptismal incorporation into Christ is, for Paul, the beginning of the true Exodus beyond (if we may speak anachronistically) global affirmations of capital and local communitarian identities—the founding of an alternative political subjectivity.

BADIOU ON RESURRECTION

For Badiou, every militant subject is induced by a truth-event, the illicit occurrence that reconfigures everything which preceded it. This subject is beyond the law, subject only to the non-literal law of love. As Badiou reads Paul, the apostle articulates just this very subject as beyond the Jewish law of identity and the Greek law of cosmic order.

The Subject of Truth

Badiou's political thought is strictly correlated to his ontology. This ontology consists of two contrasting groups of terms: being/knowledge/law and event/truth/subject. Badiou sutures his philosophy to contemporary set theory, proclaiming that "mathematics is ontology—the science of being qua being."[1] His basic term, culled from set theory, is the "multiple," such that every multiple is a collection of other multiples, or "every multiple is a multiple of a multiple."[2] Every grouping of multiples is given the philosophical term "situation." A situation is any—literally any—"presented multiplicity," from the set of cardinal numbers, to a biological organism, to the conditions of racism preceding the civil rights movement. The presentation of a multiple depends on an operation of gathering that presents each multiple as *this* multiple,[3] made up of certain "circumstances, language, and objects."[4] Each situation has its own particular being variously expounded according to the logic of multiplicities, i.e., set theory.

Within every situation there is a coordination between being and knowledge, for "in every situation, there is an encyclopedia of knowl-

1. Badiou, *Being and Event*, 4.
2. Ibid., 29.
3. Ibid., 24.
4. Badiou, "Truth: Forcing and the Unnameable," 121.

edge of the situation, linked to a language of the situation."[5] In this framework, only what is made explicit by a well-formed language is granted existence, and "whatever is not distinguished by a well-made language is not."[6] In this light, knowledge, as Badiou understands it, is linked to and authorizes the being of a given situation. Knowledge is the guaranteed being of a situation, and is therefore the law of the situation.

Now the deployment of knowledge/law within a situation seeks to minimize the excesses between presentation and *re*presentation. And while knowledge allows for no holes,[7] there are always elements of the situation that escape the law's grasp (for example, the presentation of molecules within the situation of a biological system, or an illegal immigrant eluding the count of the Census Bureau). These elements, which are presented but not *re*presented, are *singular* elements, potential sites for an event. An event is that by which something new comes into existence within a situation. Or rather, an event is the revelation of the existence of something already presented in the situation yet not represented by it. Through an event a new being "comes-forth within presentative proximity . . . subtracted from representation."[8] This coming-forth of a new being within the situation creates a truth procedure that transforms the original situation and its corresponding knowledge. As Badiou says, "a truth is always that which makes a hole in a knowledge," a hole that knowledge sought to cover over.[9] The event gives rise to a truth (but not *the* truth) that "groups together all the terms of the situation which are positively connected to the event."[10] This truth is not just some truth added to the general knowledge of the situation; it is the truth of the entire situation and of which knowledge does not know.[11] This is what Badiou calls a "truth-event."

---

5. Badiou, "Politics and Philosophy," 113–33, esp. 130. See also idem, "Eight Theses on the Universal," 146, where he says, "I call 'encyclopedia' the general system of predicative *knowledge* internal to a situation: i.e. what everyone knows about politics, sexual difference, culture, arts, technology, etc." (emphasis original).

6. Badiou, *Being and Event*, 283.

7. Ibid., 331.

8. Ibid., 177.

9. Ibid., 327.

10. Ibid. 335.

11. Ibid., 417.

A truth-event is known, and made known, through a faithful subject, or rather, through one subjected to an event. A truth always works its way through particular subjects, faithful to a singular event, investigating its results and connections. A subject does not produce truth; rather, a truth produces a subject, because the subject "in no way pre-exists the process . . . the process of truth *induces* a subject."[12] A subject is "*taken up* in the fidelity to the event, and *suspended* from truth."[13] This subject is the vanishing mediator between being and event, plumbing the depths of presentation within the situation, suspended by a truth, against the knowledge and law of representation of the situation. Therefore, while the knowledge of the being of a situation gives rise to a law of the situation, the truth of an event induces a subject.

The Resurrection of St. Paul

Now in Paul, being suspended by a truth against all laws reveals itself in Badiou's emphasis on Paul's declaration of the event of the resurrection of Christ. For Badiou, the declaration of this event of resurrection is subtracted from the Greek law of cosmic order and the Jewish law of divine exception, for "Paul's project is to show that a universal logic of salvation cannot be reconciled with any law, be it one that ties thought to the cosmos, or one that fixes the effect of an exceptional election."[14] The declaration of the Christ-event as resurrection is subtracted both from Greek knowledge and wisdom, because Paul is not trying to prove anything, and subtracted from the exception of Jewish signs and wonders, because Paul is not trying to accomplish anything.[15] Paul's militant declaration of the Christ-event is incapable of being inscribed within a Greek philosophical logos or a Jewish divine law. This will of course bring Badiou to a discussion of Paul's understanding of the law.

But before examining Badiou's understanding of law in Romans 7, we must consider more closely the themes of death and resurrection in Badiou. In the oppositions noted above between being and event, and knowledge and truth, there exists a non-dialectical relation because

12. Badiou, *Ethics*, 43 (emphasis original).
13. Badiou, *Being and Event*, 406 (emphasis original).
14. Badiou, *Saint Paul*, 42.
15. Ibid., 49.

the truth-event always irrupts unexpectedly, illicitly from within the realms of being's knowledge. The knowledge of the situation can never predict nor even acknowledge the event and its truth. For this reason, Badiou is against a Hegelian-Nietzschean capture of the resurrection as merely the sublimation of death, as the negation of negation (the object of Hegel's praise and Nietzsche's scorn). In this way Badiou argues for a de-dialecticized Christ-event, which separates out the cross and death as merely the site for the event, and resurrection as the event itself. Here Badiou references Rom 6:4–9 as indicating how our baptismal burial in Christ unites us with the death of Christ. Here is the passage in full, followed by Badiou's comment:

> "We were buried therefore with him by baptism into death, in order that, just as Christ was raised from the dead by the glory of the Father, we too might walk in newness of life. For if we have been united with him in a death like his, we shall certainly be united with him in a resurrection like his. We know that our old self was crucified with him in order that the body of sin might be brought to nothing, so that we would no longer be enslaved to sin. For one who has died has been set free from sin. Now if we have died with Christ, we believe that we will also live with him. We know that Christ, being raised from the dead, will never die again."
>
> This text is explicit: *death as such counts for nothing in the operation of salvation*. It functions as a condition of immanence.[16]

But this condition of immanence is not salvation itself. In Badiou's reading, Christ's death names the renunciation of transcendence which creates the site of reconciliation between God and man. This reconciliation through immanentization is not salvation, but merely the construction of the site of the event of salvation. Nevertheless, there is no dialectic between site and event because "the event's sudden emergence never follows from the existence of an evental site," for this would subject the event to a pre-established law. But this is impossible because the event always calls new beings into existence, resurrecting new subjects to life, beyond the purview of the existing law. For this reason the law (in this case, the Jewish law) is on the side of being, on the side of death, for

16. Ibid., 69–70 (emphasis added).

"the law is always predicative, particular, and partial," articulating the knowledge of the situation.[17]

In his explication of the law, Badiou draws heavily on Lacan's psychoanalytic theory, by equating the law with sin, such that sin names the autonomy of desire that is fixed by the law.[18] The autonomy of desire, unleashed by the law, is nothing other than the problem of the unconscious, which creates a confusion between death and life, placing the subject on the side of death, and desire/sin on the side of life.[19] The one within the law lives such that thinking is separated from doing; thought is separated from action. This type of life is really death.

In Badiou's reading of Paul, this "powerlessness of thought" is overcome when the subject is suspended by the truth-event, uniting thought and action according to a faithful declaration of the event, overcoming the gap announced by psychoanalysis. Only according to the event of resurrection does the subject return to the place of life. The unity of thought and action, overcoming the gap within the subject, is the product of the event. The event, inducing a subject and leading toward the production of a truth, is always *against the law*, the law as autonomy of desire separating thought from action (psychoanalytic), the law as divine letter (Jewish), and the law of cosmic order (Greek). According to Badiou, Paul's entire discourse on the law is enunciated for the purpose of discarding the life of the law, which is death, articulating a subject who lives according to the non-literal law of love, which is life.[20]

And indeed, it is for this very purpose that Badiou turns to Paul in the first place, to announce a "connection between a subject without

17. Ibid., 76.

18. See Lacan, *Seminar VII: The Ethics of Psychoanalysis*, 71–84, where Lacan equates the sin of Romans 7 with the psychoanalytic Thing (*das Ding*), which makes the symbolic law.

19. Badiou, *Saint Paul*, 78–79.

20. The subtext of this reading of St. Paul's relation to the law is Badiou's own movement beyond Lacan. Badiou sees Lacan as the last great figure writing in the heritage of Descartes' *cogito*. His complaint with Lacan, and any Lacanian politics, is that psychoanalysis seeks normal functioning of the subject's structure, and therefore the normal functioning of the political structure. But for Badiou true political thought is always subtracted from the political structure, from the ruling law. For Badiou, psychoanalysis places the subject within the structure, whereas politics places the subject outside the structure. See Badiou, *Being and Event*, 431–35; "Philosophy and Psychoanalysis," 60–68.

identity and a law without support," which founds "the possibility of a universal teaching within history."[21] Only this political subject, subtracted from every figure of the law and suspended by a truth-event, is capable of mobilizing against both the prevailing abstractions of statist legality and capitalist mobility, and the reaction of communitarian and particularist protests.[22] Once a subject is freed from the laws of representation, she is able to act within the situation according to what is actually presented in it, proclaiming the truth of the situation. This proclamation is presented as the generation of the universal beyond all differences. For Badiou, Paul is the founder of militant universalism, articulating a subject suspended by a truth.

ŽIŽEK ON DEATH

In contrast to Badiou, for whom a subject is *suspended* by a truth, Žižek articulates a militant subject who *suspends* the symbolic order, initiating an existence "between the two deaths." This suspending of the symbolic order does not abolish it, nor does it institute another order or law, but rather fulfills by fully realizing the law beyond its superego supplement.

Perversion and Hysteria

One way of understanding Žižek's dispute with other postmodern political theorists is through his deployment of the concepts of perversion and hysteria. Much of postmodern political theory looks to the excessive or transgressive aspects of life violently repressed by the reigning socio-political order. Inverting Hobbes, who sought to circumscribe the riotous passions of the multitude according to the law of the sovereign, these theorists seek to re-inscribe all forms of life within the political order. In this way, an ever broadening and inclusive political field will emerge through an endless re-negotiation and re-articulation of the political field, such that no one will be excluded or oppressed, but rather will be allowed to express fully their own lifestyles.[23] But the

21. Badiou, *Saint Paul*, 5.

22. Ibid., 14.

23. Žižek's main target here is Judith Butler. See his *Ticklish Subject*, ch. 5; *Welcome to the Desert of the Real*, 97–102; and also Butler, *Contingency, Hegemony, Universality*.

problem with giving free reign to all transgressive identities and life-styles through transgressive political action is that it exactly mirrors the processes of global capitalism. For the market revels in breaking every rule and crossing every line, all in the effort of creating new markets for selling new products to new consumer-subjects, who themselves are trained to transgress. Žižek complains that those promoting a "politics of multitude" as an ever-broadening of the political field exactly mimic the machinations of global capitalism. For "the subject of late capitalist market relations is perverse" in its attempt to transgress all limits, yet in its very *per*version it maintains itself as a version of capitalism.[24]

Why is this? Perversion, which Žižek uses in a technical sense drawing from psychoanalysis, stays within the political order, albeit in the seemingly exterior form of transgression. Perversion, as constant transgression against the law, enters into a morbid confusion of what counts as life and death by claiming that life (politically and subjectively) functions transgressively, and that death (politically and subjectively) comes from the law (whether they are the political laws of the land or the subjective laws of civility, sociality, sexuality, and rationality). Perversion claims to know the symbolic law, and know exactly how to resist it by transgressing it. In this way its ultimate point of reference is always the law. This means that the mutual implication of the existing political order and its own transgression are in reality an articulated whole, which therefore allows a *reasonable* form of resistance within the political order by seeking to move within the political field as a broadening, re-ordering, and re-articulation of current and future "forms of life." It does this in the form of transgression because if one were truly to move beyond, rather than merely transgress within, the socio-political order it would mean the loss all contact with reality, unhinging all systems of meaning and significance, and thus foreclosing the possibility of *reasonable* political action. But, Žižek contends, this transgressive strategy ultimately fails because it is still trapped within (because it mirrors) an economic system that feeds on transgressive forms of life even as it promotes these transgressions.

But other possible targets of this type of politics would be the more American version of radical politics represented by Jeffery Stout, Romand Coles, and William E. Connolly.

24. Žižek, *Ticklish Subject*, 248.

For Žižek, the prevailing socio-political order cannot be *transgressed* in the form of perversion, but rather must be *traversed* in the form of hysteria.[25] The hysteric is incapable of finding one's coordinates within the symbolic network, putting the symbolic order into doubt, and therefore putting oneself into doubt. The hysteric is in doubt about the symbolic law, not knowing what the law wants from her, and therefore powerless in following the law. [26] Rather than transgressing the political order in vain attempts at rehabilitating it, Žižek proposes *traversing* the political order in the mode of hysteria, or as he elsewhere calls it, through a radical "subjective destitution."[27] Rather than seeking "subjective affirmation" *from* (indicating source/origin) the political order (even in the guise of transgression), for Žižek, one ought to enact a hysterical subjective destitution *from* (indicating separation/removal) the socio-symbolic order. The figure of this subjective destitution in which "the subject accepts the void of his nonexistence" is symbolic death.[28] Only in what we might call a "psychic suicide," where one is biologically alive yet dead to the symbolic coordinates of social, political, and economic life, is one placed in "the suicidal outside of the symbolic order."[29]

Many political theorists, however, are unwilling to entertain this type of death because it seems simultaneously too *excessive* as a stepping outside the bounds of rationality, reasonability, and all other figures of political "realism," and too *moderate* in its apparently disinterested stance toward the current state of affairs. These theorists would claim that such a radical break makes it impossible to reform the political order because one is so utterly beyond it, so utterly detached from it— too ideologically minded to be any political good. But this is exactly Žižek's intention when he speaks of subjective destitution as death, for only when one considers oneself dead to the existing order will one be able to actually *act* freely with regard to it.[30] Only then will one move from piecemeal forms of transgressive resistance against the existing

25. Ibid., 265–69.

26. Žižek, *Sublime Object of Ideology*, 112–14; and *Ticklish Subject*, 247–57.

27. Žižek attributes this phrase to Lacan, but does not reference a text. See *Ticklish Subject*, 366, and *Sublime Object of Ideology*, 230.

28. Žižek, *Ticklish Subject*, 281.

29. Žižek, *Welcome to the Desert of the Real*, 99.

30. Žižek, *Ticklish Subject*, 260–64.

order toward creating the possibility of another order altogether. This subjective destitution is a radical transformation through a *traversal* of the existing order, rather than a gradual reformation through *transgressional* re-appropriations.

The Death of Christ

In the writings of Saint Paul Žižek sees one attempting to articulate just such a hysterical subject. In his first extended engagement with Paul, via a critique of Badiou, Žižek seeks to justify the place of Lacan within radical political discourse.[31] Žižek agrees with Paul about the need to die to the law in order to break out of the dialectic of law and transgression. Summarizing Lacan, he says, "One has to undergo the second, symbolic death, which involves the suspension of the big Other, the symbolic law that hitherto dominated and regulated our lives."[32] This suspension of the symbolic law breaks the morbid confusion between life and death, between law and desire. Badiou faults psychoanalysis for only being able to articulate and normalize this morbid confusion, which is death. For Badiou, it is Paul who breaks out of this separation of thought and action through recourse to the resurrection, leaving the psychoanalytic problem behind. It is here that Žižek claims that both Badiou and Paul are wrong to hastily emphasize resurrection, which for Žižek is nothing but the *in*surrection of a new master, a new beginning, a new harmony that will soon return to dominate us.

Rather than the reactionary approach of hastily instituting a new order around the truth-event of resurrection, Žižek sees in Lacan the truly radical and perpetual gesture of death, a death escaping the dialectic of law and desire. "What Death stands for at its most radical is not merely the passing of earthly life, but the 'night of the word', the self-withdrawal, the absolute contraction of subjectivity, the severing of its links with 'reality'—*this* is the 'wiping the slate clean.'"[33] This wiping the slate clean opens a space beyond the law and the order of being, but comes before the institution of a truth. For Žižek, this, then, is the space of the subject (ontologically and politically), existing "between

31. See ibid., 127–67.
32. Ibid., 151.
33. Ibid., 154 (emphasis original).

the two deaths" as one who is, as it were, among the living dead. But after this initial engagement it seems that Žižek decides not to surrender Paul so easily to Badiou's anti-psychoanalytic reading, deciding the Christian legacy is worth fighting for. Žižek begins to see in Paul one who theorizes directly the Freudian "thing" which *causes* the law and its transgressive supplement. It is not the case that the law prohibits the thing, the object and cause of desire, but rather that the thing causes the law in so far as the law protects us from the thing itself.[34] The point, for Žižek , is that Paul articulates a new relation to the thing beyond the law and its transgressive supplement. "Christianity proper is precisely to *break out* of the vicious superego cycle of the law and its transgression via Love."[35] But this *break out* via love is characterized by the radical gesture of "striking at oneself," which constitutes subjectivity as such.[36] This striking at oneself is the means by which one becomes "uncoupled" from the symbolic order, dying to one's social substance. The Pauline "new creation" (2 Cor 5:17) is linked to the Lacanian "wiping the slate clean" such that "there is a terrifying *violence* at work in this 'uncoupling,'"[37] allowing for the subject to act truly according to the necessities of each situation. This "new creation" is therefore equal parts loving and monstrous, marked as much by dying to the symbolic order as it is by killing oneself in regard to the symbolic order. In this way, albeit using a different vocabulary, Žižek emphasizes the moment of death over that of resurrection.

Žižek's reflections on Paul and death also extend toward a recovering of "the perverse core of Christianity."[38] This recovery is essentially a Lacanian reading of Christianity, and of Hegel, which posits that "both Christianity and Hegel transpose the gap which separates us from the Absolute into the Absolute itself" because Christ's death is, contra Badiou, the "negation of negation" which accomplishes redemption.[39] Throughout *The Puppet and the Dwarf* Žižek seeks to unite fall and redemption, Adam and Christ, Judaism and Christianity, law and love

---

34. Žižek, *Fragile Absolute*, 131.

35. Ibid., 145 (emphasis original).

36. Ibid., 148–50.

37. Ibid., 127 (emphasis original).

38. The subtitle of Žižek's *Puppet and the Dwarf*.

39. Žižek, *Puppet and the Dwarf*, 88.

according to this dialectic whereby the former is fulfilled by the latter, not in a new positivity, but rather through transposing the initial gap of the former into the latter itself. Ultimately, the gap separating God and humanity is internal to God himself in the cross of Christ. But rather than the death of God leading to our freedom from him, Žižek claims that the death of God, and our participation in that death, allows us to suspend the symbolic law, just as Christ did. This, then, is "the perverse core of Christianity," not that "God is dead and we have killed him," but that God is dead and we with him. Or again, we should become hysterical because God himself already is.

ST. PAUL ON CHRIST

As we have seen, both Badiou and Žižek read Paul by placing a relative emphasis on either Christ's resurrection or death, depending on the place of psychoanalysis within radical politics. Badiou ultimately rejects the Lacanian frame for understanding Romans 7 because it persists within the realm of being/knowledge/law, opting instead to see Paul as focused solely on resurrection as truth-event. Žižek, on the other hand, extends Lacan's reading of Romans 7 throughout the Pauline corpus, seeing in Paul the forerunner of the psychoanalytic community, which is itself the revolutionary collective. The problem is that both read Romans 7 as expressing an existential-ontological condition of subjectivity, reading the "I" of Romans 7 as the individual ego of Paul. But by reading Romans 7 as a proto-psychoanalytic expression of the condition of subjectivity Lacan, Badiou, and Žižek say what Paul goes to such great lengths not to say. For them the law is sin. They ultimately are forced to say what Paul refuses to say because they read the Pauline corpus through Romans 7, either for or against Lacan, instead of reading it the other way around. Or rather, they read Christ according to Romans 7, instead of reading Romans 7 according to Christ. This is what ultimately leads to either emphasizing resurrection or death to the exclusion of the other. In light of this, by turning to Romans 6 and focusing on the baptismal incorporation into Christ described there, an alternative subjectivity will be outlined, which better expresses Paul's political inspirations and aspirations. Such an alternative will begin first with situating more fully the context of Paul's texts, then turning to Romans 6.

St. Paul and the Political

By now an explicitly political reading of Paul has taken shape within Pauline scholarship.[40] Only two aspects will be noted here. The first is the dual meaning of certain terms deployed by Paul. The term "gospel" of course has extended usage throughout the Jewish Scriptures, referring to the announcement of God's promised salvation. But it is also used in the Roman world to announce the accession of the emperor, his birthday, and other grand pronouncements. Also, while "Lord" in the Jewish Scriptures refers to God, the Lord Almighty, it also functions as a title for the emperor. Words like "justice" and "parousia" also have this dual nature, referring both to the activity attributed to God by the Jewish Scriptures and the activities of the emperor according to the imperial propaganda and the imperial cult. The accumulation of these terms in Paul's writing does not necessarily indicate an anti-imperial polemic, but when they are front-loaded in the thematic introduction of Romans 1:1–17, it seems that Paul seeks to show that the imperial cult is a parody of the true worship of Christ.[41] Second, against the more individualized reading of "carrying one's cross" as referring to one's personalized trials and tribulations, imitation of the cross of Christ should rather be seen as the social and political cost of following Christ amid a society that is in rebellion against him. In this way, it is the cross of Christ that defines the new messianic community of Christ, consisting of Jews and Gentiles, within the Roman Empire. The cross is the price of social nonconformity. In this way, "carrying one's cross" is not merely an existential imitation of the way of Christ, but a political imitation of Christ and participation in an alternative community where the symbol of oppression is made into the symbol of redemption.[42]

Moving closer to our immediate text of Romans 6, we must consider the context of Romans 6–8, which N.T. Wright notes is that of a

---

40. See Horsley, *Paul and Empire*; *Paul and Politics*. But recently this consensus has been challenged, particularly by John Barclay in his 2007 SBL presentation, "Why the Roman Empire was Insignificant to Paul."

41. Wright, "Paul and Caesar," 175–77; see also idem, "Paul's Gospel and Caesar's Empire."

42. See Harink, *Paul among the Postliberals*, 105–50.

narrative retelling of the Exodus story.[43] Romans 6 begins with a discussion of baptism, which had been linked by Paul to the crossing of the Red Sea (1 Cor 10:2), a culminating moment of the Exodus. A later reference in Romans 6:16–18 to slavery (now to sin and death, rather than slavery in Egypt) further strengthens the Exodus motif. Just as after crossing the Red Sea the Israelites received the law, so also after baptism into Christ in Romans 6 there is a discourse on the law in Romans 7. Then from Romans 7 comes Romans 8, in which Paul speaks of the Spirit fulfilling the law and leading the people into the new inheritance of all of creation, rather than inheritance of the Promised Land. Wright summarizes:

> Those who were enslaved in the "Egypt" of sin, an enslavement the law only exacerbated, have been set free by the "Red Sea" event of baptism, since in the baptism they are joined to the Messiah, whose death and resurrection are accounted as theirs. They are now given as their guide, not indeed the law, which although given by God, is unable to do more than condemn them for their sin, but the Spirit, so that the Mosaic covenant is replaced, as Jeremiah and Ezekiel said it would be, with the covenant written on the hearts of God's people by God's own Spirit.[44]

In this light, therefore, we should not quarantine Romans 6–8 as merely a discourse on salvation, but as Badiou and Žižek have noted, we must read Paul as uniting the soteriological and the socio-political, which of course, every good Jewish prophet always did.

St. Paul on Death and Resurrection

As we examine Romans 6 more closely, especially the first half of the chapter, four things can be noted. First is the messianic incorporation *into*, or *with*, Christ. Paul says that we "have been baptized *into* Christ" and "*into* his death" (v. 3), just as we were "buried *with* him" (v. 4), and we "have been united *with* him" in death and resurrection (v. 5). The old self was "crucified *with* him" (v. 6) and, therefore, in verse 8, "If

---

43. Wright, "New Exodus, New Inheritance."
44. Ibid., 29.

we have died *with* Christ, we believe that we will also live *with* him."[45] This incorporation *into* Christ, and participation *with* Christ is principally linked to baptism, which unites two strands of typical Pauline thought: dying with Christ, and having union with Christ.[46] This dying with Christ is not merely a spiritualized death, but as noted above, it is the cost of social nonconformity and therefore analogous to Žižek's "subjective destitution." Similarly, union with Christ subtracts the believer from social distinctions, "for all who were baptized into Christ have clothed yourselves with Christ" (Gal 3:27) and are therefore freed from ethnic, economic, and gender hierarchies analogous to Badiou's concern for universalism.

Of course both Badiou and Žižek emphasize an incorporation and participation in Christ, but each accents a participation either in terms of the resurrection to the exclusion of death, or the reverse. And for each, Christ is but a *figure* of immanentization, and the *form* of a general process explicable without recourse to the singular narratives of Christ, or the particular history of salvation (which for them would become enmeshed in identity politics). They see participation in Christ as expressing or illustrating an immanentized ontology, devoid of specific historical content. But Paul cannot be so easily immanentized nor generalized.

This is the case because, secondly, we see Paul constantly reminding the Romans of their baptismal affirmation (6:3, 6, 9, 17), which is given fully in 1 Cor 15:3–4: "that Christ died for our sins in accordance with the Scriptures, that he was buried, that he was raised on the third day in accordance with the Scriptures." Paul's explicit reminders of this baptismal creed, along with his incorporating the scheme of "death-burial-was raised"[47] into his exhortation, indicate that the actual life, death, and resurrection of Jesus the Messiah is not so easily separated from the supposed formal movements of death and resurrection as ontological, psychological, or political categories. Add to this that Paul

45. See Moo, *Epistle to the Romans*, 391–95, for an extended discussion of *en Christo* and *syn Christo* as participation in the salvation-history effects of Christ. Unfortunately, Moo reduces this participation to forensic incorporation in Christ (emphasis added to scriptural texts).

46. Dunn, *Romans 1–8*, 312. See Gal 3:27 and 1 Cor 12:13 concerning dying with Christ, and Gal. 3:37 and 2 Cor 4:10–11 for union with Christ.

47. See Stuhlmacher, *Romans*, 90.

links this baptismal incorporation in Christ with the sweep of salvation history, indicated in his retelling of the Exodus narrative throughout Romans 6–8 in which God's redeems/rescues those enslaved, not to Egyptian masters, but to the masters of sin and death (6:16–23). In this light the revolutionary potential of Paul's thought seems strictly coordinated to God's work through particular people and communities (Israel), particular locations (the Promised Land, Jerusalem), culminating in the singular person and work of Jesus of Nazareth.

This singular incorporation in Christ (a form inseparable from the fable) leads, thirdly, to one of the most significant features of Romans 6 totally ignored by both Badiou and Žižek: the eschatological tension in which all believers live. Throughout Paul's corpus is the *already/not yet* tension seen in the typical structure of his letters moving from the indicative to the imperative. This structure, written largely through Romans 6–8,[48] is verbally manifested in the shifting from the present tense to the future in verses 5 and 8, and it is implied in the shift from past action (indicative) to present action (imperative) in verses 4 and 6. This eschatological tension is not an infinite deferral of the benefits of resurrection in Christ, but rather "the whole point of the argument is that Christians no longer belong in the world of death" but indeed presently walk in the "newness of life."[49] In this way, "The whole of this life for the believer is suspended between Christ's death and Christ's resurrection" because her transition from death to life is incomplete.[50] This incompletion is not a structural incompletion, the constitutive lack in the other which splits the subject, but rather a temporal incompletion weighed heavily on the *already* while anticipating the *not yet*. Fourthly, being suspended between Christ's death and resurrection institutes a political subjectivity freed from sin yet enslaved to God. Paul, of course, is not interested in or commenting on the modern political problem of private freedom and autonomy in relation to the need for public laws of restraint. The question for him is not whether one is a slave, but to

---

48. Dunn, in *Romans 1–8*, 303, distinguishes it in this manner:

Already/Indicative		*Not-yet/Imperative*
6:1–11	with reference to sin	6:12–23
7:1–6	with reference to law	7:7–25
8:1–9	with reference to flesh	8:10–30

49. Wright, "Letter to the Romans," 538.

50. Dunn, *Romans 1–8*, 331, also 332–33.

what or whom one is a slave (v. 16). Rather than being in bondage to sin and death, those baptized into Christ are bound to God in righteousness, according to an "obedience from the heart to the one to whom you were handed over as a pattern of teaching" (v. 17).[51] This pattern of teaching is not a new law, even a non-literal law, but is rather the very person of Christ, to whom we are "handed over" by God, having been rescued from the kingdom of darkness (sin) and brought into the kingdom of the Son (Col 1:13). But this pattern to be followed is not one of power, coercion, or force, but one united to Christ, and therefore having the same mind as Christ, which does not grasp after equality but becomes a servant of all (Phil 2:1–11). Freedom from the power, kingdom, and reign of sin institutes a subjectivity that suspends the symbolic law because the subject is suspended in Christ. This subject is not the one who suspends the law, but rather the law is suspended by Christ, in whom the subject now lives.

Suspension between death and resurrection, the eschatological tension begun in one's baptismal incorporation in Christ, unites what Badiou and Žižek separate. For while Badiou accents the resurrection of Christ tending toward an over-realized eschatology, Žižek accents the death of Christ as an under-realized eschatology.[52] On the one hand, in Badiou's over-realized eschatology it is very unclear how one remains faithful to the truth-event without tempting toward absolutism or coercion, for there is no model to imitate, nothing before the event to guide. Contra this, Paul intimately links the life of Christ, patterned as the way of the cross, to our baptismal life in Christ, which means that each one suspended between death and resurrection must live bound to God, in Christ, as a servant of all. On the other hand, in Žižek's under-realized eschatology, his "subjective destitution" forecloses the ability to judge between suicide and martyrdom, leading toward a valorization of violence.[53] Again, for Paul, the linking of death and resurrection neutralizes the fantasy of violence and death by emphasizing a participation in the life of the one who has conquered sin and death.

---

51. Dunn's translation; see *Romans 1–8*, 334, 343–44, 353–54.

52. It is interesting to note how each quotes from Romans 6:2–9. Badiou quotes Romans 6:4–9 (*St. Paul*, 69–70), and Žižek quotes Romans 6:2–4 emphasizing "death" (*Puppet and the Dwarf*, 103).

53. See Holsclaw and Long, "Martyrdom as Exteriority."

The flawed readings of Badiou and Žižek stem from prior commitments to the functioning of the symbolic law within politics, each attempting to find a new relation to the law. This emphasis on law causes them to dissipate the tension between death and resurrection that Paul unites in Christ. That tension marks the subjectivity of those in Christ, a subjectivity that is a *suspension* between his death and his resurrection. In this way, Badiou is correct that subjectivity is produced, or induced, or resurrected by a truth-event that always precedes the subject, but wrong that this subjectivity is weighted completely toward resurrection and separated from the specificity of Christ. Also, Žižek is correct that one must die to the symbolic law that sustains our identities and perpetuates our oppressions, even those identities existing in the form of transgression. But he is wrong to allow the moment of resurrection to be so fully determined by death, such that subjectivity is constituted exclusively as a "psychic suicide." Baptismal incorporation into Christ is rather the beginning of a new exodus constituting a new people, a new community. This new community cannot be sublimated according to the abstract logic of global capitalism or to the particularist rhetoric of identity politics, because it unites a universal declaration to a particular narrative through the singular person of Jesus, the Christ. Without this particular narrative, namely God's redemptive work in calling Israel, the universal declaration becomes formal and abstract, open to cooptation by capitalist economics and statist politics. Without the universal declaration, that there is neither Greek nor Jew, slave or free, male or female, the particular narrative would become insular and sectarian, merely another form of identity politics. But the universal and the particular are united in the singularity of Christ, in whom one participates through baptismal incorporation.

CONCLUSION

Now, of course, two deficiencies of the above analysis must be noted. First, Paul does not have a theory of the subject in the modern sense, and to extract from his writing such a theory is somewhat anachronistic. Be that as it may, Paul does have an understanding of corporate or communal subjectivity, rather than an individual or autonomous subjectivity. This is exactly why Paul does not have a modern theory of the subject, which attempts to ground the subject beyond tradition and community. Rather, beginning with God's work among the people of Israel, and then to all those in Christ, Paul articulates a conception of the subject in relation to others, the principal relation being with God. The reason many postmodern theorists are turning to Paul is because Paul is communal (or universal) without being bound to tradition. Second, the baptismal incorporation outlined above must necessarily be deepened through an exploration of baptism both before and after Paul. Before Paul, Christian baptism begins with John the Baptist, carrying the mantle of Elijah in the river Jordon (a little Rea Sea in the Exodus tradition), who ultimately baptizes Jesus on whom falls the Spirit of God, which is the model of Christian baptism by water and Spirit.[54] After Paul, and up to the time of Constantine's conversion, the baptismal rites and their attending declarations (eventually culminating in the Apostles' Creed) continue to deepen the theological and political significance of baptismal incorporation into Christ.

Nevertheless, it is still possible to draw a few general conclusions, politically and ontologically. Politically, baptismal incorporation in Christ enables Christians to engage in concrete political realities without being bound to the prevailing political realism. Political realism, in whatever guise, governs politics by circumscribing possibilities and suggesting appropriate means for ushering in the *eschaton* (if it hasn't already foreclosed the political by making peace with the status quo). But the eschatological tense of baptism allows one to die to this type of realism, and to hope and work toward the seemingly impossible resurrection within this very reality, trusting that only God is able to bring it about. This leads to political activity beyond activism, which is usually coupled to some ideology. Because baptismal incorporation is in Christ, rather than an idea, Christian political activity must not be merely issue driven (which tends to distort and gloss over reality, often in the name of realism), but rather must be deeply personal, integrating both the persons acting and that towards which they act. This leads to a politics of the local without parochialism, and of the national without nationalism, because neither the local nor the national are the ultimate horizon for political action. Lastly, this baptismal incorporation suggests the possibility of both protesting and collaborating with the current political regime, depending on what level one is active, local or national, and

54. Stuhlmacher, *Romans*, 97–101.

what issues are at stake. Neither protest nor collaboration is demanded or foreclosed in our baptismal incorporation because death and resurrection must always remain in tension. In these ways baptism walks between sectarian withdrawal from politics and the equating of politics with state-oriented action.

But this eschatological tension does not leave us temporally adrift. Rather, it is anchored ontologically in Christ. Eschatological tension does not lead to an understanding of a paradox or contradiction between two kingdoms or realms, and certainly not to an understanding of the separation between the natural and supernatural. The tension is resolved in Christ, who has rescued and redeemed us from the kingdom of darkness (Col 1:13–14) even as he is the one who is before all things and in whom all things hold together (Col 1:17). Christian politics is not based in an idea or an analysis, but in the one who creates and sustains the cosmos. Because the political and ontological belong to Christ, there must not be any competition between theologies of liberation and theologies of creation. Neither is more or less conservative or radical if properly situated in Christ. Baptismal incorporation in Christ, as the foundation of political subjectivity, should therefore prompt correctives and convergences within and between both Catholic and Protestant discourses which tend toward emphasizing either creation or eschatology.

As we have seen, then, both Badiou and Žižek seek to articulate a political subjectivity through a new relation to the law, subtracting from communitarian identities, capitalist equivalencies, and statist legalities. These forms of subjectivity center on resurrection or death. Each reading attempts a plundering of Paul and Christianity, on the way back to the politics and the philosophy of Athens.

Yet Paul is not so easily pillaged. For he can still be heard in the Areopagus debating the enlightened, teaching of both death and resurrection, and a more subtle relationship to the law. For political subjectivity is neither being *suspended* by a truth-event, nor *suspending* the symbolic law, but rather a *suspension* between death and resurrection according to our baptismal incorporation in Christ. In other words, political subjectivity is neither *evental* nor *hysterical*, but *baptismal*. While Badiou and Žižek help us to see again in Paul the radical dimensions of his theology as it bears on issues of politics and economics, they can only take us so far. For Paul's tension between death and resurrection affirms together the historical particularity of Israel and her God, the singularity of Christ, and the universality of those baptized into Christ, baptized "by one Spirit into one body—whether Jews or Greeks, slave or free" (1 Cor 12:13). This tension affirms history without becoming historicist as it extends toward universality without becoming abstract. Baptismal incorporation into Christ is God's culminating act of exodus. For Paul there cannot be an enlightened subjectivity, stripped from its fabled core as generalized principle, but rather, with Justin Martyr and Clement of Alexandria, the sacrament of baptism produces an illumined subjectivity, alive in the light of Christ, suspended between death and resurrection.[55] Only from within this sacrament of illumination is a true political subjectivity created, dead to the world but alive in Christ.

55. Justin Martyr, *First Apology*, 183; and Clement of Alexandria, *The Instructor*, 217.

PART IV

Agamben

CHAPTER 8

The Cross as the Fulcrum of Politics:
Expropriating Agamben on Paul[1]

by Paul J. Griffiths

Giorgio Agamben is Professor of Philosophy and Aesthetics at the
University of Verona in Italy, and has published a dozen or so books
on topics as diverse as the history of poetry and poetics, the nature
of sovereignty, the future of politics, the distinction between the human and the animal, and Paul's Letter to the Romans. He was born in
1942, and is a man of the Left, politically speaking, which means that
he was formed, like all of that European generation, by the frustrated
near-revolutions of 1968, when he would have been 26, and the fall of
the Berlin Wall in 1989 and the consequent dissolution of the Soviet
Empire. This was a generation of utopian political hopes of a broadly
Marxist kind, hopes that had to be reconfigured because of the discred-
iting of standard-issue Marxist theory. One resource for this reconfig-
uring, the most vital and these days among the most often appealed
to, is the material preserved in the Christian archive; and among this
material the Pauline literature is the most often discussed. The last fif-
teen years or so has seen a flowering of interest in the Christian archive

1. An early version of this essay was presented in Durham, England, May 2008, at
a joint conference of the theological faculties of Durham University and Duke Divinity
School. I am grateful for the critical discussion it received there, and especially for
help from John Barclay, Gerard O'Laughlin, Anastasia Scrutton, Stuart Foyle, and
Theodora Hawksley. A fuller version was given at the invitation of Douglas Harink at
a conference called "St. Paul's Journeys Into Philosophy" at the University of British
Columbia in June 2008. I am grateful to all the participants in that conference for help
in understanding Agamben, and most especially to Doug Harink, Stephen Fowl, Chris
Huebner, Creston Davis, and Charlie Collier.

by European intellectuals, many of whom are neither Christian nor Jewish, but who see in it materials they need and want. The Christian archive is for them approximately what the pagan classical archive was to Christian theorists of the first four centuries or so: indispensable, attractive, and dangerous.

Agamben reads Romans from without, therefore, writing about it neither as a church theologian nor as a member of the professional guild of New Testament scholars. He is interested in the letter as a text of foundational significance for Western thought about law and politics, and a good deal of what he writes about it is in broadly genealogical vein. He traces, for instance, the trajectory of Paul's thesis about the deactivation or emptying-out of the law, centering on the Greek verb *katargeō*, which Paul uses to describe this process, and its subsequent transformations into the Latin *evacuari* by Jerome, the German *aufheben* by Luther, Hegel's appropriation of that same term into his post-Christian dialectic, and Walter Benjamin's critique of Hegel in the "Theses on the Philosophy of History." The conceptual grammar of all this is fundamentally Pauline (or anti-Pauline), thinks Agamben; and only when this is understood can the European intellectual tradition be seen clearly. But Agamben's interest is not only genealogical; he is also interested in the Letter to the Romans constructively, taking its conceptual grammar, if I read him rightly, to provide a good solution— and perhaps the only viable solution—to the constitutive problem of political theory. Agamben, that is, endorses Paul on a particular reading of him, and in so doing approaches at least to the antechamber of theology's boudoir. This is not to say that he is Christian, or that he has anything good to say about the church, by which he seems usually to mean the Catholic Church. But it does mean that he thinks Paul is right, though usually misunderstood by the church, and in so thinking he recapitulates a trope of central importance to the history of church theology, according to which re-readings of Paul have been taken to reconstitute a lost orthodoxy.

Agamben then interprets the Christian archive—or at least this particular piece of it—from outside, as a resource for thinking through theoretical problems not, as he thinks, generated by it. In doing so, he performs an activity like what Christians have called despoiling the Egyptians, which is to say relieving the aliens of their treasure in order to put it to better use than the aliens know how to do. Efforts of this sort are, or ought to be, of considerable interest to Christians, and so, writing as one, I'd like to return Agamben's compliment, and begin the process of despoiling him for the benefit of the church.

BIOPOLITICS AND THE STATE OF EXCEPTION

The grammar of Agamben's thought has at its root a distinction between political life (*bios*) and bare, or nonpolitical life (*zōē*).[2] The former is the condition in which we humans find ourselves when we live in the city, are subject to the laws of the city, and thus, are citizens. The latter, bare life, is the pre- or non- or trans-political life we have simply as human beings, members of the species *Homo sapiens sapiens*. The constitutive political problem, then, is that of how to relate the one to the other. How is it that living human beings, conceived and born, enter into a biopolitics, one form or another of legal-political life? How, to put the same point differently, does nativity get transformed into subjection to a sovereign? And what happens when sovereignty is lost, abandoned, or otherwise dissolved?

The logic of sovereignty, thinks Agamben, evident in especially pure form in the founding texts of the modern democratic republic, which is to say those of the French and American revolutions, effectively dissolves the distinction between bare life, life as human being, and political life, life as a citizen. But it does this in a profoundly paradoxical way. The human being is depicted in these texts, and treated in the forms of political life they engender, as the bearer of inalienable rights; but the only guarantor of those rights is the state, typically the democratic republic. Outside the democratic city's walls there are other democratic cities; together they aspire and conspire to leave no territory unruled, and, therefore, no human being as a stateless noncitizen. But when the fact of being human is effectively collapsed into the fact of being a citizen, then should one fail to become a citizen, or having been one cease to be one, one becomes thereby not just stateless but also, and much more disturbingly, effectively nonhuman, a bearer of a life to which anything at all can be done. If the only life recognizable by the democratic republic is *bios*, the political life of rights and laws,

---

2. This distinction is the main theme of Agamben's *Homo Sacer*. See also his *State of Exception*, §1.3; and *Time that Remains*, 122–24 (on grace as life).

guarantees and protections, due process and proper legal procedure, positive law and constitution, then the inevitable implication is that only citizens truly live, only citizens are human. The others—the slaves, the unborn, the stateless, the refugees, the inhabitants of the camps— have lost *bios*, and in losing it have lost everything. They can be slaughtered, ignored, starved, imprisoned for life, and tortured, all without any laws being broken.

Agamben takes this absorption of *zōē* into *bios* to be intrinsic to the state rather than accidental to it, and especially clearly evident in the contemporary, late-capitalist democracy. It is inevitable, he thinks, that such forms of political life will show that they are constituted by this collapse, and that they will do so ideal-typically by establishing with a juridical gesture what he likes to call states of exception. Two examples will show what he means. First, on February 28, 1933, Hitler suspended the central articles of the constitution of the Weimar Republic, an act that the constitution of that republic itself made possible and that was thus legally performed. This act inaugurated a legal state of affairs in which the status of citizens of that republic could legally be determined by dictatorial fiat—and was. The results are too well known to need summary. Exactly parallel, argues Agamben, is the military order issued by George W. Bush on November 13, 2001, which authorized the indefinite detention, with or without trial, of those suspected of involvement in terrorist activities directed against the United States. In each of these cases we have a legal suspension of law, both constitutional and legislated, which is in Agamben's view best described as the application of a juridical claim to what lies outside the sphere of law. In legislating a state of exception, the law erases itself with its own hand, but remains visible under the act of erasure. It acts to annex lawlessness to itself, and thus, paradoxically, to give legal force—the force of law itself—to what it excepts from its own power. In legally removing all legal protections from, for example, those imprisoned at Guantánamo or those in the extermination camps in wartime Germany, they become not just outlaws, but more radically those who have nothing more than life, a life that can be—and usually will be—defined as nonhuman and treated accordingly.

If the suspension of law is itself established juridically, then there is nothing external to law: law and life, *bios* and *zōē*, now coincide without remnant, with nothing left over. Whatever might happen in the state of exception is then coincident with what's legal, and in Agamben's view the camp, whether for refugees, terrorists, kulaks, Jews, homosexuals, or gypsies, is the place in which the state of exception shows itself for what it is: a place where anything is possible because the life established there is nullified, and anything done to it will occur under the force of the law that legislates even its own suspension.

This is the fundamental grammar of Agamben's thought. It belongs, we might say, to an intensified neo-Marxism; and it generates desiderata. The most pressing among these is that of finding a way to construe human life as such (*zōē*) so that it is not juridicalized without remainder, while at the same time recognizing that the law is necessary, that the figure of the *anomos* (depicted, for example, in 2 Thess 2:3–9) by which law is destroyed and in which law is absent cannot be permitted to extinguish the law. That state of affairs, were it to happen, would be nothing other than the reverse image of the state of exception; just as the juridicalizing of law's absence makes everything possible because everything that happens when that move is made is legal, so also the simple absence of law makes everything possible because nothing is illegal. What is needed is a kind of universalism that does not fall into the statist trap of extending the juridical without remainder by legislating its own exceptions. But the conceptual resources for this are not easy to find. What is needed is a dialectical move, one that goes beyond law without erasing it, that empties law without removing it. Agamben is of course aware that the principal examples of such attempts in European thought are Hegel and Marx; but their solutions, he thinks, are shadows of a more radical and more consistent one which is to be found in Paul. And so it is to Paul that he turns for a depiction of the dialectical solution to the dissolution of *zōē* into *bios*.

It should now be clearer why Agamben, along with others, needs the Christian archive. What he needs is a way of thinking about law—and thus about politics; the two, for these analytical purposes, are not distinct, politics being just those processes by which laws are brought into being and taken out of being—that avoids two extreme positions. The first is legal universalism, which legislates even its own exceptions; this is what we now live under, he thinks. And the second is a simple absence of law, which prevents any form of biopolitics, a condition imagined by Hobbes and Rousseau in their own characteristic ways, and imagined also, in a rather different key, by the theorists of the garden, whether the garden of the first three chapters of Genesis or the *hortus conclusus* of the Song of Songs. Given the failure of the Hegelian-Marxist attempt to sublate these options, to resolve them into a synthesis in which the law remains but is in some fashion transcended, there is nowhere else to look than the dialectics of the Christian archive, evident in their most pointed form in Paul's letters. So let us now look at how Agamben construes these works.

THE CALL OF THE MESSIAH, MESSIANIC TIME, AND THE DEACTIVATION OF THE LAW

In *The Time that Remains*, Agamben prefers to construe the *klētos* (called) of Rom 1:1 with the opening clause of the verse, rendering it "Paul, called as slave of Jesus the Messiah . . ." rather than with the following clause, as most contemporary English renderings do—and as Jerome did in the Vulgate.[3] With this interpretation as springboard, and with his meditation structured around the first ten words of Romans (*Paulos doulos Christou Iesou klētos apostolos aphorismenos eis euangelion theou*) and extended into the structure of Paul's thought in general, Agamben offers an extended discussion of "calling," *klētos*, in the Pauline corpus. Agamben's lapidary formula is this: "The messianic vocation is the revocation of every vocation."[4] *Vocatio* is the Latin rendering of *klēsis*, a fact that Agamben plays with in this formula; to be called as a slave of Jesus-Messiah is to have a meta-vocation that revokes, or calls back, every other particular vocation. Calling undermines or de-energizes (removes the *energeia* from) all particular vocations, while leaving them in their form unaltered. This has special application to the vocation of being a Jew, but it applies also, and in formal terms identically, to all other vocations: being married, being male, being female, being a slave, and so on.

The *ekklēsia*, the community of the called, is then the community of those whose vocations have been revoked but not erased, emptied but not annihilated, removed from the juridical sphere to the sphere of life, of *zōē* reconfigured. Agamben appeals here to the *hōs mē*, the "as [if] not," of 1 Corinthians 7 as a way of explicating this. His understand-

3. Agamben, *Time that Remains*, 6–7.
4. Ibid., 23.

ing of the *hōs mē* is realist rather than fictional. It is not that the church's members adopt a new attitude toward their particular callings; they do not pretend, or make other fictional gestures. Rather, those vocations have been made actually different, ontologically different, emptied of legal force by a nonjuridical gesture, the gesture of slavery, of subjection to something external to and other than themselves. Notice here again Agamben's need to appeal to something external to biopolitics in order to reconstitute that same biopolitics: *bios*, biopolitical life, is for him not self-regulating. The Messiah's call to slavery, on this reading, is like the state of exception in establishing a sphere without the law; but it is profoundly unlike it because its sphere, the sphere of the church, is one in which vocations are, as Agamben likes to put it, made available for use in a reconfigured temporal order. If the camp of the condemned is the ideal-typical institutional form in the state of exception, those who live in the *ekklēsia* are in a sphere of weakness which alone makes possible the use of (rather than subjection to) their emptied but still present vocations.[5] The church is in this sense without the law; it is what Agamben likes to call the coming community, the community that occupies the time that remains.[6] For this community, the revoking of vocation reconfigures time as much as it does action, and the call by means of which this is done is not juridical, not a legal gesture.

The time that remains is not, for Agamben, a slice of time between the ascension and the parousia; it is not time extended as other time slices are. Rather, it is the time the *ekklēsia* takes to come to an end; time gathered into itself like a creature poised to spring out upon its prey; or—in an extended analogy that takes up the best part of a chapter of *The Time That Remains*—the time a poem takes to come to an end, to achieve its condition as a poem; or finally (and these are my analogies, not his), the rhythmic time of lovemaking or pregnancy, each of which has a time that it takes for its end to be achieved—the orgasm and the birth, respectively. Messianic time, *ho nun kairos*, to use the Pauline phrase, of which Agamben makes much, is therefore not a time slice but time transfigured.

Let's pause on this and look a little more closely at it. It is here, if anywhere, that Agamben's eschatology is to be found. What, then, is

---

5. See, inter alia, the discussion of freedom and use in ibid., 135–37.
6. See Agamben, *Coming Community*.

poetic time, the time that a poem takes to come to an end, to resolve itself as a poem?

Agamben takes the example of the sestina, a thirty-nine line poem in six sestets and one concluding tercet.[7] The sestina as a whole is ordered around six words: each line in each of the sestets ends with one of the six words, and the sestets are differentiated one from another by the order in which the line-ending words come. (A full statement of the rules for varying the order of the line-ending word would be superfluous here.) One example is that the word that ends the first line in any sestet ends the second line in the next sestet, while the word that ends the second line in any sestet ends the fourth in the next, and so on. Then, in the envoi, the concluding tercet, all six line-ending words occur, though not in any prescribed order. In addition, the sestina may rhyme, and may be written in a variety of metrical forms. But what defines it is not those matters, but rather the red thread of the six words. In the order of composition the envoi would be written first, and the play with the line-ending words would be worked backwards through the sestets. But in the order of reading or hearing the effect is different: if the reader knows that she is reading a sestina, by the end of the first sestet the end of the whole poem is already known, in form if not in particulars, because the six line-ending words must occur in the envoi and, in varying orders, in the intervening five sestets. In the beginning the end is already present, gathered up, folded in, and ready to unscroll.

Not only that, however. While in the order of reading or hearing the poem takes time to come to an end, the time in question is not chronological, not "one damn thing after another," not what is measured by the clock or the hourglass or the sundial. It is poetic time, in which what counts, and what is counted, is a tensive recurrence; the reader's breath and body are, metaphorically, and perhaps actually, ordered to and by the sestina's form. That form is highly formal and rule-governed, but also playful and, when it works, beautiful. The poem's playful beauty, if it is attended to, reorders the attentive reader to itself and thereby gives her entry into a poetical *kairos*, a time in which all that counts is the time the poem takes to come to an end as a poem. The reader may be male or female, Jew or Greek, slave or free; those

7. See Agamben's discussion of the sestina in *Time that Remains*, 78–87.

vocations are revoked (but not erased) in the time of the poem. And all this serves, for Agamben, as a figure for messianic time, the time of the coming community of those whose vocation has been revoked.

This is a version of the usual Christian distinction between the *already* and the *not yet*, a construal of the "as [if] not" of the *nun kairos* of the church. But it adds some depth not found in those ordinary formulations, I think. There is a *telos*, an *eschaton* that beckons; but it is one whose main function is not to point to speculation about the nature or moment of the end, but to reconfigure those who permit themselves to be drawn by it. This theme is itself often explicit in Scripture, as for example in the opening lines of the Song of Songs:

> Let me be kissed with your mouth's kiss
> for your loves are better than wine
> fragrant with your best ointments.
> Your name is oil poured out
> and so the young girls have taken delight in you.
> Drag me after you—let us run!
> May the king lead me into his storerooms
> so that we might exult and rejoice in you.
> Mindful of your loves above wine
> they rightly delight in you.[8]

The (female) beloved seeks to be reconfigured by her lover ("drag me after you") and thereby to enter into the time of exultation and rejoicing. The figure here is that of sexual play; but the time in which that occurs is in every important formal respect just like the time in which poetry is read, or that in which the Eucharist is celebrated.[9]

8. Song of Songs 1:2–4, translated from the Latin of the New Vulgate.

9. Although Agamben does not, so far as I know, discuss Augustine's understanding of time, he would have found many resonances if he had done so. The lengthy analysis of the nature of time in book XI of the *Confessions* uses the example of a poem's recitation as an index of temporal *distensio* (XI.22.28, XI.24.33); and although Augustine is not easy to understand on this question, a possible reading is that he understands the time of a poem's (or a psalm's) recitation to be analogically like the time *in toto*, time as seen *sub specie aeternitatis*: the end is present in the beginning, which fact does not abolish, for those who live in time, the temporal passage from the one to the other. What it does do is make timed living a reality that does not bind but liberates. See, for useful discussions: Wetzel, *Augustine*, 17–44; Rist, *Augustine*, 73–85; Kennedy, "Book Eleven," 167–83. See also Charles Taylor's useful formulation:

The point or purpose of reading the sestina, then, to return to Agamben's instance, is not anything consequent upon that act, just as the point or purpose of lovemaking or receiving the Eucharist is not anything consequent upon those acts. If it were, if one made love for one's health or received the Eucharist for the benefit of one's moral character, one would in fact not be doing either: these are actions that cannot be performed in subordination to calculations of consequence because to do so makes it impossible to perform them. It would be like making a promise with the fingers crossed behind the back: the promise is thereby cancelled.

There is one more point to note about the sestina as example. The structure is six-plus-one, six words and six sestets, followed by a seventh in which the preceding six are recapitulated and brought to rest. This should sound familiar: it reflects the six days of creation followed by the Sabbath. That is why Agamben chooses the sestina, just as it is why the fathers of the church chose a seven-ages schema by means of which to depict the history of the world. The time of the poem, the time that remains, is also the time of the Sabbath, a time in which rest transfigures the time of the six days, and does to those days what the revocation of the messianic call to slavery does to the vocations given in biopolitics.

But this means that the community of the called, the coming community, is without the law in rather an odd way. The opposition is not between those under the law and those not. It is, rather, between those for whom the law is something one can either be or not be under, on the one hand, and those for whom the only possibility is the double negation of not-not being under the law.[10] This is a standard dialectical move, and in Agamben's hands it yields the conclusion that in the *ekklēsia* everyone relates to what he or she is by placing that identity under negation or erasure, without thereby discovering a new identity beneath this negation that is affirmed positively and without remainder. To be a new creation in Christ, on this reading, is not exactly or

---

"His [Augustine's] instant is not the 'nun' of Aristotle, which is a limit, like a point, an extensionless boundary of time periods. Rather, it is the gathering together of past into present to project a future" (*Secular Age*, 56).

10. For the double negation see Agamben, *Time that Remains*, 44–58, on *aphorismenos*, "set apart," (*segregatus*).

simply to take on a new identity; it is to empty one's already-in-place identity of juridical significance without thereby removing it.

It is at this point that Agamben's work with the Pauline verb *katargeō* becomes relevant. He is especially interesting on the reception of this verb into the word flood of European political theory, which as he reads it is largely a series of appropriations, misunderstandings, and rejections of Paul. Understanding *katargeō* in this way permits a clear statement of the difference between the statist universalism of our democracies and the universalism of the Pauline church. According to the former, what the state guarantees you as citizen is your identity as a human being, an identity toward which you stand non-dialectically: you are identical with it, and so when the law is suspended in the state of exception the life you are left with is not yours and certainly not human. According to the latter, to Pauline universalism properly understood, *zōē*, bare nonpolitical life, has a beautiful dialectical relation to the juridical vocations of *bios*, deactivating them but not erasing them, doing to them what poetry does to prose, and thus permitting the kind of free use of them possible only when you are non-identical with them, without also postulating identity with something else. In the church, as Agamben reads it, you don't discover a transcendental identity overarching or undergirding your juridical identities; if you did, that would be one more juridical move, like the establishment of the human as a bearer of rights in the modern state. Rather, you return your juridical identity to its giver, and receive it again, transfigured— though this last formulation is mine, not Agamben's.

THE CHRISTIAN POLITICAL AGENT

Suppose now that we accept Agamben's argument that the aporias of sovereignty can only be overcome by a properly configured universalism, which means a Pauline universalism, understood as it should be. Suppose, further, that all universalisms require a fulcrum external to politics, and that there are only two lively candidates for that position, one being the assertion of rights located in the person as such, and the other being the Pauline dialectic just sketched. We might offer Marxism as a third option, but in Agamben's view—and about this I think he is right—this is just a shadow of the Pauline dialectic, reducing or (as the history of European Marxism perhaps shows) collapsing it into a vaguely leftist modulation of neoliberalism—which is what the ideology of the European Left now amounts to. So that leaves two possibilities. The first, seen most clearly in the Universal Declaration of Human Rights, is the one favored by the liberal democracies. This is an internally contradictory solution according to the argument given above, as it affirms on the one hand a law-independent bearer of rights, and on the other gives that very judgment legal form and reserves to itself the right to establish, juridically, states of exception to the judgment. Liberal democracies, then, like their totalitarian mirror images, inevitably produce fields of blood by legislatively allotting to all that lies outside themselves the status of bare life to which anything at all can be done. That leaves the Pauline dialectic, the dialectic of the vocation revoked for its proper use, as the only lively candidate. Can this be intensified in a Christian direction?

The first move in doing so is to turn to a trope noticeably absent from Agamben's reading of Paul: the cross. It is not merely that the messianic call revokes the vocation; it does so by crucifying it. The vocation of the citizen, then, which most of us have (if you don't you're in Agamben's state of exception), has been drowned in the baptismal bath along with all our other vocations, and it rises from that bath almost unrecognizable—as unrecognizable as Jesus was on the road to Emmaus. The vocation's revocation involves death. In the resurrection, the citizen—taking this term as a synecdoche now for the political agent, one who acts as advocate for or performer of particular proposals for the ordering of common life and in service of the common good—still acts as such, but with a difference that requires closer attention than Agamben gives it. He likes the tropes of play and use for what the called ones, those who belong to Jesus in the church, do with their revoked vocations.[11] But in the case of the vocation of the citizen, this is not enough. A fuller Christian analysis is that the revoked and crucified vocation of the Christian citizen should be evident in quietist political action. What fails to rise from the baptismal bath is interest

11. And not only for them: the trope of play is fundamental to Agamben's depiction of what it is to live a good life (to put one's life in play), whether or not he is thinking about Paul and the church. See, e.g., his analysis of Foucault's "Qu'est-ce qu'un auteur?" (1969) in *Profanations*, 61–72; and especially the gloss on Nastasya Filippovna's marriage play in Dostoevsky's *The Idiot*, in *Profanations*, 68–70. Compare also Agamben, *Infancy and History*, 75–96.

in the outcome of political proposals; it is just such interest that has been given its quietus, brought to rest in the arms of Jesus.[12] It should be easy enough to see why. If the question of sovereignty is insolubly aporetic in the way that Agamben suggests, then the proper response to particular questions of politics on the part of those called into the messianic community is not to attempt to dissolve the aporia, but to act in the knowledge that it cannot be dissolved—which means, among other things, acting politically without interest in the outcome of such action. This, I suggest, is the appropriate Christian gloss on what it means to act politically *hōs mē*, to be to the sphere of politics as the non-non-Jew is to the Law when that vocation is revoked.

To explain this more fully, some distinctions are necessary. To make them I leave Agamben behind with grateful thanks for his gifts, and turn, with Pascal's help, to a slightly more precise explanation of the quietism of political interest.[13] Suppose we take, as the defining mantra of quietism of all sorts, Bartleby the Scrivener's "I would prefer not to," a refusal of a direct and uncompromising kind.[14] The thing refused specifies the kind of quietism in play. In Bartleby's case, it is a complete and systematic refusal of all action and every proposal, a quietism without remainder of which he eventually dies. The quietism I'm recommending is much less radical. It is a quietism not even of political action, but only of interest in the outcome of such action: that, and only that, is what is renounced by the citizen whose vocation as such has been revoked. What gets put to rest by this quietism is a particular set of consequentialist interests, and what gets liberated is a genuinely Christian political agent, a citizen with vocation revoked, a member of the remnant who acts in the *kairos* of the messianic now.

12. For a more extended treatment of the theme of political quietism, see Griffiths, "Quietus of Political Interest."

13. I draw here upon the surviving fragments of a letter Pascal wrote to Florin Périer in June 1657. The text is in *Pascal: Oeuvres complètes*, 281. There is a very suggestive analysis in Auerbach, "On the Political Theory of Pascal." See also, though less usefully, Maritain, "The Political Ideas of Pascal."

14. On Bartleby, see Agamben, *Coming Community*, 34–36, especially the following formulation: "Bartleby, a scribe who does not simply cease writing but 'prefers not to,' is the extreme image of this angel that writes nothing but its potentiality to not-write" (36). Compare, interestingly (and quite possibly not compatibly) Agamben, *Idea of Prose*, 77–78, where he assimilates Bartleby's existence to that of the inhabitants of Limbo.

Political advocacy that is quietist with respect to interest requires of us a good deal of work. This is because prospective judgment as to the effects of writing some political proposal into law is for us ordinarily intimate with advocating or opposing that proposal, and so ascetical effort is needed to refuse such judgments and to nurture those of a different sort, or none at all, while remaining a political advocate. This difficulty is not natural: it is like neither the difficulties involved in refusing linguistic or physical intimacy with other human beings, nor like those connected with the refusal of food. There are virtuoso quietists of these kinds (the Christian desert ascetics, Kafka's hunger artist, the Buddha's ascetical teachers), that is, virtuoso practitioners of Bartleby's "I would prefer not to" in these spheres of human activity. But they have to refuse an appetite or a disposition proper to all human beings, or at least to all those not so damaged as to separate them from those appetites. The "we" to whom these difficulties apply is all, or almost all, human beings. But severing political action from interest in its outcome requires an ascetical effort of refusal only when the presence of such a connection is the ordinary thing, as it is for us. Our political formation has been, for the last three centuries or so, democratic, and it is proper to that form of political life to nurture a strong connection between deliberation as to outcome and advocacy of particular political proposals. But nurturing this connection so that it seems obvious and inevitable is not proper to all forms of political culture. Arguably (though I will not argue it) it is not proper to many premodern political forms, and it may not be proper to some contemporary ones. Perhaps, for instance, in a polis ordered by Shari'a, those who make a habit of connecting their advocacy of political proposals to prospective judgments about their effects would be as locally idiosyncratic as German tourists sunning themselves naked on Indian beaches: the locals keep their clothes on at the beach, and look askance, with a mixture of disapproval and puzzlement, at tourists who take them off.

But among us everyone sunbathes naked, and the result is that clothing ourselves in a quietism of political interest requires effort. The resulting get-up feels uncomfortable and looks odd to the locals. This sense of oddity is on its face no different from any other produced by transgressing local custom and knowledge. I think, however, that clothing ourselves in a quietism of political judgment, whether of the preliminary kind in which we eschew ordinary, consequentialist judgment, or of the more radical kind, in which we seek to become political agents altogether without judgments, has some advantages over local custom that even the locals might be able to recognize and acknowledge. Nakedness, after all, can lead to epidermal carcinomas, and wearing clothes on the beach, odd though it may look to Europeans and some Americans, may be a cover-up with some good effects.

The first advantage of quietism of the kind I have described is that those who arrive at it are likely to have a more accurate understanding of the limits of our capacity to make accurate prospective judgments about the results of enacting one political proposal rather than another, than do those whose thinking hews to the ordinary consequentialist line. These limits are especially obvious, almost unarguably so, when the proposal under discussion advocates adjustment of a complex system. Adjusting such a system in one respect always has unanticipated and often undesired effects upon other aspects of that system's behavior. This is true in economics, both micro and macro: no one appears able to predict the results of legislation (or the weather) upon the workings of financial markets, even though the rewards for successfully doing so are vast. It is true, as well, in ecological matters, even of a quite local kind: the introduction of wild parakeets into the ecosystem of Chicago forty years ago has had effects upon local bird, tree, and human life whose particulars were quite unanticipated. And it is true in matters of foreign policy: one country's or international agency's intervention in the internal affairs of another, whether militarily, diplomatically, or economically, always produces unanticipated ripples and blowbacks. Ordinary consequentialist discussion about the likely results of actualizing one political proposal or another is blind to this incapacity. It is very rare to hear mention of it in campaigns for elected office or floor debates because the grammar of political talk in democracies requires that it be occluded. If we were to acknowledge that we sometimes or often or usually have no way to assess the outcomes of the proposals we advocate, then we, as good deliberative democrats, would have to give up an essential element of our political self-understanding. This is why those committed to democracy as the preferred form of political culture will ordinarily avoid looking at this incapacity, and if they do look at it, they do so glancingly, dismissing it as an unwarrantedly excessive skepticism or a cloak for some form of totalitarianism.

It is not so difficult, however, to see that skepticism in this area is, in general, more accurate than epistemic optimism. It is not that skepticism about our capacity to predict the results of political proposals is always right; a more precise formulation is that the more complex the system to which a particular proposal advocates adjustment, the more likely skeptical disavowal is to be the right response to claims to know the results of the proposed adjustment. Quietists of political interest, then, have a distinct advantage here. It is easier for them than for consequentialists to see that thinking in consequentialist terms about political proposals aimed at the adjustment of complex systems usually cannot be done successfully, and that therefore those who advocate it do so either confusedly or deceptively. Those committed to deliberative democracy in its ordinary forms will not want to see this, and will therefore usually avert their gaze from it.

Close affinity to skeptical clarity about political prediction is not the only advantage of quietisms of political interest. An additional one is that quietists are not discouraged by, nor in any deep way concerned about, claims that the political proposals they advocate will have effects they do not want. Suppose, for example, that you advocate adjustment of the tax code in the direction of removal of tax relief on interest paid on mortgage loans. An objection to enacting this proposal might be that it would discourage home ownership, which in turn would have deleterious effects upon the stability and order of residential communities, which in turn would threaten a range of civic virtues . . . and so on. An argument in support of the proposal might be that by removing this particular federal subsidy for the middle classes more federal funds could be made available for the poor, which in turn might permit support of educational programs that would foster stability and order in towns and cities, which in turn would nurture a range of civic virtues . . . and so on. Quietist advocates of the proposal are neither discouraged by the opposing argument nor encouraged by the supportive one. Because the grounds upon which they advocate the proposal are divorced from consideration of its effects, these kinds of encouragement and discouragement are in principle irrelevant, and this separation yields a constancy of advocacy not easily available to those who support the same proposal on deliberatively consequentialist grounds.

A third advantage, close kin to the second, is that while deliberatively consequentialist political advocates are discouraged when it appears likely to them that their proposal cannot be enacted, and are as a result likely to cease advocating it and begin advocating some associated proposal that they take to have a greater chance of being enacted—democratic politics is after all the art of the possible, and a good practitioner therefore does not continue to advocate a proposal which seems impossible—their quietist counterparts are less likely to engage in such substitution. Eschewing consequentialist judgments about a proposal's enactment, as quietists of political interest do, may very easily be extended in the direction of eschewing such judgments about the likelihood of a proposal's enactment. And if that move is made, the argument that there aren't enough votes for this proposal, or that there are other apparently good reasons why it cannot be enacted, will have no purchase, however true these claims may be. Since quietists are not advocating the proposal on those grounds, they will not be troubled by such arguments—not even when they take it to be true that the proposal they advocate cannot be passed. Here too, as with the second advantage, there is a skeptical and a non-skeptical form of such a repudiation. In the skeptical form, quietists refuse to take account of arguments about the likelihood of enactment because they think that such judgments have a low probability of being true. In the non-skeptical form, they refuse because they don't care whether such judgments are true or not. Skepticism in this area is less attractive than it is in the area of judgment about the effects of enactment because the systems that govern passage or denial of a political proposal are many orders of magnitude less complex than those that proposals attempt to adjust: you stand a much better chance of predicting outcomes on the floor of the House than you do those of adjusting interest rates or ecosystems. This means in turn that quietism's affinity to skepticism in this area is less clearly an advantage over consequentialism's lack of such affinity. It is still an advantage, however.

A quietist refusal of interest in political proposals, coupled with advocacy of such proposals on other grounds, permits, then, continued advocacy in the face of both consequentialist and utopian objections. This advocacy may be activist (barricades, protests, martyrdoms) or verbal (broadsheets, blogs, street-corner speeches), and it may occur within ordinary legal bounds (voting, running for office, lobbying) or without (civil disobedience, treason, fomenting revolution). In all its variants it is impatient with or indifferent to ordinary political deliberation. And it is often, though not inevitably, skeptical about the likelihood that predictive judgments about the effects of political proposals will yield truths.

There is a fourth and final advantage that quietists of political interest have over their deliberatively consquentialist opponents: pretence can be abandoned and consistency more easily embraced. For the ordinary, post-Fordist, democracy-advocating, consequentialist politician (whether running for office or voting), the absence of political interest must either be occluded or criticized when it surfaces. Almost never can it be embraced. A candidate for elective office cannot say that she has no idea what the results of writing her programs into law will be, even if this is true and she knows it to be true; neither, usually, can she say that she advocates what she advocates for reasons (and causes) that have nothing to do with the likely results of its becoming law. (The exceptions here are the occasional appeals to unadulterated principle—results be damned—that still survive in our politics.) Rather, she must say that she advocates what she advocates because of the good it will do, and because she knows that it will bring just that good about and carry no evils in its train. But the truth is almost always otherwise. Voters rarely vote because they are convinced of, or have thought much about, the things just mentioned; instead, they vote because they like one thing or another about the features of the campaigning politician (sex, race, hair color, tone of voice, manner of speech, and so on) or because it is a matter of custom for them and the people with whom they identify to vote for a candidate who speaks in these ways, advocating proposals of these kinds. That is, voters are closet quietists of political interest in any case; and the same is true, mutatis mutandis, for those who seek office. But they remain, by and large, in the closet because the public rhetoric of our polities requires this of them. And closets, when you've lived in them for long enough, begin to feel spacious, comfortable, and above all natural—like a proper home. In the same way, lies can start to feel like the truth. Pascalian quietists of political interest, by contrast, need no closet and no lies: they can speak and act as they are. This is a deep advantage.

So, the Christian citizen who playfully uses politics without the law, as Agamben would have it, does so with political interest crucified, with a deep skepticism about her capacity to predict the results of enacting a political proposal, and with a refusal to be discouraged by predictions of failure, or of success with undesirable results. She does not expect the proposals she advocates to reduce the quantity of blood shed within the walls of the city, or in the juridicalized state of exception without those walls. She may hope for a reduction, and she must lament the failure of that hope to be realized; but she cannot, to the extent that she understands what it means for her vocation to have been revoked, expect any such reduction. She knows, after all, with Paul, that the whole of the created order groans in anticipation of the salvation to come; she must therefore groan with it, and the groaning will be long and bitter. The four notes of the political agency of the Christain citizen, then, are quietism, skepticism, hope, and lament. Together, they configure an account of political agency among the slaves of Jesus-Messiah with both more detail and more precision than any Agamben offers. It remains, of course, to provide thickly described instances of such political advocacy and agency, but that is a task for another day.

CHAPTER 9

Messianic or Apocalyptic?
Engaging Agamben on Paul and Politics

by Ryan L. Hansen

Recent postmodern philosophical accounts of Saint Paul have exposed theologians and exegetes to a vision of a political Paul that is in many ways surprising and sometimes startling. It reveals an approach to Pauline politics bounded neither by the historical-critical method nor a theology that would resemble anything like the Christian version. One such recent approach is found in the work of Giorgio Agamben. In Agamben's *The Time that Remains*, he employs Paul's letters to map out a structure of messianic time, a time in which the political subject may operate. Agamben's philosophical rendering of Paul immanentizes and absolutizes the political, brushing aside concerns for contemplating any kind of metaphysical transcendent "reality in its ontological, causal, and communicative structures,"[1] and creating a kind of unknown god. How does Christian theological thinking respond to Agamben's project? Those theologians and exegetes wishing to engage this work must, as it were, take a Pauline voyage to Athens. On such a voyage, one may indeed pass by many idols bearing various inscriptions. One may even encounter an idol devoted to the political, bearing the inscription, "To an unknown god." The Pauline theological impulse is to make this god "the one who made the earth and everything in it, the Lord of heaven and earth," known through the apocalyptic proclamation of Messiah

---

1. Pope John Paul II, *Fides et Ratio*, no. 66; quoted in Levering, *Scripture and Metaphysics*, 1.

Jesus (cf. Acts 17:22–34).[2] This essay aims to engage with Agamben's work, setting his Benjaminian messianic interpretation of Paul in conversation with a Christian apocalyptic interpretation of Paul. The broader question behind this essay is, how does theological politics proceed after modernity? It is clear that Agamben (as other recent philosophers) has offered one way forward. I will affirm Agamben's turn to Paul, but seek to show that a turn to an apocalyptic Paul, which he rejects, offers a better politics than his messianic immanentist portrayal. In doing this, I will explore the prospect and promise of a Pauline apocalyptic metaphysics, which retains concern for Agamben's immanent political, but also sets it within the broader new-creation schema of Jesus crucified and resurrected: the messianic in Paul needs the apocalyptic in Paul. The desired outcome of this engagement is to follow the Pauline theological impulse of missional engagement with secular thought in order to bear witness to and better understand the reign and rule (βασιλεία) apocalypsed in Jesus the Messiah.

AGAMBEN, BENJAMIN, AND THE MESSIANIC

Agamben's work on Paul is set within the larger framework of his *Homo Sacer* project where concepts that are at the heart of *The Time that Remains*—sovereignty, law, the exception—are set out and defined. In *Homo Sacer* he explains that there were two ways to express the concept of life in Greek: *zōē* and *bios*.[3] These words held apart the idea of the general act of living (*zōē*), and a qualified form of life particular to an individual or community (*bios*), in essence defining a canon for the Western political tradition.[4] Agamben argues that with the rise of modernity, natural or bare life begins to be included or captured in state power, with politics evolving into biopolitics.[5] This entry of life as such into the political for Agamben represents the defining moment

---

2. Indeed it seems that Paul has not completed a proper journey into philosophy until Christian theology engages philosophy's appropriation of Paul. Rather than the journey coming to its end in philosophy's appropriation, Christian theology's response to that appropriation is itself Paul's journey into philosophy.

3. I have retained Agamben's transliterations of the Greek where engaging him.

4. Agamben, *Homo Sacer*, 1–2.

5. Ibid., 3. Agamben turns to the work of Hannah Arendt and Michel Foucault to trace this genealogy.

of the modern and radically redraws the classical meaning of what it means to be political.[6] The modern is always seeking to define the *bios* (form of life) of *zōē* (life as such) and consequently the two become nearly indistinct.[7] This is spelled out concretely in the concept of the citizen. Alluding to the 1789 Declaration of the Rights of Man and of the Citizen, Agamben argues, "the very natural life that . . . is placed at the foundation of the order vanishes into the figure of the citizen, in whom rights are 'preserved.'"[8] Natural birth immediately gives way to nation, bare life becomes *bios* such that *zōē* becomes the immediate bearer of sovereignty. Agamben argues that rights are given to the human person only to the extent that this human subject vanishes into the subject of the citizen.[9] Biological life gives way to political life, the right of citizenship, governed by the sovereign.

A second and concomitantly significant feature of modern politics according to Agamben is its concept of sovereignty—spelled out by Carl Schmitt—where the sovereign is the one who can decide on the exception, who can suspend the law, making oneself simultaneously inside and outside the law. Modernity, according to Agamben, is where the exception becomes the rule, so to speak. Thus the sovereign becomes the one who is both inside and outside the law, keeping the law by not keeping the law.

The problem as spelled out by Agamben is that bare life, living existence in itself, by entering into the political, is "entirely transformed into law."[10] In essence, bare life is made into a political form of life; rather than a pure given, bare life is made a right in modernity. When coupled with the other distinct characteristic of the modern, the exception, life as such, conceived in terms of rights, can be suspended and thus receives a capacity to be killed.[11] Indeed this capacity to be killed under the ban or exception is the definition of *homo sacer*, the sacred

---

6. Ibid., 4.
7. Ibid., 9–10.
8. Ibid., 128.
9. Ibid.
10. Ibid., 55.
11. Ibid., 123.

human subject who is at once included in the law by exclusion such that he or she may be killed but not sacrificed or executed politically.[12]

This leads Agamben to declare that the fundamental paradigm of modern Western politics is not the city but the concentration camp.[13] Once bare life has become a political form of life, it can be revoked in the state of exception, paving the way for the camp as modern political space. The political task for Agamben is to learn to recognize the camp in its many "metamorphoses and disguises,"[14] and it is for this task that Agamben turns to Walter Benjamin as one who calls for serious analysis and confrontation with modern politics as a normalized state of exception. Agamben's work in *The Time that Remains* may be seen as an attempt to respond to Benjamin's Thesis VIII, "On the Concept of History":

> The tradition of the oppressed teaches us that the 'state of emergency' in which we live is not the exception but the rule. We must attain to a conception of history that accords with this insight. Then we will clearly see that it is our task to bring about a real state of emergency, and this will improve our position in the struggle against Fascism.[15]

This alternative conception of history is Benjamin's messianic "now-time" (*Jetztzeit*), and Agamben seeks to understand the structure of this messianic time by turning to Benjamin's "Theses on the Philosophy of History," whose "entire vocabulary," Agamben suggests, "appears to be truly stamped Pauline."[16] Indeed, Agamben's task is to relate Paul's Letter to the Romans to Benjamin's "Theses" such that Paul's letters are restored to the "fundamental messianic text for the Western tradition."[17] Following the line of thought laid out for his work on *Homo Sacer*, he intends Paul, and specifically the structure of his messianic time, to be an aid in thinking through a politics of exception to the normalized state of exception.[18]

12. Ibid., 8.
13. Ibid., 123.
14. Ibid.
15. Löwy, *Fire Alarm*, 57 58.
16. Agamben, *Time that Remains*, 144.
17. Ibid., 1.
18. In *Homo Sacer*, Agamben turns to Benjamin as a messianic alternative to

In *The Time that Remains* Agamben sets to work to "restore Paul's letters to the status of the fundamental messianic text for the Western tradition."[19] His concern for what he calls the messianic comes first and foremost with Walter Benjamin's work in his "Theses on the Philosophy of History" and secondarily from Paul's use of *Christos*. For Agamben, his task essentially entails reading Paul's letters, especially Romans and 1 Corinthians, under a Benjaminian matrix. Agamben is primarily interested in spelling out the concept of messianic time as found in Paul's letters and he does this via an examination of the first ten words of the book of Romans.[20]

The structure of messianic time is essentially time contracted, or the remnant of time that is left in the time that time takes to end—the time that remains before time ends. Agamben understands this as the meaning of Paul's urgent exhortation in 1 Cor 7:29–32: "But this I say, brethren, time contracted itself, the rest is . . . ."[21] There is play here with the notion of conceptualizing time in approaches to Paul's messianic thought. Agamben notes a distinction between linear, representable time, and the real experience of time. He argues that linear time is representable but unable to be thought, while reflecting on a real experience of time renders something thinkable but unrepresentable.[22] This issues in a crisis of how to both think *and* exist in Pauline messianic time—one may do one or the other, but not both. With this he comes to the problem of all philosophy: How does one experience what is thought, and how does one think the unthought, the unthinkable real experience? Bridging these two phenomena is the question of philosophy.

Agamben bridges this gap between thought and experience with what he calls "operational time," a concept he borrows from linguist Guillaume. Operational time, and specifically, the operational time

---

modernity's politics; in *Time that Remains* he turns to Paul as an aid in spelling out Benjamin's messianic politics.

19. Agamben, *Time that Remains*, 1.

20. The ten words serve as jumping-off points into all kinds of Pauline themes and philosophical side roads, such that his exegesis is not limited to determining the meaning of those ten words alone.

21. Agamben, *Time that Remains*, 23. This is Daley's translation of Agamben's translation of Paul.

22. Ibid., 64.

which is messianic time, is the "time in which we take hold of and achieve our representations of time."[23] What we can conceive of as time, in other words our representations of time, are seized in this contracted time and lived out. The contracted messianic time is the use of represented time in experienced time. There is a coinherence of *chronos* and *kairos* in this model: Agamben states, "*chronos* is that in which there is *kairos*, and *kairos* is that in which there is little *chronos*."[24] The *kairos* that is seized is nothing other than the contracted and remnant *chronos*.[25]

This conception of seized time in Agamben's work is drawn from Walter Benjamin's concept of the redemption of history. For Benjamin, the representation of time *is* the concept of history, or more specifically, of those in history crushed by "every historical infamy as a necessary stage in the triumphal march of Reason, as an unavoidable moment of humanity's Progress towards the Consciousness of Freedom."[26] Benjamin speaks in Thesis IX of an angel who, turned towards the past, sees "one single catastrophe" piling "wreckage upon wreckage" at its feet; this angel is being driven into the future by a storm called "progress."[27] Progress for the modern is the mystifying force of history, and Benjamin seeks to challenge this head on. The angel would prefer to be able to aid the human sacrifices of this progress, but it is blown further and further forward by the triumphal march of the victors.[28] The messianic revolutionary task is not to bring about more or better progress, but "to activate the emergency brake."[29] Thus the task of the revolutionary is to seize one's concept of history, a concept decidedly for the trampled in history, and make this concept of history one's experience of time. This is precisely what Agamben is after in his

23. Ibid., 68.

24. Ibid., 68–69. Agamben here is quoting from the *Corpus Hippocratum*.

25. Agamben, *Time that Remains*, 69.

26. Löwy, *Fire Alarm*, 64.

27. This translation of Benjamin's thesis and all further translations of the theses are taken from Löwy, *Fire Alarm*, here 60, 62. The angel in this thesis is inspired by Paul Klee's *Angelus Novus*.

28. Löwy, *Fire Alarm*, 64–65. Löwy argues that Benjamin is confronting the Hegelian philosophy of history, namely that "World history [is] the world's court if judgment."

29. Ibid., 67.

definition of operational time; the representation of time in the defeats of the revolutionary past (*chronos*) are taken up and seized and made to be our experience in present, abridged time (*kairos*). To demystify progress and form a constellation with the oppressed of the past is to be out of joint. This is why Agamben's operational time is not added to represented time, but is laid alongside of it, creating a disjointedness wherein which one can seize the instant and accomplish temporal redemption.[30]

This out-of-joint character brings Agamben back to the key theme in his work in *Homo Sacer* and in Benjamin's theses: the state of emergency. As quoted earlier, Benjamin's task in Thesis VIII is to call for a state of exception to the normalized state of exception, the latter being what has allowed fascism to go largely unchallenged not from a lack of desire but from a lack of understanding. In other words, Benjamin wants to posit that fascism is possible only because of the twentieth century's fixation with progress; rather than an aberration, fascism is the logical production of a modern politics of progress. What is needed is a conception of history that does not assume a general progress, but remembers the victims of history and interrupts the chain of human wreckage that "progress" leaves in its wake. Hence, Benjamin's task is to raise the fire alarm in the mid-twentieth century in order to wake people up to these "progressivist illusions."[31] Of these illusions, the most menacing to Benjamin is the assumption that fascism would just automatically disappear in the course of historical progress. The "real state of exception" is the task of interrupting, by uprising and revolt, "if only for a brief moment, the triumphal procession of the powerful."[32]

For Agamben, this interrupting is the seizure of messianic time. How does one live in this messianic state of exception? According to Agamben, the answer can be found in Paul's logic of messianic inoperativity (*katargeō*). Agamben explores this in Paul's use of *klēsis* and

---

30. Cf. Agamben, *Time that Remains*, 70–71: "Paul uses this term [*parousia*] to highlight the innermost uni-dual structure of the messianic event, inasmuch as it is comprised of two heterogeneous times, one *kairos* and the other *chronos*, one an operational time and the other a represented time, which are coextensive but cannot be added together. Messianic presence lies beside itself, since, without ever coinciding with a chronological instant, and without ever adding itself onto it, it seizes hold of this instant and brings it forth to fulfillment."

31. Löwy, *Fire Alarm*, 59.

32. Ibid., 60.

hōs mē in 1 Cor 7:17–22 and his discussion of the law in Romans 7. Agamben appropriates Paul's use of these phrases to show how one makes use of what is given in order to live into this notion of messianic operational time. Calling *klēsis* a technical term in Paul's messianic vocabulary, Agamben argues that *klēsis* is what relates every juridical status and worldly condition to the messianic event.[33] But Agamben is careful to emphasize that the messianic vocation does not have a positive content. Rather it is the use of the time that remains to make one's representation of time real. The messianic *klēsis* is not a call to another vocation, place, or time but simply the use of one's present condition.[34] Thus, primarily, the messianic calling is a nullification, or as Agamben puts it, "*the revocation of every vocation.*"[35]

This concept of revocation is meant in the double sense here, not only in the sense of recalling or taking back, but also in the sense of calling again, giving a second call to every vocation. Agamben makes this clear when he relates Paul's use of *hōs mē* to the idea of *klēsis* and revocation. For Paul, the "as not" or *hōs mē* does not set one's factical condition in the world over against another condition. Instead, the call to live "as not" sets one's status and condition against itself.[36] For Paul it is not that those who are weeping should rejoice, rather those who are weeping are those "as not" weeping, those who are rejoicing are those "as not" rejoicing. This undermines one's status and condition without altering its form; it is a re-vocation, a taking away and a renewing of the vocation.[37] Thus, Agamben argues against an ontological understanding of the new creation: "This expropriation [of the juridical-factical properties of existence] does not, however, found a new identity; the 'new creature' is none other than the use and messianic vocation of the old."[38]

This phenomenon becomes more focused in Agamben's exploration of Paul's term *katargeō*. Almost exclusive to Paul in the New

---

33. Agamben, *Time that Remains*, 22.

34. Cf. ibid., 22–23: "The messianic vocation does not, however, have any specific content; it is nothing but the repetition of those same factical or juridical conditions *in which* or *as which* we are called."

35. Ibid., 23 (emphasis original).

36. Ibid., 24.

37. Ibid.

38. Ibid., 26.

Testament *katargeō*, for Agamben, conveys the relation between the messianic and the law. Agamben argues that Paul employs the term to mean "I make inoperative, I deactivate, I suspend the efficacy."[39] The term has the sense of taking the energy out of something. Pointing to Rom 7:5–6, Agamben argues that the messianic *katargeō* deactivates the subject from the law.[40] Set within the context of his discussion of the state of exception in *Homo Sacer* and the need for an exception to it, *katargeō* becomes a very important term for Agamben. Messianic power deactivates the works of the law, not by annihilation or destruction, but by making them inoperative or no longer in effect.[41] With this Pauline inoperativity, Agamben finds his new politics, his exception to the normalized exception: "Paul radicalizes the condition of the state of exception, whereby law is applied in disapplying itself, no longer having an inside or an outside."[42] In terms of his larger project, the new political subject is deactivated from the law of exception by exception to it, no longer making *homo sacer* or the camp the norm. The law is preserved by excepting the exception to it.

In this way the messianic vocation creates a remnant. The remnant is the people who do not coincide with themselves, who instead live in the *hōs mē* vocation and take up at the decisive moment the vocation of bringing time to an end by realizing their representation of time and history. In other words, the remnant people are the ones who dwell messianically within the remnant time. The messianic remnant cannot coincide with itself, because they are a people out of joint, a people who refuse to become part of the "triumphant procession" of sacrifice for progress.[43] They are also out of joint with themselves in relation to those in history who have been sacrificed in the name of progress; they are identified with and view history from the standpoint of the downtrodden, defeated, and disenfranchised.[44]

This notion of a people out of joint, never coinciding with themselves, leads Agamben to what he describes as a concrete example and

39. Ibid., 95.
40. Ibid., 96.
41. Ibid., 97.
42. Ibid., 106–7.
43. Löwy, *Fire Alarm*, 49.
44. Ibid., 51–55.

small-scale structure of messianic time: the rhyme. Specifically, he has in mind the sestina, a six stanza poem where the last word of each stanza is gathered, and these six words are then strewn throughout one final stanza of three lines in what is called the *tornada*.[45] The end of the poem, which is a contracted time before the poems ends, takes up words found throughout the poem and rhymes with the past of the poem. Agamben's use of the poem crystallizes all we have been examining thus far. The recitation of the poem is in a sense a messianic gesture; it is a machine that strains towards its end, the time it takes to come to the end of the poem. But because of its structure, where the end words are repeated and recapitulated in the last three lines or *tornada*, the sestina mirrors Agamben's temporal structure of the messianic vocation. The finale of the poem rhymes or echoes moments strewn throughout the rest of the poem. Similarly, the messianic vocation is to echo or rhyme with moments throughout a particular representation of history, excepting itself from the dominance of progress. Thus, the messianic gesture is to rhyme with moments where modernity's procession of death and progress is temporarily interrupted, and the rhyming within the messianic *tornada* will make time end, will bring that specific representation of history to life.[46]

The messianic politics of deactivation from the law works with Agamben's larger project of finding a politics where the human person doesn't immediately vanish into the figure of the citizen. By making oneself inoperative to the law, the messianic political agent is no longer subject to the suspension of that law as the norm for politics. The messianic exceptional politics sets itself against every factical condition in the world so that the citizen exists as not the citizen. The now-time of the messianic allows the subject to identify with the oppressed of the past and so to deactivate oneself from the dominant progressivist politics of the modern. In this a messianic remnant of time is opened up

---

45. The sestina, like all poetry, is done injustice when described with prose.

46. For Agamben's discussion of rhyme and the sestina see *Time that Remains*, 78–87. On interrupting the flow of "progressism" see Löwy, *Fire Alarm*, 101: "The 'splinters (*Splitter*) of messianic time' are the moments of revolt, the brief instants that save a past moment, while effecting a fleeting interruption of historical continuity, a break in the heart of the present. As fragmentary, partial redemptions, they prefigure and herald the possibility of universal salvation."

where one may fulfill the past and simultaneously un-fulfill the present, charging it with messianic potential.[47]

Agamben sets this messianic Pauline politics in opposition to an apocalyptic reading of Paul. Rather than forming a dialectical constellation with the past and presenting an exception to the modern, apocalyptic "is situated on the last day, the Day of Wrath. It sees the end fulfilled and describes what it sees."[48] He differentiates the messianic and the apocalyptic by designating the former the time of the end and the latter the end of time.[49] The apocalyptic, as being *already* fulfilled, cannot present a politics of exception because it cannot deal with the remaining time before the end. The messianic vocation for Agamben is a "movement of immanence"[50] and requires the formation of a constellation with those in the past who have been done violence by the politics of the state of exception.[51] The messianic creates a remnant of exception and opposition within the flow of history; the apocalyptic is seen as already fulfilled outside of the flow of history—at its end.

PAULINE APOCALYPTIC METAPHYSICS

Agamben's messianic politics are immanentized, assuming a metaphysics of univocity. This univocity emphasizes a "determinate sameness" to all political existence, where opposition or resistance is trapped within the same plane as that which it opposes.[52] Here I wish to explore and advocate a Pauline apocalyptic politics, which assumes a different metaphysics. I will argue that only an apocalyptic Pauline politics and metaphysics is capable of a truly new politics because only it provides a politics and citizenship that is not captured by the immanent flow of history. The apocalyptic is truly an other politics because it arrives not in opposing itself to anything else, but in arriving fills up the whole. The apocalyptic impulse in Pauline thought is not captured by the immanent, but shows how the immanent is caught up and opened to

---

47. Cf. Agamben, *Time that Remains*, 97–99.
48. Ibid., 62.
49. Ibid.
50. Ibid., 25.
51. Cf. ibid., 145.
52. Cf. Desmond, "Neither Servility nor Sovereignty," 158.

the fullness of God's apocalypse, Jesus the Messiah. Paul's apocalyptic thought will show how, just as progressivist illusions are doomed to failure, so too is a politics that sets itself up against the modern in an immanent antagonistic struggle, because it is a politics capable of being captured by the logic of the modern. An apocalyptic metaphysics will be informed by what William Desmond calls the metaxological. Metaxological metaphysics is not the cartoon version of Platonism, where the immanent and transcendent worlds are rigidly separated, but rather, "a metaphysics [that] asks for a practice of philosophy that, even in the immanences of everyday life, recalls us to a porosity to transcendence as other."[53] By examining Paul's apocalyptic within this metaphysical frame, I hope to show how Paul offers a different sense of metaphysics and politics where a beyond can contain within itself immanent politics and transform it. In other words, although Agamben's messianic politics needs an immanent univocal metaphysics, to say that metaphysics is beyond politics is not to make an anti-political statement.[54] Instead, Paul's apocalyptic logic will confirm with Desmond that "the loss of the beyond of metaphysics, as going with the absolutization of the political, tends to lead to the loss of the wisdom of the immanent that is the genuine art of the political."[55] I will argue that Agamben's *hōs mē* does not accomplish a truly new politics without a Pauline apocalypticism informed by Desmond's metaxological.

Paul makes very clear in the first chapter of Romans that the very heart of his gospel is apocalyptic. In the gospel, the salvation of the cosmos is "apocalypsed" (ἀποκαλύπτεται, 1:17).[56] Similarly, the wrath of God is "apocalypsed" on account of those who refuse to give honor and worship (δόξα) to God (1:18–21; cf. 3:23). This wrath is for the purpose of showing forth the salvation God has revealed (3:21), in order that the created cosmos might be rightly ordered toward God once again— that is, that it might be inseparable from the love of God (Romans 8). Douglas Harink notes how for Paul, "apocalypse" is shorthand for "Jesus Christ." In other words, what is revealed in Jesus is "the action of

53. Ibid., 158; cf. 155: "In this [Nietzschean] caricature we find the univocal fixation of (metaphysical) difference in terms of rigidly separated worlds: the world here and the beyond world. 'Metaphysics' deserts the world here for the beyond world."

54. Ibid., 173.

55. Ibid., 156.

56. "Apocalypsed" is a borrowed term from Douglas Harink and J. Louis. Martyn.

God . . . as both determining and revealing 'the grain of the universe.'"[57] Jesus shows and sets in motion the rightly ordered creation.

The idea of a rightly ordered creation is a quintessentially apocalyptic notion, and it shows up repeatedly in Paul's letters.[58] In Galatians the cosmos is crucified with Christ, such that there is a new creation (Gal 6:14–15). In Paul's admonition to Philippian Christians that they shine like stars in the universe, the emphasis is less on light and brightness, and more upon being in place among a crooked generation that is out of place, out of joint (Phil 2:15). In an apocalyptic framework the celestial bodies are created with the ability to worship God by obeying the right order of creation, and by doing so singing God's praises.[59] This is also the logic behind Paul's startling phrase that people of the Spirit (πνευματικός) will "judge angels" (1 Cor 6:3; cf. 2:10—3:3; 10:3–4). In apocalyptic texts like 1 Enoch angels are portrayed as in charge of the right operation and interrelation of cosmic and celestial bodies; thus those who are "spiritual" in Paul's terminology, who are most in tune with God's redemptive "grain of the universe" revealed in the crucified Jesus, will be rightly ordered enough to judge the order that angels keep over creation.

This kind of mindset does not and cannot result from a univocal sense of being, the sense of being to which Agamben adheres. For Paul, as for Agamben, history is on a wrong course. But for Paul it cannot be corrected or redeemed from within its immanent condition. This is the logic of the transition in Romans from the seventh to eighth chapter. The immanent, out-of-joint condition (which Paul refers to as both sin and σάρξ) cannot be interrupted from within its own immanence. The interruption, the redemption of the past here for Paul is the acknowledgement that he does not want to do evil, yet he cannot help but be interlocked with it. On a purely univocal and competitive plane, Paul is always defeated because he finds that σάρξ is always victorious. "With my mind I am a slave to the law of God, but with my flesh I am a slave to the law of sin" (Rom 7:25b).[60] Paul here is referring to the same law

57. Harink, *Paul among the Postliberals*, 69.

58. Cf. Hahne, *Corruption and Redemption of Creation*, 9, 38–39.

59. Hahne (ibid., 104) demonstrates that in 1 Enoch 38–44 nature is not clockwork set in motion by God, but is comprised of personal conscious beings with the capacity to obey God's commandments, thus singing praises and giving glory to God.

60. Biblical quotations in this essay are primarily drawn from the NRSV.

but speaking about it in two ways. Here is immanence par excellence, the univocal. Or perhaps the struggle here is somewhat dialectical, but even dialectic draws difference into a "mediated sameness" and hence tends towards a univocity.[61] But this immanent univocity always results in the victory of σάρξ. Good immanence cannot triumph over bad immanence, so to speak. Paul realizes the futility of his immanent situation; there is a war raging in his immanent self and there is no way out of it. No interruption from the inside will be able to defeat, even momentarily, the logic of destruction present in Paul's σάρξ. Nor will any seizure of time allow Paul to take up past victories and redeem them. All the past and all the present in Paul are consumed by this dialectical and hence univocal logic of sin and σάρξ.

However, when Paul considers what has been apocalypsed in the gospel of Jesus Christ, he realizes that there is another law at work, the "law of the Spirit of life" (8:2). This law has liberated those trapped in the immanent struggle with the law of sin and death. Again, it is important to note that the "law of God" and the "law of sin" are the same thing in chapter 7. The only new thing is the law of the Spirit. This law is a new-creational law, not trapped within the immanent struggle. It comes from beyond, which is why it can triumph over sin and death. The advent of the law of the Spirit abolishes the immanent struggle between the good law and the law of the flesh.

J. Louis Martyn discerns a similar apocalyptic logic at work in Paul's letter to the Galatians. The antinomies that defined the old creation are swept away when the apocalyptic revelation of the crucified and resurrected Christ arrives. Martyn writes, "finding the law to be an enslaving power precisely in its opposition to the Not-Law, Paul denies the existence of numerous pairs of opposites that, in one form or another, are identified by all people as the beacons from which one gains one's bearings [in the world]."[62] The immanent antinomies, which seemed so integral to the debate at hand, have been swept away with the old creation, says Martyn. Instead of antinomies that, though seemingly different, were really univocal in their opposition, Paul bears witness to a new logic, the logic of the beyond, the transcendent. But to

---

61. Cf. Desmond, *Being and the Between*, 177.

62. Martyn, *Theological Issues*, 119.

what degree is the old creation really swept away or killed?[63] Martyn perceives a new antinomy at work, an apocalyptic antinomy that is now the primary binary opposition to the flesh. It is not immanent law against law, but new creation or Spirit against flesh.[64] But does this do justice to Paul's high opinion of the function of the law after the advent of the apocalypse of Christ crucified and raised?[65]

I suggest again that the issue is a metaphysical one. The kind of transcendence that Paul bears witness to in his understanding of the law of the Spirit is not one that once again moves towards univocal immanence and antinomy—to have the immanence and transcendence on the same competitive plane cancels out the true transcendence, the true sense of the beyond of the law of the Spirit.[66] The law of the Spirit really is a new creation [κτίσις], not something that is still stuck in struggle with the old. This flattening of the beyond of the law of the Spirit into a kind of univocity is best avoided if we wish to follow Paul's apocalyptic logic. The beyond of the law of the Spirit and the new creation is a kind of non-competitive transcendence.[67] This means that the law of

63. N. T. Wright's discussion on apocalyptic interruption and covenantal fulfillment is helpful here: "One of the things which is 'unveiled' is precisely *how the covenant plan has been worked out*, how God has at last done what he said he would do . . . In the messianic events of Jesus' death and resurrection Paul believes *both* that the covenant promises were at last fulfilled *and* that this constituted a massive and dramatic irruption into the processes of world history unlike anything before or since" (*Paul*, 53–54).

64. Martyn, *Theological Issues*, 119–21.

65. Cf. ibid., 180: "Paul's words about the Law in Galatians 3:19–25 and his similar and dissimilar words about the Law in Romans 7 have usually combined to form a fish-bone in the throat of every interpreter who has attempted to formulate a coherence in Paul's understanding of the Law."

66. Cf. Desmond, "Neither Servility nor Sovereignty," 155: "Being beyond [after] metaphysics may have 'transcending' but it must be this-worldly. If for postmetaphysical thinking there is any transcendence, it must be entirely immanent."

67. On the idea of non-competitive transcendence see Barron, *Priority of Christ*, 191–229: "The very attempt to gather God and creatures together under one metaphysical canopy effectively separated them, turning them . . . into rivalrous 'beings'" (195). Also, "[The Christian understanding of God] is the understanding of God as the Creator of all that is, a reality existing in a modally different way from any creature or collectivity of creatures, otherly other than the nondivine and hence capable of the most intimate and noninvasive relationship with the nondivine" (203). Again, "God's otherness from the world cannot be construed in such a manner that God and what is not God are comparable within a common frame of reference or according to shared properties univocally interpreted" (205). Additionally, "Any and all of the

the Spirit can infuse itself into the immanent law and share the same space without displacing or competing with the other. They can exist together because they are not of one entity but truly other to each other. According to William Desmond, this kind of transcendence is metaxological. "Meta-" here is employed in the double sense of being beyond and being between.[68] Hence, we might say that the transcendence of the law of the Spirit, or the logic of the new creation, does not kill or sweep away the immanent old, but instead opens it up beyond itself; it comes to immanence and leavens it with transcendence.[69] Rather than a competitive antagonism, which tends towards univocity, the law of the Spirit and the immanent law have a metaxological relationship. The law of the Spirit comes to the immanent law from beyond, informing and liberating it, at the same time setting free the persons trapped in immanence to be a new creation and hence *keep the commandments of God.* This is the logic of 1 Corinthians and Galatians put together: "Neither circumcision nor uncircumcision is anything, but a new creation and keeping the commandments of God is everything" (Gal 6:15 and 1 Cor 7:19)![70]

That "everything" is the fullness of God's apocalypse of Jesus Christ. It would be wise to revisit the concept of *katargeō*, a Pauline term that Agamben found crucial to his messianic politics and examine it under a Pauline apocalyptic matrix. First Corinthians 13:8–13 is a crucial passage for Paul's use of *katargeō*. Paul has just proclaimed that the love displayed in the apocalypse of Christ is the fullness of God's

---

supreme beings proposed by either philosophers or concocters of myth would exist competitively over and against other lesser beings in the world" (214). Finally, "Unable to appreciate how the God of Aquinas is some*how* else, [William] James had to make God some*where* else" (221).

68. Cf. Desmond, "Neither Servility nor Sovereignty," 155.

69. Desmond, *Being and the Between*, 182: "The metaxological sense is mindful of *openings in* the happening of the between. It is also mindful of *the opening of* the between itself, beyond all boundaries of finite determination. Transcendence transcends the happening of the between, even while the between, metaxologically understood, marks an opening beyond itself towards the most ultimate other, whose integrity for itself can never be determinately mastered. The immanent middle opens beyond itself to unconditional transcendence." Desmond continues, "What is being denied is any totalism of univocity that might claim to subsume completely the ontological enigma of the singular being as given to be" (183).

70. And Paul might say that this is all summed up in "faith working through love" (Gal 5:6).

new creation: "Love never ends." He then proceeds to use a string of various forms of *katargeō*. Love, for Paul, fills up the whole, such that everything else will cease or come to an end. But Paul is not pitting love and prophecy or love and knowledge on a competitive plane; rather love, being the fullness of God's new creation, fills the whole. Paul illustrates this logic when he writes, "For we know only in part and we prophesy only in part; but when the complete comes, the partial will come to an end" (1 Cor 13:9–10). The complete and the partial cannot compete against each other, for if they did the complete would not be complete. Paul's apocalyptic, unlike Agamben's messianic, cannot be placed on a competitive plain with any other politics. The apocalypse is not against anything because for Paul there is nothing outside of God's new creation in Christ—"everything has become new" (2 Cor 5:17). Thus, the deactivation at work in Paul's use of *katargeō* is not directly antagonistic; rather, the deactivation or making inoperative is a side effect of God's work in Jesus.

This kind of non-competitive transcendence is further illustrated by turning once again to Paul's σάρξ/πνεῦμα distinction as found in 1 Corinthians. It is not that now, because of the apocalyptic situation, flesh and Spirit are locked together in a different but similar univocal struggle. Nor is the flesh meant to be physical as opposed to something non-physical. For Paul, the goal is not the eradication of σάρξ but the hallowing of the body (σῶμα)—sanctification (Rom 6:19; 1 Cor 6:11; 1 Thess 3:13; 4:1–8).[71] Here, rather than being one part of a binary opposition, σάρξ for Paul is pure immanence. Σάρξ is not diametrically opposed to Spirit, but instead cut off from Spirit, cut off from its source of life and freedom.[72] Instead of being two elements in a binary opposition or antinomy, flesh infused with Spirit signifies a transformation and a transcendence that is beyond and between. Transcendence and immanence will not be separated or divorced in this metaphysi-

71. The flesh is not dishonored or disgraced but is indwelt, exalted and hallowed. Cf. the logic of exaltation of the immanent into the superior in Desmond, *Being and the Between*, 222.

72. Paul would have understood this aspect of σάρξ from the Hebrew scriptural tradition of *bāśār*. H. W. Wolff describes *bāśār* as having the sense of "flesh" but also "weakness" or "infirmity." Thus, *bāśār* or σάρξ is a state of pure immanence, the state of weakness apart from the gift of God's Spirit. Wolff writes, "In complete contrast to this 'flesh' is the 'spirit' (Isa. 31:3); but the spirit is also the flesh's hope (Joel 2.28)" (*Anthropology of the Old Testament*, 31; cf. 26–31).

cal construal.[73] This points towards a Christian metaphysics of non-competitive transcendence. More than a mere dialectic, which draws difference towards a univocity, Paul's conception of the πνευματικός is one whose σάρξ is leavened with πνεῦμα.[74] In other words, there is not a competition between two things existing on one immanent plane, but an immanence that is leavened with transcendence. The πνευματικός is not one that is opposed to the σάρξ but one who dwells in between σάρξ and πνεῦμα, in the porosity between flesh and Spirit.[75] This σάρξ/πνεῦμα matrix that Paul traces out apocalyptically runs counter to the logic Agamben discerns in the distinction between the two. The distinction between Spirit and flesh does not make an exception to the exception, dividing the division the law makes. This would place God's

73. Desmond, *Being and the Between*, 201: "[Being beyond totality] refers to the beyond of superior otherness, transcendence itself as in excess of every immanent self-transcendence. Transcendence is redoubled in the metaxological: transcendence in innerness, transcendence in the between, transcendence beyond reduction to immanence, and yet at work in the intimacy of immanence." Cf. Desmond, "Neither Servility nor Sovereignty," 156: "I think it is not so simple, and not so easy to get the political into wise focus, if the sense of the 'beyond' of politics is lost, or betrayed, and the 'political' is tempted to assume sole sovereignty for the immanent organization of the powers of the 'to be.'" And again, ibid., 157: "One's care will be different if the excellences of immanence, in the enjoyment and joy they offer, are also signs of what cannot be exhausted by immanence."

74. Desmond, "Neither Servility nor Sovereignty," 159: "I would put the primary accent . . . on being in-between; and on our thinking as an intermediating that, once again, is directed primarily not to an inclusive whole of thought thinking itself but to a mindful porosity to the transcendence of being, as both other and yet in intimate relation to us. I think that metaphysics, most fundamentally, is metaxological, and that mindful attention to the equivocities of given immanence is one of its important tasks." Desmond also notes that to speak of the beyond is to speak hyperbolically, to emphasize the *hyper*; cf., Desmond, *Being and the Between*, 222: "The *huper* itself ruptures self-mediation, throws the self back onto itself. Now the communicative self is with itself differently, for it is then thrown beyond itself. This is the movement of agapeic mindfulness into radical humility before transcendence itself. It is also a movement of exaltation into the superior." This sounds quite similar to Agamben's messianic self-out-of-joint-with-itself, except Agamben assumes a univocal metaphysics where Desmond posits a metaxological beyond, an excessive source of the to-be of the self, an other which gives what cannot be self-produced. Cf. Desmond, *Being and the Between*, 205. This hyperbolic logic is akin to the Thomistic *via eminentiae*, which P. Travis Kroeker (see "Whither Messianic Ethics?," 45) identifies in Breton's approach to Paul.

75. On the concept of porosity, see Desmond, "Neither Servility nor Sovereignty," 158.

work in an antagonistic and competitive relationship with the divisions in the law.[76] The porosity of the immanent σάρξ to the transcendent πνεῦμα will not allow for a competitive univocal construal of the two. A metaxological metaphysics may also help to temper and inform some of the talk of dualism in approaches to the apocalyptic Paul, and thus aid attempts to spell out the true break with immanence and the old cosmos.[77] Without the metaxological, portraits of Pauline apocalyptic like Martyn's run the risk of falling back into a kind of immanent antagonistic univocity, becoming enfolded once again back into the old creation of antinomy and dialectic.[78]

This logic of porosity between immanent and transcendent is aptly demonstrated by Paul's discussion of history and the two aeons in 1 Corinthians 10. In the material leading up to this chapter, Paul spells out the new way of being in light of the apocalypse of Christ. There is a new epistemology due to this revelation, but also a new ontology—it is not just that we perceive the cosmos differently, but the cosmos is and has been revealed to be actually ontologically different.[79] In chapter 10 Paul is continuing to warn those who still view the cosmos with old-creation epistemological lenses that the immanent logic and wisdom of the world just will not do justice to God's new creation in the crucified Christ. Here Paul uses the example of those baptized into Moses who ate and drank the "same spiritual food and drink" as the Corinthians (10:2–4). Yet Paul warns, God was not pleased with them because they looked upon the world, and upon the rock that was Christ (10:4) with the old-cosmos immanent logic. This immanent logic caused them to become idolaters (10:7; cf. 1 Cor 2–4, 8) and misconstrue the body and sex (10:8; cf. 1 Cor 5; 6:12–20; 7) and put the Lord to the test (10:9; cf.

---

76. Agamben, *Time that Remains*, 49.

77. Cf. e.g., Martyn, *Theological Issues*, 120, 178; Beker, *Paul's Apocalyptic Gospel*, 39–44. But see Beker, *Paul the Apostle*, 146, where the dualism is peripheral because the fullness of redemption and the fullness of time has occurred in Christ.

78. This logic is at work in Martyn when he says that the Galatians who have gone back to the ways of the Teachers are no longer living in the real cosmos, the new apocalyptic Christological cosmos (see *Theological Issues*, 121). However, without the metaxological metaphysics, his dualistic emphasis veers back dangerously toward dialectic, and hence univocity. The new world enters into the old, not abolishing it, but abolishing its old immanence; the new comes from beyond and informs the old to live between immanent and transcendent.

79. Cf. Martyn, *Theological Issues*, 89–110.

1 Cor 6:1–8). Paul writes, "If you think you are standing, watch out that you do not fall" (10:12). He writes this as warning to those who are still measuring reality according to the old-cosmic bearings, the old antinomies. The old-cosmos logic of worldly power and wisdom is idolatry for Paul after the apocalypse. The old-cosmos logic of what the body is for in sex is immorality for Paul after the apocalypse. And the old-cosmos logic of legal rights against one another is complaining and putting Christ to the test for Paul after the apocalypse. This is why, according to Paul, those who think they are measuring by the Spirit, but who are really measuring by a false measurement—an immanent transcendence—are not truly standing, even if they think they are. Their transcendence is still measured by the univocal immanent logic of the old cosmos, apart from the truly other apocalyptic logic of Christ crucified.

For Paul, there is no sense of relating to the past in a seizure of *kairos* in order to redeem the past and the present. The past is caught up in an immanent logic, and is irredeemable by immanence. The life of the Corinthian church as spelled out in the letter confirms this; their immanence "rhymes" with the immanence of those baptized into Moses. Immanent redemption, Paul argues, is not redemption at all, for it gets caught up in a univocal struggle with sin; and this immanent univocal struggle only increases the stranglehold that sin has on the entire cosmos. But Paul does have redemption in mind, for the apocalypse has revealed and effected the "grain of the universe" as found in the crucified Christ. Paul explicates the redemptive logic in verse 11: "These things happened to them to serve as an example, and they were written down to instruct us, on whom the ends of the ages have come." The old ways of measuring served as an example that the old ways of measuring were inadequate. This is visible now because Paul and the Corinthians are a people who live under the sign of the apocalypse, they are a people over whom the ends of the ages have come to overlap.[80] The apocalyptic people found in Christ are those who live between the immanence of the old and the transcendence of the new; they live in the porosity of the two ages. This is the apocalyptic logic of a metaxological metaphysics. The end of one age and the other end of the other age exist on the

---

80. See the discussion of τά τέλη τῶν αἰώνων in Thiselton, *First Epistle to the Corinthians*, 743–45.

same plane in a non-competitive transcendence, such that the old is opened up and made porous to the new, non-antagonistically. This is perhaps why the flesh (in itself) is opposed to the Spirit, but the Spirit sanctifies the flesh.[81]

On our way to spelling out the promise of the apocalyptic Paul for a Christian politics, it may be helpful to examine apocalyptic counterparts for Agamben's messianic construals of existing *hōs mē* and the concept of rhyme. First, it is clear that a univocal and immanent understanding of the calling to remain *hōs mē* will not do for the apocalyptic Paul. For Agamben, the people of the *hōs mē* are those who remain in an immanent struggle with the forces of oppression and domination. The *hōs mē* sets the immanent person against their immanent self, in other words a univocal struggle is envisioned—a struggle that exists on the same competitive plane. But in an apocalyptic matrix, the *hōs mē* people are in their condition "as not" because they are not in their condition immanently (κατὰ σάρκα; Rom 8:5–13; 1 Cor 1:26). Those weeping exist "as not" weeping because they are saturated by a logic of the beyond, the logic of new creation which transforms their condition and opens it up to exist between immanence and transcendence. What the *hōs mē* indicates is precisely other than immanence; it indicates that one's actions are done in openness to the apocalyptic logic of the Spirit, which infuses the condition and makes it a new creation. Or to put it differently, the logic of the beyond is the complete, such that the partial immanent condition ceases to hold sway on the person.

We may also trace out an indication of a concept of apocalyptic "rhyme." The openness of the immanent condition to the non-competitively transcendent allows that condition to "rhyme" with the beyond. This rhyme is the being of the between, the existence of flesh infused

---

81. I take this to be the logic of Gal 5:17—"For what the flesh desires is opposed to the Spirit, and what the Spirit desires is opposed to the flesh; for these are opposed to each other, to prevent you from doing what you want." Apocalyptically and metaxologically this would read, "For immanence alone is opposed to openness to the transcendent beyond, and the transcendent beyond is opposed to immanence alone, for these two ways of being are opposed to each other, to prevent you from doing the good you want to do." That is, these two are opposed only when immanence places itself on a competitive plane with the beyond. Flesh is always opposed to Spirit, but Spirit is only opposed to flesh insofar as flesh opposes itself, sets itself against Spirit. But Paul follows this up with his apocalyptic announcement that the old cosmos is being crucified and raised to life by the life giving Spirit—new creation.

with Spirit, the appearance or apocalypse of a new creation in Christ. Metaxological apocalyptic rhyme opens up a space for a politics that can rhyme with a sense of redemption that is truly other to the long list, and ever growing heap, of injustice and horror we call human history. For Paul, an immanent struggle with this history just leads to further entanglement in its univocal logic. Resisting sin and death on a competitive plane, on its own terms, is futile. But the apocalypse has occurred, the revelation of a new creational logic in Christ crucified and resurrected has appeared, and the immanent is now infused with and inscribed within the beyond of the Spirit of Christ's resurrection life. The apocalyptic agent's mind is now gifted and given to rhyme with the Christ-mind. And the political mind that becomes obedient to death, even death on a cross, can rhyme with the mind of the one with the name above all other names—wholly other unto every other notion of the political, and yet non-competitively so, such that the political gains the potential to be opened up and transformed, even hallowed.[82]

A sanctified politics is, finally, the promise of an apocalyptic Pauline metaphysics. The apocalyptic approach demonstrates that under Pauline logic, Agamben's messianic is still captured in the immanent flow of history because it assumes a competitive metaphysics in its politics of exception. To make oneself inoperative from modernity's law of exception is still to be trapped in its logic, because one's politics is still within the schema of the modern, still inscribed by it. Thus to be against the politics of fascism or the politics of the state of exception is still to be caught up in them. Agamben's messianic movement of immanence contains within its very immanence the logic of its capture by that which it opposes. Gianni Vattimo understands this to be the logic of modernity itself; struggling over against modernity is to further the foundations of modernity itself: progress and overcoming.[83] Indeed, the linear timeline that Agamben assumes lends itself to continuing modernity's project. Vattimo writes, "It is very likely that the idea of thought's progress and emancipation through 'critical overcoming' is

82. Cf. Barron, *Priority of Christ*, 215: "I do not think it is merely coincidental, by the way, that there is a close relationship between Anselm's mysterious name for God and a 'naming' of Christ that takes place in Paul's letter to the Philippians . . . That than which no greater can be thought is tightly correlated to the one than whom no greater can be named."

83. See Vattimo, *End of Modernity*, 4.

closely related to a linear conception of history."[84] If the best politics is the politics of competitive exception, where is the room for tending to the immanent activities of time and language? Are they not captured by the logic of antagonism and competition? With William Desmond we may ask, "Without religious finesse for the primal porosity, is the art of politics weakened in its wise negotiation of immanent porosities and boundaries in the finite between?"[85]

A Pauline new-creational apocalyptic ontology also offers a better alternative to the problem of *homo sacer*. The question of the citizen and the human may be addressed from Paul's perspective in Philippians. Twice in his letter to the Philippians Paul mentions a citizenship that is from heaven (Phil 1:27; 3:20–21). Modernity's politics of exception evaporates the human into the figure of the citizen, where this citizenship, and also one's humanity, can be suspended. Agamben's answer to this is a disengagement with, or a counter suspension to, modernity's factical condition. A Pauline apocalyptic offers a better citizenship rather than an immanent disengagement. Whereas modernity offers a citizenship that is irresistible but can be revoked, for Paul God has acted in Christ to offer a citizenship that can be freely refused or accepted. Furthermore, this gospel of heavenly apocalyptic citizenship does not replace one's created status as human but fills up the lacks in it. In other words, modernity offers a citizenship in place of one's humanity, the apocalyptic citizenship to which Paul bears witness offers a citizenship that perfects one's humanity.

Also, Pauline apocalyptic offers a better hope for politics in that it is not against anything, not the exception to anything. Christ is revealed and an entire world, an entire creation is put forward. In the apocalypse of Christ, argues Paul, the complete has come, leaving no room for the partial (1 Cor 13:10). This means that the complete is not set in opposition to the partial, it does not have to compete for the same space in a zero-sum equation. The apocalypse of Christ fills up the whole for Paul in such a way that there is no remainder (cf. Eph 1:15–23). All is to be situated (or radically unsituated) in Christ. A Pauline apocalyptic politics is filled with positive content—the new creation is ontologically bursting at the seams. The promise of Pauline apocalyptic politics

84. Ibid., 179.
85. Desmond, "Neither Servility nor Sovereignty," 177.

is (paradoxically) that it is neither for nor against anything like fascism or empire or anything else.[86] Paul's gospel is radically *for* the reign and rule of God in the Messiah Jesus, because it *is* that reign and rule, and this fills up the whole of the new creation.

This apocalyptic approach may give exegetes and theologians opportunity and cause to revisit the almost canonical *already/not yet* rubric of Pauline thought. Even Agamben turns to this rubric to demonstrate "the paradoxical tension . . . that defines the Pauline concept of salvation. The messianic event has *already* happened, salvation has already been achieved according to believers, but, nevertheless, in order to truly be fulfilled, this implies an additional time."[87] But can there be anything that is *not yet* for the apocalyptic Paul?[88] If so, then this *not yet* remains outside the purview of the apocalypse of Jesus, it retains a kind of competitive outside-ness to the fullness of Christ. For Paul this cannot be, his apocalyptic theology leaves nothing in all creation untouched. Douglas Harink understands Paul's apocalyptic theology as leaving no remainder:

> [A]pocalyptic theology is theology "without reserve," that is, theology which leaves no reserve of space or time or concept or aspect of creation outside of or beyond or undetermined by the critical, decisive, and final action of God in Jesus Christ. . . . [T]o "contextualize" Paul's apocalyptic as the "conditioned" product of his time, is to escape the grip of his message.[89]

Paul's "apocalyptic without reserve" calls for a reexamination of theologians' and exegetes' commitment to the *already/not yet* schema. Might there be a better way of formulating Paul's thoughts according to his

86. Cf. Wright, "Paul's Gospel and Caesar's Empire," 164: "Paul, in other words, was not opposed to Caesar's empire primarily because it was an empire . . . but because it was Caesar's, and because Caesar was claiming divine status and honors which belonged only to the one God." Wright is on track here, but I think in light of the fullness of the apocalypse in Christ, I would hesitate to say Paul's gospel is opposed to empire at all, simply that because God's fullness has come in Christ, the empire is the partial that makes its exit from the Christian political stage.

87. Agamben, *Time that Remains*, 69.

88. This need not be read along the lines of Pauline enthusiasts who, I would argue, live only in the transcendent. This of course betrays the middleness of an apocalyptic metaxological metaphysics. Pauline Christians live in the between, but this does not mean that there is anything for them that remains outside the dominion of Christ.

89. Harink, *Paul among the Postliberals*, 69.

apocalyptic logic that leaves no part of God's new creation outside of Christ? The question for now must remain an open one.[90]

Conclusion

The promise of apocalyptic for Christian politics is clear: it makes the immanences of life matters of discernment and discipleship. Time, language, community, and ethics, rather than being defined in opposition to other immanent construals of the same, are all to properly find their place in Jesus the Messiah. Paul's is a radical call not to fit the apocalypse of Jesus into politics as usual but to begin to understand the very definition of politics by looking to the new creation in Christ. The challenge of Paul's apocalyptic metaphysics is to fight the assumption that one can even know what politics is before one has moved out to the crucified and resurrected Messiah. Lest this raise worries of a new type of fascism or totalizing discourse we may be reminded that the apocalypse of Christ is about the weakness of the cross rather than power, about seeking the peace of the city, rather than securing it as property over which to rule. When one moves out to that Messiah, one moves to where that Messiah goes: the neighbor, the stranger, and the poor (Gal 5:14; Rom 12:9–21; 1 Thess 5:15). We must also remind ourselves that if, as Agamben argues, "two thousand years of translation and commentary coinciding with the history of the Christian church have literally cancelled out the messianic . . . from Paul's text,"[91] then surely Christian thought is also capable of betraying the apocalyptic given to it in Paul's letters. This heightens the urgency of the call to leave nothing outside of the revelation of Christ, as it seeks to eschew turning to any kind of politics outside the fullness of Christ. Agamben's work with

90. Something like apocalyptic simultaneity might be worth examining in more detail. Cf. Wright, *Paul*, 57: "A sense that God's ultimate future has come forwards into the middle of history, so that the church is living within—indeed, is constituted precisely by living simultaneously within!—God's new world and the present one. The age to come has already arrived with Jesus; but it will be consummated in the future. The church must order its life and witness, its holiness and love, along that axis." Another proposal worth exploring would be how Beker formulates it: "Christ not only 'ratifies' the Old Testament 'promises' but also opens them up anew as 'hope,' because in Christ the promises have been given a new basis . . . [they] are not made obsolete by the Christ event but are taken up in hope" (Beker, *Paul the Apostle*, 148).

91. Agamben, *Time that Remains*, 1.

Paul can certainly help theologians and exegetes focus their thought in that direction. We can all await his further work as we seek to understand how Christ's call touches even what Agamben has to offer toward a Pauline apocalyptic politics, while understanding that Paulinism is a very fruitful place for theological politics to turn after modernity.

PART V

Hermeneutics, Ecclesia, Time

Hermeneutics of Unbelief: Philosophical Readings of Paul

by Jens Zimmermann

INTRODUCTION

When philosophers read Scripture, it is particularly appropriate to examine their hermeneutical presuppositions in approaching a sacred text whose influence on Western thought has been immense and which is so deeply embedded in a religious context and its secularization. In this article, I will attempt to assess the presuppositions that guide recent philosophical interpretations of the apostle Paul, with the help of Hans-Georg Gadamer's philosophical hermeneutic.[1] Gadamer's philosophical hermeneutic is an especially appropriate analytical tool because he examines what occurs in the process of understanding by focusing on the encounter of two horizons: that of the text and that of the interpreter. In this encounter, hermeneutical analysis pays particular attention to the interpreter's "historically effected consciousness"; Gadamer uses this term to indicate that historical influences govern not only the reader's initial interest in and projected meaning of a text, but these influences also continue to shape his interpretation even while straining to let the text speak.[2] To acquire an awareness of one's own historical prejudices, says Gadamer, is extremely difficult because we never stand outside of our own situation and "hence are unable to have objective knowledge of it. We always find ourselves within a situation, and throwing light on

---

1. I am using the singular "hermeneutic" to adhere to Gadamer's own term, "*philosophische Hermeneutik.*"

2. Gadamer, *Gesammelte Werke* (hereafter abbreviated as *GW*), 1:301. All translations from German works are my own unless an English version is cited first.

it is a task that is never entirely finished."[3] Recognizing and legitimizing this subjective element as part of the encounter with an object of interpretation allows Gadamer to say that "all understanding is always also self-understanding."[4] Understanding takes place when the reader's horizon fuses with the life-world and meaning horizon of the text, which is always an act of translation whose success depends on the interpreter's ability to identify the question asked by the text. Indeed the confluence of the subjective and objective elements of interpretation is expressed in the hermeneutical maxim that a text is an answer to a question, and an adequate interpretation identifies the question that animates a given communication and therefore defines its subject matter. It is along these lines too that Gadamer identifies perennially valid or classical texts as those which have shaped and continue to shape our understanding because they constitute answers to abiding human questions across cultural and linguistic boundaries.[5]

These familiar hermeneutic axioms are repeated here to assess recent philosophers' appropriations of Paul within the framework of philosophical hermeneutics. No doubt, Paul's text is classical in that it touches on abiding questions concerning the meaning and purpose of human existence. It is equally beyond question that interpretations of Paul have changed, depending on the cultural horizon within which he has been interpreted. The questions we identify in Paul and how we understand him obviously depend very much on our own historically specific horizon, on what Gadamer calls "the historically effected consciousness" with which we approach this text. This concept on the one hand addresses the fact that the text speaks to us because we are participating in a historically grown socio-linguistic concept, but it also entails, on the other hand, that we can never fully penetrate this web of historical effects in our interpretation of texts. Gadamer's insistence that "the historically effected consciousness is more being than being aware" is of special importance for our hermeneutical assessment of Paul's philosophical interpreters.[6] Our guiding concern is whether philosophical readings can do justice to the Pauline text given

3. Gadamer, *GW* 1:301.

4. Gadamer, *GW* 2:130.

5. Gadamer, *GW* 2:223–24.

6. See Gadamer, "Zwischen Phänomenologie und Dialektik—Versuch einer Selbstkritik" (Between Phenomenology and Dialectic—A Self-Critique), *GW* 2:11.

the kind of consciousness beholden to secularism and individualism that seems to mark recent philosophical appropriations of Paul. Given the complexity of past horizons and the ever shifting direction of our own cultural context, Gadamer rightly refuses the possibility of a single authoritative interpretation. Yet this refusal does not endorse relativism. A good interpretation is measured by its faithfulness to the text's own horizon and its plausible integration into our present one so that our self-understanding is changed.[7] How hard do these philosophical interpreters struggle to let Paul's horizon confront their own? Recall, for instance, what reading Paul as a classic text means for Alain Badiou: "No transcendence, nothing sacred, perfect equality of this work with every other, the moment it touches me personally."[8] Already one detects a number of unthematized modernist assumptions such as the rejection of transcendence and the priority of the individual.

Assessing philosophical readings of Paul with the help of philosophical hermeneutics entails two basic questions. First, what motivates and shapes the philosophical interpretations of Paul that have abounded at least since Spinoza[9] and Nietzsche? The second question is whether philosophical readings of Paul do justice to his specific horizon of meaning; that is, whether such overtly secular readings of Paul as those of Agamben, Badiou, Žižek, and Taubes are a reasonable approximation to Paul's socio-historical horizon of interpretation.

I will try to answer these two central hermeneutical questions by, first, locating the historically effected consciousness of these philosophical exegetes within the horizon of Continental philosophy after the religious turn, in order to determine how fruitful the philosophical engagement with Paul is within this horizon. Second, I will isolate the central christological elements of incarnation and participation

---

7. See Gadamer's explanation of this process in "Vom Zirkel des Verstehens," *GW* 2:57–66.

8. Badiou, *Saint Paul*, 1.

9. Spinoza draws on Paul, for example, in the fourth chapter of his theological-political treatise, making Paul an example of accommodating historically contingent truths (such as God's attributes as merciful, or as judge, or as law giver) for the sake of preserving and declaring historically independent eternal truths of necessity (hereby joining scriptural exegesis to the monistic ontology which merges God and nature into one immanent system; Spinoza, *Theologico-Political Treatise*, 65). Spinoza reduces the nature of apostolic doctrine to ethics (162), thus anticipating the moral Christ of the nineteenth century.

in Paul's writings that philosophical readings tend to overlook on account of their particular historically shaped interpretive horizon. By neglecting Paul's incarnational and participatory high Christology, philosophical interpreters fail to let the Pauline horizon confront their own, and thus they fall short of a productive hermeneutical engagement with theology.

THE HISTORICALLY EFFECTED CONSCIOUSNESS OF CONTINENTAL PHILOSOPHY

In terms of historically effected consciousness, as far as one may claim such a stereotypical overview, philosophical readings of Paul stem from a relatively homogenous readership. From Nietzsche through Spinoza, from Kierkegaard all the way to Jacob Taubes, Agamben, Badiou, Lyotard, and Žižek, these interpretations remain within a basic Western, Judeo-Christian framework, even if, or precisely if, this framework has been secularized and changed in principle to a framework of unbelief. Nonetheless, the coordinates of this paradigm continue to be very much the interpretive themes which have shaped Western culture decisively at least since the Protestant Reformation, and we can observe this in the questions the respective philosophers find in Paul's text. For the sake of assessing more recent philosophical readings of Paul, we will focus on the historical effects of this paradigm as exemplified by Continental philosophy.

Arguably the most comprehensive question within current philosophical thinking as determined by the religious turn within the Continental philosophical tradition is the correlation of transcendence and immanence in relation to the human subject. The debates in Continental philosophy in its continuing fascination with religion boil down to this basic relation. All other questions concerning the universal and the particular, concerning freedom, authority, politics, ethics, human dignity, guilt, identity and difference, the nature of truth—all these are determined by the kind of transcendence-immanence relation we allow to define human selfhood and existence.

This claim is both sweeping and terribly abstract, but perhaps the following example of Lévinas and the use of more theological language will make this point a little more clear. Lévinas's ethical philosophy engages critically, for the sake of human dignity, both philosophical idealism and Heideggerian ontology—the former as a wrong kind of humanism which seeks to understand the self out of the self, and the latter as a monstrous attempt to overcome idealism by making human dignity dependent on the impersonal voice or directives of being.[10] In opposing not only Heidegger but also any totalizing constructs of human knowledge, including hermeneutics, Lévinas takes flight from ontology and seeks to escape from being by locating ethics in the personal encounter with the other by whom I am called to responsibility to the point of substitution. Because of this starting point, even though one can understand this choice, Lévinas struggles throughout his work to reconcile ethics and ontology. Being, or ontology, remains a necessary but dangerous medium for the appearance of the ethical; the ethical relation that determines the truly human subject is always in danger from the ontological structures that allow its appearance. To use Lévinas's terms, the ethical "saying" rises rather precariously within the ontological "said" of culture, language, and writing. This attitude of unease, even hostility, towards the immanent, to history and ontology, makes Lévinas one of what Jacob Taubes has called "zealots of the absolute"[11] or, to paraphrase him for the purpose of our argument, "zealots of transcendence."

At the same time, however, Lévinas retains the Hebrew sensibility for expressing transcendence uncompromisingly in personal, ethical terms. Since his ethical philosophy rests ultimately on the personal transcendence of God as reflected in the face of the other, he abhors any abstract notion of consciousness or any form of knowledge that compromises this personal call of the other toward responsibility. Other zealots of the transcendent are not so particular. Derrida, together with other advocates of what one may call atheistic transcendence (such as Simon Critchley and Alain Badiou), abstracts from the concrete personal ethical transcendence a structural transcendence, reducing transcendence beyond all particularity to a formal absolute.

10. I follow Gadamer's less "mystical" understanding of Heidegger's being: philosophy asks what the *being* of human self-understanding is and with this question the subject transcends itself, and philosophy opens itself "to a hitherto closed experience which transcends the thinking from subjectivity, an experience Heidegger calls being [*Sein*]" (*GW* 1:105). Gadamer finds here an experience that allows us to experience the transcendence of art through its historicity.

11. Taubes, *Political Theology*, 62.

Lévinas clearly recognizes this tendency in Derrida and accuses him of an inverted Platonism, of favoring the theoretical over the ethical.[12] One can see this secularization of Lévinas and its effect on ethical transcendence in Derrida's notion of the messianic, for example, which secularizes and thus profoundly changes Lévinas's ethical, and biblical, concept of justice to a formal ideal. The messianic is merely structural, abstract, and not concrete. In fact it cannot be concrete because then it is already objectified, co-opted by some ontology or interpretation and hence reduced to sameness. In other words, to say it with Badiou, Derrida favors the universal and, ironically, for all his talk about difference, sacrifices the particular on the altar of an ineffable and—this is important—an impersonal abstract universal ideal.[13] Designating this ideal as indeconstructible justice or messianic does nothing to mitigate the impersonal emptiness of this purely structural notion.

This example, however, has already carried us too far into details, and before we lose a sense of what my actual concern is with respect to philosophical readings of Paul, I had better state my argument as clearly as I can: The philosophical horizon of Continental philosophy is determined by a quest for transcendence, but this quest is still hampered by a modernist framework that is unable to engage the incarnational and participatory concepts that are vital to Paul's theology.

Interpretations of Paul at least from Friedrich Nietzsche onward through Heidegger all the way to Jacob Taubes are very much about defining the human self in light of some greater reality than the self.[14]

---

12. Lévinas, *Alterity and Transcendence*, 173: "I have often wondered, with respect to Derrida, whether the *difference* of the present which leads him to the deconstruction of notions does not attest to the prestige that eternity retains in his eyes, the 'real present,' *being*, which corresponds to the priority of the *theoretical* and the truth of the *theoretical*, in relation to which temporality would be a failure." Instead, Lévinas reads in time the ethical encounter of the other. For Gadamer's similar comment concerning Derrida's obsession with the Platonic, see Gadamer, "Frühromantik, Hermeneutik, Dekonstruktivismus" (Early Romanticism, Hermeneutics, Deconstruction), *GW* 10:129–30. Gadamer argues that Derrida's equation of understanding with assimilation betrays itself as "an idealistic and logocentric position."

13. As Badiou puts it, "[T]here can be no ethics without God the ineffable. To believe that we can separate what Lévinas's thought unites is to betray the intimate movement of this thought, its subjective rigour" (*Ethics*, 22).

14. I concur at this point with Taubes's reading of Nietzsche. Taubes sees even in Nietzsche's resolute immanentism the desire for an ecstatic experience of eternal recurrence that de-centers the self (Taubes, *Political Theology*, 85).

All of these readings are a crusade against philosophical idealism and complacent political liberalism. Nietzsche's Dionysian affirmation of the self in the greater context of eternal recurrence, Heidegger's Being, Derrida's indeconstructible justice, Badiou's "event" and his quest for "materialist grace,"[15] and Agamben's messianic—all aim at redefining the subject in relation to some form of transcendence. At the same time, this redefinition is conducted with an eye to undermining liberal democracy and unthinking rule of law in the name of a greater cause. We can see this intent, for example, in Heidegger's alignment with Hitler's illusions of Germanic greatness in his *Introduction to Metaphysics*[16] and we detect a similar subversive desire in the questioning of state authority and the rule of law in Taubes's, Agamben's, and Badiou's political readings of Paul, which take up Carl Schmitt's suggestion that law and state are founded on an exception.[17] Continental philosophy, in short,

15. Badiou, *Saint Paul*, 81.

16. Heidegger depicts the German people as destined to take a stand in the eternal struggle (*polemos*) between being and becoming in the history of being (*Introduction to Metaphysics*, 62). This very task is the mission of the German nation, which "as a historical nation must move itself and thereby the history of the West beyond the center of their future 'happening' and into the primordial realm of the powers of being" (38).

17. See Agamben, *Time that Remains*, 118. In Badiou this thesis plays itself out as the Pauline event of grace against the letter of the law which Badiou defines as the unthinking "letter of automatism, of calculation . . . Every letter is blind and operates blindly. When the subject is under the letter, or literal, he presents himself as a disconnected correlation between an automatism of doing and a powerlessness of thought" (Badiou, *Saint Paul*, 85). Grace, by contrast, means that law or automatism, or thought, "cannot wholly account for the brutal starting over on the path of life in the subject, which is to say, for the re-discovered connection between thinking and doing." "Salvation is the unchaining of the subjective figure whose name is sin" (84). This happens through the event, something "that exceeds the order of thought," Badiou's interpretation of the law: "'Grace' names the event as condition for an active thought" (85). Taubes in particular recognizes the radical subversive power of Pauline theology. Paul, he argues, is not some neo-liberal but a zealous Pharisee: "Paul is a zealot, a Jewish zealot. . . . The spiritual costs that he must bear he doesn't take upon himself for the sake of some blather in the spirit of this great nomos liberalism. . . . Rather, this is someone who answers the same thing in a completely different way, that is, with a protest, with a transvaluation of values: it isn't *nomos* but rather the one who was nailed to the cross by *nomos* who is the imperator! This is incredible, and compared to this all the little revolutionaries are *nothing*" (Taubes, *Political Theology*, 24). Taubes is certainly a long way ahead of Badiou in recognizing the personal nature of the universal: "Sure, Paul is also universal, but by virtue of the 'eye of the needle' of the crucified one, which means: transvaluation of all the values of this world. This is nothing like

struggles to define subjectivity against some kind of transcendence, but has difficulty doing so with an open acknowledgment and full engagement of the religious context that forms Paul's horizon of meaning.

This discrepancy causes problems for philosophically viable concepts of the human self, because a truly human notion of subjectivity (and a host of other philosophical notions) requires the balancing of immanence and transcendence while retaining at the same time Lévinas's emphasis on the personal or ethical dimension of the self. Philosophical readings of Paul are generally marked by the inability to correlate immanence and transcendence. Paul becomes either a materialist or a zealot of the universal absolute, and this polarity has serious hermeneutical consequences, not least because both extremes tend to neglect or even obviate the hermeneutical discernment required for human freedom and responsibility.[18] Richard Kearney's warning against the postmodern sublime as an empty, impersonal cipher also applies to philosophical readings of Paul: "[H]ow could we ever recognize a God stripped of every specific horizon of memory and anticipation? . . . Is there really no difference, in short, between a living God and a dead one, . . . between messiahs and monsters?" Pure materialism and pure event forgo the correlation of transcendence and they bid "adieu" to interpretive discernment by replacing the incarnate God with openness to the monstrous.[19] My argument is that none of the philosophical readings manage to uphold the successful correlation of transcendence and immanence we find in Paul because they ignore or downplay the one thing that determines Pauline thought: Christology. More specifically, philosophical readings fail to grasp the fundamental importance of the incarnation and of participation in Paul's Christology.

---

nomos as *summum bonum*. This is why this carries a political charge; it's explosive to the highest degree" (24).

18. As Richard Kearney has pointed out, Badiou's analysis of Paul's *dynamis* results in paradoxes "completely irreducible to hermeneutic mediation or understanding of any kind" ("Paul's Notion of *dynamis*," 24).

19. Kearney, *God Who May Be*, 76.

PAUL'S INCARNATIONAL AND PARTICIPATORY HORIZON OF MEANING

In New Testament studies the concepts of incarnation and participation, while not uncontroversial, seem generally firmly established as a Pauline development of Jewish messianism.[20] While Gordon Fee, drawing partially on the work of Richard Bauckham, is bolder in affirming a high Christology and incarnational theology[21] than, for example, James Dunn, both scholars demonstrate the importance of the incarnation for Paul's Christology. According to Dunn, Paul's central thought is the idea that in the gospel Jesus embodies a continuity not only "with Israel, but with humankind (Adam) as a whole. The gospel (*euangelion*) which stemmed from and focused on this Jesus could therefore speak not simply to the Israel of old but to the world at large. Which also means that for Paul salvation was intended to fulfill the purpose of creation. And to achieve that, God had reached down to the depths of human impotence under the power of sin and death and had identified himself in an unprecedented way (incarnation?) with the man Jesus."[22] N. T. Wright helpfully links the incarnational motif in Paul to the traditional Old Testament critique of idolatry: "Against the age-old attempts of human beings to make God in their own (arrogant, self-glorifying) image, Calvary reveals the truth about what it meant to be God. Underneath this is the conclusion, all-important for current Christological debate: incarnation and even crucifixion are to be seen as *appropriate* vehicles for the dynamic self-revelation of God."[23]

---

20. Bauckham, *God Crucified*. Bauckham argues for the continuation of a genuinely Jewish understanding of God in Christian theology by pursuing a "Christology of divine identity." He insists that "this Christology of divine identity is not a mere stage on the way to the patristic development of ontological Christology in the context of a trinitarian theology. It is already a fully divine Christology, maintaining that Jesus Christ is intrinsic to the unique and eternal identity of God. The Fathers did not develop it so much as transpose it into a [Greek conceptual framework]" (viii).

21. Fee, *Pauline Christology*, 12.

22. Dunn, *Theology of Paul*, 206.

23. Wright, *Climax of the Covenant*, 84 (emphasis original). See also Gorman, *Apostle*, 102–5. Gorman, like many others, draws on Philippians 2:6–11 as a summary of Paul's "master story," a portrayal of Christ's self-emptying humiliation and subsequent exaltation. See also Gordon Fee on this passage, especially on the phrase "by coming in human likeness": "With that in hand, Paul then emphasizes the reality of Christ's incarnation by starting the next sentence with an echo of the preceding one,

This self-revelation of God is a "package deal," an organic unity of the Messiah's work and its cosmic, universal effects. Incarnation, crucifixion, and resurrection go together. They inaugurate a new creation and a new humanity, and being a Christian is nothing less than ontological participation in this reality.

For the sake of our argument concerning philosophical readings of Paul, we need to emphasize this organic unity of the Christ event, its cosmic effects, and the Christian's participation in them *as a new creation* for two reasons. First, this unity is not a matter of interpretive preference but constitutes the very fabric of Paul's thinking. Second, because this unity is intrinsic to the integrity of the Pauline corpus, the distortion or neglect of this unity in interpreting Paul, no matter from what philosophical perspective, will inevitably miss the radical import of the Pauline gospel not only for theology but also for philosophy and politics. Take, for example, Alain Badiou's denial of the incarnation. He claims that in Paul the sending of the son in no way entails "that Christ is the incarnation of God, or that he must be thought as the becoming-finite of the infinite."[24] Badiou willingly gives up the correlation of personal transcendence and ontological immanence in Paul to suit his own philosophical leanings toward a revolutionary event divorced from historical particularity. Badiou's disincarnate philosophy is imposed on Paul, who, according to Badiou, battles ontology in the name of transcendence: "The Christ event testifies that God is not the god of Being, is not Being." In this ontological subversion, an anticipation of Heidegger's denunciation of onto-theology, "non-being is the only legitimizable affirmation of being."[25] It is not so much Badiou's atheism[26] but its philosophical and social consequences that require careful attention: by severing the event from ontology, Badiou subordinates the human subject to an impersonal, (at best) ethically neutral event.

---

which repeats the emphasis on the genuineness of his humanity. . . . Any reading of this passage that does not take seriously its implied and expressed emphasis on Christ's incarnation is to read the text apart from the context in which Paul has told the story" (Fee, *Pauline Christology*, 507).

24. Badiou, *Saint Paul*, 74.

25. Ibid., 47.

26. See Badiou, *Ethics*, 25: "Let us posit *our axioms*. There is no God . . . The only stopping point is the void."

To claim that "Paul's thought dissolves incarnation in resurrection"[27] tears asunder what Paul had joined together in Christian experience by linking the event to the self-denying crucified God who died for the redemption of humanity, who died out of love for concrete human beings. One shudders to think what a post-Maoist radical subject will justify in pursuing radical fidelity to an event not qualified by the ontological manifestation of compassion and mercy in the Messiah's life and death.

Jesus as the identification of God with humanity in the unique historical incarnation as the Jewish Messiah[28] and the Christian's *participation* in this event are inseparably bound together in Paul. What philosophers either miss or all too easily dismiss is what Badiou has called the fourth discourse or mystical element in Paul, an experience of "secret communion with truth."[29] Except that Paul's secret is not the subjectivistic, gnostic secret that turns Paul into Badiou's living aporia between the particular and the universal. Because Badiou's subject is founded by the declaration of the event within a modernist cosmos without mystery or relationality, he never grasps the intrinsic connection between this participatory element and Paul's public apostolic mission of proclaiming the gospel.[30] For Paul, this communion with truth is intrinsically part of his declaration of the gospel, and not merely a private experience that founds his subjectivity.[31] Aside from Paul's understanding of the Christ event within the messianic history and categories of Judaism, the communal language with which he refers

---

27. Badiou, *Saint Paul*, 74.

28. N. T. Wright at least has no qualms in asserting that "it is now, I think, largely recognized that this passage [Philippians 2:6–11] does indeed express a very early, very Jewish and very high Christology, in which Paul understands the human being Jesus to be identical with one who from all eternity was equal with the creator God, and who gave fresh expression to what that equality meant by incarnation, humiliating suffering, and death" (*Paul*, 93). Wright feels confident to conclude that passages like Romans 5:6–11 only make sense as expressions of the love of God "if Jesus is understood as the very embodiment of the one God" (95).

29. Badiou, *Saint Paul*, 51.

30. As shown, for example, in Paul's link between the indwelling of the Spirit in Christians and the redemption of creation in Romans 8; it is in this context that Paul serves God with his "whole heart in preaching the gospel of his Son" (Romans 1:9 NIV), who, as Paul just declared in the letter's opening, is the fulfillment of Jewish and thus also of the world's hopes.

31. Badiou, *Saint Paul*, 52–53.

to the worshippers of Christ as the true Israel, because they embody the true faith of "our" forefather Abraham, demonstrates the natural interconnectedness of "being *in* Christ" and the body of Christ: "If *we* have been united with him like this in his death, *we* will certainly also be united with him in his resurrection" (Rom 6:5). The phrase "united with [Christ]" once again demonstrates the participatory nature of Pauline theology. By participatory I mean everything indicated by such participatory phrases as "in Christ" (*en Christo*) and "in the Lord" (*en Kyrio*).[32] As James Dunn points out, there are several usages and meanings of this motif in Paul's writings, the meaning of which cannot be limited to describing the "objective saving work of Christ," nor is it simply shorthand for saying "Christian." Rather, as Dunn explains, in conjunction with the idea of indwelling, captured by the phrase in Col 1:27, "Christ in you, the hope of glory," these phrases denote "existential participation in the new reality brought about by Christ."[33] Participation in Christ founds the Christian community and determines its ongoing existence as its very source of life; or, to say it philosophically, faith is not first a mental assent but an ontological state, or mode of being, namely "being in Christ."[34]

When one examines the participatory phrases in Paul's writings, one cannot, as Dunn explains, "avoid talk of something like a mystical sense of the divine presence of Christ within and without, establishing and sustaining the individual in relation to God. Likewise we can hardly

32. Taking the Pauline corpus as a whole, an integrative reading of his theology shows the virtual ubiquity of participatory language (however covenantal or mystical one may want to interpret it): Eph 2:13; 3:17; Gal 2:20; Col 2:6; 3:16; 1 Cor 12:27 (the body metaphor); 2 Cor 5:17, etc. Similarly, commentators are increasingly comfortable with the thought that Paul's theology is inherently social because it is Trinitarian. See, for example, Gorman, *Cruciformity*, especially ch. 4, "The Triune God of Cruciform Love" (63–74).

33. Dunn, *Theology of Paul*, 400.

34. While its Pauline authorship is not accepted by many scholars, the letter to the Colossians fits into this participatory concept by portraying the dependence of creation on the Messiah, God the Son, "the one working *in* me in power (*dunamis*)" with whose "*energeia*" Paul conducts his apostolic ministry (Col 1:29). The same energy is also at work in the Colossians by the Spirit, whose work Paul outlines for the Roman church as the indwelling of the *Christos*, qualifying "Christ in you" as sonship and Trinitarian participation: "And if the Spirit of him who raised Jesus from the dead is living in you, he who raised Christ from the dead will also give life to your mortal bodies through his Spirit, who lives in you" (Rom 8:11).

avoid speaking of the community, a community which understood itself not only from the gospel which had called it into existence, but also
from the shared experience of Christ, which bonded them as one."[35]
As Ernst Käsemann puts it, there is some sense of a union with the
Messiah, but one has to be careful to delineate exactly what this union
entails. Whatever the final definition of this notion may be, Käsemann
confirms the absolute centrality of Christology for understanding this
mystical element in Paul,[36] and already makes the important point for
our argument, namely that this participatory notion combines elements of an ongoing personal relationship with the integration of the
"Christian and the community" into the "ongoing effects of a historical
event,"[37] an event Paul understands as "the beginning of a new age."[38]

No matter how difficult it may be for us moderns to understand
"Paul's imagery of incorporation into another person," this reality is
an essential part of Paul's Christology and pneumatology. James Dunn
even claims that the "study of participation in Paul leads more directly into the rest of Pauline theology than justification."[39] In Pauline
thought, participation in Christ is what holds together the unique historical Christ event within history with its universal effects; it is the
conjoining of immanence and transcendence by virtue of participating
in the cosmic effects of the incarnation, death, and resurrection of the
Messiah. Incarnation and participation in the Messiah as taking part
in the new order of creation—this union of the personal and the universal is expressed in Paul's "Christ devotion." The who and the what,

---

35. Dunn, *Theology of Paul*, 401. We will see this later, but clearly, if this sharing is
participation to an equal degree in the communion of Father, Son, and Spirit, as Paul's
interchangeable usage of these names in Corinthians and Romans seems to indicate,
the cherished opposition between Father and Son that writers like Badiou and Žižek
import from Freud into their reading of Paul collapses.

36. Käsemann, *An die Römer*, 211.

37. Ibid., 212. Käsemann's following chapters, "Das Sein im Geiste als Stand in
der Kindschaft" and "Das Sein im Geiste als Stand in der Hoffnung," also clearly tie
together Christology and pneumatology. Käsemann insists that pneumatology has to
be determined christologically (214), and also opposes Bultmann's separation of the
existential self from the physical body (218).

38. Ibid., 183.

39. Dunn, *Theology of Paul*, 395.

personal relation and participation in the inbreaking, ongoing event of God's kingdom, are inseparable.[40]

This theological context and the content of participation are well captured by Douglas Harink's summary of Paul's theology in Galatians: "The Father's decisive and invasive action through the Son opens up a new space in the world—new-creation space. . . . That space is indicated by the phrase *in Christ*. The new creation is in the first place Jesus Christ himself; in the second place it is the cosmos delivered of enslaving powers through the crucifixion; in the third place it is the Galatian Gentiles participating in Christ's death and resurrection through baptism into his community and living life in the Spirit . . ." This, Harink explains, is Paul's "apocalyptic gospel," with its central message that "God is remaking the cosmos and humanity in Christ and the Holy Spirit, and human beings are being invited to participate in that triune remaking through the *ekklesia*."[41] N. T. Wright identifies the same central elements in Paul: "God had acted in Jesus the Messiah to usher in the new age, to inaugurate the new covenant, to plant the seeds of new creation. The preaching of the gospel was the means whereby the Spirit worked in the hearts and minds of both Jews and Gentiles, not just to give them a new religious experience, not even just to bring them salvation, but to make them the people in whom the new age, the Age to Come of Jewish eschatological expectation, had come to birth."[42]

If the unity of reconciled communion with God and new creation are indeed central to Paul's thought, what does this unity of incarnation and participation mean for philosophical notions of the human subject? It means that philosophical interpretations of Paul have to recognize the meeting of finite and infinite through personal and relational categories in his theology. These categories not only found the subject in its communal structure, but in locating the subject as participation *in* the Messiah and therefore *in* the new historical and cosmic realities, Paul's thought inaugurates a radical innovation. For now the subject is defined by an actual call hailing from, yet not restricted to, a historical event within ontology, but this event and the call originate from a personal man-God, from the Messiah in whom God has put in motion

40. See Gordon Fee's section "Christ Devotion and Soteriology—2 Corinthians 5:14–6:2" in *Pauline Christology*, 196–97.

41. Harink, *Paul among the Postliberals*, 80–82.

42. Wright, *Paul*, 147.

an *already* but *not yet* transformation of creation and humanity already ultimately defined by the fact—at least for Paul it is a fact—of personal, sacrificial love. Ontology and ethics, the particular and the universal, come together not as impersonal pure event without direction, but as a reality determined by incarnation, cross, and resurrection, a reality in which the Christian participates.

One obvious symptom of failing to recognize these aspects of Pauline Christology is the subordination of the human subject in these philosophical interpretations to an impersonal principle. Even in Jacob Taubes's decidedly messianic Jewish reading of Paul, he ends up suggesting a purely historical and Freudian reading that reduces Paul's gospel to an abstract sense of guilt that "has taken on universal, economically universal form."[43] For Badiou, the subject is defined by the eventual structure of "not . . . but," and in Agamben this principle is changed into the messianic temporal structure of "as if" (*hōs mē*). In the final analysis, these philosophical readings tend to deperson-alize and immanentize the human subject. If Jacob Taubes is correct, and modernity is "an immanent cosmos,"[44] then all of these readings remain profoundly modernist in their neglect of Paul's actual source of transcendence: the Messiah as living, personal reality in whom the believer participates through the Spirit.

My thesis is, in short, that Paul's theology ultimately depends on an incarnational Christology that achieves a correlation of immanence and transcendence defined in personal and hence ethical terms, and that without this Christology central concerns of philosophical read-ings of Paul remain unclear at best, or become dehumanizing at worst. For, by dismissing Paul's Christology as either mythological remnant or fable, philosophical readings betray their own historically effected modern consciousness, and in their laudable attempt to define the sub-ject in relation to something greater either succumb to immanence and

43. Taubes, *Political Theology*, 93. Note also that Taubes accepts Freud's insight that Paul's own contribution to the oriental mind is the sense of "dark traces of the past" in the mind which are "ready to break through into its more conscious regions" (91). Taubes wants to "defend the claim that Freud, who is involved with the basic experi-ence of guilt, is a direct descendant of Paul" (89).

44. Taubes's remarks are refreshingly candid in rejecting any pretensions to the contrary. He also seems to say that this immanent cosmos is wrong (*Political Theology*, 84) and demonstrates Nietzsche's complete awareness that Christianity threatens this immanence and an autonomous, self-defining ego (87–88).

reductive Freudian-Marxist categories or advocate an impersonal transcendence without determined ethical, human contours (sometimes
both occur in the same writer).

In his recent book, *A Secular Age*, Charles Taylor classifies the
social imaginary behind recent philosophical readings of Paul as "exclusive humanism," that is, a historically grown, secularist worldview
characterized by an absence of a personal transcendent. According
to Taylor, cultural developments beginning with church reforms in
the eleventh century and continuing all the way to deism[45] and the
Enlightenment effected a loss of the premodern worldview, which had
defined human existence in some way as communion with the divine
or a higher reality. The human condition, argues Taylor, "was more
and more understood in terms of impersonal orders; and this process
was grasped in historical consciousness which saw the impersonal as
superseding earlier, more personal forms."[46] Louis Dupré makes the
same argument but emphasizes that this development entails the loss of
participation in or communion with the divine.[47] Hence, the dismissal
of Paul's participatory, incarnational concepts derives from a historically effected consciousness for which such ideas seem to go against
the grain of their life world. For us, "orthodox, communion-defined
Christianity really belongs to an earlier age," a return to which seems
like regressing.[48] Based on this secularist hermeneutic, the current
readings of Paul remain, with many challenging and profound (and for
the Christian profitable) insights notwithstanding, on the whole rather
undialogical "requisitions" of Paul,[49] resembling less context-honoring
interpretations than prooftextings of one's own position. This failure to
allow a genuine confrontation with Paul's incarnational and participatory horizon of meaning deprives Continental philosophy of important
Pauline insights concerning philosophy's own quest for a subject defined
by transcendence. I want to end by mentioning some possible examples
of how philosophy could learn from Paul if it listened more carefully to
his definition of faith as participation. Paul's christologically grounded

45. See Taylor, *Secular Age*, 288.

46. Ibid., 282–83.

47. Dupré, *Religion and the Rise of Modern Culture*, 42.

48. Taylor, *Secular Age*, 289.

49. I am indebted for this term to Alain Gignac, whose excellent essay "Taubes,
Badiou, Agamben" has provided the starting point for my own reflections.

participatory ontology provides important clues for post-metaphysical, relational concepts of the human subject, the correlation of immanence and transcendence, and, finally, for the relation of faith and politics.

WHAT PAUL COULD DO FOR PHILOSOPHY

Subjectivity

Continental philosophy since Nietzsche is pursuing a subject that is fully in the world but also, to use Badiou's phrase, "oversteps finitude."[50] Ontological materialism and de-ontological ethics (either personal— Lévinas; or impersonal—Derrida et al.) oppose each other. Badiou's "materialism of grace" and Žižek's "Pauline materialism" stand over against Lévinas's ethical transcendence or Derrida's messianic justice.

Besides this immanence-transcendence dichotomy, the subject is also torn between impersonal and personal wombs giving birth to the self. Agamben's work stands out in this regard, for his initial work on *homo sacer* is directed against the politicization of the subject. His philosophy seeks to articulate a concept of the political in which the human is not defined by politics or law.[51] Consequently, he defines Paul's messianic in contradistinction to Badiou's and any other neo-Marxist subordination of the self to anarchic principles and revolutionary events.[52] Yet even Agamben cannot seem to break through to Paul's no-

50. Badiou, *Saint Paul*, 81.

51. Eva Geulen, in her introduction to Agamben's work, argues that Agamben fights the increasing tendency to define humanity legally, a process stemming partially from restricting genetic manipulation and mutation of the human, resulting in the definition and purpose of human life becoming increasingly politicized and codified by law (Geulen, *Giorgio Agamben*, 10). Agamben's figure of the *homo sacer* is intended to expose the nexus between this legal codification and simultaneous stripping of rights of the human [*Verrechtlichung und Entrechtung*] (11) and the innermost solidarity of totalitarianism and democracy (12). Agamben believes that the human sciences provide and wrestle with concrete forms of life rather than abstractions and calculations, and so, "at a time when life seems to belong exclusively to the jurisdiction of the biological sciences, Agamben reminds us (*klagt ein*) of the potential and competence of the human sciences" (13). And yet Agamben often does not seem to find the way into concrete History but works with notions as a kind of image he wants to use (27) in the service of his new articulation of a truly human life (31).

52. Agamben, *Time that Remains*, 43. Taubes also rejects the kind of discourse theory advanced by Badiou: "In order to be able to present the Jewish experience and not to remain in the abstract—I have absolutely no use for 'Discourses on . . .'" (Taubes, *Political Theology*, 28).

tion of participation, which grounds eschatological tension, suffering, and living between the ages, in the identity the Pauline subject derives from an ongoing personal relation with the Messiah through the Spirit. For Agamben the messianic form of life remains more important than the Messiah,[53] wherefore he never quite accomplishes his goal to answer the question of what it means for Paul "to live in the Messiah," and "what the messianic life is like."[54] Badiou, as we have seen, recognizes a mystical element in Paul, but subordinates it to the impersonal messianic eventual structure and declaration. For Paul, and contrary to Badiou, "the real of faith" is precisely *not* "an effective declaration," but first of all new life, a mode of being.[55]

By contrast, Paul defines Christian existence as participation in the messianic event consisting of incarnation, cross, and resurrection; this participation is not an impersonal principle nor is it first of all structural, but it constitutes an ongoing relational encounter with the Messiah through the Spirit. Based on this encounter the subject gains its communal, ethical, historical, and yet transcendent identity, an identity secured by being known without possessing complete knowledge, defined by an Other who grounds humanity in the divine and defines it as charity. It is in this participatory structure that Badiou's "no-but" and Agamben's "as not" structures could gain their ethical grounding.

---

53. For Agamben, the *hōs mē* is not merely a negative term, but "it is for Paul the only possible use of worldly conditions. The messianic call is neither a right [*Recht*] nor does it constitute an identity; it is a general potentiality, which one uses without being its proprietor." To live in this call does not, however, found a new identity. The "new creation" is only "the use and messianic call of the old" (*Time that Remains*, 37). What exactly this new use is, Agamben does not state here, though there is a hint in a footnote (ibid., note on p. 39) that he will talk about this. We will have to watch his use of identity, for surely there is in the personal call, —at least for Lévinas, and I think also for the Christian (see Bonhoeffer)—very much the foundation of a new identity in Christ, which incorporates but also supersedes the older identities and, in this sense, transforms them. For a more theological understanding of 1 Cor 7:29–31, and the difference between Stoicism and Pauline Christianity, see Hays, *First Corinthians*, 127–28.

54. Agamben, *Time that Remains*, 29.

55. Badiou, *Saint Paul*, 88.

Universality and Particularity

The ability of Paul's incarnational Christology to correlate transcendence and immanence could also clarify philosophy's problems with the relation of the particular to the universal. Take Badiou, for example, who has made this topic the explicit theme of his commentary on Paul. For him, Paul's gospel manages to correlate a particular historical event, Christ's resurrection, with universal significance. Paul is, therefore, in Badiou's words, "a founder, in that he is one of the very first theoreticians of the universal."[56] Yet Badiou, because of his historically effected consciousness, also has to oppose this theoretical to the real. In his reading, the resurrection is a fable, not actually grounded in ontological reality.[57] This formalist abstraction from personal transcendence is systemic in secularist hermeneutics and points to the heart of the hermeneutical issue at stake. Unlike Paul, secularist hermeneutics cannot actually hold together the particular and the universal but will always privilege one or the other. To cite Badiou again, while he asserts that "the universal is not the negation of particularity," his pursuit of an abstract universal has precisely that effect: he ends up opposing not only law and gospel,[58] but also inner subjective truth and its historical expression in "rites and external markings."[59] As prophet of "universal eventalism," Badiou emerges as a profoundly non-hermeneutical thinker precisely because he does not understand the epistemological yield of the incarnation for philosophy.

Badiou's philosophical reading of Paul fails to correlate individuality and totality, the personal particular and the universal, in a balanced way. Consequently both the divine and the human subject be-

---

56. Ibid., 108.

57. "What Paul must be given exclusive credit for establishing is that the fidelity to such an event exists through the termination of communitarian particularisms and the determination of a subject-of-truth who indistinguishes the One and the 'for all.' Thus, unlike effective truth procedures (science, art, politics, love), the Pauline break does not base itself upon the production of a universal. Its bearing, in a mythological context implacably reduced to a single point, a single statement (Christ is resurrected), pertains rather to the laws of universality in general. This is why it can be called a *theoretical* break, it being understood that in this instance 'theoretical' is not being opposed to practical but to *real*" (Badiou, *Saint Paul*, 108; emphasis added on "real").

58. Ibid., 76.

59. Ibid., 22.

come distorted. In the history of Western thought, Paul's incarnational Christology may well be the only premise to offer a subjectivity with a distinct identity (in Christ, called and known by God) that is rooted in a personal divine transcendent universal of definite ethical character (love to the death), which on account of the incarnation nonetheless can be experienced and articulated only within communal and historical terms (but not reduced to them). Henri de Lubac, for example, is convinced that "nowhere outside the influence of Christianity has man ever succeeded in defining its conditions; he has always wavered between the imagining of an individual survival in which beings remain separated and a theory that absorbs them into the One." No abstract logic, says Lubac, will ever overcome this dilemma. Only Christianity has successfully offered the proper "bond between the personal and the universal."[60]

Yet even more hermeneutical readers of Paul, such as Jacob Taubes, overlook the possibilities offered by Paul's incarnational Christology for overcoming the inherent opposition between the particular and the universal which characterizes the social imaginary of Freudian and Lacanian psychoanalysis. Both thinkers view reality as the struggle between the big universal and legalistically oppressive father Other and the smaller, particular, me-affirming son. Lacan continues this profoundly non-incarnational tradition by suggesting that entering the symbolic order of language causes identity problems, which throws the human self into all kinds of tensions as it emerges from childhood into the social world. The Pauline harmony of Father and Son (and Spirit), whether proto-Trinitarian or not, challenges these oppositions of son and father, of the real and of the symbolic or legal order.

While Jacob Taubes is certainly correct to point out the anthropological value of Paul's gospel, surely Paul's gospel cannot be reduced to a universal Freudian experience of guilt?[61] Turning Paul into Kafka is already a questionable move insofar as it tends to affirm a certain cliché about the Jewish life-world as one determined by guilt, and hence an open invitation to persecution;[62] the bigger question is how wise it is to put Paul on Freud's couch, because this step ignores the biblical mes-

60. Lubac, *Catholicism*, 341.

61. Taubes, *Political Theology*, 88.

62. On this phenomenon, which is explicitly acknowledged by Jewish writers such as George Steiner, for example, see Sagiv, "George Steiner's Jewish Problem," 144–45.

sianic context of Paul, which is not yet expressed through the psycho-analytical prism of a primordial father-son rivalry.[63] Taubes's Freudian gospel, even if getting at something true in human nature, ignores—aside from the larger cosmic dimensions of Paul's gospel—the Pauline harmony of Father and Son. And Taubes's Freudian reading still thrives in psychoanalytic interpretations of Paul and Christianity from Julia Kristeva to Badiou and especially Žižek. Žižek's "Pauline materialism," the idea that Christianity rids us of the big transcendent Other and there-fore fulfills the goal of psychoanalysis, shows two things at once: first, that Freudian or Lacanian readings consistently reduce Christianity to immanence, and second, that this reduction derives from the residual belief characteristic of secularist hermeneutics, namely that traditional Christianity constitutes an abandoning of this world.[64] If not only psy-choanalytical but also deconstructive readings and Lévinasian ethical readings would realize Paul's understanding of the incarnation, either psychoanalytical-Marxist materialism or deconstructive-ethical criti-

---

63. Taubes, *Political Theology*, 92–94. Taubes here cites Freud's *Moses and Monotheism*: "Christianity, having arisen out of a father-religion, became a son reli-gion. It has not escaped the fate of having to get rid of the father." Taubes seems quite convinced that Freud is right: that "[t]he Christian accusation is that of *deicide*." It is on the basis of Freud's work that "only now can an interpretation of Freud be begun—on an entirely new level" (94).

64. Žižek's whole idea is that Christianity gets rid not only of the Father God but of God altogether, since God always sends us off to another world instead of dealing with the concrete realities of this one: "The point of this book is that, at the very core of Christianity, there is another dimension. When Christ dies, what dies with him is the secret discernible in 'Father, why hast thou forsaken me?': the hope that there is a father who has abandoned me. The 'Holy Spirit' is the community deprived of its support of the big Other. The point of Christianity as a religion of atheism is not the vulgar humanist one that the becoming-of-man-of-God reveals that man is the secret of God (Feuerbach et al.); rather, it attacks the religious hard core that survives even in humanism, even up to Stalinism, with its belief in History as the 'big Other' that decides on the 'objective meaning' of our deed" (Žižek, *Puppet and the Dwarf*, 171). Christianity's destiny and actual message is the heroic gesture of self-eradication: "in order to save its treasure, it has to sacrifice itself—like Christ, who had to die so that Christianity could emerge" (ibid.). No matter how benignly one wants to read this as a much needed deconstruction of possibly destructive, ossified cultural forms of Christianity, the "perverse core" of Christianity is ultimately its complete demise, not its constant self-renewal. Christianity is for Žižek a form of psychoanalysis, fulfilling its goal to get rid of the big Other (ibid., 170–71), which seeks to determine and fetter me. There simply is no God after this procedure.

cism could be transformed toward a reading that does more justice to human reality and to a non-secular understanding of religion.

Paul, Politics, and Ethics

Finally, a word on the political subversiveness of Paul's messianism. None of the philosophical readings seems to grasp the complex combination of beliefs that actually motivates Christian dissent in politics. Jacob Taubes's insistence on Paul's elevation of the crucified Messiah over Caesar[65] and on Paul's radical act of founding a new people in Christ[66] comes a lot closer to the theological sources of political dissent than Badiou and Žižek, who turn Paul into a Marxist guerilla fighter gathering fellow revolutionaries. Yet even Taubes misses the "package deal" of Paul's Christology, in which participation in the Messiah links the Christian as a new creation through life in the Spirit to the eschatological realities of the *already* and *not yet* kingdom. In other words, we can't get at the subversive power of Christianity against misappropriated state authority by isolating certain elements of Pauline theology while disregarding his christological religious convictions.

We all too easily forget, for example, that Dietrich Bonhoeffer's political resistance to the Nazi regime was founded on the very unity of incarnation and participation we find in Paul. For Bonhoeffer, Christian existence is defined as participation in the messianic work of God and therefore of universal, historical significance for humanity as a whole. In the incarnation, God becomes human to represent humanity, to affirm it, to judge it, and to renew it, so that henceforth the resurrected Christ defines true humanity as participation in God. This emphasis is found in Bonhoeffer's earliest theological work and persists into his unfinished book on Christian ethics. Stressing the ontological participation in the new humanity of Christ, Bonhoeffer calls the church "Christ existing as community,"[67] the new humanity drawn into communion with God through Christ,[68] and concludes, "The church is nothing but

65. Taubes, *Political Theology*, 24.

66. Ibid., 28.

67. Bonhoeffer, *Sanctorum Communio*, 127. Hereafter abbreviated as *DBW* (*Dietrich Bonhoeffer Werke*) 1.

68. *DBW* 1: 113: "the new human being (*Mensch*), who is drawn into the community of God."

a piece of the new humanity, in which Christ has truly taken shape. . . . The church is the new human being who has been incarnated, judged, and brought to new life in Christ."[69]

Bonhoeffer takes up the Pauline theme of a new humanity and, much like the church fathers, emphasizes the universal or cosmological and social dimensions of Christology. Yet unlike the philosophical readings of Paul under discussion, Bonhoeffer's universal, the new humanity, is neither a human possibility nor an abstract concept, i.e., not a humanistic ideal (*Humanitätsideal*)[70] but an empirical fact of profoundly changing social relations among actual human beings who are drawn into communion with God through Christ by the power of the Holy Spirit. Because of God's reconciliation with humanity through the substitutionary work of Christ, the Spirit transforms social relations by endowing the new creature with the ability to love another above himself.[71] Via participation in Christ, the character of the new humanity's originator, "being-for-another" is imparted to the new creatures in Christ: "The being with each other of the church community and its members through Christ already entails their being for each other. Christ is the measure and standard of our conduct . . . and our actions are the actions of members of the body of Christ, that is, they possess the power of the love of Christ, through which each may and ought to become a Christ to the other."[72]

The church as the new humanity, as the *kainos anthropos,* is enabled by God to exist as one collective person, as an organism that nonetheless maintains the individuality of each member.[73] In *Act*

---

69. *DBW* 6: 84.

70. *DBW* 1: 108. English translation in *Dietrich Bonhoeffer Works 1* (hereafter abbreviated *DBWE*), 167: "Christian love is not a human possibility."

71. *DBW* 1: 111, 112.

72. *DBW* 1: 120 (*DBWE* 1: 182).

73. *DBW* 1: 128: "In all dem ist die Einzeln-Einsamkeit jedes Gliedes nicht aufgehoben." This collective is not, as Bonhoeffer makes clear, based on any kinship of souls or ontological sameness, but rather exists in God's Word by faith and precisely therefore allows the crassest external opposites to dwell in unity. Church unity is not about "agreement in the Spirit" but "unity of Spirit," that is, about the objective unity given in Christ (129). He also repeatedly asserts that this concept of participation has little to do with "mystical union" (*mystischer Verschmelzung*; 197). See also Bonhoeffer's lectures on the church in 1935 for his seminarians: "Die sichtbare Kirche," in *DBW* 14: 435–36.

and Being, Bonhoeffer takes up this conception of "Christ as existing in community," in order to address what he perceives to be the most fundamental problem of modern theology, namely, the inability to correlate revelation and ontology. He solves modern theology's dualistic opposition of being and reflection by defining faith as participation in the new humanity, the *deuteros anthropos*, brought about by the incarnation, death, and resurrection of Jesus the Christ and manifested in the church.[74] the solution to the dualistic opposition of being and reflection he diagnoses as the basic problem of modern theology, namely the inability to correlate revelation and ontology. In his effort to establish an ontological realism in which the Christian participates in God's transcendence without compromising genuine historicity, Bonhoeffer correlates act and being by defining Christian existence as "that historical human being, who knows himself transposed from the old into the new humanity, who is what he is through the membership in the new humanity, a person newly created by Christ."[75]

This participatory quality of Bonhoeffer's christological ontology makes possible two things: First, ontology and revelation, being with and reflection about God, are joined without rift. Unlike Continental philosophy, Bonhoeffer no longer proceeds from the polarity of God and world.[76] Zealotry of the absolute and materialist idolatries of God are equally avoided. Secondly, the self is no longer an isolated ego, but the individual human subject is now linked in Christ to humanity as a whole yet without relinquishing individual personhood.[77]

The connection between the individual Christian, the church as the body of Christ, and humanity as a whole is crucial for Bonhoeffer's universalism. Especially in his Christology lectures, in his final work, *Ethics*, and even in an apparently new phase in Bonhoeffer's "prison"

---

74. *DBW* 2: 108–9. See also *DBW* 4: 232: "The Church is one being. All who are baptized are 'one in Christ' (Gal 3:28; Rom 12:5; 1 Cor 10:17). The church is 'human being.'"

75. *DBW* 2: 117.

76. *DBW* 2: 117 (but also pp. 37 and 38 for stating the problem). Bonhoeffer also emphasizes this in his summary of his habilitation in his inaugural university lecture in 1930. The title of this summary lecture, "Die Frage nach dem Menschen in der gegenwärtigen Philosophie und Theologie," also indicates Bonhoeffer's general focus on the question of human identity. See *DBW* 10: 377.

77. *DBW* 2: 118–19.

theology, the infamous idea of "religionless Christianity,"[78] we find a link between the individual Christian, the church, and the world, through Christ as the recapitulation of humanity and his presence in Christians.

The link between church and world becomes particularly clear in Bonhoeffer's emphasis on the church as an embodiment of the new humanity in terms of the *imago Dei*. The Trinity, argues Bonhoeffer in *The Cost of Discipleship (Nachfolge)*, indwells each believer and therefore constitutes a new human self as part of the collective new humanity: "It is indeed the holy Trinity who dwells within Christians, who permeates them and changes them into the very image of the triune God. The incarnate, crucified, and transfigured Christ takes on form in individuals because they are members of his body, the church. The church bears the incarnate, crucified, and risen form of Christ. Within the body of Christ, we have become 'like Christ.'"[79] Bonhoeffer clearly describes the being of the Christian as participation in Christ: "We are *in him* in the power of his having become human."[80] Christ does not rest, says Bonhoeffer, until he has brought to completion in us the entire form of Christ (*Christusgestalt*), of the one who "has become human, crucified and glorified." It is "in the becoming human of Christ" that the "entire humanity regains the dignity of being made in the image of God (*Gottesebenbildlichkeit*)."[81] The true revelation of the *imago Dei* in Christ now urges upon the Christian to view all of humanity in the light of Christ, thus personalizing and intensifying the ethical imperative already contained in the Old Testament notion of *imago Dei*:

> Whoever from now on attacks the least of the people attacks Christ, who took on human form and who in himself has restored the image of God for all who bear a human countenance. In community with the incarnate one, we are once again given

78. Bonhoeffer argues that Christ's nature is to be in the middle of things, of our existence, of history and of nature, with, obviously, important implications for church-state relations in *DBW* 12: 307. Especially in the sections titled "positive Christology," Bonhoeffer emphasizes the importance of keeping the mystery of the incarnation constantly before us, in order to ensure a proper ecclesial understanding of the new humanity as Christians (*DBW* 12: 340–48).

79. *DBWE 4*: 287.

80. *DBW 4*: 273.

81. *DBW 4*: 301 (*DBWE 4*: 285). Translation slightly altered to emphasize the "becoming human." The translation in *DBWE* has "incarnation" and "incarnate one."

our true humanity. With it, we are delivered from the isolation caused by sin, and at the same time restored to the whole of humanity. Inasmuch as we participate in Christ, the incarnate one, we also have a part in all of humanity, which is borne by him. Since we know ourselves to be accepted and borne within the humanity of Jesus, our new humanity now also consists in bearing the troubles and the sins of all others. The incarnate one transforms his disciples into brothers and sisters of all human beings. . . . The form of the incarnate one transforms the church community into the body of Christ upon which all of humanity's sin and trouble fall, and by which alone these troubles and sins are born.[82]

Bonhoeffer's interpretation of Pauline incarnational Christology led him directly into the resistance against Hitler's regime. Segregation within the church (between Aryans and Jews) and the general dehumanizing of people did not merely offend a sense of honor and virtue but touched the very heart of the evangel. His famous statement, "only he who cries out for the Jews may also sing Gregorian chant," captures the essence of this theology. For the Nazis to reintroduce ethnic distinctions as a barrier to this participation in Christ was in effect to undo God's redemptive work for humanity, of which the church was to be an expression. One doubts that Badiou's eventual rupture, Žižek's self-cancellation of Christianity, or even Taubes's notion of universal guilt provide an equally valid foundation for human action.

Indeed, political life and ethics are most properly founded in Paul's ideas of incarnation and participation. We could do worse than to draw here on Bonhoeffer's notion of the state's divine mandate to uphold the subservience of all spheres of public life to the human dignity affirmed in the Incarnation. The mandates as Bonhoeffer conceives of them observe a fine distinction between state and government and therefore endorse neither statism nor nationalism in the name of faith.[83]

Participation in Christ as the new human being has also been traditionally the source of Christian ethics, defined not principally as rules but as restoration of the divine image in humankind through the indwelling of the Spirit. Ethics, as Bonhoeffer describes it, is not a tem-

---

82. *DBWE* 4: 285.

83. Zerner draws attention to this important point in Bonhoeffer's understanding of church-state relations in her essay "Church, State and the 'Jewish Question,'" 199.

plate of rules but dynamic "Christ-formation" through participation in the one who died for the life of the world. The Christian existence is therefore ontologically structured after Christ as being-for-the-other— not a private experience, but, as N. T. Wright calls it, "living in the new age."[84] When political values turn against humanity, the Christian is called to resist by means of the most humane political means possible. Pauline Christianity as lived by Bonhoeffer, for example, never forgets that this political activity is intrinsically a matter of interpretive discernment, a standing in the midst of the world with Christ; *Nachfolge*, or discipleship, is hermeneutical because it follows the incarnational patterns laid down by God himself.[85]

CONCLUSION

Our hermeneutical assessment of recent Pauline studies by philosophers may be summed up thus: these readings obviously offer penetrating insights that may well sharpen or challenge standard theological readings of this important classical figure in the history of ideas. However, until Pauline theology is allowed to challenge in turn philosophical frameworks that remain committed to psychoanalytical, materialist, Marxist, or other predetermined ways of filtering human experience—in other words, until Paul's thought is allowed to shape secularist hermeneutics rather than being unilaterally shaped by them—the transformative impact of such readings for either philosophy or culture will be negligible and will merely serve to confirm either theological or secularist philosophical readings in their respective positions. That Paul's monotheistic religious vision does not have to signify intolerant bigotry or theocratic fundamentalism, but that, on the contrary, it provides the very basis for a common, universal concept of being human without sacrificing particularity—this possibility will only emerge if philosophy allows itself to be challenged by Pauline theology, which is something that, as far as I can see, has not yet taken place. And yet only such a dialogue could show that Paul's vision, even in secular translation, holds the key to truly human concepts of existence, including the one of such high importance for our time, namely the relation of religion and politics.

84. Wright, *Paul*, 147.

85. This is the gist of Bonhoeffer's description of the Christian life as "Realistic Responsibility" in *Ethics*. See especially *DBWE* 6: 253ff.

CHAPTER 11

On the Exigency of a Messianic Ecclesia:
An Engagement with Philosophical Readers of Paul

by Gordon Zerbe

Introduction

Theodore Jennings Jr., in an essay titled "Paul and Sons"—a title that plays on Jacques Derrida's reflections on proprietary rights to Marx— suggests that there is currently a battle being waged over inheritance rights to Paul.[1] This continues his repeated claim in his earlier book *Reading Derrida/Thinking Paul* (2006), that Paul must be liberated from the imprisoning clutches of his ecclesiastical, theological, and exegetical readers, Paul's so-called "friends."[2]

To be sure, we have the recent claim of Giorgio Agamben that Walter Benjamin has effected the *Aufhebung* of Paul, fulfilled and thereby nullified in a moment of *tornada*, recapitulation—taken out of, even away from, his original context. Agamben's *The Time that Remains* "originates in the conviction that there is a kind of secret link, which we should not miss at any price, between Paul's letters and our epoch. From this perspective, one of the most often read and commented texts of our entire cultural tradition undoubtedly acquires a new readability which displaces and reorients the canons of his interpretation."[3] For his

---

1. Jennings, "Paul and Sons," 85–114.

2. Jennings, *Reading Derrida/Thinking Paul*, 2–4.

3. As cited in Žižek, *Puppet and the* Dwarf, 107, from the back cover of the French edition, which Žižek suspects must have been written by Agamben since it "provides such a precise résumé of the book." Cf. Agamben, *Time that Remains*, 144–45: "this orientation toward the past characteristic of Benjamin's messianism finds its canonic

part, Slavoj Žižek concludes his *The Puppet and the Dwarf* with this claim:

> In what is perhaps the highest example of Hegelian *Aufhebung*, it is possible today to redeem this [subversive, emancipatory] core of Christianity only in the gesture of abandoning the shell of its institutional organization (and, even more so, of its specific religious experience). The gap here is irreducible: either one drops the religious form, or one maintains the form, but loses the essence. That is the ultimate heroic gesture that awaits Christianity: in order to save its treasure, it has to sacrifice itself—like Christ, who had to die so that Christianity could emerge.[4]

At the beginning of the book he asserts, "my claim is not that the subversive kernel of Christianity is accessible also to a materialist approach; my thesis is much stronger: this kernel is accessible *only* to a materialist approach—and vice versa: to become a true dialectical materialist, one should go through the Christian experience." The first thesis of Benjamin is turned around: the puppet called theology can win all the time, if it enlists the service of historical materialism, which today has to stay underground.[5]

Žižek and Agamben, along with Alain Badiou and Jacob Taubes,[6] are examples of recent thinkers who have appropriated Paul into their theoretical undertaking, none on specifically Christian grounds. But their contributions are not just interesting or provocative. They in fact provide considerable potential for Christian theological reflection, offering numerous points of insight, illustration, and even inspiration. That is, Christian readers of Paul need not make any counter territorial claims on Paul. Indeed, the more substantial divide among readers of Paul is one between historicist readers of Paul, who would like Paul imprisoned within the first century, and all those readers who wish to place Paul in the midst of contemporary political and theological

---

moment in Paul"; "these two fundamental messianic texts of our tradition, separated by almost two thousand years, both written in a situation of radical crisis, form a constellation whose time of legibility has finally come today."

4. Žižek, *Puppet and the Dwarf*, 171.

5 Ibid., 3, 6.

6. Badiou, *Saint Paul*; Taubes, *Political Theology*.

discourse, whether interested ecclesially-theologically and/or theoreti-
cally-philosophically (even non-theistically).[7]

What makes dialogue with these four post-Marxist thinkers particularly interesting is that they share with post-Christendom Christian
theology some crucial points of fundamental convergence: (a) a radical
critique of the present world order, including some form of resistance
and dissent, and (b) some notion of the strongly utopian and interruptive, yet non-progressivist hope at the root of the tradition. In this essay
my focus will be on just one aspect of their thought, namely, ecclesial
theory. I will be treating the notion of an ecclesial community not so
much as a mid-point between individual subjectivity and society in
general, even less as an aggregate of those caught up in a new messianic
subjectivity. Rather, it is the question of some midpoint existing in the
tensive polarity between what now exists in the wake of the new revelation and what will or must obtain in the eschatological utopia to which
the revelation witnesses.[8] What, then, is the exigent necessity of the notion of an ecclesial community, whether founded on a new subjectivity
of radical unplugging (Žižek); a truth procedure toward a universal
singularity evident in the militant figure (Badiou); a vision for the coming community, a community of messianic callings, a messianic form
of life (Agamben); or a messianic community that is "free of rule," with
which all oppressed groups can identify (Taubes)? Given this limited
scope, I will be reading these theoreticians as they read Paul, and as
Paul reads his own sacred texts: schematically, selectively, typologically,
and without complete contextual and genealogical regard.

To anticipate our results, the ecclesial thinking of these theorists can
be placed into a three-fold typology, representing options that continue
to entertain radical Christian ecclesial theorists. (1) For Agamben the
messianic community is primarily an abstract aggregate of messianic
callings, a somewhat serendipitous and certainly non-institutional, or
non-boundable reality, a remnant that through auto-suppression only
knows itself as the not-all, conscious of existing only to lose itself in
the fullness (redemption) of the all. (2) In Taubes we find a messianic

7. This was illustrated at the 2005 Syracuse University conference on "Saint Paul
among the Philosophers," where Badiou and Žižek were in attendance. My impression
is shared by Gignac in "Taubes, Badiou, Agamben," 155–211, esp. 200–201, n. 5.

8. For a similar concept, see Epstein, "Politics of Prefigurative Community,"
333–46.

ecclesia that, as an apparently socially identifiable entity, has primarily a representational function, alongside its fundamental task of counter-imperial delegitimation. (3) In Žižek and Badiou the messianic movement or impulse has a more transformational vocation relative to the whole of society, even as it refuses to be characterized by bounded markings other than fundamental fidelity, and even as it seeks to resist both institutionalizing, self-preoccupied, dogmatic or undemocratic betrayals and faulty utopian dreams, while still nourished by utopian notions.

AGAMBEN ON THE MESSIANIC COMMUNITY:
THE ANARCHIC-NIHILISTIC MESSIANIC CALLING

Agamben's *The Time that Remans* is an erudite discourse on numerous themes in Paul's writings, especially in the treatment of the analogous (or homologous) afterlife of these themes in later political-philosophical writers. But while displaying considerable sensitivity to the particularity of Paul's thought itself, the book ultimately paints a Paul assimilated to the thought of Walter Benjamin. As the conclusion to the book makes clear, in Benjamin Paul's messianism has found its "canonic moment," its truest "time of legibility" (144–45)—Paul is the actual invisible (and un-cited) hunchback for Benjamin's historical materialist puppet (138–39).[9]Agamben's ecclesial thinking in *The Time that Remains* continues his earlier treatment of "the coming community," his glad tidings that provide a counterpart to his more pessimistic analysis of the current state of biopolitics, with its foundational violence that separates "naked life" from "form of life" and operates in a perpetual state of exception. Naked life must become form of life (the good life, the happy life, *eudaimonia*) in "the coming community," the coming politics. Crucial elements of this vision include: (a) an emancipation from the division between naked life and form of life, (b) an "irrevocable exodus from any sovereignty," (c) "pure mediality without end intended as the field of human action and of human thought," (d) release from the "figure of the law" as the sole orientation of politics, and (e) a conception of community that does not presuppose commonality, common prop-

---

9. Here and in the remainder of this section on Agamben, parenthetic page number references refer to *The Time that Remains*.

erty or identity as a condition of belonging, but rather allows for the "co-belonging" of "whatever singularities." The "coming community" cannot be a retreat to mystical communion, nor does it entail a nostalgic return to some location of Gemeinschaft. Rather, "form of life" emerges in the very process of exclusion and inclusion that constitutes the biopolitical exception (e.g,. enclosures like the detention camp), and designates an exemplary life through "the impotent omnivalence of whatever beings." It will emerge not in the struggle between states, but in the struggle between the state and humanity as such, heralded by events of "whatever singularity" such as Tiananmen.[10] The Time that Remains, then, represents an articulation of "form of life" in "the coming community" specifically on messianic terms.[11] The messianic life, life in the Messiah, is the answer to the naked life of biopolitics.

Special interest in the notion of a messianic community appears explicitly from the opening pages of The Time that Remains. Seeking to restore Paul as a fundamental messianic text for the Western tradition, he charges that "anti-messianic tendencies were doubtlessly operating within the Church as well as the Synagogue" (1). Both have had an interest in expunging or muting Paul's Jewish messianic thought. He observes: "a messianic institution—or, rather, a messianic community that wants to present itself as an institution—faces a paradoxical task" (1): to have the Messiah either perennially ahead of you, or always behind you, is equally discomforting. The question that is raised, then, is whether or not a messianic community can take on concrete, institutional form without betraying its messianic character and vocation.

---

10. See Agamben, Coming Community, 1–4, 11, 44, 85–86, 107; and Means without End, 3–11, 57–58, 116–17. An interesting treatment of the figuration of humanity at the end of history, in which form of life it will not be possible to isolate bare life as the biopolitical subject, appears in his Open: Man and Animal, a reflection on an image of the messianic banquet of the righteous on the last day (preserved in a thirteenth-century Hebrew Bible) in which the righteous are pictured with animal, not human heads. This opens a reflection on the enigma of the ultimate reconciliation of humans with their animal nature, taking up a Pauline theme of Romans 8:19. The righteous, however, "do not represent a new declension of the man-nature relation," but indicate a zone of non-knowledge that allows them to be outside of being, "saved precisely in their being unsavable" (Open, 92).

11. This is anticipated in his essay "In This Exile," in Means without End, 135–36: "The task that messianism has assigned to modern politics—to this human community that would not have (only) the figure of the law—still awaits the minds that might undertake it."

Agamben identifies the following problematic features that beset "a messianic community that wants to present itself as an institution"[12]:

(1) as an institution, a messianic community becomes preoccupied with a new identity for messianic life, seeking a replacement, not a fundamental transformation (re-vocation), of all worldly vocations, estates and identity;

(2) it begins to claim rights and prerogatives for itself, as the thing in itself;

(3) it organizes itself around codified systems of laws, creating a new law; as such it merely replaces or emulates existing institutions of power;

(4) it is disciplined around systems of right doctrine, exclusively denotative systems of thought for what it believes, hopes, and loves, losing the performative immediacy of these;

(5) it loses its character of auto-suppression and its true vocation of mere instrumentality (pure means, use) for the sake of the all, ultimately betraying its mission on behalf of the all.

Agamben applies this critique in two directions: on the one hand to the church, but also to the (political) party, its secularized double. As for the church: this is what happens when the Messiah is entirely seen in the past, as founder, and not as a critical principle that shatters boundaries in a new constellation (the "Bild" of Benjamin). As he puts it in *Means without End*, "The church has frozen the messianic event, thereby handing the world over to the power of judgment."[13] That is, by losing its true vocation for the all, it has damned the rest of the world. A serious indictment indeed.

The related question is whether or not a political theology can only be negative, negating both a statist political theology (against Carl Schmitt) and its double, an institutionally constituted positive revolutionary political agency or program. Is there any room for a (socially) identifiable, not merely abstract ecclesia under that negation? Is the answer only in a purely "anarchic-nihilistic" messianism, the form of messianism Agamben articulates?

12. Agamben, *Time that Remains*, 1.
13. Ibid., 135.

Messianic Time

For Agamben the crucial framework for conceptualizing a messianic community is in "the very structure of messianic time and the particular conjunction of memory and hope, past and present, plenitude and lack, origin and end that this [messianic time] implies" (1–2). Only after Paul's understanding of messianic time has been appreciated "can we raise the question of how something like a messianic community is in fact possible" (2). Distinguishing sharply between messianism and apocalypse, then, Agamben argues that Pauline messianic time is not the end of time, but the time of the end.

> What interests the apostle is not the last day . . . but the time that contracts itself and begins to end (1 Cor. 7:29), or if you prefer, the time that remains between time and its end. . . . Messianic time, the time in which the apostle lives, the only time that concerns him, is . . . neither chronological time nor the apocalyptic *eschaton*. . . . [It is] the time that remains between these two times, when the division of time is itself divided (62).

A key feature of this time is its form as "recapitulation": "the messianic . . . is a caesura that divides the division between times and introduces a remnant, a zone of undecidability, in which the past is dislocated into the present and the present is extended into the past" (74). Thus it is less oriented to the future, as to the "contraction of past and present," to "the present as the exigency of fulfillment" (76–78).

Features of the Messianic Community

Within this understanding of messianic time, what then are the specific features of the messianic community, the messianic "form of life"? Three critical aspects can be identified.

First, taking his cue from the linguistic correspondence between *klēsis* ("calling," thus "vocation") and *ekklēsia* ("assembly," that which is "called out"), Agamben argues that the Pauline ecclesia is a "is a community of messianic vocations," with an emphasis on the multiplicity of individual messianic subjectivities (31–33). The crucial text for Agamben is 1 Cor 7:17–22, 29–33a, which brings together the notions of *klēsis* ("calling," thus "vocation"), living *hōs mē* ("as not"), "remaining in a calling," and *mallon chrēsai* ("rather make use"). The messianic "as not" constitutes a revocation (in a double sense) and transformation of all juridical and social conditions (identities, estates, vocations, etc.), by undermining them and hollowing them out without altering their form, expropriating them under the form of "usage" and "pure praxis" without possession and ownership (22–42). "The messianic vocation is not a right, nor does it furnish an identity; rather, it is a generic potentiality that can be used without ever being owned" (26). The paradigmatic case is Onesimus, who, while remaining a slave, is *hyper doulon* ("more than a slave"), for Agamben a "super slave" (Phlm 16; pp. 13, 29).

Furthermore, aware of the arbitrariness and gratuitousness of one's condition (31), the subject (and thus the messianic community) lives by auto-suppression, in that the subject's complete redemption coincides with his/her complete loss (Rom 6:6; 8:11; p. 31). The entire subject is both dislocated and nullified in the messianic vocation (Gal 2:20; p. 41). In connection with this notion, and in response to the possible charge that his conception of the messianic calling may imply nothing more than a "mental reserve," a "Marranism,"[14] Agamben (following Benjamin) emphasizes that the prime modality of the messianic vocation is "exigency," in particular the exigency of the lost, oppressed, and defeated (39–42). This "weak" messianic modality involves an "assimilation to what has been lost and forgotten" (1 Cor 1:26–28; 4:13) "on both the collective and individual levels," and is expressed as a "groaning" along with the caducity (*mataitēs*) of all creation (Rom 8:20–22, 28; pp. 40–41): "the capacity to remain faithful to that which having perpetually been forgotten, must remain unforgettable" (39). Insofar as

14. In this connection, Agamben, in *Time that Remains*, identifies three non-messianic interpretations of the Pauline "as not": (a) as eschatological "indifference" to the world, as proposed by Max Weber (20–22); (b) the model of Christendom, in which the "as not" is merely a mental reserve, a spiritualist indifference that is really an affirmation of dominant politics (33); and (c) various philosophical modes of discourse in modernity (including Heidegger, Adorno, Kant, Forberg, Hegel, structuralism, deconstructionism, and Derrida) that imply some form of Stoic mental reserve and detachment, and at worst suggest an acquiescence and accommodation to the world as it is (33–39). Agamben is especially antagonistic to the transformation of the "as not" into an "as if," the reduction of religion and ethics into the mere embrace of fiction. Agamben is not so much worried about the matter of whether or not the messianic claim might be fiction as such; rather, he is more concerned about the ecclesial-political consequence of such a position. Such an approach is unable to "conceive of restoring possibility to the fallen," and contrasts with Paul's own claim that "power is actualized in weakness" (2 Cor 12:9) (38).

this especially backward-looking assimilation is absolute, the question of "presumed identities and ensuing properties" is finally settled (41). Indeed, any move to organize or institutionalize a messianic community, even (and especially) for purposes of constituting a vanguard, is to create something "distinct" from the real "community of messianic vocations" (even though pretending to coincide with it) and constitutes one of its most serious betrayals (33).[15]

Second, the messianic community is marked by a separation that fundamentally negates other separations, including its own, through the notion of the remnant, which is ever situated as a "not-all."[16] Applying this to the concepts of a people, democracy and the proletariat (57–58), and sharply critical of Badiou's universalism,[17] Agamben emphasizes that the remnant is in constant tension with the all:

15. In this framework, Agamben, in *Time that Remains*, admits that Marx's original rendering of the Pauline "as not" is truly messianic, in that it rejects the individual-political disjunction, positing the coincidence of individual revolt and political revolution through the vehicle of the proletariat. In this case, the fulfillment of individual and egoist need coincides with a political revolution. Crucial is the idea of the redemptive function of the proletariat, which in itself incarnates the split between the individual and his social figure under capitalism; the revolution aims toward the dissolution of all estates, but only through the auto-suppression of the proletariat. But this view necessarily founders by the aporia created by the party, namely in the notion of the working class or of the vanguard as the embodiment or vehicle for the dictatorship of the proletariat (31–33): (1) The identification of the proletariat with the working class is a most serious betrayal of Marx; for Marx this is only a strategic identification, "a historical figure contingent on the proletariat." (2) There is the theoretical problem of the party as identical to the working class while simultaneously different from it: that is, if ego need and social revolution coincide, why is a party needed? (3) There is the problem of organization, with the inevitable introduction of rule and its discipline. The party acknowledges that it is distinct from the messianic community, and yet pretends to coincide with it. (4) The organization inevitably succumbs to "right theory" as its criterion for inclusion, with resulting claims of infallibility, and necessary purges. (5) As a true and proper social identity which claims prerogatives and rights for itself, it is no longer a "historical figure contingent on the proletariat" and loses its revolutionary vocation. It establishes a rule and a law, that emulates the very rule of that which it seeks to oppose. For Agamben, then, any form of organizational vanguardism inevitably betrays the messianic.

16. According to Agamben, Paul negates other separations "in the name of another separation that is no longer a separation according to the *nomos*, but a separation according to the messianic proclamation" (*Time that Remains*, 46). Insofar as the law operates primarily in instituting divisions and separations, the messianic community is comprised of the division of the division (47).

17. Agamben rejects Badiou's conception of Paul that there is a universalism above

> [T]he remnant is closer to being a consistency or figure that
> Israel assumes in relation to election or to the messianic event.
> It is therefore neither the all, nor a part of the all, but the impos-
> sibility for the part and the all to coincide with themselves or
> with each other. *At a decisive instant, the elected people, every*
> *people, will necessarily situate itself as a remnant, as not-all.* (55,
> emphasis original)

Drawing especially on Romans 11, Agamben asserts that the remnant
is "not any kind of numeric portion or substantial positive residue;" it
is rather a division "without ever reaching any final ground" (50–52).
Moreover, the remnant "functions as a very peculiar kind of soteriological machine. . . , not so much the object of salvation as its instrument." It "is precisely what prevents divisions from being exhaustive
and excludes the parts and the all from the possibility of coinciding
with themselves." Nevertheless, the remnant "only concerns messianic
time and only exists therein. In the *telos*, when God will be 'all in all'
(Rom 11:36; 1 Cor 15:28), the messianic remnant will not harbour any
particular privilege and will have exhausted its meaning in losing itself
in the *plērōma* [fullness]" (56).

Third, the messianic life and vocation, and thereby the messianic
community, is marked by the de-activation (*katargēsis, Aufhebung*)
of *nomos*. The messianic "state of exception," is never an occasion for
assimilation to state power (107–9), and is instead characterized by a
"tendentious lawlessness" (111). The messianic state of exception returns to the conditions of pre-law, and entails (a) a contraction of the
law, marked by an indeterminacy between inside and outside, an un-
observability, and an unformulability; (b) a recapitulation in the figure
of love (108); (c) an orientation toward gratuity, with fidelity as the
instance of the justice of the law; and (d) a "form of life," a community,
not a new text with dogma, as the instantiation of the new covenant
(2 Cor 3:2; p. 122). Taking an analogy from Franciscan thought, he
observes that what mattered was "to create a space that escaped the
grasp of power and its laws, without entering into conflict with them
yet rendering them inoperative. . . . They implicitly put forth the idea
of a *forma vivendi* that was entirely subtracted from the sphere of the
law" (27).

---

the cuts and divisions; for Agamben the universal will always be a remnant in messianic time (*Time that Remains*, 51–53).

As a counterpart to the *Aufhebung* of law, the messianic community is marked by a recovery of "faith" in its performative, not denotative functions (113–37). This means a rejection of "codified systems of norms and articles of faith," and of the "juridicizing of all human relations," whether in law or in religion (135). It is in the in the performative dimension of what we may believe, hope and love that "language suspends its own denotation" (133). In the experience of the "nearness of the word," a divided faith is re-established, restored (135). Just as importantly, in the experience of "pure word" we have (through revocation and usage) "the act of a potentiality that fulfills itself in weakness." As oriented to the pure power of saying, "messianic power finds its *telos* in weakness" (2 Cor 12:9–10; 1 Cor 1:27), against all formulation of dogma, accumulation of knowledge, denotative propositions, and desire for efficacy (136–37).

Assessment

Agamben's construction of Paul is particularly insightful for Christian ecclesial reflection in the caution against betrayals implicit in "institutionalizing," the emphasis on messianic weakness evident in the assimilation to the lost and forgotten (in both an intellection and sociopolitical sense), and the notion of the ecclesia primarily as a remnant aware of itself only as "not-all" and as mere instrument for the redemption of the all through which it ultimately loses itself (in the same manner as for Christian reflection the church is ultimately absorbed into the reign of God).

But one should also identify some significant demurrers, beginning with Agamben's notion of messianic time, which is crucial for his understanding of the ecclesial calling and community. It is quite true that contracted time is the time in which the apostle claims to live: to use terms of J. Christiaan Beker, it is the proleptic realization of the telic triumph of God inaugurated in the resurrection.[18] But it is certainly mistaken to suggest that this is the only time that "concerns" or "interests" him. There remains in Paul an undeniable eschatological passion, for the imminent, inexorable, and universal arrival of the reign of God, as discomforting as that may be. There is a polarity in Paul which

18. Beker, *Paul the Apostle*, 135–81, 303–49.

precludes a favoring of the contraction of time between resurrection and *parousia* over against the vision of the arrival of the *telos* itself. The notion of the *telos* (end/goal) itself is crucial to Paul's messianism. As J. Taubes puts it, apocalypse renders the inexorable end of history to be "not in an indeterminate future, but entirely proximate."[19]

Clearly what is at stake for Agamben, and many others since the big non-event of the *parousia* (or the communist utopia), is that any focus on the final *eschaton* immediately signals a perpetual deferment of the messianic, "in which nothing can be achieved" (69, citing G. Scholem's disenchantment with utopian messianism).[20] The inevitable and implicit delay in any future-oriented eschatological hope "renders unreachable the end that it supposedly produces" (70).

This matter of coming to terms with Paul's eschatological vision continues to cause stumbling. As many before him, Agamben is forced to come up with a form of iteratively realized eschatology, via Benjamin. He embarks on a significant reinterpretation of *parousia* as messianic "presence," against any implicit deferment: messianic time is "operational time pressing within the chronological time," a time that "may even interrupt secular time here and now" (73). Thus the *parousia* simply becomes "each instant" when the Messiah might pass though the door, an assimilation to the last thesis of Benjamin.[21]

Certainly the notion of the realization of an eschatological moment should be harnessed, as should the notion that the reign of God appears in moments little recognized, outside the social or temporal boundaries of what is supposed to be, or supposed to happen. Yet, to lose hold of a firm grasp toward the final, exigent vision of cosmic recreation is also troubling. But there is a crucial nub here: Agamben is not the only one who hesitates in the face of the millennial utopian anticipation. Indeed, the true scandal of Paul's thought for us is not just its cruciform character, but the unrealized and apparently unrealizable *eschaton* (at least for Western thought, whether Christian or Marxist).[22]

19. Taubes, *Abendländische Eschatologie*, 10; cited in Gold, "Jacob Taubes," 155.

20. Scholem, *Messianic Idea*, 1–36.

21. Agamben, *Time that Remains*, 70–71, 100.

22. The disenchantment with thoroughgoing eschatology seems closely correlated with a comfortable political-social location, but also with a concomitant capitulation to a progressivist, immanentist consciousness of nature's necessity and cycles. For

To anticipate remarks below, in contrast to Agamben, J. Taubes maintains a more robust consistent apocalyptic eschatology as the framework for his delegitimation of sovereignty and law and his world-nihilism,[23] and Žižek resists the collapsing of the *not yet* into the "actualizable" (claiming to favor a Christian eschatological version compared to the Judaic); and even Badiou maintains a more positive attitude toward Paul's thoroughgoing eschatological comportment. Meanwhile, among Christian theologians, J. C. Beker proposes that Paul's thoroughgoing apocalyptic must be embraced in the midst of its mythological and apparently obscurantist character, resisting a collapsing of eschatology into Christology, via spiritualization and/or by institutionalization (and salvation-history solutions).[24]

Furthermore, by privileging 1 Cor 7:29–32 as Paul's "most rigorous definition of the messianic life" (23), an assertion which surely can be contested, Agamben is able to sustain the argument that the messianic vocation can never constitute a new identity, but instead only hollows out existing ones (by both destroying and using them). Thus in Agamben, not only does the messianic absorb eschatology, but in addition the notion of the messianic vocation absorbs any notion of an ecclesia with any concrete shape. Even the discussion on justice as a prime marker of the ecclesia is very much muted (107, 120). Not surprisingly, Žižek complains that in Agamben's Pauline theory we have little more than formalism.[25]

For Agamben, the messianic calling does not have its own positive content, but is what happens in the revocation of all worldly, secular conditions, especially those determined juridically. Agamben emphasizes that the messianic vocation can never constitute any new identity (other than a nullification of existing ones), because otherwise one immediately goes down the path of the pursuit of privilege, prerogatives, and rights. But as a result of the privileging of the messianic primarily as a form of negation, and by limiting himself to 1 Corinthians 7, not only does the messianic vocation have no specific positive content, but in addition there is no vocation for the messianic community as a cor-

---

an appropriation of the Pauline (Christian) millennial vision in Filipino theology of struggle, see Zerbe, "Constructions of Paul."

23. Taubes, *Political Theology*, 53.

24. Beker, *Paul the* Apostle, 135–81, 303–49.

25. Žižek, *Puppet and the Dwarf*, 109–13.

porate body, apart from being in general an "instrument of salvation." Agamben does not know of the Pauline "calling" to be a consecrated and distinct people of character ("holy": Rom 1:7; 1 Cor 1:12; cf. 1 Thess 4:7), the "calling" to an alternative dominion (1 Thess 2:12; Phil 3:14; cf. 1 Cor 1:9) and a mental transformation toward its imperatives (Rom 8:28; Rom 12:1–2) and toward the animation of justice (Rom 6:13, 15–23), the "calling" to express the realities of freedom and peace (Gal 5:13; 1 Cor 7:15), the "calling" to be in one body (Col 3:15), nor finally the "calling" that involves being known (identified) by attachment to Messiah Jesus in particular (1 Cor 1:7, 9; cf. Rom 9:24–26).

It should also be observed that Agamben's use of the Onesimus paradigm does not correspond with Paul's own imperative to Philemon in regard to Onesimus. Onesimus is not a model of the one who is to "remain" in a hollowed out juridical condition as a "super slave." Paul actually uses the phrase "more than a slave" (*hyper doulon*) to describe how Onesimus will be valuable to his present owner in his new status "no longer as a slave," precisely "in the flesh" (Phlm 16), that is, as a consequence of his manumission, which Paul clearly advises while not saying so directly in the letter. The letter to Philemon thus stands in a certain tension with 1 Corinthians 7, not as providing its paradigmatic case.

It is certainly a significant corrective to 2,000 years of Christian history and identity formation to emphasize that Paul promotes the displacement of all identity privileging through the messianic. But what is missing is at least a counterpart acknowledgment that in Paul the messianic vocation fundamentally involves a loyalty that necessarily involves some form of positive corporate politics. For instance, Paul's thesis in Philippians is this: "collectively practice your citizenship, practice your politics, singularly according to the glad announcement [*euangelion*] of the Messiah" (Phil 1:27). This thesis is then unpacked decisively in terms of the corporate life of the assembly, both in its kenotic-cruciform aspects (1:27—2:9; 3:2–10) but also in its corresponding universal-cosmic dimensions (2:9–11; 3:11–21). The messianic fidelity is thus oriented to a "dominion in heaven" (3:20), which undermines identity formation both via ethnic particularities (3:2–14) and via a consumerist, ascendant, triumphalist, coercive and statist universalism (3:18–21), since the orientation of a heavenly dominion means immediately that the one loyal to the messianic announcement is a global, cosmic citizen (3:21–21; 2:9–11). Fidelity is not simply hollowed out of identity, but redirected in God's love story of reclaiming a creation toward the establishment of full justice, peace, and *eudaimonia*,[26] that is, toward the good life, as embodied proleptically in a community of those whose fidelity is founded gratuitously on the fidelity of the Messiah himself (with messianic fidelity being the prototype of all subsequent fidelity).[27]

JACOB TAUBES: A REPRESENTATIONAL ECCLESIA

While Agamben claims Taubes as the prime exemplar of his "anarchic-nihilistic" appropriation of Paul's messianism, some elaboration of Taubes's own views is appropriate to nuance this matter. While Taubes rightly rejects the sovereignty of the historical reading of a text, the legacy of Spinoza, his own reading of Paul, as expressed in his 1987 Heidelberg lectures but also in his earlier work,[28] is certainly the most historically sympathetic and plausible among the so-called philosophical readings of Paul. He quite naturally understands Paul both within his Judaic context and in the context of the legacy of imperial assault on that community. In other words, he naturally thinks from below, worried more about any chaos from above than chaos from below (142).[29] There are two distinct aspects to Paul's political theology according to Taubes: on the one hand, what can be described as a "negative political theology,"[30] and on the other, a positive form, focused on an alternative community formation. Taubes specifically reads Romans "politically" as opposed to "existentially," as evident from the syllabus title for a course on Romans: "On the Political Theology of Paul: From Polis to Ecclesia." He interprets Romans "as the legitimation and formation of a new social union-covenant [*Ver-Bund*], of the developing ecclesia against the Roman Empire, on the one hand, and on the other hand,

26. Cf. Rom 14:17; Paul's word for *eudaimonia* is *chara*, joy.

27. E.g., Hays, *Faith of Jesus Christ*.

28. Taubes's basic line of approach to Paul is already evident in his 1947 doctoral dissertation, *Abendländische Eschatologie*. See Gold, "Jacob Taubes," 140–56, n. 48 for citation of essays that discuss influences on Taubes's reading of Paul.

29. Here and in the remainder of this section on Taubes, parenthetic page references refer to *The Political Theology of Paul*.

30. Terpstra and de Wit, "No Spiritual Investment," 320–53.

of [against] the ethnic unity of the Jewish people" (117).Thus Taubes does not reject political theology as such, only a positive political theology (along with Karl Barth, against Carl Schmitt). According to Marin Terpstra and Theo de Wit, Taubes recognizes that Paul seeks a more radical intervention than either establishing a sound political system or attempting to replace one through revolution. Rather, Paul seeks "a theological *delegitimation* of all political power [including that of the church] as a *political* attitude."[31] In *The Political Theology of Paul*, Taubes argues that Romans opens and closes with a messianic declaration of war on Caesar (13–16), and that Paul's attack on the law is not anti-Judaic polemic, but part of his assault on the use of law as ordering power in any sovereignty, whether political, churchly, or natural (23). According to W-D. Hartwich, A. Assmann and J. Assmann (the editors of his lectures on Paul), Taubes understands that because Paul's political theology has no positive form as such, it can be claimed and identified with by all oppressed groups.[32]

At the same time, a crucial issue for Paul is "the establishment and legitimation of a new people of God" (28, 40). Paul's apocalyptic anarchism is of a particular sort: messianic sovereignty can only be represented in a people, and a crucial mark of the alternative community is that it must be "free of rule" (*Herrshaftsfrei*), oriented sociologically as opposed to cratologically.[33] Taubes rejects both a privatization of the messianic, and a supposed Pauline quietism that endorses the prevailing political order. Romans 13 has a purely pragmatic occasion, that of mere survival; its apparent acquiescence is a function of an apocalyptic nihilism that refuses to engage in open warfare but also refuses to grant legitimacy and ultimate obedience to any political regime (54).[34] The ecclesia is thus a third type of community formation alongside and in opposition to both the ethnic community and the Roman imperial order. He calls this a "new union," a "new intimacy" (52), a "community of solidarity" (*Solidaritätsgemeinschaft*), or a "kinship of the promise"

---

31. Ibid., 324 (emphasis original). They argue that Taubes is equally against an imperialistic secularism, which resists the incursion of political theology in the world, and against a political theology on behalf of the ruling order (Schmitt), but not against all political theology.

32. Hartwich, "Afterword," 121–22.

33. Ibid., 140–41.

34. On this two-fold refusal, see further Gold, "Jacob Taubes," 142–50.

(28). An alternative conception of universalism emerges with the messianic, one that signifies "the election of Israel," but nevertheless an Israel "transfigured" as an inclusive "all Israel" that is open to all who obey the commandment to love the neighbour (24–25, 41, 52–53). This universalist orientation for a transfigured "all Israel" is based on fidelity to and "faith in" the Messiah, a paradoxical faith that is contradicted by the evidence and yet brings "a total and monstrous inversion of the values of Roman and Jewish thought" (6–10).

The two primary constituting principles of the ecclesia are *pneuma* and *agapē*, in both its forms as love of neighbour (Rom 13:8–10) and as love of the enemy (Rom 11:28–32; Taubes, 25, 41–49).[35] *Pneuma* is completely contrary to Hegel's notion of the immanent *Geist* (38–43), but is instead "a force that transforms a people and that transforms the text" (45). And, as Taubes's editors put it, *Geist* represents a logic that goes beyond the natural order of the given and is "the decisive category for transcending the continuity and the normative claim of the tradition and the ethnic limits of the people of God."[36]

J. Gold observes that these themes are already evident in Taubes's *Abendländische Eschatologie*, his doctoral dissertation of 1947. In that work Taubes claims that Paul envisions a collective whose members "have freed themselves from all natural, organic attachments—from nature, art, cult, and state—and for whom emptiness and alienation from the world, as well as the separation with secularism, accordingly reached a high degree."[37] Paul sees a hitherto unknown spiritual nation coming into existence, one based on "the *pneumatic We*," a community that rejects all legal-political determinations of identity (state, law, etc.). "In contrast to the old, fully-grown attachments, the Messianic community (*Gemeinde*) is an inorganic, subsequent, 'pneumatic' togetherness (*Zusammensein*) of individuals."[38]

In general terms, one might observe that in contrast to Agamben (and Benjamin) Taubes admits to Paul's consistent, thoroughgoing eschatology, and does not seek to absorb it completely into the

---

35. For Paul there is only *one* love commandment, "an absolutely revolutionary act" relative to the powers that be, not a dual commandment as in the Jesus tradition (Taubes, *Political Theology*, 53). See also Hartwich, "Afterword," 128–31.

36. Hartwich, "Afterword," 128.

37. Cited in Gold, "Jacob Taubes," 153; from *Abendländische Eschatologie*, 64.

38. Gold, "Jacob Taubes," 153.

messianic;[39] nor does he collapse the messianic community completely into the aggregate of messianic callings. Taubes's ecclesia in fact looks much like that of John Howard Yoder, in its primarily representational function and in the refusal to grant it much of a transformational role (relative to society's public politics) other than that of "witness" (cf. the primacy of delegitimation of all rule in Taubes).[40]

Slavoj Žižek and Alain Badiou: A (Cautiously) Vanguard Ecclesia

Similar to Taubes, and also in contrast to those who read the Pauline *not yet* as denoting eschatological "indifference" to the world, there are those who not only emphasize the apocalyptic-eschatological component in Paul's thought, but also refuse to understand this as resulting necessarily in a passivity that preempts some form of political presence in the world. Indeed, it is proposed that active working is sustained precisely by this very eschatological passion. Žižek and Badiou (for different reasons) represent such a view, analogously very close to the ecclesial reading of Paul by Pauline scholar J. Christiaan Beker, who likens the Pauline ecclesia to the "avant-garde" in service of (and modelling) the "reign of God."[41] Thus, in contrast to the "anarchic-nihilistic"

39. Ibid., 142, 144, 148–51, shows that in his earlier *Abendländische Eschatologie*, Taubes includes as chief marks of (Pauline) apocalyptic (a) a modality of interpretation—reading (the signs of the times) and speaking (witnessing); (b) the interiorization of the Messianic via *pneuma* (in a manner parallel to, but distinct from Gnosticism); (c) the conferral of significance to the act of decision in the context of distress, versus capitulation to necessity, cycle, and inevitability; and (d) an eschewing of both the temptation to force the course of events, and the retreat to a passive comportment, against the self-immolating flames of eschatological intensity.

40. E.g., Yoder, *Politics of Jesus*. For Yoder's treatment of Paul's ecclesial themes, see also Harink, *Paul among the Postliberals*, 105–49.

41. Beker, *Paul the Apostle*, 135–81, 303–49. Crucial to Beker's approach to Paul is the thoroughgoing embrace of Paul's apocalypticism as the critical carrier and center of his thought. If there is a problem of social conservatism in Paul, it is not one of fundamental theory, but instead, one of failure of nerve. There is certainly in Beker a more heightened interest in the "transformative vocation" of the messianic community in the rest of society than in pure alternative community formation and the delegitimation of all sovereignty (as compared to Taubes and Agamben). Beker specifically resists the collapsing of futurist eschatology in the church into either spiritualization and/or a salvation-history oriented ecclesiologizing and institutionalizing, as occurred especially under the influence of Origen and Augustine (ibid., 139), though admittedly

appropriation that appears to be Agamben's own, and to the more purely representational notion of an ecclesia in Taubes, the ecclesial theory of these interpreters comes closer to the Marxian notion of the coincidence of the political and the subjective, and its consequential vanguardism. That is, they display a much more optimistic view of the transformative role and power of the messianic community relative to the all or the utopia. Not surprisingly, then, both Žižek and Badiou are quite comfortable with the Paul-Lenin analogy.[42] At the same time, however, they observe grave dangers when any vanguard ceases to see itself as provisional and contingent.

I will not seek to contextualize fully Žižek's ecclesial thinking, except to say he is certainly interested in making radical Christianity and historical materialism allies on the same side of the barricade. Against Badiou's formalism, he wishes any historical materialist also to go through the "Christian experience," that is, to reckon with its substantive logic. He similarly finds Agamben's messianism not sufficiently engaged with the substance of Christian (Pauline) thought, and leaning toward a formalism.[43] And while he invites Christianity to heroically lose itself in order to save its treasure, he does appear to offer some positive role for certain forms of Christianity.[44] It is in the subversive

---

underway already in the NT: "The vocation of the church is not self-preservation for eternal life but service to the created world in the sure hope of the world's transformation at the time of God's final triumph" (313). "If God's coming reign will establish an order of righteousness that encompasses the created order (Rom. 8:19–21), and if the Pauline hope is not to be identified with a Gnostic discontinuity between the material and the spiritual (so that the material will simply perish and is therefore 'indifferent'), then one would expect that the church as the blueprint and beachhead of the kingdom of God would strain itself in all its activities to prepare the world for its coming destiny in the kingdom of God. . . . If the world is to be the scene of the "worship" of the Christian, then the church exists for the world in the world. Unless this is true, the sighing of the Christian for the redemption of the world (Rom. 8:19–21) is simply reduced to a faint ecclesial whisper" (326–27).

42. E.g., Žižek, *Fragile Absolute*, 2.

43. Žižek, *Puppet and the Dwarf*, 108.

44. E.g., ibid., 3: "One possible definition of modernity is: the social order in which religion is no longer fully integrated into and identified with a particular cultural life-form, but acquires autonomy, so that it can survive as the same religion in different cultures. This extraction enables religion to globalize itself . . . ; on the other hand, the price to be paid is that religion is reduced to a secondary epiphenomenon with regard to the secular functioning of the social totality. In this new global order, religion has two possible roles: *therapeutic* or *critical*. It either helps individuals to function better

form of Christian thought and practice that he has some hope, and he finds considerable homology between Christian messianic thought and revolutionary process.[45]

In further contrast to Agamben, Žižek emphasizes the more activist strain of Christian apocalyptic messianism: the arrival of the Messiah implies "the urge to act"; messianic "arrival functions as a signal which triggers activity," in accordance with the conclusion, "we must help God."[46] As such, Christian messianism is to be distinguished, in his view, from passive forms in Judaism (echoing Scholem's admission that in Judaism, forms of messianism tend toward the passive variety). Moreover, he appears unsatisfied with the anarchic-nihilistic version of politics, especially with any posture that does not exhibit a clear positive political project.[47] Indeed, Žižek appears to accept some notion of vanguardism more readily than Agamben, although the true revolutionary needs equally to be concerned about the cure of the soul through Lacanian psychoanalysis.[48]

The Community of the "Holy Spirit"

Žižek's ecclesial thinking is expressed succinctly at the conclusion of *The Fragile Absolute*. In opposition to both the "ghost of the past" (whether fundamentalisms, traditionalist religion, or communitarianism, all metaphored by the Balkans) and to the "spectral ghost of the capitalist present," there still comes

---

in the existing order, or it tries to assert itself as a critical agency articulating what is wrong with this order as such, a space for the voices of discontent—in this second case, religion *as such* tends toward assuming the role of a heresy." That is, "heresy" especially related to state- or society-demanded orthodoxy.

45. Ibid., 133–34.

46. ibid., 136.

47. Žižek, *Ticklish Subject*, 171–72. He expresses an equal distaste for traditionalist communitarians (Taylor), universalists (Rawls, Habermas), and postmodern "dispersionists," all of whom share a reduction of the political.

48. While Žižek is sympathetic to Badiou's attempt to argue for a conception of universality in opposition to both a capitalist globalism and communitarian logic, he rejects Badiou's claim that Lacanian psychoanalysis is unable to provide the foundation for a new political practice (see *Ticklish Subject*, 3, 127–244). For his engagement with Agamben, see esp. *Puppet and the Dwarf*, 107–21, 134.

the brief apparition of a future utopian Otherness to which every authentic revolutionary stance should cling. . . . the third
modality of ghosts is none other than the Holy Ghost itself, the
community of believers *qua* 'uncoupled' outcasts from the social order—with, ideally, authentic psychoanalytic and revolutionary political collectives as its two main forms.[49]

Crucial to Žižek's ecclesiology, then, is the Lacanian notion of the Holy
Spirit.[50] For Žižek, the Holy Spirit replaces God as the transcendent
"big Other." Through divine self-limitation God in effect assures the
reality of the Holy Spirit as the symbolic community immanent in the
world. "The 'Holy Spirit' is the community deprived of its support in
the big Other."[51] This means that the subject is deprived of all structures of social legitimation or support, including overtly theological
ones. For Christianity, this includes the repudiation of its "institutional
organization"—in order to save its treasure, it has to sacrifice itself.[52]

The Gesture of Separation: Uncoupling

Christian logic as exemplified by Paul, then, calls for the emergence
of an "alternative community": a subjectivity and a collectivity "un-
plugged" and "uncoupled" from the social order, from the balance of
the All, from the organic community, from the domain of established
social mores, and from the social structure of our being.[53] And this unplugging assumes a radical subjective conversion, involving the freeing
of subjects from superego, libidinal, and spectral-ideological domination, and thus from the commodity-fetishism associated with the political and economic order. The unplugging can never be reduced to an
"inner contemplative stance" which nonetheless supports participation

49. Žižek, *Fragile Absolute*, 160.

50. For a definition, see Žižek, *Puppet and the Dwarf*, 9–10.

51. Ibid., 171.

52. Žižek does not resolve the problem of how the immanent Holy Spirit can
keep itself from becoming merely another big Other. While certainly suspicious of
the Marxian notion of the communist utopia (insofar as it is founded on the notion
of unbridled productivity and the notion of a balanced, self-restrained society), and
certainly wary of the possible co-opting of the revolution by the party, he still maintains a decisive place for the transformative vocation of an emerging revolutionary
community.

53. Žižek, *Puppet and the Dwarf*, 118–21; *Fragile Absolute*, 128–29.

in the social game. The uncoupling from the hierarchy of the social order means that it will be treated as fundamentally irrelevant; indeed, it
moves the subject in an Other space, but is nevertheless not escapist.[54]
Žižek certainly sides with Agamben in asserting that 1 Corinthians 7 is
by no means a "legitimation of the existing power conditions"; rather,
it represents an ignoring of distinctions not relevant to the struggle, as
characteristic of any "thoroughly engaged fighter."[55]

In particular, it is the "the active *work* of love which necessarily
leads to the creation of an *alternative* community."[56] It is love that enjoins the gesture of separation, calling us to "unplug from the organic
community into which we were born."[57] The alternative community is
founded on the prototypical act of love in the event of Jesus, through
its primordial and disruptive violence. Yet, this uncoupling contrasts
with a Fascist carnivalesque unplugging from the established symbolic
rules: *"the proper Christian uncoupling suspends not so much the explicit
laws but, rather, their implicit spectral obscene supplement."*[58]

The All and the Part

This alternative community (the part) has a complex relationship with
the all: the alternative community exists only for the all, the whole that
it longs for. Hence crucial to the separation is also the gesture of recognizing the insignificance of the part relative to the whole. While this
may sound similar to Agamben's criticism of vanguardism, Žižek is not
entirely comfortable with Agamben's notion of dividing the division.
He queries in response to Agamben, "What if the only way to invest a
new universality is precisely through overcoming the old divisions with
a new, more radical division which introduces an indivisible remainder
into the social body?"[59] Taking up the notion of the "remnant," he promotes the motto of the proletarian revolution: "We were nothing, we
want to become All." From the perspective of redemption, the remnant

---

54. Žižek, *Fragile Absolute*, 120, 158–59.
55. Žižek, *Puppet and the Dwarf*, 111–12; *Fragile Absolute*, 129.
56. Žižek, *Fragile Absolute*, 129 30 (emphasis original).
57. Ibid., 121.
58. Ibid., 130 (emphasis original).
59. Žižek, *Puppet and the Dwarf*, 108.

counts as nothing within the established order: "it is irrevocably lost, thrown into nothingness." Yet "the remainder of this order, its part of no part, will become All."[60]

Eschatological Passion:
"the brief apparition of a future utopian Otherness"

Žižek argues further, in homology with Christian messianic apocalypticism, that the revolutionary (ecclesial) process must retain an eschatological passion. True eschatological messianism has an activist strain. He cites Rosenzweig approvingly: "The future is no future without this anticipation and the inner compulsion for it, without this 'wish to bring about the Messiah before his time' and the temptation to 'coerce the kingdom of God into being'; without these, it is only a past distended endlessly and projected forward."[61] Moreover, this action cannot wait for the "right moment," but involves constant risk taking on its behalf. Revolutionary time proper cannot be translated into objective historical time, with clearly identified phases and transitions between phases. It is only through premature attempts that the subjective conditions for the right moment might come. As a result, "in an authentic revolution, predestination overlaps with radical responsibility"; the real, earnest work begins after the initial eschatological event.[62]

ALAIN BADIOU: EVENTAL TRUTH OF UNIVERSAL SINGULARITY AND PAUL THE MILITANT FIGURE

In contrast to the three previous authors, Badiou's book on Paul displays no overt interest in ecclesial theory. What interests Badiou is Paul as the exemplar of his theory of universalism, and the subjective figure of the true militant. Paul is the prime and foundational illustration of a "truth procedure" toward universality in an "evental site" (22).[63] Nevertheless,

60. Ibid., 133.

61. Ibid.; citing Rosenzweig, Star of Redemption, 227.

62. Žižek, Fragile Absolute, 135.

63. Here and in the remainder of the chapter, parenthetic page references refer to Badiou's Saint Paul. For the notion of evental truth, see further Badiou, Being and Event. "Truth procedures" apply to the domains of politics, art, science, and love, but not to religion-theology.

he still offers some explicitly ecclesial comments, and moreover, as I will argue, there is an ecclesiology implied in his presentation of modes of discourse and subjective positions appropriate to them (albeit, certainly a purely formal one, as is his figure of the militant individual).

The Foundation of Cells:
Admiration for Paul's Activist-Organizational Work

Badiou emphasizes with considerable admiration that the founding of communities, groups, cells, was the focus of Paul's life's work (20–21, 95). His letters, while displaying the agility of a superlative theoretician, are nevertheless "interventions . . . possessed of all the political passion proper to such [political] interventions." His letters point to the fundamental "concerns and passions of collective intervention." Badiou thus praises Paul's impressive Lenin-like combination of theoretician and activist-community organizer (20–21, 31–33).

According to Badiou, these cell groups were "envisioned in terms of a small group of militants"; they represented a "small core of the constituted faithful," "enclaves of the faithful." Members addressed each other as "brothers [and sisters]," "an archaic form of our 'comrades'" (20). Playing midwife to these cells, Paul ascribed to them the special status of "the real" proper to any location (in the way he addressed them as Corinthians, Philippians, or Galatians). But by favoring interruption over preservation, and pure fidelity over the stabilization of external or secondary "markings" of fidelity, Paul displays a "universal and de-centered vision of the construction of Christian enclaves" (34).

"Co-workers" and "Son-subjects": Shared Egalitarianism

Badiou goes further than this, emphasizing that the correlate of Paul's theoretical universality is practical "equality"—the occasion for naming all fellow militants as "co-workers." Furthermore, he explains that the "evental declaration filiates the declarant," just as the "resurrected Son filiates all humanity" (59). Paul, according to Badiou, thus rejects "filiation" via the "disciple-subject" (which implies mastery) and instead embraces filiation via the "son-subject." "All post-evental universality equalizes sons through the dissipation of the particularity of the fathers" (59), which would be otherwise impossible through disciple-

subjects and consequential structures of mastery. Thus "all equality is that of belonging together to a work" and "those participating in a truth procedure are co-workers in its becoming" (60). The figure of the law too is relieved for the sake of a "shared egalitarian endeavor."

Eschatological Universality Mediates Identity: Local Victories as Universal

Badiou defines the messianic community in Paul as one that embraces the modalities of fidelity, agape, and hope. Badiou gives the last a special emphasis. Paul's apocalyptic universalism is not, however, one that is preoccupied with some "satisfaction that feeds on the punishment of the wicked." Rather, it is hope as the subjective modality toward the victory of a universal by which Paul can say, "all Israel will be saved" (Rom 11:25–26). "Each victory won, however localized, is universal." And the economy of salvation is truly universal: Paul knows that he himself is justified only insofar as everyone is—"I identify myself in my singularity as subject of the economy of salvation only insofar as this economy is universal" (96).

Hence "for Paul, universality mediates identity. It is the 'for all' that allows me to be counted as one. Wherein we rediscover a major Pauline principle: the One is inaccessible without the 'for all'" (97). From this perspective, hope does not simply have to do with the future: "It is a figure of the present subject, who is affected in return by the universality for which he works" (97).

This apocalyptic universalism in the mode of hope also means, therefore, that there can never be a contentment with any (historical) realization of that hope, nor with any preoccupation in a new identity apart from the hope for the universal. Paul's "clearest conviction is that the eventual figure of the Resurrection exceeds its real, contingent site, which is the community of believers such as it exists at the moment. The work of love is still before us; the empire is vast. . . . Paul's universalism will not allow the content of hope to be a privilege accorded to the faithful who happen to be living now. It is inappropriate to make distributive justice [which focuses on the punishment of the wicked] the referent of hope" (95).

A Community of Weakness? Badiou and the Path of the Cross

One might also say that Badiou's figure of the militant implies or demands the formal figure of a militant community that can lead what he calls for, namely a new "cultural revolution" between the polarity of "abstract homogeneity of capital" and "identitarian protest." His notions of the diagonal cut, the divided subject, and evental rupture do entail some form of militant community founded on that very subjectivity.[64] And Badiou does correlate the divided subject ecclesially in connection with the notion of continuous separation and remnant. One would expect further that this remnant community would be of the same order as the messianic mode of discourse that he presents, and the new subjectivity appropriate to it. That is, his argument would appear to imply a form of militant community marked by folly, scandal, weakness, and humiliation in contrast to that of mastery, power, glorification, or worldly status. But here Badiou stops short. He cannot fully embrace the close interrelationship of cross and resurrection in Paul, appearing especially worried about the spectre of some Nietzschean resentment, hatred of life, as a driving force in Paul's life and thought.[65] For Badiou, evental truth declaration in the modality of weakness does not correspond to one of lived weakness. At that point, only the triumphant path of resurrection holds. Unlike Taubes, he cannot appreciate Paul's emphasis on true solidarity with the world's outcasts as the prime mode of messianic existence. Badiou cannot distinguish between, on the one hand, the embrace of the path of the cross as a mode of messianic being, and on the other hand, a masochistic embrace of suffering, which extols the virtues of suffering in and of themselves or ascribes to suffering an intrinsically redemptive function. The cross can be the focal point and feature of a mode of discourse, but not a true subjective path, never mind an ecclesial one (73); death is merely a mode that helps to define the divided subject. Death is only on the side of flesh

---

64. See Badiou, *Saint Paul*, 11–14, 55–64, 98–107.

65. See the lengthy analysis of this theme in Badiou by Žižek in *Ticklish Subject*, 145–58. In my view, when it comes to understanding Paul's politics, it is indeed crucial not to understand Paul's counter-imperial perspective as deriving from some envy or resentment. Paul's approach derives from his articulation of the messianic glad tidings, not from a reflex of discontent (as in the Nietzschean version); Paul refuses to make Rome as such the singular enemy or particular target.

and law, and "cannot be the operation of salvation" (66–68). At this point, Badiou has seriously misunderstood Paul.

Concluding Reflections

In 1902 Alfred Loisy propounded his famous dictum, "Jesus announced the kingdom, and what arrived was the church."[66] Despite his conflict with the Roman Catholic hierarchy (while also rejecting the solutions of liberal Protestantism), he truly believed that Jesus did intend to form some kind of society or community; it was the aping of civil government in its institutionalization that he doubted Jesus intended.[67] Around the same time, Vladimir Lenin published his classic pamphlet *What Is To Be Done?* (1901–2), promoting organizational vanguardism as a way to assure the necessary arrival of the communist utopia.[68]

But the project of the vanguard has not brought the dream to realization. Christianity and Marxism have had to confront a similar ghost: the non-arrival of the *telos*. Christianity survived by reorienting its foundational messianism, by spiritualizing messianic glad tidings and by institutionalizing itself. For a while, it looked like Marxism might also survive in institutional, statist forms that, while claiming a heritage in Marx, were for many a betrayal of the vision. But now it would appear that, in contrast to Christianity, it no longer has significant institutional form in its classic statist realizations (Russia, China), and in the North it is only represented by small conventicles of thinkers and activists seeking to arouse the faithful.[69] It may be that Christianity will also have to return to its foundational messianic form and messi-

66. Loisy, *Gospel and the Church*, 166.

67. Ibid., 165–69.

68. Lenin, *Essential Works*. Lenin argues for the establishment of an organization (party) at the center of the revolution: to direct the efforts of the working class (identified as the proletariat) in the socialist revolution, to help achieve the dictatorship of the proletariat, and eventually the communist society. He posits a central organization to establish discipline according to "the most advanced theory," and rejects the more anarchist voices that favored "spontaneity," "freedom of criticism," and "democratic" process. As a result, the document created a split in the international socialist movement, leading to the formation of the Third International in 1919, which was in turn eventually co-opted by its statist, Stalinist incarnation.

69. See now Žižek, *In Defence of Lost Causes*.

anic fidelity in the coming generations, and may also only exist among small, outcasted conventicles of the faithful.

In the meantime, there is much that Christians can take from these politico-philosophically oriented interpreters of Paul. Proponents of radical messianic fidelity in Christian terms will continue to wrestle with the relative merits of the three forms of ecclesiology articulated by these philosophers: the anarchist-ethical version (Agamben), the primarily representational version (Taubes), and the more activist-vanguard version (Badiou, Žižek). In particular, as these interpreters suggest, when the church forgets or refuses to admit that it is "a purely contingent historical figure," a merely "strategic identification" in the drama of the reconstitution of a new people of God in which all humanity becomes "all Israel," it is in danger of losing its true vocation and instrumentality (pure use) toward the fulfillment of the cosmic drama, God's love story with all creation. It loses its character of necessary "auto-suppression" relative to the vision of the reign of God. It forgets that it ultimately has identity only in the universal, eschatological economy of salvation when God will be all in all. When the church seeks to maintain an absolute church-world distinction, despite the *telos* of the universal-eschatological-messianic drama, it is in danger of becoming a mere obscurantist haven for the (self)righteous.

This is not to say that the church as seeking to establish itself as a messianic community cannot have some institutional form. But in its self-conscious preoccupation with its own reality and identity, it walks a never-ending tightrope. In the very gesture of separation founded on messianic love and fidelity, there must be a corresponding embrace of all that is lost, all that is other. And it still seems more appropriate to try to stay on the tightrope than to seek to remain on the apparently firm ground of the alternatives, whether basking in the security of mystical or individualist subjectivity, or retreating into identitarian communal havens, or embracing the coercive universalisms of Christendom or the state, or acquiescing to the niceties and comforts of liberalism and global capital, or being content with reality reduced to the merely historical-material.

CHAPTER 12

Time and Politics in Four Commentaries on Romans

by Douglas Harink

> Love is the fulfilment of the law. And this is because you know
> the time: it is the hour to awake from sleeping, for now our sal-
> vation is nearer than when we believed. The night is far gone;
> the day is near. . . . Put on the Lord Jesus Christ.
>
> (Rom 13:10–12, 14; author's translation)

INTRODUCTION

Modern theology characteristically displays its modernity when it
contextualizes the gospel within a wider secular history. In modern
theology the gospel is "understood" insofar as it is graspable as another
event and factor within secular history, and perhaps also, for those who
wish to assert something theological, as an interpretative extra above
and beyond that history. In any case, the gospel is defined by its relation
to a time that exceeds the time of the gospel and is defined prior to and
apart from it. According to Stanley Hauerwas, the secular is

> the name given to that time, and the correlative politics, in
> which time is no longer . . . interwoven with a higher time. . . .
> The habits that now constitute the secular imagination are so
> imbedded in how Christians understand the world we no lon-
> ger have the ability to recognize the power they have over us.
> That power . . . is exemplified by the assumption that time qua
> time names a duration that precedes the Gospel. As a result

time is ontologically presumed to name the ground on which
the Christian narrative of redemption occurs.[1]

Like modern theology, modern biblical scholarship, as modern, is governed by the same "habits that now constitute the secular imagination." Most Paul scholarship is modern in that sense.[2]

But Paul does not know another time than that contained within and qualified by the gospel. For Paul the time of the gospel both interrupts and exceeds—interrupts *because* it exceeds—the flow of worldly time. Paul writes his Romans letter, he says, "to proclaim the gospel to you also who are in Rome" (1:15).[3] That gospel is the revelation of the "time" (*kairos*), the "hour" (*hōra*), the "now" *(nun)*, the "day" (*hēmera*) (13:11–12) in which "the whole world" (*pas ho kosmos*) is brought "under judgment" (*hypodikos*) (3:19–20); it is the revelation of the justice of God in Jesus Christ, which is now made known as God's mercy to Israel, to the nations, and to all creation. The time of the *apokalypsis Theou* in Jesus Christ is uncontained and unconditioned by any other time or hour or day or now; rather, the time of the gospel precedes and exceeds and conditions every other time, entering into and exploding the "times and the seasons," however they may be defined, whether by Israel or the nations. Paul's proclamation of the gospel, which is what the Letter to the Romans is (1:15), is the announcement of God's time, the time of Jesus Christ.

No wonder then that someone like Karl Barth comes upon a *postmodern* gospel when he comes upon Romans. Or, more recently, Walter Lowe, asking the question, "Is There a Postmodern Gospel?," turns to Paul's apocalyptic gospel and finds there the fundamental premise by which modern theology's secularized time might be questioned and qualified:[4]

1. Hauerwas, "State of the Secular," 170, 174.

2. For a critique of modern biblical scholarship along these lines, see Milbank, *Theology and Social Theory*, 110–21.

3. The Letter to the Romans is a proxy for Paul's personal proclamation of the gospel to the Romans (1:8–15). He hopes to come to Rome soon to do that, but is delayed by another, rather lengthy plan to take the collection from the Gentile churches to Jerusalem (15:22–29). Unfortunately Paul's self-declared reason for writing Romans— to proclaim the gospel to those who are in Rome—is often ignored by biblical scholars seeking out the reasons for Romans.

4. Lowe, "Is There a Postmodern Gospel?" Lowe answer's his question by drawing on J. Louis Martyn's work on Paul.

> The rationalist [i.e., modern] response to apocalyptic is to treat it, or belief in it, as a historical phenomenon. In doing so, the historian asserts a priori the very continuity of history which apocalyptic would question—into the dustbin of history goes the notion that history is headed for the dustbin. But a similar distortion occurs when believers inscribe apocalyptic within a cosmic timeline, be it ever so celestial. . . .
>
> Reason spontaneously seeks to contextualize that with which it deals. But Christian theology depends upon the quite different premise that we ourselves have been contextualized; and not just conceptually, but actually. It is we who have been inscribed.[5]

"Christian theology depends upon the quite different premise" of the Epistle to the Romans. The entirety of Paul's epistle seeks to bring about just such a contextualization of time and history, to "inscribe" Israel and all the nations—indeed, all creation—and therefore also all those who hear or read the letter, into the time of the gospel. Commenting on Galatians, J. Louis Martyn writes, "Paul wrote Galatians in the confidence that *God* intended to cause a certain event *to occur* in the Galatian congregations when Paul's messenger read the letter aloud to them . . . The author we see in the course of reading Galatians is a man who *does* theology by writing in such a way as *to anticipate* a theological *event.*"[6] As with Galatians, so with Romans: the hearer or reader of Romans is addressed as one brought by God into the sphere of God's apocalyptic action. Romans anticipates a "theological event" in which the time of hearing or reading the letter is itself assumed by God into the singular, apocalyptic, contextualizing time of the gospel and transfigured—becoming the time in which the messianic power of the Spirit is released and the obedience of faith is created among God's people. Further, if we are speaking of "apocalyptic action," "messianic power," and "the obedience of faith," we must say that the theological event that Romans anticipates is also intrinsically and simultaneously a political event, *an event that creates and activates messianic political agency* that participates in and corresponds to the faithfulness of Jesus the Messiah. If that is so, it raises questions about the modern practice

5. Lowe, "Prospects for a Postmodern Christian Theology," 23.

6. Martyn, "Events in Galatia," 161 (emphasis original); see also Martyn, *Galatians,* 105–6.

of commentary on Romans. Do the usual historicist habits of modern biblical interpretation blind the commentator to the apocalyptic transfiguration of time and politics? Can a modern commentator who does not recognize and participate in that transfiguration, *precisely in the practice of commentary*, truly grasp the message of Romans or communicate it to the contemporary reader? Must a Romans commentary itself, if it is to be true to Paul, finally aim in form and content to be such an act of recognition and participation?

In this essay I examine four recent commentaries on Romans (by Robert Jewett, N. T. Wright, Karl Barth, and Giorgio Agamben) with those questions about time and its transfiguration by the apocalyptic time of the gospel in mind. How do these commentators understand the time of Paul's writing, and the time of our hearing, reading, and interpreting Romans, in relation to the apocalyptic time of the gospel that the letter announces and in which (according to Paul) it is caught up? Further, how does the understanding of time and history presupposed by the commentator determine the fundamental character of the commentary that is written? Finally, what kind of politics is implicitly or explicitly assumed and anticipated by the understanding of time operative in the commentary, and how is the commentary itself an instrument of that politics?

1. Gospel Time in Secular History

Modern historical criticism in biblical scholarship is marked by the deployment of historicist reason in understanding the Bible.[7] With respect to Romans, it seeks to situate Paul's writing of the letter within the historical causes and aims of Paul's apostolic mission, the history, sociology and politics of the messianic congregations in Rome at the time of Paul's writing, and the social, cultural, and political contexts in which both Paul and the Roman congregations lived and worked. These factors are analyzed and brought together to develop a picture of the reasons *for* Romans—the historical conditions through which and into which Romans was written—which in turn form the backdrop for understanding something of the reasoning *of* Romans—how the letter

---

7. By "historicist reason" I mean, following Hauerwas, the attempt to describe a situation without reference to a "higher time." Since Ernst Troeltsch that has been the mode of historical reason in theology and biblical interpretation.

works and what it says as an argument, and indeed how the letter itself became and might again become a factor in the flow of history.[8] Robert Jewett sums up such a procedure compactly and representatively in the first paragraph of his recent massive commentary on Romans in the Hermeneia series:

> This commentary employs all of the standard methods of historical-critical exegesis. This includes historical analysis; text criticism, form criticism, and redaction criticism; rhetorical analysis; social scientific reconstruction of the audience situation; an historical reconstruction of the situations in Rome and Spain, historical and cultural analysis of the honor, shame, and imperial systems in the Greco-Roman world; and a theological interpretation that takes these details into account rather than following traditional paths formed by church traditions.[9]

Thus employed, the various methods of historical-critical analysis and reconstruction enable the reader to contextualize Paul's gospel in its time, to see how it is conditioned by, and itself enters into, the causal flow of history as another factor within it, aiming to bring about certain socio-political effects that themselves further condition history's movement and outcomes. Through historical reason the reader is able to form an idea of the basic historical origins and purpose of the letter and its overall message. Romans as a communicative act is evoked by a historical situation that Paul wants to affect, as well as a new situation in history he wants to effect, by means of the gospel. Thus Jewett describes the basic purpose of Romans in this way: "The basic idea in the interpretation of each verse and paragraph is that Paul wishes to gain support for a mission to the barbarians in Spain, which requires that the gospel of impartial, divine righteousness revealed in Christ be clarified to rid it of prejudicial elements that are currently dividing the congregations in Rome."[10] The overall message of Romans fits into that basic historical purpose (gaining support for Paul's mission, cancelling prejudicial misunderstandings of the gospel), and becomes the means of bringing about a new situation: the religious and social equality among Jewish and Gentile believers in Rome. "In the shameful cross,

8. See the important and influential examples of this strategy in Wedderburn, *Reasons for Romans*; and Donfried, *Romans Debate*.

9. Jewett, *Romans*, 1.

10. Ibid.

Christ overturned the honor system that dominated the Greco-Roman and Jewish worlds, resulting in discrimination and exploitation of barbarians as well as poisoning the relations between the congregations in Rome. The gospel offered grace to every group in equal measure, shattering the imperial premise of exceptionalism in virtue and honor."[11] Jewett concludes his opening paragraph by stating that the methods of historical-critical exegesis work together to help us understand these aims of Paul in the letter: "In the effort to *follow Paul's attempt to persuade and transform* the Roman congregations, one should bring to bear all of the available historical and cultural information. So the first matter on which such an accounting should be given is the nature of the commentary's approach to the stubborn details of history and culture."[12] The task of the commentator is to deploy historical reason in the construction of a historical narrative in which Paul's letter makes sense both as a product of its time and as another causal factor making its own contribution to the historical course of events. Jewett offers a brilliant and highly instructive—indeed paradigmatic—performance of the historical-critical task; it is difficult to imagine a more thoroughly researched and carefully argued commentary in the modern tradition. Every word, phrase, and section of the letter is meticulously located within and related to its first-century context. The more detailed that contextualization is, the more successful is the commentary in historical-critical terms; the thousand and more pages of text attest to the success of Jewett's work.

But we may pause for a moment when Jewett also declares his intent to provide "a theological interpretation that takes these [historically-critically discerned] details into account." What might that mean? For Jewett it too means a description of Paul's theological claims in their first-century context, locating them in the context of the religious ideas and claims of Second Temple Judaism, the Jesus tradition, and the Roman Empire. As a commentator Jewett does not engage in theological exegesis as his own theological participation in the same divine origin, aim, and power which calls Romans into being, invoking historical-critical methods for occasional illumination insofar as the history of Paul's time as well as the time of the interpreter is assumed into

11. Ibid.
12. Ibid. (emphasis added).

the singular apocalyptic time of the gospel designated by Paul with the terms "hour," "day," "now." Rather, for Jewett theological interpretation itself remains commentary in the modern historicist mode, as should we expect it to since, as Jewett notes, the series for which the commentary is written itself requires historicism of its contributors: "Although I remain faithful to the Hermeneia format by leaving the contemporary application up to my readers, I hope that the extraordinary relevance of Romans to the situation of cultural, religious and imperial conflicts is easily discernable."[13] Summing up his own commitment to historical-critical exegesis, Jewett writes:

> The linguistic, intellectual, and religious horizon of the first century can thus be used to guard against imposing later ideological agendas back onto Romans. This hermeneutical principle promises a measure of accountability and testability in discerning Paul's intended argument; readers are offered a frankly acknowledged set of hermeneutical assumptions and methods to evaluate and correct. My goal is to sharpen the ancient horizon of the text so that it can enter into dialogue with the modern horizons of our various interpretive enterprises.[14]

Historical criticism thus practiced, Jewett hopes, will provide critical leverage ("a counterweight") over against "unacknowledged ideologies," "hegemonistic agendas," and "traditional views" held by "particular churches and groups" in their readings of the letter, so that what Paul writes in his own time (clarified by historical criticism) might be brought to bear anew on the present cultural, religious, and political situation.[15] The commentary as such, however, maintains the conceit of objective historical research rather than unapologetic theological and political witness in the present evoked by the letter. Jewett does not seek to comprehend both the letter and the commentary within the singular time of the *apokalypsis Theou*, and engage in commentary as a "theological event" that Paul anticipates God will bring about through the reading of Romans.

The aim and practice of modern biblical commentary could hardly be more clearly displayed. Past and present are horizons separated

13. Ibid., xv.
14. Ibid., 3.
15. Ibid., 2–3.

by temporal distance on a temporal-causal continuum. Commentary paves the way for a "dialogue" between past and present, but does not aim to do that work itself. The aim of the commentary itself is to situate Romans thoroughly in the past in the hope that, thus situated, its "relevance" for the present might become clear. The present day reader of Romans, acting within secular time (the only time there is), might in turn take up the same kind of (liberal progressivist) non-discriminatory, egalitarian politics, practices, and actions as those encouraged by Paul in the letter. Contemporary theological interpretation, if it is engaged at all (for it is strictly secondary to the main aim of commentary), must try to join together what is separated by historicist reason in seeking out situations and actions in our own time that correspond to those of Paul's.

2. Gospel Time in Salvation History

Jewett's commentary represents a high point of historical-critical exegesis, though not likely its end. A different and increasingly influential exegetical proposal is that of N. T. Wright. Wright also deploys the "the standard methods of historical-critical exegesis" in his studies of Paul, though he is by no means uncritical of the secular assumptions of such methods.[16] With respect to Romans, however, he provides a remarkably brief introduction in his commentary on the letter, treating hardly any of the matters that occupy Jewett for nearly a hundred pages.[17] Wright is clear that there are historical and political contingencies with respect to empire, city, and synagogue, Jews and messianic Gentiles, in Rome that shed light on Paul's mission and his purpose in writing the letter. In fact, for Wright as for Jewett reconstruction of the history and politics of the Jews in Rome, as well as the imperial theopolitics preceding and at the time of Paul's writing, "produces a situation into which Romans fits like a glove."[18]

---

16. Wright engages in an extended discussion and critique of the assumptions of the historical-critical method in *New Testament and the People of God*, 81–120.

17. Wright, "Letter to the Romans." Wright's introduction is in pp. 395–408; its brevity is in some measure a factor of the type of commentary *The New Interpreter's Bible* is—more ecclesially than academically oriented, as Wright himself notes (408).

18. Wright, "Letter to the Romans," 406.

But for Wright the focus of the commentary lies elsewhere than in trying to discern the religious, social, or political situation of Romans and to locate the letter within that. Rather, his emphasis is on what we might call the *theological situation* of the letter and the theological reasoning that that engenders in the letter and in its readers. Thus Wright aims at a certain kind of theological commentary. For Wright the argument of Romans is finally explicable only in terms of the description of a much larger divine drama, a cosmic-historical divine plan to which Paul constantly, though often allusively rather than directly, refers. The commentator's primary task is to grasp the contours and movement of that divine cosmic-historical drama behind the text of Romans which is always presupposed by Paul (and, according to Wright, widely shared in Second Temple Judaism, from which Paul learned much of the story), and then to plot the arguments of Romans within and with reference to that larger divine cosmic-historical narrative. According to Wright, Paul's task in Romans is to show how the gospel is located within and marks a new stage of that narrative.

> It is not simply that Paul alludes to a number of well-known narratives [in Israel's scriptures] . . . I want to insist that Paul's whole point is precisely that with the coming, the death and the resurrection of Jesus the Messiah *a new chapter has opened within the story* in which he believed himself to be living, and that understanding what that story is and how this chapter is indeed a radically new moment within it provides one of the central clues to everything else he says . . .
>
> [T]he great stories of Abraham, of Exodus, of David . . . and of exile and restoration . . . create not merely a rich narrative backcloth from which motifs can be drawn at will to produce a resonant typology but also, much more so, *a single narrative line*, containing typological recapitulations but not reducible to them, in which Paul believed that he and his contemporaries were living.[19]

The *apokalypsis Theou* in Jesus the Messiah is indeed for Wright something "radically new," but rather than itself constituting the singular time within which Israel's scriptures are to be read, it is "a new chapter" in a larger history already well under way.

19. Wright, *Paul*, 9 (emphasis added).

[I]n Paul's day the [shared] story [of Israel] was in full swing. He and many of his Jewish contemporaries were eager to discover where precisely the plot had got to and what role they were called to play within it.

This in turn is grounded . . . on the belief that the one true God is the creator, the ruler and the coming judge of the whole world. Monotheism of the Jewish style (creation, providence, final justice), which Paul re-emphasizes as he refashions it, generates just this *sense of underlying narrative, the historical and as yet unfinished story* of creation and covenant, to which the individual stories such as those of Abraham and the Exodus contribute, and whose flavour they reinforce, but which goes beyond mere typology into *strong historical continuity.*[20]

To substantiate this proposal, Wright's reading of Romans plots each of its argumentative moves with reference to the supposed wider theological-historical timeline.[21] Romans requires a kind of "narrative interpretation" in which what Paul proclaims in the letter is contextualized within the larger divine cosmic-historical narrative derived from the Old Testament and the writings of Second Temple Judaism; the task of commentary is to make explicit the many allusive references in Romans to that narrative and to show how Romans itself is advancing it. Such interpretation, Wright argues, is necessary not only for theological reasons, but also because the "facts of history" conditioning the very production of the letter demand it:

The [recent] turn to narrative is . . . one of the most significant developments [in Paul scholarship]. I want to insist that this be seen both as part of the developing 'new perspective' and as a central, not merely illustrative or peripheral, element in Paul. But, equally, it is important to stress that it is also a matter of sheer *history*: understanding how stories worked in the ancient world, and how a small allusion could and did summon up an entire implicit narrative, including narratives within

---

20. Ibid., 12 (emphasis added).

21. While Paul himself does from time to time draw a brief narrative from Israel's scriptures into his arguments, usually reading them typologically, one searches his letters in vain for any indication that a "large-scale" narrative of Israel is constitutive for any of his arguments, or for his theology as a whole. Yet much of Wright's commentary is taken up with reconstructing that narrative from the letter.

which speaker and hearer believed themselves to be living, is a vital tool.[22]

Wright cites Richard Hays's *The Faith of Jesus Christ* as a key work in the move to narrative interpretation of Paul's letters.[23] But while Hays in that work focuses attention primarily on the *christological* story implicit in the argument of Galatians, Wright argues that there is a much larger narrative at work behind Paul's writings, evident most particularly in Romans (chapters 9–11 especially). Drawing again on the work of Hays, this time on his theory of how biblical allusions work in Paul,[24] Wright proposes that the narrative implicitly and often explicitly at work in Paul's arguments, surfacing particularly through Paul's scriptural quotations, is the whole progressive sweep of cosmic and covenantal history from Genesis to Kings, from creation to covenant, from exile to return, and through to the prophetic anticipations of the messianic age. Over against Hays's emphasis on typology, however, Wright insists "that Paul saw scripture as story and as prophecy, *not* in the abstract sense of mere typological prefigurement between one event and another, according to which in principle the two events could stand in any chronological relation to each other, but in the sense of a very specific story functioning in a very specific way. For Paul, the story is always moving toward a climax; . . . it was a story whose climax, Paul believed, *had now arrived.*"[25] Typology in Paul merely enhances the flavor of his telling of that single overarching salvation-historical story. For Wright, mention of the names of Abraham or Moses or David (or any other biblical character) in Romans goes far beyond typology; it requires that the interpreter recall the larger scriptural narratives that those names "summon up," in order to fill in and fill out in the fullest possible way the single divine drama or plan that Paul is invoking, telling, and retelling in the letter. The purpose and message of Romans become fully understood only by making that (often implicit) drama explicit and showing how the letter moves its storyline forward. Wright's commen-

---

22. Wright, *Paul*, 8 (emphasis original).

23. Hays, *Faith of Jesus Christ.*

24. Hays, *Echoes of Scripture.*

25. Wright, *Climax of the Covenant*, 264 (emphasis original): "I still find Hays' picture incomplete, and leaving Paul looking more arbitrary in his handling of the Jewish Bible than I think exegesis actually suggests . . ."

tary is characterized above all by the attempt to show how the various words, phrases, and sections of Romans constitute the narration of a cohesive, comprehensible, and continuous drama of God's working in the world.

If we can accept what seems like an oxymoron, we may think of Wright as engaging in a kind of theological historicism. Secular versions of historical causality are uninteresting to him (and in fact he would regard them as mistaken). But the discernment of a *successive and progressive divine causality in history* (i.e., God's faithfulness to his covenantal promises) in which both the letter and the reader participate is crucial for Wright in understanding Paul. Wright's emphasis on divinely ordained "strong historical continuity," rendered also as a "single narrative line," in Paul's "underlying theology" has a significant impact on how he construes history and apocalyptic in Paul's theology. He sets his own understanding of apocalyptic in contrast to that proposed by J. Christiaan Beker and J. Louis Martyn:

> According to this way [i.e., the apocalyptic interpretations of Paul by Beker and Martyn], the divine solution to the problem of the world is simply to break in to an otherwise unfruitful and corrupt ongoing historical process and to do something radically new. Over against any idea that *God was quietly and steadily working his purposes out as year succeeded to year*, this would-be 'apocalyptic' theology insists that, for Paul, God broke into history, the history of Israel, the history of the world, in his action in Jesus and particularly in his cross; and God will do so again, very soon from Paul's perspective, in the second coming through which what God accomplished through Jesus will be brought to completion. In this kind of 'apocalyptic' we find the very opposite of a 'covenant' theology in which the *age-old promises are to be fulfilled through the long unwinding of Israel's and the world's story*. On the contrary: God is doing a new thing. Jesus bursts onto the scene in a shocking, unexpected, unimaginable fashion, the crucified Christ offered as a slap in the face to Israel and the world, folly to Gentiles and a scandal to Jews. The result is new creation, not so much *creatio ex vetere* but a fresh *creatio ex nihilo*.[26]

26. Wright, *Paul*, 50–51 (emphasis added). Wright "intends to sum up" and "not to caricature" Beker and Martyn with this description of their apocalyptic interpretation. But it is indeed caricature in good measure. Elsewhere Wright also attempts to temper the linear-progressivist tone that generally characterizes his covenantal-historical in-

Wright's own construal of the *apokalypsis Theou*, precisely as a kind of *creatio ex vetere*, proposes the arrival of Jesus Christ as *the next event in a sequence*, albeit a climactic, determinative, even "irruptive" event, arising out of the "long unwinding" of Israel's history. Christ is the one in whom "God's long and many-staged plan of salvation has come to fruition."[27]

The language of *God's plan* dominates Wright's approach to time, history, and apocalyptic in Paul's reasoning. "The shorthand phrase *Iesous Christos . . .* enables Paul to draw together several narratives at the heart of his thinking. God's plan for Israel and the world had come to its fulfilment in Jesus of Nazareth, Israel's Messiah and the world's true Lord, in whom Israel's destiny had been accomplished and in whom, therefore, Jew and Gentile alike could inherit the promises made to Abraham."[28] Over against Israel's "failure" to fulfill its purpose in God's plan, "God must stick to the plan." Therefore, in contrast to unfaithful Israel, "[p]recisely as Messiah, he [Jesus] offers God that representative faithfulness to the plan of salvation through which the plan can go ahead."[29] This, Wright argues, is in keeping with first-century Jewish ways of thinking about the messianic arrival in relation to historical time. The coming "end" is "not simply . . . a bolt from the blue, descending into an otherwise undifferentiated and irrelevant historical sequence. They saw it precisely as the climax, the denouement, of a story, a plot which had been *steadily unfolding in the mind of God and on the ground in the Middle East.*"[30]

---

terpretation: "We cannot expound Paul's covenant theology in such a way as to make it a smooth, steady progress of historical fulfilment; but nor can we propose a kind of 'apocalyptic' view in which nothing that happened before Jesus is of any value even as preparation. In the messianic events of Jesus' death and resurrection Paul believes *both* that the covenant promises were at last fulfilled *and* that this constituted a massive and dramatic irruption into the processes of world history unlike anything before or since. And at the heart of both parts of this tension stands the cross of the Messiah, at once the long-awaited fulfilment and the slap in the face for all human pride. Unless we hold on to both parts of this truth we are missing something absolutely central to Paul" (*Paul*, 54; see also 57). This qualification notwithstanding, Wright's own emphasis is consistently on the *continuity* in covenant history.

27. Ibid., 53.

28. Ibid., 46–47.

29. Ibid., 47.

30. Ibid., *Paul*, 134 (emphasis added). Wright's interpretation of Romans 9–11 is especially dominated by this narrative reasoning: "Within Romans 9–11, it is often

Wright, as much as Jewett, presents us with a contextualized gospel in Paul. The interpretation of Romans for Wright proceeds on the
assumption that Paul's proclamation in Romans is primarily about a
divine cosmic-historical drama in which the crucifixion and resurrection of Jesus Christ is another, the next, albeit "climactic" stage in the
chronological sequence of God's plan. The coming of Christ follows
the previous stages "leading up" to it, and indeed it will be followed
by yet the next stage, the stage of the church in which the next act of
the divine drama is played out. The previous, preparatory stages of the
divine cosmic-historical drama recede ever further into the past of the
narrative-historical continuum. The contextualizing apocalyptic "day,"
"hour," "now" of the gospel we find in Paul is instead contextualized
and qualified in Wright's interpretation not by time as secular history
(as in Jewett) but by time as progressive salvation-history. For Wright
the task of commentary is to show how that providential historical narrative is the single timeline on which creation, Israel, Jesus Christ, Paul,
the Letter to the Romans, the church, and the present-day Christian
all have their discreet temporal places. The contemporary reader of
Romans is enabled through such a commentary to discern his or her
place and action within God's continuously unfolding work in history
through the church. Politically (with reference to Wright's comments
on Romans 13), this may mean that Christians refuse to avenge themselves "at a purely personal level" for injustices done to them. At the
level of conflict among nations, it may mean that "the only way forward
is the establishment of a worldwide justice system that will carry moral
weight across different cultures and societies," with Christians and the
churches adding their influence however possible to achieving that "way
forward."[31] For Wright, Christian readers of Romans find themselves

---

not noticed that Paul's large-scale argument consists of a retelling of the story of Israel
[cf. "a massive retelling of the scriptural narrative," 125], from Abraham, Isaac and
Jacob through Moses and the Exodus to the prophets and the exile . . . and then, with
a glance at the remnant, to the Messiah. *Telos gar nomou Christos* in Romans 10:4 ('the
Messiah is the . . . end? goal? of the law') relates directly both to 9:5 and to the whole
narrative of which it forms the climax—and 'climax' is in fact a good translation for
telos here. The entire narrative is, arguably, messianic from start to finish, in the sense
that Paul understands the story of Israel to be reaching its climax with the coming
and achievement of the Messiah . . ." (ibid., 43–44). See also Wright, "Letter to the
Romans," 622; and the entire commentary on Rom 9–11 (626–99).

31. Ibid., 723.

participating in God's salvation-historical work among the people of God, and in turn seeking to influence and transform the life of cities, peoples, and nations according to God's plan in order to bring about greater justice in social, economic, political, and international orders. Wright's narrative-driven commentary may therefore be understood politically as displaying, proposing, and contributing to a (chastened) version of Christendom—Christians influencing the current structures to bring about a continuous transformation of society.

3. Gospel Time as the Apocalypse of Eternity

Strangely, the one commentary on Romans in the modern era that turned out to be truly revolutionary, theologically and politically speaking, is the second edition of Karl Barth's *Römerbrief*—a commentary written virtually without regard either to "the ancient horizon of the text" (Jewett) or to the steadily unfolding salvation-historical "plan" of God (Wright). Barth's commentary is *apocalyptically* charged through and through.[32] Commenting on the theme of Romans as set forth in 1:16–17, Barth writes, "The Gospel is the victory by which the world is overcome. By the gospel the whole concrete world is dissolved and established" ("Sie [die Heilsbotschaft] ist als Aufhebung und Begründung alles Gegebenen der Sieg, der die Welt überwindet").[33] On Rom 3:21 Barth writes,

> **But now.** We stand here before an irresistible and all-embracing dissolution of the world of time and things and men, before a penetrating and ultimate KRISIS, before the supremacy of a negation by which all existence is rolled up. The world is the

32. Barth, *Romans*. German quotations are from Barth, *Römerbrief*. It should be noted, however, that Barth studiously avoids the term "apocalyptic" in the commentary (a point first brought to my attention by J. Louis Martyn). I have argued elsewhere, dependent largely on the work of Martyn, that Paul's thinking is thoroughly "apocalyptic" in tone and substance from beginning to end (see Harink, *Paul among the Postliberals*, ch. 2). I would further suggest that Barth's "dialectical theology" of "*Krisis*" in *Romans* is a way of rendering a "non-identical repetition" of Paul's apocalyptic thinking. Barth's words from the preface to English edition confirm that suggestion: "My book deals with one issue only. Did Paul think and speak in general and in detail in the manner in which I have interpreted him as thinking and speaking? Or did he think and speak altogether differently?" (*Romans*, x).

33. Barth, *Romans*, 35; *Römerbrief*, 11.

world; and now we know what that means (i.18—iii.20). But whence comes this KRISIS? . . . Our origin evokes in us a memory of our habitation with the Lord of heaven and earth; and at this reminiscence the heavens are rent asunder, the graves are opened, the sun stands still upon Gibeon, and the moon stays in the valley of Ajalon. *But now* directs our attention to time which is beyond time, to space which has no locality, to impossible possibility, to the gospel of transformation, to the imminent Coming of the Kingdom of God, to affirmation in negation, to salvation in the world, to acquittal in condemnation, to eternity in time, to life in death—*I saw a new heaven and a new earth; for the first heaven and the first earth are passed away.* This is the Word of God.[34]

In the time of "but now," there is no secular-historical progression or salvation-historical narrative leading up to the arrival of the gospel. Rather, the "but now" of the gospel contextualizes all times and histories. The ordinary markers of historical sequence—hours, days and years, birth and death, the rise and fall of nations—are fundamentally disturbed, indeed dissolved, before the "penetrating and ultimate KRISIS," which is the gospel. The "imminent Coming of the Kingdom of God" is "the time which is beyond time," the "higher time" (Hauerwas) in terms of which all other times are disclosed and judged and justified. "By the gospel the whole concrete world is dissolved and established."

Commenting on Rom 3:1–20, in which Paul writes that "there is none righteous," and "every mouth is stopped" and "the whole world" is placed under God's judgment, Barth has this to say about history (whether secular or *heilige*):

History is the display of the supposed advantages of power and intelligence which some men possess over others, of the struggle for existence hypocritically described by ideologists as a struggle for justice and freedom, of the ebb and flow of old and new forms of human righteousness, each vying with the rest in solemnity and triviality. Yet one drop of eternity is of greater weight than a vast ocean of finite things . . .

The judgement of God is the end of history, not the beginning of a new, a second epoch. By it history is not prolonged, but done away with. The difference between that which lies beyond the judgement and that which lies on this side of it is

34. Barth, *Romans*, 91–92 (emphasis original).

not relative but absolute; the two are separated absolutely. God speaks: and He is recognized as the Judge. By His speech and by His judgement a transformation is effected so radical that time and eternity, here and there, the righteousness of men and the righteousness of God, are indissolubly linked together. The end is also the goal; the Redeemer is also the Creator; He that judgeth is also He that restoreth all things . . . What is new is also the deepest truth of what was old. The most radical ending of history, the negation under which all flesh stands, the absolute judgement, which is the meaning of God for the world of men and time and things, is also the crimson thread which runs through the whole course of the world in its inevitability . . .

And so it follows that every impress of revelation in history, however little cause there may be in it for boasting of human righteousness, however little peace and security it affords, is not extinguished and destroyed as it passes through the judgement, but is thereby authorized, established and confirmed [bestätigt, bewährt und bekräftigt]. For in the radical dissolution of all physical, intellectual, and spiritual achievements of men, in the all-embracing 'relativization' of all human distinctions, their true and eternal meaning is made known.[35]

The apocalyptic dissolution and establishment of time and history is the characteristic mark of Barth's dialectical theology in Romans. As Bruce McCormack writes, the theology of the second edition of the commentary is characterized by a "radically futurist 'consistent' eschatology according to which the Kingdom of God is understood as that which brings about 'the dissolution of all things, the cessation of all becoming, the passing away of this world's time.'"[36] Or, in the phrase of Walter Lowe, Barth's Romans is "apocalyptic without reserve."[37]

---

35. Barth, Romans, 77–78; Römerbrief, 51–52.

36. McCormack, Karl Barth's Critically Realistic Dialectical Theology, 208 (the internal quote is from Barth). McCormack further specifies Barth's "dialectical theology in the shadow of a consistent eschatology" as one in which the "basic intention" is "to speak of a presence of God (revelation, the Kingdom of God, the new humanity, etc.) in history in such a way as to make it clear that these realities are not of history" (209, emphasis original). McCormack thus rightly identifies Barth's dialectical theology as the way in which Barth was seeking to be faithful to New Testament eschatology, and not vice versa.

37. The phrase comes from the subtitle of Lowe, "Prospects for a Postmodern Christian Theology: Apocalyptic without Reserve."

Barth's commentary on Romans is thoroughly apocalyptic because he believes that Romans itself is an apocalyptic text through and
through, that is, a text in which God's *Aufhebung* and *Begründung* of
all things through the crucifixion and resurrection of Jesus Christ is
the very subject matter of Paul's gospel, and constitutes the *one* time
in which not only Paul but also the hearers and readers of Romans,
whether past or present, are living. Barth writes the commentary within
that singular time of the gospel. The eternal God and the revelation of
God's justice in the gospel is the singular theme, *die Sache*, of Romans.
It is that theme that Barth seeks to bring to expression in *and as* his
own commentary, in an attempt to witness faithfully to the theological
event in which the letter is born, and which the letter in turn anticipates
bringing about in its readers.[38]

The apocalyptic tone of the commentary is a result of Barth finding himself under apocalyptic pressure from the God of Paul's gospel.
Rather than contextualizing Paul's apocalyptic gospel within secular or
salvation-historical time, Barth's aim in the commentary is to speak of
the contextualizing power of the gospel in Romans not only in what he
writes about Romans, but in the very manner in which he writes the
commentary. In a discussion of the place of historical-critical method
in the preface to the first edition, Barth writes:

> Paul, as a child of his age, addressed his contemporaries. It is,
> however, far more important that, as Prophet and Apostle of
> the Kingdom of God, he veritably speaks to all men of every
> age. The differences between then and now, there and here,
> no doubt require careful investigation and consideration. But
> the purpose of such investigation can only be to demonstrate
> that these differences are, in fact, purely trivial. The historical-
> critical method of Biblical investigation has its rightful place:
> it is concerned with the preparation of the intelligence—and
> this can never be superfluous . . . Nevertheless, my whole en-
> ergy of interpreting has been expended in an endeavour to see
> through and beyond history into the spirit of the Bible, which
> is the Eternal Spirit. What was once of grave importance, is so
> still. What to-day is of grave importance . . . stands in direct

38. "Barth . . . does not consider *Romans* a book about method in theology, or neo-
Protestantism, or cultural criticism after the war; speaking strictly, we might say that
Barth does not consider it a book *about* anything, but only a commentary that speaks
with and through Paul" (Sonderegger, *That Jesus Christ Was Born a Jew*, 19).

connexion with that ancient gravity. If we rightly understand
ourselves, our problems are the problems of Paul; and if we be
enlightened by the brightness of his answers, those answers
must be ours.[39]

Historical-critical method can be only a prolegomenon (serving to
determine "what stands in the text") to the real task of biblical commentary, which is to discern and speak the *subject matter* of the text:
"Criticism [*krinein*—Barth begins his sentence with this Greek word,
which more accurately means "judgment"] applied to historical documents means for me the measuring of words and phrases by the standard of that about which the documents are speaking—unless indeed
the whole be nonsense."[40] Here historical-critical method is itself contextualized and judged by the subject matter of the text, in the case of
Romans by the apocalypse of God and God's justice in Jesus Christ.
In Barth's commentary the rationalism, historicism, and progressivism
taken as criteria of the real by theological modernism are exposed and
defeated. As Lowe says of the *Römerbrief,* "Gone [is] the ontotheological
order which had grounded Western confidence in an all-encompassing
reason. Gone the unintrusive god of theism, sublime guarantor of an
ultimate good. And gone the autonomous subject, font of human progress by its emergent divinity."[41] What is set before the reader instead is
the intrusive, disturbing, dissolving God of *apokalypsis*, the God of the
gospel by whom all supposed secular and sacred times are shattered,
judged, taken up, and transfigured.

What about the idea of salvation-history in Barth? Is there any
sense in which the apocalypse of God in the coming of Christ is seen
as the fruition of a progressively unfolding, divinely planned historical sequence, beginning with creation, moving through Israel, kings,
prophets and exile, and having as its outcome the arrival of Christ and
the era of the church? We have already seen that Barth imagines no
"second epoch" following the crisis of the gospel. The *apokalypsis Theou*
in Jesus Christ is not the next act in a long unfolding *heilsgeschich-
tlich* drama, inaugurating a new and improved historical sequence.
The church does not succeed and supersede Israel as a new and higher

39. Barth, *Romans,* "Preface to the First Edition," 1.

40. Ibid., "Preface to the Second Edition," 8; *Römerbrief,* xii.

41. Lowe, "Prospects for a Postmodern Christian Theology," 17.

theological-historical-political development. Indeed, in his remarkable discussion of Romans 9–11, Barth makes no distinction between historical Israel and the church *vis a vis* God and the gospel.[42] "Israel" does not represent a prior or outdated reality with respect to the church. The church occupies no other time or history than Israel with respect to the gospel's *Aufhebung* and *Begründung*. Barth writes on Rom 9:4–5:

> It is . . . a quite sober statement that Paul is making when he asserts that the other Pharisees know and say and represent and possess all that he knows and says and represents and possesses of the Gospel. Nothing that MEN can say or know of the Gospel is 'new'; for everything which they possess is identical with what Israel possessed. . . . If it is a matter of being Israelites, of possessing the adoption, the glory, the covenants, the fathers, the giving of the law, the service of God, the promises, and the Christ according to the flesh, does not the Church also possess precisely all this? Is anything that we can possess more than the whole fullness of the Old Testament? . . . Israel—the Church—even possesses 'God'.[43]

As an apostle of Christ, therefore, Paul does not separate himself from his Israelite kindred *kata sarka* but stands in fundamental solidarity with them in the time of the gospel (Rom 9:3). He reckons himself even now the "remnant" in which all Israel is embodied: "So then also in the now-time a remnant, chosen by grace, has come into being (*houtōs oun kai en tō nun kairō leimma kat' eklogēn charitos genonen*)" (Rom 11:5 DH). The distinction the gospel creates between the elect and rejected, between "the Church of Jacob" and "the Church of Esau," is not a line of division running between the historical church on the one hand and the historical people Israel on the other. Rather, the gospel creates a fundamental distinction between the single entity Israel/church as an "observable, knowable, and possible" religious-political community on the one hand (i.e., Israel/church in its solidarity with the "world"), and the "unobservable, unknowable, and impossible" reality that "has neither place, nor name, nor history"[44] on the other (i.e., Israel/church

---

42. For this reason I will frequently use the term "Israel/church" to indicate the fact that what Barth writes in the commentary about Israel applies precisely also to the church, and vice versa. See further Harink, "Barth's Apocalyptic Exegesis."

43. Barth, *Romans*, 338–39.

44. Ibid., 341–42.

"in the eternal 'Moment' [when it] dawns in Christ"[45]). There is no possibility of a sequential, successive, supersessive historical transition (a divine cosmic-historical drama) from one chosen people (e.g., the elect as Israel of old) to another (e.g., the elect as the church or the "new" or "true" Israel). In the *apokalypsis Theou* Israel and the church are a single entity that is simultaneously rejected and elected.

For Barth the *apokalypsis Theou* in Jesus Christ confronts the history of Israel/church as its "tribulation"; as the revelation of God's righteousness, the gospel *hardens* Israel/church in its opposition to God insofar as it is a power in world history, and confirms its solidarity with the present age that is passing away. But by God's *mercy* alone—and against all intrinsic or emergent religious-historical possibilities—Israel/church is also chosen by God to stand as a sign to the world of God's "impossible" election and righteousness, as a sign of the redemption of history in the age to come. It is precisely as it stands *against* the "success" of Israel/church in sustaining itself through history and as a viable contributor to its "progress" (i.e., in its capacity as a "religion") that the gospel is revealed as a word of judgment and dissolution. By contrast, to the "stumbling" of Israel/church—that is, to its incapacity to be an agent contributing to the higher development of history—God brings about its justification, and with it the justification of the whole world. God's hardening and rejection of Israel/church (its "tribulation"), for the sake of the world, brings about nothing less than the reconciliation of the world. When God by his mercy redeems Israel/church from its self-sustaining journey in history, and removes its hardening, this is nothing less than "the dawning of the Day of Jesus Christ, with the manifestation of the glory of God—for which we now hope, and can only hope—and with the world redeemed by God."[46]

For Barth there is no divine cosmic-historical narrative, no linear sequence leading from creation to Israel, from Israel to Christ, from Christ to the church, from the church to the eschaton. Rather, the gospel of Jesus Christ cancels that supposed linear salvation-historical "plan" and renders the whole of past, present, and future immediate to the time of the gospel. Israel and the church, Paul and his readers, the letter and the commentator, exist together *in one and the same time*, the

45. Ibid, 360.
46. Ibid, 407.

time of the gospel, the time of judgment and redemption. By refusing to contextualize Paul within either a secular historical or a salvation historical framework, Barth marks a decisive break with modernity and opens the way for another kind of commentary, one in which the simultaneity of the letter and the commentator in apocalyptic gospel time creates the conditions for commentary as a "theological event." Not only Paul's letter, then, but also the commentary on it, is written in such a way as to anticipate a corresponding event in the life of the reader, the event of the obedience of faith.

If we ask about the political character of the obedience of faith envisaged by Barth's commentary, it does not take the form of conservative, liberal, or violent revolutionary action to bring about in history (whether gradually or suddenly) a new order of things. "What man has the right to propound and represent the 'New', whether it be a new age, or a new world, or even a new—spirit? Is not every new thing, in so far as it can be schemed by men, born of what already *exists*? The moment it becomes a human proposition, must it not be numbered among the things that are?"[47] Negatively, obedient political action does not "set what exists against what exists"; rather, it takes the form of a "not-doing," an "action void of purpose": "Its meaning is that men have encountered God, and are thereby compelled to leave the judgment to him. The actual occurrence of this judgment cannot be identified with the purpose or with the secret reckoning of the man of this world."[48] In other words, obedient political action does not strive by whatever means to bring about its "good" end in history. The end of political action is given over to eternity.

Positively—and simultaneously—obedient political action therefore takes the form of love. "Love of *one another* ought to be undertaken as the protest against the course of this world, and it ought to continue without interruption."[49] If love alone is action without interruption, love is the participation of time in eternity:

> Time is . . . irreversible; and of this the irrevocable hurrying away of the past and the relentless approach of the future are a parable. But a parable of it also is the completely hidden, un-

47. Ibid, 480 (emphasis original).
48. Ibid, 483–84.
49. Ibid, 492.

observable, intangible present which lies 'between' the times. Facing, as it does, both ways, each moment in time is a parable of the eternal 'Moment'. Every moment in time bears within it the unborn secret of revelation, and every moment can be thus qualified.—*This do, knowing the time* [Rom 13:11]. And so, the known time—apprehended and comprehended in its transcendental significance—provides the occasion for the incomprehensible action of love. . . . Love builds no tabernacles [or new and improved socio-political structures], for it seeks to create nothing that abides, nothing that 'exists' in time. Love does what it does only in the knowledge of the eternal 'Moment'. Love is therefore the essentially revolutionary action.[50]

Commentary on Romans is for Barth neither practicing objective historical research, nor narrating the grand story of God's cosmic-historical plan. Commentary itself can be nothing other than a revolutionary action, participating as such with Paul in the revolutionary action of God in Jesus Christ, in which "the unborn secret of revelation" is released upon the world and time, to bring about their death and resurrection.

4. Gospel Time in Type and Recapitulation

A constitutive feature of Paul's Letter to the Romans is his use of Israel's scriptures. As we saw above, Wright takes Paul's scriptural references as clues to the grand cosmic-historical narrative background that funds Paul's whole theological project, and that finally makes sense of the arrival of the Messiah. Barth, on the other hand, more or less absorbs Paul's scriptural references seamlessly into Paul's own writing, and gives no explicit attention to or account of how Paul uses Israel's scriptures. Nevertheless, Paul's use of the scriptures, particularly his typological use, may be a significant clue to the relation between the messianic-apocalyptic time of the gospel and the history of Israel, the church and the world. Giorgio Agamben makes that case in his philosophical commentary on Romans, *The Time that Remains*.[51]

---

50. Ibid, 497–98.

51. Agamben's "commentary" is shaped directly only by the first ten Greek words of Romans (1:1), a point to which I shall return. A good deal of *The Time that Remains* takes up texts from elsewhere in the Pauline corpus, especially from 1 Corinthians.

Agamben is interested (as part of a larger project in political philosophy) in understanding the character of messianic time and messianic agency in Paul. Providing something of a definition of messianic time, he writes: "[T]he messianic is not the end of time, but *the time of the end* . . . What interests the apostle is not the last day, it is not the instant in which time ends, but the time that contracts itself and begins to end (*ho kairos synestalmenos estin*; 1 Cor. 7:29), or if you prefer, the time that remains between time and its end."[52] "For Paul the contraction of time, the 'remaining' time represents the messianic situation par excellence, the only real time."[53] Here we may recall Paul's reminder in Rom 13:11–12: "Besides this, you know what time (*kairos*) it is, how it is now the moment (*hōra*) for you to wake from sleep. For salvation is nearer to us now (*nun*) than when we became believers. The night is far gone, the day (*hēmera*) is near." Given the *kairos*, Paul instructs us to "put on the armor of light" and to "put on the Lord Jesus Christ"—that is, to live in the time of the end as the only real time because it is the time of the *apokalypsis Theou*. To "put on" *Christos* is to be clothed in his crucified, resurrected and exalted reality which alone determines the *nun kairos*, the present messianic time. That time is not another time than *chronos*; it is, rather, *chronos* laid hold of and taken up by Jesus the Messiah into his own enduring reality. Messianic time is the time of the Messiah.[54]

Agamben provides a further definition that now includes the messianic subject: "[M]essianic time, an operational time in which we take hold of and achieve our representations of time, is the time *that* we ourselves are, and for this very reason, it is the only real time, the only time we have."[55] In messianic time "what we take hold of when we seize *kairos* is not another time but a contracted and abridged *chronos*… That messianic 'healing' happens in *kairos* is evident, but this *kairos* is

52. Agamben, *Time that Remains*, 62 (emphasis original). Agamben further explains the concept of "the time that contracts itself and begins to end" with reference to the poem, in particular the sestina (78–87). See the essay by Paul Griffiths in this volume for further reflection on Agamben's use of the sestina to illustrate messianic time.

53. Ibid., 5.

54. Agamben himself stops short of affirming that Jesus is *the* Messiah, crucified, risen, living and present as the Lord of time; that is, affirming the actuality and indeed the determination of "the messianic" in the singular Messiah Jesus.

55. Ibid., 68 (emphasis original).

nothing more than seized *chronos*."[56] Agamben's analysis here is important for describing the messianic subject's experience of and relation to time. The "day" of the Messiah's coming is a time qualitatively different from the measurable days of *chronos*.

> The Messiah has already arrived, the messianic event has already happened, but its presence contains within itself another time, which stretches its *parousia*, not in order to defer it, but, on the contrary, to make it graspable. For this reason, each instant may be, to use Benjamin's words, the 'small door through which the Messiah enters.' The Messiah always already had his time, meaning he simultaneously makes time his and brings it to fulfillment.[57]

In this messianic stretching of the *parousia*, *chronos*-history in the historicist and progressivist senses (whether secular or theological) is opened up and made permeable to the *kairos* of the Messiah. "In Paul, messianic time, as operational time, implies an actual transformation of the experience of time that may even interrupt secular time here and now."[58]

The messianic transformation of time brings about a fundamental alteration in Paul's reading of Israel's scriptures. The proclamation of the gospel (which the letter to the Romans is) constitutes the "time of legibility" of Israel's scriptures,[59] the decisive moment of reading the scriptures "in the Messiah" in which the prophetic writings *now* (and only now) speak their timely word about the Messiah, and thus find their messianic fulfillment. In the messianic now-time the figures and patterns of Israel's scriptures are taken up and become "legible" or recognizable for what they are, anticipations or types of the Messiah, who is himself the "time of the now" in which all of the figures and types are "recapitulated." Origen (if we may draw him in here for a moment) captures the idea of the messianic "time of legibility" exactly: "Before

56. Ibid., 69.

57. Ibid., 71.

58. Ibid., 73.

59. The phrase and the idea of "the time of legibility" is from Walter Benjamin, quoted in Agamben, *Time that Remains*, 145. Agamben provides a helpful analysis of Benjamin's idea of *Jetztzeit* ("now-time") and *das Jetzt der Lesbarkeit* ("the now of legibility"). Benjamin's probing of the concept of messianic time in his "Theses" is profound and germane to the discussion of messianic interpretation touched upon here.

the sojourn of Christ, the law and the prophets did not contain the proclamation which belongs to the definition of the gospel, since he who explained the mysteries in them had not yet come. But since the Savior has come and has caused the gospel to be embodied, he has by the gospel made all things as gospel."[60]

Agamben points to typology as the means by which Paul defines the "innermost relation of messianic time to chronological time."[61] In Paul's typological interpretation of Israel's scriptures the messianic "now-time" creates an inversion of the past and the future; the past becomes, in a sense, alive again, open to the future: "the past (the complete) rediscovers actuality and becomes unfulfilled, and the present (the incomplete) acquires a kind of fulfillment."[62] Time is transformed in the typological relation, making the past alive and open to its fulfillment in the messianic present. Agamben draws attention to 1 Cor 10:6, 11, where Paul brings brief narratives of Israel's past together with the current life of the church in Corinth with the concept of *typos*: "Now these things occurred as types for us [*typoi hēmōn*]" (v. 6—the NRSV translates *typoi* lamely as "examples"). "Now these things happened to them as types [*typikōs*], and they were written down to instruct us, on whom the ends of the ages have come" (v. 11). The typological and the messianic are brought together here to render "a tension that clasps together and transforms past and future, *typos* and *antitypos*, in an inseparable constellation. The messianic is not just one of two terms in this typological relation, *it is the relation itself*."[63] History's truth is born in messianic time; yet it is the truth that was always waiting to be born in this time. Typological relations between past and future are frequently invoked in Romans, particularly in chapter 9, where Isaac and Jacob become types of the nations (*ethnē*) who in the now-time are receiving mercy, while Pharaoh becomes a type of Israel which is in the now-time "hardened" to the message about Messiah Jesus. Paul is in no sense describing a divinely governed linear-historical drama with these references to the characters in Israel's stories (cf. N. T. Wright). Rather, these characters are given life again in the relation between Israel and

60. *Commentary on John* 1.33; quoted in Behr, *Mystery of Christ*, 91.

61. Agamben, *Time that Remains*, 73.

62. Ibid., 75.

63. Ibid., 74 (emphasis original).

the nations established in the Messiah: in messianic time the *chronoi* of Isaac and Jacob and Pharaoh are taken up into the present *kairos* of the Messiah and fulfilled.[64]

Agamben further identifies "recapitulation" (*anakephalaiōsis*) as another Pauline concept that defines the relation between messianic time and chronological time. Referring to Eph 1:10, Agamben writes: "What Paul says here is that insofar as messianic time aims toward the fulfillment of time . . . it effectuates a recapitulation, a kind of summation of all things, in heaven and on earth—of all that has transpired from creation to the messianic 'now,' meaning the past as whole."[65] Agamben notes that in Rom 13:9–10 Paul brings in the idea of *anakephalaiōsis*

---

64. I should note, in contrast to Agamben, that Paul's typological reading of Israel's scriptures is his way, in relation to Israel's scriptures, of rendering the reality of *Jesus'* messianic *lordship* over time, of Jesus the Messiah's co-temporality with Israel "of old" in which he, as Israel's Lord, takes Israel up into his own messianic reality, the *nun kairos*, and *reactivates* Israel's past as a living messianic witness. It is important to emphasize, in contrast to Agamben, that for Paul "the messianic" is not an indeterminate concept, but is defined and determined by the life, crucifixion, resurrection, and exaltation of Jesus (Phil 2:6–11). Agamben thoroughly immanentizes the theological concept of the messianic (see the discussion in De la Durantaye, *Giorgio Agamben*, 367–71) because he (unlike Paul) deliberately turns the discussion away from the actuality of Messiah Jesus who is the Lord of time. But for Paul it is not messianic subjects but this messianic *Lord* who in the first place "takes hold of," and "seizes," time, makes it his own by judging and redeeming it, and in turn *gives* it as that "contracted and abridged *chronos*," the time that remains, in which messianic subjects enact a cruciform history as a participation in the Messiah. That Jesus Messiah is himself Lord of time is crucial for grasping that messianic time is the only properly real time not only for the messianic subject, but also for all humanity. Thus, for example, Paul's discussion of "what time it is" in Rom 13:11–14 follows close on the heels of his discussion of the time of the empire (13:1–7). For Paul, even the time of the empire is laid hold of by the *kyrios*, the Messiah Jesus. God "hollows out" the "factical condition" of the empire and the powers that be—the "history makers" according to their own vaunted self-understanding as *kyrioi*—and puts it to use for God's own purpose. Despite their own lack of knowledge and acknowledgement that they live in messianic time, the "governing authorities" are nevertheless, in the now-time, conscripted as God's *diakonoi*, not for the glorious purpose (as they think) of bringing in the age of "peace and justice" (because that age has already been apocalyptically inaugurated by God through the crucified and risen Messiah), but for the rather inglorious purpose of executing God's "wrath" on evildoers. Messianic subjects, on the other hand, *know and acknowledge* what time it is: while they live under the empire, they do not live in imperial time and the regime that it establishes, but in the "day" of the Lord which has now arrived. They have clothed themselves in its light as in armor. They have "put on the Lord Jesus Christ"—they live in the Messiah's time and the regime that he establishes.

65. Agamben, *Time that Remains*, 75–76.

to speak of the relationship of the various commandments to the one commandment to "love your neighbor as yourself." In this way, love is the *plērōma* of the law. Here again, the temporal relation is not that of sequence but of simultaneity:

> What is decisive here is that the *plērōma* of *kairoi* is understood as the relation of each instant to the Messiah—each *kairos* is *unmittelbar zu Gott* . . . , and is not just the final result of a process . . . each time is the messianic now . . . , and the messianic is not the chronological end of time, but the present as the exigency of fulfillment, what gives itself 'as an end' . . . In this sense, recapitulation is nothing else than the other facet of the typological relation established by messianic *kairos* between present and past.[66]

Here again we might reflect on Romans 9–11, in particular 11:25–32. If Romans 9 is characterized by messianic typology, Romans 11 is characterized by messianic recapitulation. Paul envisages the coming in of the *plērōma* of the nations as well as the salvation of *pas Israēl*, and envisages this recapitulation of the history of Israel and the nations—a history recapitulated now as the one for the sake of the other (11:28–32)—precisely as the arrival of the Messiah: "Out of Zion will come the Deliver" (11:26).

Agamben's analysis of messianic time in Paul enables us, via typology, to return to the historical and narrative details (the *chronoi*) of Israel—and not only Israel, but also the nations (Rom 13:1–7) and all creation (Rom 8:18–25)—and find them being opened up to the *kairos* of the messianic in which the *chronoi* will not be finally abandoned to the destructive powers of sin and death. The *chronoi* of Israel, the nations, and all creation is seized, judged, taken up, and fulfilled in the "stretched" *nun kairos* of the Messiah. That is something that we do not find happening in the vision of secular time presupposed by Jewett and the historicist reading of Romans. Nor do we find it in the "on-going" linear time of salvation history in Wright, in which, for example, Israel "according to the flesh" is superseded by Christ and the church and left in its past. In both Jewett and Wright the *chronoi* set the conditions and context for the messianic *kairos*, rather than the other way around. By contrast, Barth's radical contextualization of his-

66. Ibid., 76.

tory by the gospel in the dialectic of time and eternity has the effect of rendering all times co-present to eternity; nevertheless, it also in some measure has the corresponding effect of canceling out all of the details of historical occurrence, rendering every actual difference in time null and void. Agamben's recovery of Pauline typology and recapitulation reveals how in the apocalyptic-messianic time of the gospel nothing is lost, no time is lost, in the now-time of the gospel. Nothing is lost, but everything is altered in the moment of messianic arrival. Messianic action cannot bring about that messianic alteration as an end; rather, acting in "weak messianic power" in the time that remains, it awaits the Messiah's arrival.

For Agamben the message of Romans must itself be grasped and rendered in "the time that remains between time and its end." Romans has its own "time of legibility." "The possibility of understanding the Pauline message coincides fully with the experience of such a [messianic] time; without this, it runs the risk of remaining a dead letter."[67] The very character of Agamben's book, a "commentary on Romans," is therefore an attempt to read Romans messianically. As I have noted, it is in fact commentary "only" on the first ten Greek words of the letter, rather than on the whole text. "But," writes Agamben, "since we do not have time for such an endeavor [commentary on the whole text] . . . we will have to place our stakes in this brief time, on this radical abbreviation of time that is the time *that remains*." That endeavor "depends on a preliminary wager: we will be treating this first verse [of Romans] as though its first ten words recapitulate the meaning of the text in its entirety."[68] As we have seen, recapitulation is central to Paul's way of rendering the idea of messianic time. The first ten words may then be taken as Paul's own messianic act of recapitulation: "each word of the incipit contracts within itself the complete text of the Letter, in a vertiginous recapitulation."[69] Agamben's commentary on these words is therefore his own corresponding messianic performance. He turns away from commentary as tour de force, the powerful, persuasive, "irresistible," interpretation of the whole—the mode that in one way or

67. Ibid., 2.
68. Ibid., 5–6 (emphasis original).
69. Ibid., 6.

another characterizes the commentaries of Jewett, Wright and Barth—
and writes commentary as an act of weak messianic power.

Conclusion

Writing commentary is a work in time. The commentary that comes to
be written, as we have seen, displays in the very character of its production and writing a particular understanding of time and human agency,
whether that is made explicit in the commentary or not. Of our four
commentators, Jewett seems to be the least reflective about the character of time that his commentary presupposes. That likely reflects the
fact that secular time is so deeply and widely assumed in our age that it
requires a labor of attention and discernment to think time in any other
way. It is, further, the character of time assumed by the Hermeneia
commentary series (and imposed upon the contributors to it), and no
doubt by Jewett himself as a scholar fundamentally shaped by modernity. It is clearly not the character of time assumed by the Letter to the
Romans. It leaves Jewett to work out his relation to Romans and his
task as a commentator in historicist terms, and thus finally, despite all
the obvious brilliance in research and synthesis, to miss the point of the
letter. Wright, on the other hand, seeks to give an explicitly theological
account of time as the divinely directed linear sequence of events: the
cosmic-historical drama that comes to a climax (but not an end) in
Jesus Christ, a drama to be continued along the same sequence in the
covenantal history of the church in the world. Wright proposes that
account of time as the background story of Romans and seeks to plot
the "story" of Romans within that larger story and as itself a further
explication of it. The apocalyptic-messianic character of Paul's gospel
in Romans is read as a significant feature of one climactic event (the
coming of Christ) in the larger story, but not as constitutive of the very
character of time itself. Paul and Romans are therefore, for Wright,
characters located firmly in the salvation-historical past, no less to be
read from a temporal distance than they are by Jewett. The work of
commentary is to mediate the temporal gap.

Barth is the first modern commentator on Romans to take the
apocalyptic-messianic tone of Romans as constitutive for understanding the character of time, and to write a commentary that aims both to
participate in and give display to time as thus constituted. For Paul time

is neither constitutively closed off from the divine (as in historicism), nor a steady linear progression under divine agency (as in salvation-historicism). Rather, time is permeable, malleable, redeemable, because it is taken up into the crucifixion and resurrection of Jesus the Messiah, who is the Creator and Lord of time. The vehicle Barth uses to render this apocalyptic construal of time is the dialectical relationship of eternity and time. The problem here, though, is that finally there can be no true dialectic in that relationship: eternity (as Barth construes in the commentary) is the overwhelming reality and cannot but ultimately overcome time rather than establish its reality. Barth's commentary often resists that outcome insofar as he follows Paul's text; but his practice of dialectic always tends, in the "Moment," toward a cancellation of time and the particularities of history by eternity. By contrast, Agamben's understanding of the moment of messianic time as "stretched," shown in his analysis of typology and recapitulation, enables us to understand time and history, apocalyptically and messianically constituted, as open to healing and redemption through figuration and anticipation. The particularities of temporal existence are taken up—resurrected—in the Messiah's arrival which renders the past "legible." Agamben's own work of commentary seeks to participate in messianic time and enact a form of messianic agency by taking the time to dwell in the first ten words of Romans as dwelling in the whole of Paul's messianic gospel. At the same time, however, Agamben himself falls short of grasping how it is the messianity of Jesus in particular—that is, that Jesus *is* the Messiah—that is at the heart of Paul's understanding of time. "Messianic" is finally not something intrinsic to the nature of time (which Agamben might also say), but is the character of time given by the Lord of time, Jesus the Messiah. If we were to dwell on this last point, however, we would be led again to Barth, this time to the *Church Dogmatics*, and the christological-pneumatological theology of time he develops at length in its pages.[70] But that is for another time.

70. See especially *Church Dogmatics* II/1, §14; III/2, §47; IV/1, §62.3; IV/3.2, §72.1.

Bibliography

Adams, Edward, and David G. Horrell, editors. *Christianity at Corinth: The Quest for the Pauline Church*. Louisville: Westminster John Knox, 2004.

Agamben, Giorgio. *The Coming Community*. Translated by Michael Hardt. Theory out of bounds 1. Minneapolis: University of Minnesota Press, 1993.

———. *Homo Sacer: Sovereign Power and Bare Life*. Translated by Daniel Heller-Roazen. Meridian: Crossing Aesthetics. Stanford: Stanford University Press, 1998.

———. *Idea of Prose*. Translated by Michael Sullivan and Sam Whitsitt. Intersections. Albany, NY: SUNY Press, 1995.

———. *Infancy and History: The Destruction of Experience*. Translated by Liz Heron. New York: Verso, 2007.

———. *Means without End: Notes on Politics*. Translated by Vincenzo Binetti and Cesare Casarino. Theory out of Bounds 20. Minneapolis: University of Minnesota Press, 2000.

———. "The Messiah and the Sovereign." In *Potentialities: Collected Essays in Philosophy*, edited and translated by Daniel Heller-Roazen, ch. 10. Meridian: Crossing Aesthetics. Stanford: Stanford University Press, 1999.

———. *The Open: Man and Animal*. Translated by Kevin Attell. Meridian: Crossing Aesthetics. Stanford: Stanford University Press, 2004.

———. "Der Papist ist ein weltlicher Priester." Interview by Abu Rieger. *Literaturen*, June 2005, 21–25.

———. *Profanations*. Translated by Jeff Fort. New York: Zone Books, 2007.

———. *Potentialities: Collected Essays in Philosophy*. Edited and translated by Daniel Heller-Roazen. Meridian: Crossing Aesthetics. Stanford: Stanford University Press, 1999.

———. *State of Exception*. Translated by Kevin Attell. Chicago: Chicago University Press, 2005.

———. *The Time that Remains: A Commentary on the Letter to the Romans*. Translated by Patricia Dailey. Meridian: Crossing Aesthetics. Stanford: Stanford University Press, 2005.

Alexander, Philip S. "Predestination and Free Will in the Theology of the Dead Sea Scrolls." In *Divine and Human Agency in Paul and His Cultural Environment*, edited by John M. G. Barclay and Simon J. Gathercole, 27–49. Early Christianity in Context, Library of New Testament studies 335. London: T. & T. Clark, 2006.

Asmis, Elizabeth. "Choice in Epictetus' Philosophy." In *Antiquity and Humanity: Essays on Ancient Religion and Philosophy: Presented to Hans Dieter Betz on His 70th Birthday*, edited by Adela Yarbro Collins and Margaret M. Mitchell, 385–412. Tübingen: Mohr/Siebeck, 2001.

Auerbach, Erich. "On the Political Theory of Pascal." In *Scenes from the Drama of European Literature*, 101–29. Theory and History of Literature 9. Minneapolis: University of Minnesota Press, 1984.

Badiou, Alain. *Being and Event*. Translated by Oliver Feltham. New York: Continuum, 2005.

———. "The Communist Hypothesis." *New Left Review* 49 (2008) 29–42.

———. "Eight Theses on the Universal." In *Theoretical Writings*, edited and translated by Ray Brassier and Alberto Toscano, 143–52. Athlone Contemporary European Thinkers. New York: Continuum, 2004.

———. *Ethics: An Essay on the Understanding of Evil*. Translated and introduced by Peter Hallward. Wo es war. New York: Verso, 2001.

———. *Infinite Thought: Truth and the Return of Philosophy*. Edited by Justin Clements and Oliver Feltham. New York: Continuum, 2003.

———. "Philosophy and Politics." In *Infinite Thought: Truth and the Return of Philosophy*, edited by Justin Clements and Oliver Feltham, 52–59. New York: Continuum, 2003.

———."Philosophy and Psychoanalysis." In *Infinite Thought: Truth and the Return of Philosophy*, edited by Justin Clements and Oliver Feltham, 60–82. New York: Continuum, 2003.

———. "Politics and Philosophy." *Angelaki* 3:3 (1998) 113–33.

———. *Saint Paul: The Foundation of Universalism*. Translated by Ray Brassier. Stanford: Stanford University Press, 2003. Cultural Memory in the Present. Originally published as *Saint Paul: La Fondation de l'universalisme* (Paris: Presses Universitaires de France, 1997).

———. "Truth: Forcing and the Unnameable." In *Theoretical Writings*, edited and translated by Ray Brassier and Alberto Toscano, 119–34. Athlone Contemporary European Thinkers. New York: Continuum, 2004.

Barclay, John. "Why the Roman Empire Was Insignificant to Paul." Paper presented to the Pauline Epistles section of the SBL annual meeting, San Diego, November 19, 2007.

Barron, Robert. *The Priority of Christ: Toward a Postliberal Catholicism*. Grand Rapids: Brazos, 2007.

Barth, Karl. *Church Dogmatics III/2: The Doctrine of Creation*. Translated by H. Knight, G. W. Bromiley, J. K. S. Reid, and R. H. Fuller. Edinburgh: T. & T. Clark, 1960.

———. *The Epistle to the Romans*. Translated from the 6th ed. by Edwin C. Hoskyns. Oxford: Oxford University Press, 1968. German ed.: *Der Römerbrief* (Zürich: EVZ, 1940).

Bauckham, Richard. *God Crucified: Monotheism and Christology in the New Testament*. Didsbury Lectures 1996. Grand Rapids: Eerdmans, 1999.

Behr, John. *The Mystery of Christ: Life in Death*. Crestwood, NY: St. Vladimir's Seminary Press, 2006.

Beker, J Christiaan. *Paul the Apostle: The Triumph of God in Life and Thought*. Philadelphia: Fortress, 1980.

————. *Paul's Apocalyptic Gospel: The Coming Triumph of God*. Philadelphia: Fortress, 1982.

Bell, Daniel. "Badiou's Faith and Paul's Gospel: The Politics of Indifference and the Overcoming of Capital." *Angelaki* 12:1 (2007) 97–111.

————. "The Politics of Fear and the Gospel of Life." In *Belief and Metaphysics*, edited by Conor Cunningham and Peter M. Candler, 426–51. Veritas. London: SCM, 2007.

Benjamin, Walter. *The Arcades Project*. Edited by Rolf Tiedemann, translated by Howard Eiland. Cambridge, MA: Belknap Press/Harvard University Press, 1999.

————. "Critique of Violence." In *Reflections: Essays, Aphorisms, Autobiographical Writings*, edited by Peter Demetz, translated by Edmund Jephcott, 277–300. New York: Schocken, 1978.

————. "Even the Sacramental Migrates into Myth." In *Selected Writings*, edited by Marcus Bullock and Michael W. Jennings, translated by Howard Eiland and Edmund Jephcott, 1:402–3. Cambridge, MA: Belknap Press/Harvard University Press, 1996–2006.

————. "Fate and Character." In *Reflections: Essays, Aphorisms, Autobiographical Writings*, edited by Peter Demetz, translated by Edmund Jephcott, 301–11. New York: Schocken, 1978. German ed.: "Theologisch-politisches Fragment," in *Illuminationen: Ausgewählte Schriften* (Frankfurt: Suhrkamp, 1977).

————. *Gesammelte Schriften*. Edited by Rolf Tiedemann and Hermann Schweppenhäuser. 7 vols. Frankfurt: Suhrkamp, 1972–89.

————"Goethe's 'Elective Affinities.'" In *Selected Writings*, edited by Marcus Bullock and Michael W. Jennings, translated by Howard Eiland and Edmund Jephcott, 1:297–360. Cambridge, MA: Belknap Press/Harvard University Press, 1996–2006.

————. *Illuminations*. Edited by Hannah Arendt. Translated by Harry Zohn. New York: Schocken, 1968.

————. "Paralipomena to 'On the Concept of History.'" In *Selected Writings*, edited by Marcus Bullock and Michael W. Jennings, translated by Howard Eiland and Edmund Jephcott, 4:402–3. Cambridge, MA: Belknap Press/Harvard University Press, 1996–2006.

————. *Reflections: Essays, Aphorisms, Autobiographical Writings*. Edited by Peter Demetz, translated by Edmund Jephcott. New York: Schocken, 1978.

————. *Selected Writings*. Edited by Marcus Bullock and Michael W. Jennings, translated by Howard Eiland and Edmund Jephcott. 4 vols. Cambridge, MA: Belknap Press/ Harvard University Press, 1996–2006.

————. "Theologico-Political Fragment." In *Reflections: Essays, Aphorisms, Autobiographical Writings*, edited by Peter Demetz, translated by Edmund Jephcott, 312–13. New York: Schocken, 1978. German ed.: "Theologisch-politisches Fragment," in *Illuminationen: Ausgewählte Schriften* (Frankfurt: Suhrkamp, 1977).

————. "Theses on the Philosophy of History." In *Illuminations*, edited by Hannah Arendt, translated by Harry Zohn, 253–64. New York: Schocken, 1969. Originally published, New York: Harcourt, Brace & World, 1968.

————. "Ueber den Begriff der Geschichte," in *Illuminationen: Ausgewählte Schriften* (Frankfurt: Suhrkamp, 1977), 251–61.

———"World and Time." In In *Selected Writings*, edited by Marcus Bullock and Michael W. Jennings, translated by Howard Eiland and Edmund Jephcott, 1:226–27. Cambridge, MA: Belknap Press/Harvard University Press, 1996–2006.

Blanton, Ward. "Disturbing Politics: Neo-Paulinism and the Scrambling of Religious and Secular Identities." *Dialog* 46:1 (2007) 1–13.

Bobzien, Susanne. *Determinism and Freedom in Stoic Philosophy*. Oxford: Oxford University Press, 1998.

Boer, Martinus C. de. "The New Preachers in Galatia. Their Identity, Message, Aims, and Impact." In *Jesus, Paul, and Early Christianity: Studies in Honour of Henk Jan de Jonge*, edited by Rieuwerd Buitenwerf et al., 39–60. Supplements to Novum Testamentum 130. Leiden: Brill, 2008.

———. "Paul and Apocalyptic Eschatology." In *The Encyclopedia of Apocalypticism*, edited by Bernard McGinn, John J. Collins, Stephen J. Stein, 1:345–83. New York: Continuum, 1998.

———. "Paul and Jewish Apocalyptic Theology." In *Apocalyptic and the New Testament: Essays in Honor of J. Louis Martyn*, edited by Joel Marcus and Marion L. Soards, 169–90. JSNTSup 24. Sheffield: JSOT Press, 1989.

Boer, Roland. *Marxist Criticism of the Bible. A Critical Introduction to Marxist Literary Theory and the Bible*. London: Sheffield Academic, 2003.

Bonhoeffer, Dietrich. *Dietrich Bonhoeffer Werke*. Munich: C. Kaiser, 1986–99.

———. *Dietrich Bonhoeffer Works*. Edited by Wayne Whitson Floyd Jr. Minneapolis: Fortress, 1996–.

Bornkamm, Günther. *Paul*. Translated by D. M. G. Stalker. New York: Harper & Row, 1971.

Boyarin, Daniel. *A Radical Jew: Paul and the Politics of Identity*. Contraversions 1. Berkeley: University of California Press, 1994.

Breton, Stanislas. *Saint Paul*. Philosophies 18. Paris: Presses Universitaires de France, 1988.

———. *The Word and the Cross*. Translated by Jacquelyn Porter. Perspectives in Continental Philosophy 22. New York: Fordham University Press, 2002.

Butler, Judith, et al. *Contingency, Hegemony, Universality: Contemporary Dialogues on the Left*. Phronesis. New York: Verso, 2000.

Cavanaugh, William T. *Torture and Eucharist: Theology, Politics, and the Body of Christ*. Challenges in Contemporary Theology. Malden, MA: Blackwell, 1998.

Clement of Alexandria. *The Instructor*. In *The Ante-Nicene Fathers*, edited by A. J. Robertson and James Donaldson, 2:207–98. Peabody, MA: Hendrickson, 1999.

Davis, Mike. *Planet of Slums*. New York: Verso, 2006.

De la Durantaye, Leland. *Giorgio Agamben: A Critical Introduction*. Stanford: Stanford University Press, 2009.

De Ste. Croix, G. E. M. *The Class Struggle in the Ancient Greek World: From the Archaic Age to the Arab Conquests*. Ithaca, NY: Cornell University Press, 1980.

Derrida, Jacques. *Margins of Philosophy*. Translated by Alan Bass. Chicago: University of Chicago Press, 1982.

Desmond, William. *Being and the Between*. SUNY Series in Philosophy. Albany, NY: SUNY Press, 1995.

———. "Neither Servility nor Sovereignty: Between Metaphysics and Politics." In *Theology and the Political*, edited by Creston Davis, John Milband, and Slavoj Žižek, 153–82. SIC 5. Durham, NC: Duke University Press, 2005.

Donfried, Karl P., editor. *The Romans Debate*. Rev. ed. Peabody, MA: Hendrickson, 1991.

Duff, Paul Brooks. "Metaphor, Motif, and Meaning: The Rhetorical Strategy behind the Image 'Led in Triumph' in 2 Corinthians 2:14." *Catholic Biblical Quarterly* 53 (1991) 86–89.

Dunn, James D. G. "The New Perspective on Paul." *Bulletin of the John Rylands Library* 65 (1983) 95–122.

———. *Romans 1–8*. Word Biblical Commentary 38A. Dallas: Word Books, 1988.

———. *The Theology of Paul the Apostle*. Grand Rapids: Eerdmans, 1998.

Dupré, Louis. *Religion and the Rise of Modern Culture*. Erasmus Institute Books. Notre Dame: University of Notre Dame Press, 2008.

Eagleton, Terry. *Ideology: An Introduction*. New York: Verso, 1991.

Eisenbaum, Pamela. "Paul, Polemics, and the Problem of Essentialism." In *Paul between Jews and Christians*, edited by Mark Nanos, 224–38. *Biblical Interpretation* 13:3 (2005).

Ellacuría, Ignacio. "The Crucified People." In *Mysterium Liberationis: Fundamental Concepts of Liberation Theology*, edited by Ignacio Ellacuría and Jon Sobrino, 580–603. Maryknoll, NY: Orbis, 1993.

Elliott, Neil. "The Apostle Paul's Self-Presentation as Anti-Imperial Performance." In *Paul and the Roman Imperial Order*, edited by Richard A. Horsley, 67–88. Harrisburg, PA: Trinity, 2004.

———. *The Arrogance of Nations: Reading Romans in the Shadow of Empire*. Paul in Critical Contexts. Minneapolis: Fortress, 2008.

———. *Liberating Paul: The Justice of God and the Politics of the Apostle*. Bible and Liberation Series. Maryknoll, NY: Orbis, 1994; Minneapolis: Fortress, 2006.

Epstein, Barbara. "The Politics of Prefigurative Community: The Non-Violent Direct Action Movement." In *Cultural Resistance Reader*, edited by Stephen Duncombe, 333–46. New York: Verso, 2002.

Fee, Gordon D. *Pauline Christology: An Exegetical-Theological Study*. Peabody, MA: Hendrickson, 2007.

Fitzgerald, John T. "Virtue/Vice Lists." In *Anchor Bible Dictionary*, 6:857–59. New York: Doubleday, 1992.

———, and L. Michael White. *The Tabula of Cebes*. Texts and Translations 24. Chico, CA: Scholars, 1983.

Fredriksen, Paula. *From Jesus to Christ: The Origins of New Testament Images of Jesus*. New Haven: Yale University Press, 1988.

Fukuyama, Francis. *The End of History and the Last Man*. New York: Penguin, 1992.

Gadamer, Hans-Georg. *Gesammelte Werke*. 10 vols. Tübingen: Mohr/Siebeck, 1985–95.

———. "Vom Zirkel des Verstehens." In *Gesammelte Werke*, 2:57–66. Tübingen: Mohr/Siebeck, 1993.

———. "Zwischen Phänomenologie und Dialektik—Versuch einer Selbstkritik." In *Gesammelte Werke*, 2:3–23. Tübingen: Mohr/Siebeck, 1993.

Galinsky, Karl. *Augustan Culture: An Interpretive Introduction*. Princeton: Princeton University Press, 1996.

Garnsey, Peter, and Richard Saller. *The Roman Empire: Economy, Society, and Culture*. Berkeley: University of California Press, 1987.

Gaston, Lloyd. *Paul and the Torah*. Vancouver: University of British Columbia Press, 1987.

Geulen, Eva. *Giorgio Agamben zur Einführung*. Zur Einführeng 304. Hamburg: Junius, 2005.

Gignac, Alain. "Taubes, Badiou, Agamben: Contemporary Reception of Paul by Non-Christian Philosophers." In *Reading Romans with Contemporary Philosophers and Theologians*, edited by David W. Odell-Scott, 155–211. Romans through History and Culture Series. New York: T. & T. Clark, 2007.

Goethe, Johann Wolfgang von. *Elective Affinities*. Translated by Judith Ryan. New York: Suhrkamp, 1988.

Gold, Joshua Robert. "Jacob Taubes: Apocalypse from Below." *Telos* 134 (2006) 140–56.

Gooding-Williams, Robert. *Zarathustra's Dionysian Modernism*. Atopia. Stanford: Stanford University Press, 2001.

Gorman, Michael J. *Apostle of the Crucified Lord: A Theological Introduction to Paul and His Letters*. Grand Rapids: Eerdmans, 2004.

———. *Cruciformity: Paul's Narrative Spirituality of the Cross*. Grand Rapids: Eerdmans, 2001.

Gottwald, Norman K. *The Hebrew Bible: A Socio-Literary Introduction*. Minneapolis: Fortress, 2002.

Griffiths, Paul. "Christ and Critical Theory." *First Things*, August/September 2004, 46–55.

———. "The Quietus of Political Interest." *Common Knowledge*, 15/1 (2009) 7–22.

Habermas, Jürgen. "Walter Benjamin: Consciousness or Rescuing Critique." In *On Walter Benjamin: Critical Essays and Recollections*, edited by Gary Smith, 90–128. Studies in Contemporary German Social Thought. Cambridge, MA: MIT Press, 1995.

Hahne, Harry Alan. *The Corruption and Redemption of Creation: Nature in Romans 8.19–22 and Jewish Apocalyptic Literature*. Library of New Testament Studies 336. New York: T. & T. Clark, 2006.

Halivni, David. *Midrash, Mishnah, and Gemara: The Jewish Predilection for Justified Law*. Cambridge, MA: Harvard University Press, 1986.

Hallward, Peter. *Badiou: A Subject to Truth*. Minneapolis: University of Minnesota Press, 2003.

Hamacher, Werner. "Guilt History: Benjamin's Sketch 'Capitalism as Religion.'" Translated by Kirk Wetters. *Diacritics* 32 (Fall 2002) 81–106.

Hanssen, Beatrice. *Walter Benjamin's Other History: Of Stones, Animals, Human Beings, and Angels*. Weimar and Now 15. Berkeley: University of California Press, 2000.

Harink, Douglas. "Barth's Apocalyptic Exegesis and the Question of Israel in *Römerbrief*, chs. 9–11." *Toronto Journal of Theology* 25:1 (2009) 5–18.

———. "False Universal? Badiou's Paul *sans* Jesus, Israel and the Church." Unpublished paper presented to the Theology and Continental Philosophy group at the AAR annual meeting, San Antonio, November 2004.

———. *Paul among the Postliberals: Pauline Theology beyond Christendom and Modernity*. Grand Rapids: Brazos, 2003.

———. "Paul and Israel: An Apocalyptic Reading." *Pro Ecclesia* 16:4 (2007) 359–80.

Hart, David Bentley. *The Beauty of the Infinite: The Aesthetics of Christian Truth*. Grand Rapids: Eerdmans, 2003.

Hartwich, Wolf-Daniel, et al. "Afterword." In Jacob Taubes, *The Political Theology of Paul*, edited by Aleida and Jan Assmann, translated by Dana Hollander, 115–42. Cultural Memory in the Present. Stanford: Stanford University Press, 2004.

Hauerwas, Stanley. "The State of the Secular: Theology, Prayer and the University." In *The State of the University: Academic Knowledges and the Knowledge of God*, 165–86. Illuminations: Theory and Religion. Malden, MA: Blackwell, 2007.

Hays, Richard B. *Echoes of Scripture in the Letters of Paul*. New Haven: Yale University Press, 1989.

———. *The Faith of Jesus Christ: An Investigation of the Narrative Substructure of Galatians 3:1—4:11*. 2nd ed. The Biblical Resource Series. Grand Rapids: Eerdmans, 2002.

———. *First Corinthians*. Interpretation. Louisville: John Knox, 1997.

Heidegger, Martin. *Being and Time*. Translated by John Macquarrie and Edward Robinson. New York: Harper & Row, 1962.

———. *Introduction to Metaphysics*. Translated by Ralph Manheim. New Haven: Yale University Press, 2000.

———. *Nietzsche*. Translated by David Farrell Krell. 2 vols. San Francisco: HarperCollins, 1991.

———. *The Phenomenology of Religious Life*. Translated by Matthias Fritsch and Jennifer Anna Gosetti-Ferencei. Studies in Continental Thought. Bloomington: Indiana University Press, 2004.

Hersh, Seymour M. *Chain of Command: The Road from 9/11 to Abu Ghraib*. New York: HarperCollins, 2004.

Hodge, Caroline Johnson. "Apostle to the Gentiles: Constructions of Paul's Identity." In *Paul between Jews and Christians*, edited by Mark Nanos, 270–88. *Biblical Interpretation* 13:3 (2005).

———, and Denise Kimber Buell. "The Politics of Interpretation: The Rhetoric of Race and Ethnicity in Paul," *Journal of Biblical Literature* 123:2 (2004) 233–51.

Holsclaw, Geoffrey, and D. Stephen Long, "Martyrdom as Exteriority: Politics after Bare Life." In *Witness of the Body: The Past, Present, and Future of Christian Martyrdom*, edited by Michael L. Budde and Karen Scott, n.p. Grand Rapids: Eerdmans, forthcoming 2009.

Horsley, Richard A., editor. *Paul and Empire: Religion and Power in Roman Imperial Society*. Harrisburg, PA: Trinity, 1997.

———, editor. *Paul and Politics: Ekklesia, Israel, Imperium, Interpretation: Essays in Honor of Krister Stendahl*. Harrisburg, PA: Trinity, 2000.

Hunsinger, George. *How to Read Karl Barth: The Shape of His Theology*. Oxford: Oxford University Press, 1991.

Jacobson, Eric. *The Metaphysics of the Profane: The Political Theology of Walter Benjamin and Gershom Scholem*. New York: Columbia University Press, 2003.

Jameson, Fredric. "On Interpretation." In *The Political Unconscious: Narrative as a Socially Symbolic Act*, 17–102. Ithaca, NY: Cornell University Press, 1981.

———. *Postmodernism, or, The Cultural Logic of Late Capitalism*. Post-contemporary Interventions. Durham, NC: Duke University Press, 1991.

Jennings, Theodore W., Jr. "Paul and (Post-modern) Political Thought." Paper presented to the Paul and Politics section of the SBL annual meeting, November 2003.

———. "Paul and Sons: (Post-modern) Thinkers Reading Paul." In *Reading Romans with Contemporary Philosophers and Theologians*, edited by David W. Odell-Scott,

85–114. Romans through History and Culture Series. New York: T. & T. Clark, 2007.

———. *Reading Derrida/Thinking Paul: On Justice*. Cultural Memory in the Present. Stanford: Stanford University Press, 2006.

Jewett, Robert. *Romans: A Commentary*. Hermeneia. Minneapolis: Fortress, 2007.

Justin Martyr. *First Apology*. In *The Ante-Nicene Fathers*, edited by A. J. Robertson and James Donaldson. 1:159–87. Peabody, MA: Hendrickson, 1999.

Kafka, Franz. "On Parables." In *The Basic Kafka*, translated by W. and E. Muir. New York: Simon & Schuster, 1979.

Kahl, Brigitte. *Galatians Re-Imagined: Reading with the Eyes of the Vanquished*. Paul in Critical Contexts. Minneapolis: Fortress, 2009.

Käsemann, Ernst. *An die Römer: Handbuch zum neuen Testament*. Edited by Günther Bornkamm. 3rd ed. Tübingen: Mohr/Siebeck, 1973.

Kearney, Richard. *The God Who May Be: A Hermeneutics of Religion*. Indiana Series in the Philosophy of Religion. Bloomington: Indiana University Press, 2001.

———. "Paul's Notion of *dynamis*." In *St. Paul among the Philosophers*, edited by John D. Caputo and Linda Martin Alcoff, 142–69. Indiana Series in Philosophy of Religion. Bloomington: Indiana University Press, 2009.

Kennedy, Robert P. "Book Eleven: The Confessions as Eschatological Narrative." In *A Reader's Companion to Augustine's Confessions*, edited by Kim Paffenroth and Robert P. Kennedy, 167–83. Louisville: John Knox Press, 2003.

Kierkegaard, Søren. *The Concept of Anxiety: A Simple Psychologically Orienting Deliberation on the Dogmatic Issue of Hereditary Sin*. Edited and translated by Reidar Thomte and Albert B. Anderson. Kierkegaard's Writings 8. Princeton: Princeton University Press, 1980.

———. "The Difference between a Genius and an Apostle." In *The Book on Adler*, edited and translated by Howard V. and Edna H. Hong. Kierkegaard's Writings 24. Princeton: Princeton University Press, 1998.

———. *Philosophical Fragments; Johannes Climacus*. Edited and translated by Howard V. and Edna H. Hong. Kierkegaard's Writings 7. Princeton: Princeton University Press, 1985.

———. *The Sickness unto Death: A Christian Psychological Exposition for Upbuilding and Awakening*. Edited and translated by Howard V. and Edna H. Hong. Kierkegaard's Writings 19. Princeton: Princeton University Press, 1980.

———. *Works of Love*. Edited and translated by Howard V. and Edna H. Hong. Kierkegaard's Writings 16. Princeton: Princeton University Press, 1995.

Kroeker, Travis. "Is a Messianic Political Ethic Possible?" *Journal of Religious Ethics* 33:1 (March 2005) 141–74.

———. "Whither Messianic Ethics? Paul as Political Theorist." *Journal of the Society of Christian Ethics* 25:2 (2005) 37–58.

Lacan, Jacques. *Seminar VII: The Ethics of Psychoanalysis*, translated by Dennis Porter. New York: Norton, 1986.

Lenin, Vladimir. *Essential Works of Lenin: "What Is To Be Done?" and Other Writings*. Edited by Henry M. Christman. New York: Dover, 1987.

Levering, Matthew. *Scripture and Metaphysics: Aquinas and the Renewal of Trinitarian Theology*. Challenges in Contemporary Theology. Oxford: Blackwell, 2004.

Lévinas, Emmanuel. *Alterity and Transcendence*. Translated by Michael B. Smith. European Perspectives. New York: Columbia University Press, 1999.

Liew, Tat-Siong Benny. "Margins and (Cutting-) Edges: On the (Il)legitimacy and Intersections of Race, Ethnicity, and (Post)Colonialism." In *Postcolonial Biblical Criticism: Interdisciplinary Intersections*, edited by Stephen D. Moore and Fernando F. Segovia, 224–38. The Bible and Postcolonialism. New York: T. & T. Clark, 2005.

Lindemann, A. "Die biblische Toragebote und die paulinische Ethik." In *Studien zum Text und zur Ethik des Neuen Testaments: Festschrift zum 80. Geburtstag von Heinrich Greeven*, edited by Wolfgang Schrage, 242–65. Berlin: de Gruyter, 1986.

Loisy, Alfred. *The Gospel and the Church*. Edited by Bernard B. Scott. Lives of Jesus Series. Philadelphia: Fortress, 1976.

Long, A. A., and D. N. Sedley. *The Hellenistic Philosophers*. 2 vols. Cambridge: Cambridge University Press, 1987.

Lopez, Davina C. *Apostle to the Conquered: Reimagining Paul's Mission*. Paul in Critical Contexts. Minneapolis: Fortress, 2008.

Lowe, Walter. "Is There a Postmodern Gospel?" In *The Blackwell Companion to Postmodern Theology*, edited by Graham Ward, 490–504. Blackwell Companions to Religion 4. Malden, MA: Blackwell, 2001.

———. "Prospects for a Postmodern Christian Theology: Apocalyptic without Reserve." *Modern Theology* 15 (1999) 17–24.

———. *Theology and Difference: The Wound of Reason*. The Indiana Series in the Philosophy of Religion. Bloomington: Indiana University Press, 1993.

Löwy, Michael. *Fire Alarm: Reading Walter Benjamin's "On the Concept of History."* Translated by Chris Turner. New York: Verso, 2005.

Lubac, Henri de. *Catholicism: Christ and the Common Destiny of Man*. Translated by Lancelot C. Sheppard and Elizabeth Englund. San Francisco: Ignatius, 1988.

Malherbe, A. J. "Hellenistic Moralists and the New Testament." *Aufstieg und Niedergang der römischen Welt* II.26/1 (1992) 267–333.

———. *Paul and the Popular Philosophers*. Minneapolis: Fortress, 1989.

Maritain, Jacques. "The Political Ideas of Pascal." In *Redeeming the Time*, by Jacques Maritain, translated by Harry Lorin Binsse, 29–45. London: G. Bles, 1943.

Martyn, J. Louis. "Apocalyptic Antinomies." In *Theological Issues in the Letters of Paul*, 111–24. Nashville: Abingdon, 1997.

———. "Epistemology at the Turn of the Ages." In *Theological Issues in the Letters of Paul*, 89–110. Nashville: Abingdon, 1997.

———. "Events in Galatia: Modified Covenantal Nomism versus God's Invasion of the Cosmos in the Singular Gospel: A Response to J. D. G. Dunn and B. R. Gaventa." In *Pauline Theology*, vol. 1: *Thessalonians, Philippians, Galatians, Philemon*, edited by Jouette M. Bassler, 160–79. Society of Biblical Literature Symposium Series 4. Minneapolis: Fortress, 1991.

———. *Galatians: A New Translation with Introduction and Commentary*. Anchor Bible 33A. New York: Doubleday, 1997.

———. Review of *Paul and the Hermeneutics of Faith* by Francis Watson. *Scottish Journal of Theology* 59 (2006) 427–38.

———. *Theological Issues in the Letters of Paul*. Nashville: Abingdon, 1997.

McCormack, Bruce. *Karl Barth's Critically Realistic Dialectical Theology. Its Genesis and Development, 1909–1936*. Oxford: Clarendon, 1995.

Meeks, Wayne A. *The Origins of Christian Morality: The First Two Centuries*. New Haven: Yale University Press, 1993.

Meggitt, Justin J. *Paul, Poverty and Survival.* Studies of the New Testament and Its World. Edinburgh: T. & T. Clark, 1998.

Milbank, John. *Being Reconciled: Ontology and Pardon.* London: Routledge, 2003.

———. "The Invocation of Clio: A Response." *Journal of Religious Ethics* 33 (2005) 3–44.

———. "The Sublime in Kierkegaard." In *Post-Secular Philosophy: Between Philosophy and Theology,* edited by Philip Blond, 68–81. New York: Routledge, 1998.

———. *Theology and Social Theory: Beyond Secular Reason.* Signposts in Theology. Cambridge, MA: Blackwell, 1990.

Moo, Douglas J. *The Epistle to the Romans.* New International Commentary on the New Testament. Grand Rapids: Eerdmans, 1996.

Nanos, Mark D. *The Mystery of Romans: The Jewish Context of Paul's Letter.* Minneapolis: Fortress, 1996.

Nietzsche, Friedrich Wilhelm. *The Anti-Christ.* In *The Portable Nietzsche,* edited and translated by Walter Kaufmann, 565–656. New York: Penguin, 1968. German ed.: *Der Antichrist,* in *Nietzsche Werke: Kritische Gesamtausgabe,* edited by Giorgio Colli and Montinario (Berlin: de Gruyter, 1969).

———. *Daybreak: Thoughts on the Prejudices of Morality.* Edited by Maudermarie Clark and Brian Leiter, translated by R. J. Hollingdale. Cambridge: Cambridge University Press, 1997.

———. *Ecce Homo.* In *The Anti-Christ, Ecce Homo, Twilight of the Idols, and Other Writings,* edited by Aaron Ridley and Judith Norman, translated by Judith Norman, 71–151. Cambridge Texts in the History of Philosophy. Cambridge: Cambridge University Press, 2005.

———. *The Gay Science.* In *The Portable Nietzsche,* edited and translated by Walter Kaufmann, 93–102. New York: Penguin, 1968.

———. *Thus Spoke Zarathustra.* In *The Portable Nietzsche,* edited and translated by Walter Kaufmann, 103–439. New York: Penguin, 1968.

———. *Twilight of the Idols, or, How One Philosophizes with a Hammer.* In *The Portable Nietzsche,* edited and translated by Walter Kaufmann, 463–563. New York: Penguin, 1968.

———. *Writings from the Late Notebooks.* Edited by Rüdiger Bittner, translated by Kate Sturge. Cambridge Texts in the History of Philosophy. Cambridge: Cambridge University Press, 2003.

Pascal, Blaise. *Pascal: Oeuvres complètes.* Edited by Louis Lafima. Paris: Éditions du Seuil, 1963.

Perelman, Chaïm, and Lucie Olbrechts-Tyteca. *The New Rhetoric: A Treatise on Argumentation.* Translated by John Wilkinson and Purcell Weaver. Notre Dame: University of Notre Dame Press, 1969.

Pickstock, Catherine. *After Writing: On the Liturgical Consummation of Philosophy.* Challenges in Contemporary Theology. Oxford: Blackwell, 1998.

Plato. *Phaedrus.* Translated by R. Hackforth. In *The Collected Dialogues of Plato, Including the Letters,* edited by Edith Hamilton and Huntington Cairns, 475–525. Princeton: Princeton University Press, 1963.

Price, S. R. F. *Rituals and Power: The Roman Imperial Cult in Asia Minor.* Cambridge: Cambridge University Press, 1984.

Rist, John M. *Augustine: Ancient Thought Baptized.* Cambridge: Cambridge University Press, 1994.

Robbins, Jeffrey W. "The Politics of Paul." *Journal for Cultural and Religious Theory* 6:2 (2005) 89–94.

Rosenzweig, Franz. *The Star of Redemption.* Translated by William W. Hallo. Notre Dame: University of Notre Dame Press, 1985.

Sagiv, Assaf. "George Steiner's Jewish Problem." *Azure* 5763 (Summer 2003) 144–45.

Schmitt, Carl. *The Concept of the Political.* Translated by George Schwab. Chicago: University of Chicago Press, 1996.

———. *Political Theology: Four Chapters on the Concept of Sovereignty.* Translated by George Schwab. Cambridge, MA: MIT Press, 1985.

Scholem, Gershom Gerhard. *The Messianic Idea in Judaism and Other Essays on Jewish Spirituality.* New York: Schocken, 1971.

Schwartz, Regina M. "Revelation and Revolution." *Crosscurrents* (Fall 2006) 376–82.

Sobrino, Jon. *No Salvation outside the Poor: Prophetic-Utopian Essays.* Maryknoll: Orbis, 2008.

Sonderegger, Katherine. *That Jesus Christ Was Born a Jew: Karl Barth's "Doctrine of Israel."* University Park: Pennsylvania State University Press, 1992.

Spinoza, Benedict de. *Theologico-political Treatise.* In *Chief Works,* vol. 1, translated by R. H. M. Elwes, 1–265. New York: Dover, 1951.

Starr, James, and Troels Engberg-Pedersen, editors. *Early Christian Paraenesis in Context.* Beihefte zur Zeitschrift für die neutestamentliche Wissenschaft und die Kunde der älteren Kirche 125. Berlin: de Gruyter, 2004.

Stendahl, Krister. *Final Account: Paul's Letter to the Romans.* Minneapolis: Fortress, 1995.

———. *Paul among Jews and Gentiles, and Other Essays.* Philadelphia: Fortress, 1976.

Stuhlmacher, Peter. *Paul's Letter to the Romans: A Commentary.* Translated by Scott J. Hafemann. Louisville: Westminster John Knox, 1994.

Taubes, Jacob. *Abendländische Eschatologie: Ad Jacob Taubes.* Edited by Richard Faber, Eveline Goodman-Thau, and Thomas H. Macho. Würzburg, Ger.: Königshausen & Neumann, 2001.

———. *The Political Theology of Paul.* Translated by Dana Hollander. Cultural Memory in the Present. Stanford: Stanford University Press, 2004.

Taylor, Charles. *A Secular Age.* Cambridge, MA: Belknap, 2007.

Terpstra, Marin, and Theo de Wit. "'No Spiritual Investment in the World as It Is': Jacob Taubes's Negative Political Theology." In *Flight of the Gods: Philosophical Perspectives on Negative Theology,* edited by Ilse N. Bulhof and Laurens ten Kate, 320–53. Perspectives in Continental Philosophy II. New York: Fordham University Press, 2000.

Thiselton, Anthony C. *The First Epistle to the Corinthians: A Commentary on the Greek Text.* New International Greek Testament Commentary. Grand Rapid: Eerdmans, 2000.

Vattimo, Gianni. *The End of Modernity: Nihilism and Hermeneutics in Postmodern Culture.* Translated by Jon R. Snyder. Parallax: Revisions of Culture and Society. Baltimore: Johns Hopkins University Press, 1991.

Vollenweider, Samuel. *Freiheit als neue Schöpfung: Eine Untersuchung zur Eleutheria bei Paulus und in seiner Umwelt.* Forschungen zur Religion und Literatur des Alten und Neuen Testaments 147. Göttingen: Vandenhoech & Ruprecht, 1989.

Wan, Sze-Kar. "Collection for the Saints as Anti-Colonial Act: Implications of Paul's Ethnic Reconstruction." In *Paul and Politics: Ekklesia, Israel, Imperium,*

Interpretation: Essays in Honor of Krister Stendahl, edited by Richard A. Horsley, 191–215. Philadelphia: Trinity, 2000.

Watson, Francis. *Paul and the Hermeneutics of Faith*. New York: T. & T. Clark, 2004.

Webster, John. *Barth's Ethics of Reconciliation*. Cambridge: Cambridge University Press, 1995.

Wedderburn, A. J. M. *The Reasons for Romans*. Minneapolis: Fortress, 1991.

Welborn, Lawrence. *That There May Be Equality: The Radicality of Paul's Economics in 2 Corinthians*. Minneapolis: Fortress, forthcoming 2010.

Wetzel, James. *Augustine and the Limits of Virtue*. Cambridge: Cambridge University Press, 1992.

Whittaker, C. R., and P. D. A. Garnsey, editors. *Imperialism in the Ancient World: The Cambridge University Research Seminar in Ancient History*. Cambridge Classical Studies. Cambridge: Cambridge University Press, 1978.

Wolff, Hans Walter. *Anthropology of the Old Testament*. Translated by Margaret Kohl. Mifflintown, PA: Sigler, 1996.

Wolin, Richard. *Walter Benjamin: An Aesthetic of Redemption*. New York: Columbia University Press, 1982.

Wright, N. T. *The Climax of the Covenant: Christ and the Law in Pauline Theology*. Minneapolis: Fortress, 1994.

———. "The Letter to the Romans." In *The New Interpreters Bible*, 10:393–770. Nashville: Abingdon, 2002.

———. "New Exodus, New Inheritance: The Narrative Structure of Romans 3–8." In *Romans and the People of God: Essays in Honor of Gordon D. Fee on the Occasion of His 65th Birthday*, edited by Sven K. Soderlund and N. T. Wright, 26–35. Grand Rapids: Eerdmans, 1999.

———. *The New Testament and the People of God*. Christian Origins and the Question of God 1. Minneapolis: Fortress, 1992.

———. *Paul: In Fresh Perspective*. Minneapolis: Fortress, 2005.

———. "Paul and Caesar: A New Reading of Romans." In *A Royal Priesthood?: The Use of the Bible Ethically and Politically: A Dialogue with Oliver O'Donovan*, edited by Craig Bartholomew et al., 173–93. Scripture and Hermeneutics 3. Grand Rapids: Zondervan, 2002.

———. "Paul's Gospel and Caesar's Empire." In *Paul and Politics: Ekklesia, Israel, Imperium, Interpretation: Essays in Honor of Krister Stendahl*, edited by Richard A. Horsley, 160–83. Harrisburg, PA: Trinity, 2000.

Yoder, John Howard. *The Politics of Jesus: Vicit Agnus Noster*. 2nd ed. Grand Rapids: Eerdmans, 1994.

Zanker, Paul. *The Power of Images in the Age of Augustus*. Translated by Alan Shapiro. Jerome Lectures, 16th ser. Ann Arbor: University of Michigan Press, 1988.

Zerbe, Gordon. "Constructions of Paul in Filipino Theology of Struggle." *Asia Journal of Theology* 19 (2005) 188–220.

Zerner, Ruth. "Church, State and the 'Jewish Question.'" In *The Cambridge Companion to Dietrich Bonhoeffer*, edited by John W. de Gruchy, 190–205. Cambridge: Cambridge University Press, 1999.

Žižek, Slavoj. *The Fragile Absolute, or, Why Is the Christian Legacy Worth Fighting For?* Wo es war. New York: Verso, 2000.

———. *In Defense of Lost Causes*. New York: Verso, 2008.

———. *The Puppet and the Dwarf: The Perverse Core of Christianity.* Short Circuits. Cambridge, MA: MIT Press, 2003.

———. *The Sublime Object of Ideology.* Phronesis. New York: Verso, 1989.

———. *The Ticklish Subject: The Absent Centre of Political Ontology.* Wo es war. New York: Verso, 1999.

———. *Welcome to the Desert of the Real!: Five Essays on 11 September and Related Dates.* New York: Verso, 2002.

Index of Names

Adorno, Theodor W., 261n14
Agamben, Giorgio, 1–3, 5, 7–9, 13, 47,
49, 58–60, 90, 94n8, 112n31, 120,
137, 141–42, 142n22, 143–45, 179,
179n1, 180–81, 181n2, 182–86,
186n7, 187, 187n9, 188–90, 190n11,
191, 191n14, 196–97, 198–99,
199n3, 199n5, 200–1, 201n18, 202–
3, 203n24, 204–7, 207n46, 208–10,
213–15, 215n74, 218–23, 229–30,
233, 241, 243, 243n51, 244, 244n53,
254, 254n3, 255–57, 259–61,
261n14, 262, 262–63n15–17, 263–
68, 270, 271n41, 272–73, 273n48,
275, 281, 285, 304, 304–5n51–52,
305, 305n54, 306, 306n59, 307–8,
308n64, 309–10, 312
Althusser, Louis, 140
Anselm, Saint, 219n82
Arendt, Hannah, 199n5
Aristotle, 141, 187–88n9
Assmann, Aleida, 269
Assmann, Jan, 269
Auerbach, Erich, 43n23, 191n13
Augustine, Saint, 37, 45n28, 187–88n9,
271n41
Badiou, Alain, 1–2, 5–8, 13, 39–40,
40n8, 41–43, 56–57, 64–67, 120–21,
121n3, 121n5, 122–23, 123n7,
124–29, 129–30n14–16, 130–32,
132n18, 133, 137, 137n4, 139–41,
141n19, 143–44, 146, 146n32–33,
147, 147n37, 148–49, 149n46,

150–51, 154, 155–57, 157n5, 158–
60, 160n20, 161, 164–66, 168–71,
171n52, 172, 174, 229–32, 232n13,
233, 233n17, 234n18, 236–37,
239n35, 241, 243, 243n52, 244–45,
247–48, 252, 255–56, 256n7, 257,
262, 262n17, 266, 271–72, 273n48,
276–79, 279n65, 280–81
Barclay, John, 167n40, 179n1
Barth, Karl, 9, 61, 61n78, 66, 70n21,
269, 283, 285, 296, 296n32, 297–98,
298n36, 299, 299n38, 300–1,
301n42, 302–4, 309, 311–12
Bauckham, Richard, 235, 235n20
Baur, F. C., 149
Beker, J. Christiaan, 2, 146n34, 222n90,
264, 266, 271, 271n41, 293, 293n26
Bell, Daniel M., 121n3, 123n7, 131–
32n17–18, 137
Benjamin, Walter, 1–5, 38–39, 39n4,
43–44n23, 49, 50n50, 51–54, 56n66,
58–60, 60n76, 90, 90n3, 91, 91n4,
92, 92n6, 93–94, 94n8, 95–97,
97n12–13, 98–100n17–19, 99–104,
104n22, 105–7, 109–10, 110n25,
111–12, 112n30–31, 113–15, 180,
201, 201–2n18, 202–3, 203n27–28,
204, 254, 254n3, 255, 257, 259, 261,
265, 270, 306, 306n59
Blanton, Ward, 138
Boer, Martinus C. de, 2, 20n13, 27,
27n24

Bonhoeffer, Dietrich, 8, 244n53,
    248–49, 249n73, 250, 250n76, 251,
    251n78, 252, 252n83, 253, 253n85
Bornkamm, Günther, 149n46
Boyarin, Daniel, 64–65, 119–20,
    127–28
Breton, Stanislas, 46, 56–58, 62, 67,
    149n46, 215n74
Bultmann, Rudolf, 239n37
Bush, George W., 38, 182
Butler, Judith, 161n23
Clement of Alexandria, Saint, 175
Coles, Romand, 161–62n23
Connolly, William E., 161–62n23
Constantine, 46, 173
Critchley, Simon, 231
de Wit, Theo, 269
Derrida, Jacques, 74, 74n36, 231–32,
    232n12, 233, 243, 254, 261n14
Descartes, René, 160n20
Desmond, William, 8, 209, 213,
    213n69, 215n74, 220
Dostoevsky, Fyodor, 55, 190n11
Dunn, James D.G., 136n3, 170n48,
    171n51, 235, 238–39
Dupré, Louis, 242
Eckhart, Meister, 62
Ellacuría, Ignacio, 151
Elliott, Neil, 6
Engberg-Pedersen, Troels, 119
Epictetus, 17, 17n6
Fee, Gordon, 235, 235n23
Forberg, Friedrich Carl, 261n14
Foucault, Michel, 95, 141, 190n11,
    199n5
Fowl, Stephen, 6, 179n1
Freud, Sigmund, 55, 239n35, 241n43,
    246, 247n63
Gadamer, Hans-Georg, 8, 227, 227n1,
    228–29, 229n7, 231n10, 232n12
Gaston, Lloyd, 136, 136n2, 149
Geulen, Eva, 243n51
Gignac, Alain, 137n5, 242n49, 256n7
Goethe, Johann Wolfgang von, 97n12
Gold, Joshua Robert, 270
Gorman, Michael J., 253n23
Gottwald, Norman, 144n27

Gramsci, Antonio, 140
Griffiths, Paul J., 7, 120n1, 121n5, 137,
    146n33, 305n52
Guillaume, Gustave, 202
Habermas, Jürgen, 113n33, 273n47
Hahne, Harry Alan, 210n59
Hallward, Peter, 139n13
Hansen, Ryan L., 7–8
Hanssen, Beatrice, 112n31
Harink, Douglas, 9, 15, 15n4, 124–25,
    179n1, 209, 209n56, 221, 240
Hartwich, Wolf-Daniel, 269
Hauerwas, Stanley, 282, 285n7, 297
Hays, Richard, 292, 292n25
Hegel, Georg Wilhelm Friedrich, 159,
    165, 180, 183, 261n14, 270
Heidegger, Martin, 1, 4–5, 40n8, 42, 49,
    64, 68, 72–89, 112n31, 231, 231n10,
    232–33, 233n16, 236, 261n14
Hitler, Adolf, 182, 233, 252
Hobbes, Thomas, 161, 183
Holsclaw, Geoffrey, 6–7
Horsley, Richard., 143n26
Jameson, Fredric, 140, 144n27, 151–53
Jennings, Theodore, Jr., 137n5, 147n37,
    254
Jerome, Saint, 180, 184
Jewett, Robert, 9, 285–89, 295–96, 309,
    311
Justin Martryr, Saint, 134, 175
Kafka, Franz, 61, 61n78, 192, 246
Kahl, Brigitte, 145n29
Kant, Immanuel, 56n67, 61, 261n14
Käsemann, Ernst, 2, 239, 239n37
Kearney, Richard, 234, 234n18
Kierkegaard, Søren, 4, 40n8, 43, 47,
    47n35, 48, 50n50, 52, 55–56, 71n24,
    75, 230
Klassen, Justin, 5
Kristeva, Julia, 247
Kroeker, Travis, 4, 215n74
Lacan, Jacques, 155, 160, 160n18,
    160n20, 163n27, 164, 166, 246
Lenin, Vladimir, 129n15, 272, 277, 280,
    280n68
Levinas, Emmanuel, 130n16, 230–32,
    232n12–13, 234, 243, 244n53

Loisy, Alfred, 280
Lopez, Davina C., 145n29
Lowe, Walter, 15, 283, 283n4, 298, 298n37, 300
Löwy, Michael, 203n28
Lubac, Henri de, 246
Luther, Martin, 45n28, 54, 180
Lyotard, Jean-François, 230
Mao Tse-tung, 129
Marcus, Joel, 24n19
Martyn, J. Louis, 1–2, 4, 6, 125, 209n56, 211–12, 216, 216n78, 283n4, 284, 293, 293n26, 296n32
Marx, Karl, 60, 102, 111, 139, 144, 151, 183, 254, 262n15, 280
McCormack, Bruce, 298, 298n36
Meggitt, Justin J., 147n36
Milbank, John, 66, 69–70, 70n21, 71, 71n25, 72, 72n28, 73–76, 87–88, 103
Moo, Douglas J., 169n45
Nietzsche, Friedrich Wilhelm, 4, 37, 40n8, 41–48, 48n36, 49–50, 50n50, 53–54, 54n60, 55–56, 59–60, 159, 229–30, 232, 232n14, 233, 241n44, 243
Origen, 134, 271n41, 306
Pascal, Blaise, 7, 191, 191n13
Périer, Florin., 191n13
Phaedrus, 73–74
Philo, 13, 128, 153, 153n56
Pickstock, Catherine, 73–75, 81, 83, 85–86
Poettcker, Grant, 5
Pol Pot, 129
Prodicus, 17, 17n8
Rawls, John, 273n47
Robbins, Jeffrey W., 137n5
Robespierre, Maximilien, 129
Rosenzweig, Franz, 276
Rousseau, Jean-Jacques, 183
Schmitt, Carl, 38, 91, 200, 233, 259, 269, 269n31
Scholem, Gershom Gerhard, 98–99n17, 265, 273
Schwartz, Regina M., 129
Sobrino, Jon, 151

Socrates, 73
Spinoza, Benedict de, 229, 229n9, 230, 268
Staiger, Emil, 59
Steiner, George, 246n62
Stendahl, Krister, 136n1
Stout, Jeffrey, 161–62n23
Taubes, Jacob, 1, 8, 39, 42, 49, 54–55, 58–59, 137, 229–32, 232n14, 233, 233n17, 241, 241n43–44, 243n52, 246–47, 247n63, 248, 252, 255–56, 265–66, 268, 268n28, 269, 269n31, 270–71, 271n39, 271n41, 272, 279, 281
Taylor, Charles, 187n9, 242, 273n47
Terpstra, Marin, 269
Tertullian, 134
Thiselton, Anthony C., 119
Thomas Aquinas, Saint, 212–13n67
Troeltsch, Ernst, 285n7
Trudeau, Pierre, 38
Vattimo, Gianni, 219
Weber, Max, 60, 70, 88, 261n14
Welborn, Lawrence, 147n36
Wolff, Hans Walter, 214n72
Wolin, Richard, 97n13, 99–100n18
Wright, N.T., 9, 167–68, 212n63, 221n86, 235, 237n28, 240, 253, 285, 289, 289n16–17, 290–91, 291n21, 292–93, 293n26, 294, 294n30, 295–96, 304, 307, 309, 311
Yoder, John Howard, 58n70, 271, 271n40
Zerbe, Gordon, 8–9
Zerner, Ruth, 252n83
Zimmermann, Jens, 8
Žižek, Slavoj, 1–2, 3n3, 6–7, 9, 92n6, 120, 137, 155, 161, 161n23, 162–63, 163n27, 164–65, 165n38, 166, 168–71, 171n52, 172, 174, 229–30, 239n35, 243, 247, 247n64, 248, 252, 254n3, 255–56, 256n7, 257, 266, 271–73, 273n47–48, 274, 274n52, 275–76, 279n65, 281
Zohn, Harry, 91n4, 93n7

Index of Subject Keywords

Abraham, 6, 127–28, 133–34, 238,
    290–92, 294, 294–95n30
Adam, 52, 165, 235
advocacy, 75, 192, 194–95, 197
agapē, 52, 130–31, 215n74, 270, 278
Antichrist, 39, 52, 80–82, 87
antinomy, 211–12, 214, 216–17
antiphilosopher, antiphilosophy, 1,
    122, 136, 137n4, 150
anxiety, 5, 68, 75, 84–86, 88–89
apocalypse, 2, 9, 32, 53, 56, 99–100n18,
    109, 111, 125, 209, 212–14,
    216–17, 219–21, 221n86, 222,
    260, 265, 300
apocalypsed, 4, 199, 209, 209n56, 211,
apocalyptic, Pauline apocalyptic, 1–4,
    6–9, 13–14, 14nn.2–3, 27,
    27n24, 28–29, 32n30, 38, 43,
    46–47, 51, 54, 60–61n76, 90–91,
    92n6, 94, 109, 125, 125n12,
    126–28, 136, 147–48, 153, 198–
    99, 208–12, 212n63, 213–16,
    216n78, 217–18, 218n81, 219–
    21, 221n88, 222, 222n90, 223,
    240, 260, 266, 269, 271, 271n39,
    273, 278, 283–85, 288, 293, 293–
    94n26, 294–96, 296n32, 298–99,
    303–4, 308n64, 310–12
    theology, 9, 14, 136, 221, 293
apocalypticism, 95, 154, 209, 271n41,
    276
apokalypsis, 2, 300
    Theou, 2, 4, 9, 283, 288, 290, 294,
    300, 302, 305

assent, 14, 24, 32, 87, 238
Aufhebung, 254–55, 263–64, 296, 299,
    301
authenticity, 72–73; *see also*
    inauthenticity

Barnabas, 21
beauty, 49n42, 76, 88, 186
becoming, 39–40, 40n8, 41–42, 45,
    47–51, 51n51, 52–56, 61, 63, 78,
    233n16, 298
Begründung, 296, 299, 301
Benjaminian, 92n6, 93, 99–100n18,
    114, 199, 202
biopolitics, 141, 181, 183, 185, 188,
    199, 257–58, 258n10
biopower, 142–45, 147
bios (political life), 181–83, 185, 189,
    199–200
body of Christ, *see* Christ, body of

capitalism, 121–22, 137, 138n8, 139–
    41, 152, 155, 162, 172, 262n15
Catholicism, 96, 100, 100n19, 103
causality, 42, 43n23, 44–45, 45n28,
    52–53, 55–56, 112, 293
choose, 17–20, 23, 25–26
Christ
    body of, 31, 46, 144, 238, 249–52
    resurrection of, 7, 109, 125, 127,
    130, 134, 150, 158, 169, 171,
    239, 250, 290, 295, 299, 312; *see
    also* resurrection

Christendom, 38–39, 46–48, 54–55,
138, 256, 261n14, 281, 296
Christology, 230, 234–35, 235n20,
237n28, 239, 239n37, 241, 245–
46, 248–50, 251n78, 252, 266
chronos, chronoi, 59, 62, 203–4,
204n30, 305–6, 308, 308n64,
309
circumcision, 21–25, 30, 109–10, 213
citizen, citizenship, 8, 103, 144, 154,
181–82, 189–91, 196–97, 200,
207–8, 220, 267–68
communion with God (with
Christ), 240, 242, 248–49
communist, 139–40, 265, 274n52, 280,
280n68
"Communist hypothesis," 139–40
community, the church as, 31, 137, 172,
184–85, 188, 238–39, 248–52,
256, 260, 280; *see also* messianic
community
community-destroying Desire of the
Flesh, 24–25
consequentialism, consequentialist,
191–96
contextualization, 9, 14, 22, 56–57n67,
284, 287, 309
contextualize, contextualizing, 15,
15n4, 22, 221, 272, 282, 284,
286, 291, 295, 297, 299–300, 303
Corinthians, Letters to the, 5, 13–14,
21, 23, 31–32, 32n30, 37, 39,
41–43, 46–47, 49, 52–53, 56–60,
61n78, 62, 79, 107n23, 115,
122, 131–32, 146, 146n30, 147,
149–50, 152–54, 165, 168–69,
169n46, 175, 184, 202, 205, 210,
213–14, 216–18, 220, 238n32,
239n35, 244n53, 250n74, 260–
61, 261n14, 263–64, 266–67,
275, 304n51, 305, 307
1 Cor 7, 13, 58–60, 61n78, 62, 115,
132, 153–54, 184, 202, 205, 213,
216, 244n53, 260, 266–67, 275,
305
cosmic-historical narrative/drama,
290–91, 295, 302, 311

cross/*stauros*, 1, 5–6, 24n18, 29–30, 32,
41–42, 45–48, 51, 56–58, 67,
123, 125, 145, 150, 159, 166–67,
171, 190, 219, 222, 233n17, 241,
244, 279, 286, 293, 293–94n26
word of the, 1, 5, 32, 57
crucifixion, 2, 4, 7, 29–31, 43, 46,
54, 123n7, 127, 144–45, 147,
147n37, 235–36, 240, 295, 299,
308n64, 312

David, 290, 292
death, 2, 4, 7, 16, 18, 24–25, 29–30, 41,
46, 49, 55, 58–59, 67–68, 74–76,
83–88, 98, 99n18, 107n23, 109,
123, 123n7, 124, 127, 130–31,
131n17, 133–34, 141–42, 145–
46, 146n30, 147, 155, 158–66,
168–71, 171n51, 172, 174–75,
190, 207, 211, 212n63, 219, 235,
237, 237n28, 238–40, 246, 250,
279, 290, 293–94n26, 297, 304,
309
by crucifixion of the cosmos, 4, 30,
210, 218n81, 240
decide, 17, 38, 141, 200
despair, 80, 82–83, 86–87
Deuteronomy, 18–21
dialectic, dialectical, 9, 54, 90n3, 158–
59, 164, 166, 180, 183–84, 188–
90, 208, 211, 215–16, 216n78,
296n32, 298, 298n36, 310, 312
image, 90, 90n3
materialism, 139, 255
Dionysian, 42, 45, 47–49, 51, 233
divine, 2–5, 14, 18–20, 27, 32n30,
41–43, 43n23, 44, 46–50, 52,
54–59, 61n78, 62, 66, 82, 88, 91,
96–97, 99–100n18, 103, 104n22,
106, 108–9, 110n26, 114, 137,
144–45, 148, 153, 153–54n56,
158, 160, 221n86, 235n20, 238,
242, 244–46, 252, 274, 286–87,
290–91, 293, 307, 311–12
drama, 290, 292, 295, 302
violence, 101, 103, 106, 109–10,
110nn25–26, 111–12, 114

dual agency, 28, 28nn25–26, 29–32
    and the cross, 29–30
    of the community, 31–32

ecclesia, ecclesial, 8–9, 100n19, 137n5,
    138, 251n78, 254, 256–57, 259–60,
    261n14, 264, 266, 268–71, 271n40,
    271–72n41, 272–73, 276–77, 279,
    289n17
Elijah, 173
election, 59, 96, 122, 126, 158, 263, 270,
    302
epistemology, 13–14, 74, 216
Esau, 301
ethics, 17, 38, 61, 75, 222, 229n9, 230,
    231, 232n13, 241, 243, 248, 252,
    261n14
    relationship with ontology, 231, 232n12,
    241, 243, 248, 252–53; *see also*
    ontology
euangelion, 1, 14–15, 184, 235, 267
Eve, 46
event, evental (Badiou), 1–2, 7, 39–42,
    65–66, 109, 121, 121nn4–5,
    122–24, 126–29, 129n14, 130–31,
    133, 146, 146n32, 148, 150–51,
    156–61, 164, 166, 171–72, 174,
    233, 233n17, 236–37, 241, 243–45,
    245n57, 252, 276, 276n63, 277–79;
    see also messianic event
Ezekiel, 168

faith, 1, 5, 25, 29, 32, 32n30, 33, 46,
    48–49, 58, 67–70, 72, 75, 87–88,
    130, 213n70, 238, 242–44, 249n73,
    250, 252, 264, 270, 284, 303;
    see also new humanity, faith as
    participation in
faithful, the, 277–78, 280–81
"false brothers," 21, 23
fate, 19, 98, 98–99nn.17–18, 105–6,
    247n63
flesh, 24–28, 43, 46, 52, 67, 103, 109,
    115, 128, 170n48, 210–12, 214,
    214nn71–72, 215, 218, 218n81,
    267, 279, 298, 301, 309
"form of this world," 13, 115

Freudian, 165, 241–42, 246–47
fruit borne by the Spirit, *see* Spirit, fruit
    borne by

Galatian(s) (the people/church), 22–30,
    103, 211, 216n78, 240, 277
Galatians, Letter to the, 21–22, 23n17,
    24–31, 54, 62, 64, 103, 111,
    121, 126, 128, 132–33, 146n30,
    148–49, 169, 169n46, 210–11,
    212n65, 213, 213n70, 218n81,
    222, 238n32, 240, 250n74, 261,
    267, 284, 292
    5:13–25, 24–28, 28n26, 29, 31
gnostic, Gnosticism, 42, 76, 90–91,
    99–100n18, 237, 271n39,
    271–72n41
gospel, the, 1, 14–15, 15n4, 16, 21–23,
    25–27, 31–32, 32n30, 33, 126,
    148, 167, 209, 211, 220, 235,
    237, 237n30, 239–40, 245, 247,
    282–83, 283n3, 284–87, 290,
    295–97, 299–304, 306–7, 310;
    see also Paul's gospel
    generative power of, 32
    invasive meeting with
        philosophy, 14–16, 26, 28
    truth of, 22, 25
Greek
    discourse, 65, 122–23, 148
    Market Place, 15, 21

Hegelian, 159, 184, 203n28, 255
hermeneutic(s), hermeneutical, 8,
    27n23, 43n23, 63, 114, 227,
    227n1, 228–32, 234, 234n18,
    242, 245–47, 253, 288; *see also*
    interpretation
historical-critical, 9, 76–77, 79, 198,
    286–89, 289n16, 299–300
historical
    criticism, 285, 288
    materialist, materialism, 3, 53, 92–
        93, 95, 100, 102, 110, 112–14,
        255, 257, 272
historically effected
    consciousness, 227–30, 241–42,
    245

historicism, 5, 39, 71–72, 74–75, 98n15,
   112–13, 288, 293, 300, 312
historicist, 9, 52, 71, 91, 97n13, 111–12,
   112n30, 113, 175, 255, 285,
   285n7, 288–89, 306, 309, 311
Holy Spirit, *see* Spirit, Holy
hope, 5, 62, 68–69, 76, 78–80, 82,
   86, 89, 147, 173, 197, 214n72,
   222n90, 237n30, 238, 247n64,
   256, 259–60, 265, 271–72n41,
   273, 278, 302
human
   autonomy, 19–20, 29, 170
   responsibility, 72, 108, 231, 234,
   276
humanity, the new, *see* new humanity

identity, 9, 18, 40–41, 56–57, 59–60,
   71n25, 81, 105, 110, 114, 120,
   126, 128–29, 132, 149, 156,
   161, 169, 172, 188–89, 205,
   230, 235n20, 244, 244n53, 246,
   250n76, 258, 259, 261–62, 266–
   68, 270, 278, 281
ideological, 6, 136, 140–41, 143–45,
   145n29, 146, 151–54, 163, 274,
   288
   constraint, 143, 144n27, 152–53
ideology, 146–47, 150–54, 173, 190,
   288, 297
imago Dei, 251
immanence, 8, 48–49, 67, 73, 115, 159,
   208–14, 214–15nn.72–74, 215–
   16, 216n78, 217–18, 218n81,
   219, 222, 230, 234, 236, 239,
   241, 241n44, 243, 245, 247; *see
   also* transcendence
immanent, immanentist, 8, 43, 45, 49,
   51, 53–54, 66–67, 69–70, 70n21,
   88, 92n6, 93, 95, 98–99, 99n18,
   101, 106, 111, 114, 123, 159,
   169, 198–99, 208–12, 212n66,
   213, 213n69, 214n71, 215,
   215n73, 216, 216n78, 217–20,
   222, 229n9, 231, 232n14, 241,
   241n44, 265n22, 270, 274,
   274n52, 308n64

inauthenticity, 73, 85–86; *see also*
   authenticity
incarnation, 8, 229–30, 232, 234–35,
   235–36n23, 236–37, 237n28,
   239–42, 244–48, 250, 251n78,
   251n81, 252–53; *see also*
   participation in Christ
interpretation, 2, 4, 15n5, 24,
   43–44n23, 53, 55, 58, 91, 98–
   99nn.17–18, 128, 148, 151–52,
   184, 199, 227–30, 232, 233n17,
   240–42, 247, 247n63, 252, 254,
   261n14, 265, 271n39, 285,
   285n7, 286–89, 291–93, 293n26,
   294n30, 295, 306–7, 310; *see also*
   hermeneutic(s)
indifference to differences, 123, 129–30,
   130n16, 131–33
Isaac, 294–95n30, 307–8
Israel, 6, 18, 18n9, 19, 30, 58–59, 126–
   28, 132, 134, 137, 144n27, 153,
   170, 172–73, 175, 235, 238, 263,
   270, 278, 281, 283–84, 290–91,
   291n21, 293–95, 294–95n30,
   300–301, 301n42, 302, 304,
   306–7, 308n64, 309

Jacob, 294–95n30, 301, 307–8
Jeremiah, 168
Jerusalem church, 21–23
Jewish discourse, 65, 122–23, 126, 148
John the Baptist, 173
Judaism, 4, 126–28, 148–49, 165, 237,
   273, 287, 290–91
juridical, 38–40, 47–48, 56n66, 60, 106,
   108, 182–85, 189–90, 197, 205,
   205n34, 261, 266–67
justice, 91–92, 104, 106, 108–9, 120,
   167, 212, 216, 219, 228–29,
   232–33, 243, 248, 263, 266–68,
   278, 283, 291, 295–97, 299–300,
   308n64
justification, 51n51, 67, 136n2, 239, 302

kairos, nun kairos, 59, 62, 153, 185–87,
   191, 203–4, 204n30, 217, 283,
   305–6, 308, 308n64, 309

katargēsis, 43, 46, 47n35, 52, 54, 263
kenosis, kenotic, 47, 47n35, 49, 49n42,
    57, 61–63
Kierkegaardian skepticism, 76, 86, 88

Lacanian, 160n20, 165–66, 246–47,
    273, 273n48, 274
Law, 7, 18–19, 23–25, 29–30, 58, 191,
    212n65
law, 7, 39–41, 43, 46–47, 47n35, 51, 54,
    58, 63, 103, 107n23, 108–11,
    115, 121–24, 129–30, 140,
    149–50, 153–60, 160n20, 161,
    164–66, 168, 170n48, 171, 174,
    180, 185, 188, 205–7, 210–13,
    215–16, 233n17, 245, 257, 269,
    282, 294–95n30, 301, 307, 309
  Greek, 156, 158, 160
  Jewish, 22, 111, 148–49, 156,
    158–60
  Mosaic, 103, 107, 107–8nn23–24,
    108–10
  Sinaitic, 18–19, 23–24
  social, political, 38, 91, 103–8,
    108n24, 109–10, 110n26, 114–
    15, 141–42, 145, 161–63, 170,
    172, 174, 180–84, 189, 192, 196,
    199–201, 206–7, 219, 233, 243,
    243n51, 245, 257, 257n11, 259,
    262nn15–16, 263–64, 266, 270,
    278, 280
  of the Spirit, 211–13
  symbolic, 160n18, 162–64, 166,
    171–72, 174
love, 7, 19, 25, 28–31, 38, 47, 47–48n35,
    49, 49n42, 50–51, 57, 59–60,
    60–61n76, 62–63, 75, 88, 97,
    97n12, 98–99, 101, 124, 129–31,
    134, 156, 160, 165, 187–88,
    209, 213, 213n70, 214, 222n90,
    237, 237n28, 241, 245n57, 246,
    249, 249n70, 259, 263–64, 268,
    270, 270n35, 275, 276n63, 278,
    281–82, 303–4, 309

martyr, martyrdom, 42, 48, 55, 59, 151,
    171, 195
Marxism, 140, 183, 189, 280

Marxist, Marxian, 5–6, 53, 94, 137–40,
    144, 144n27, 151–52, 179, 184,
    242–43, 247–48, 253, 256, 265,
    272, 274
mastery, 4, 39–41, 53, 56, 65, 67, 101,
    148, 277–79
materialism, 123, 234, 243, 247; *see
    also* dialectical materialism;
    historical materialist
Messiah, messiah, 1–2, 4–6, 10, 39,
    40n8, 42, 43–44n23, 46–49,
    51–54, 56–61, 91, 100–102, 115,
    134, 137, 150, 152, 168–69, 184–
    85, 197–99, 209, 221–22, 234,
    236–37, 238n34, 239–41, 244,
    248, 258–59, 265, 267–68, 270,
    273, 276, 284, 290, 293–94n26,
    294, 294–95n30, 304–5, 305n54,
    306–8, 308n64, 309–10, 312
messianic, 2–6, 8–9, 37–40, 40n8,
    41–43, 43–44n23, 46–47, 47n35,
    48–50, 50n50, 51–62, 90–92,
    92n6, 94, 98–100nn17–19,
    100–102, 105, 109–13, 115, 128,
    168, 184, 188, 190–91, 199, 201,
    201–2n18, 202–4, 204n30, 205,
    205n34, 206–9, 213–14, 215n74,
    218–19, 222, 232–33, 237, 241,
    243–44, 244n53, 248, 254–55n3,
    256–58, 258n10, 259–61, 261–
    62nn14–16, 262–71, 271n39,
    273, 279, 279n65, 280–81, 284–
    85, 289, 292, 294, 294–95n30,
    305, 305n54, 306, 306n59, 307,
    308n64, 309–12
  agent, agency, 5, 62, 112, 305, 312
  apocalypse, 2–3, 9, 56, 91, 99–
    100n18, 109, 276, 304, 310–11
  community, 2, 4–5, 10, 59, 115, 167,
    191, 256, 258–62, 262nn15–16,
    263–64, 266, 270–71, 271n41,
    272, 278, 281
  event, 1, 9, 39, 42, 60, 204n30, 205,
    212n63, 221, 244, 259, 263,
    293–94n26, 306
  time, 39, 53, 59, 61–62, 113, 185,
    187, 198, 201–5, 207, 207n46,

260, 262–63n17, 263–65, 304–5,
305n52, 306, 306n59, 307–8,
308n64, 309–10, 312
messianism, 2, 4, 38–39, 42, 47, 55,
56–57n67, 109, 235, 248, 254n3,
257, 258n11, 259–60, 265, 268,
272–73, 276, 280
meta-suspicion, 69–70
metaphysics, 8, 199, 208–9, 209n53,
212n66, 215, 215n74, 216,
216n78, 217, 219, 221n88, 222
metaxological, 8, 209, 213, 213n69,
215nn73–74, 216, 216n78, 217,
218n81, 219, 221n88
moral
competence, 17, 25–26
drama
militant, apocalyptic, three-
actor, 4, 26–27, 27n24,
28–29, 32n30
Sinaitic form of, 21–26, 30
irresponsibility, 19
Mosaic law, *see* law, Mosaic
Moses, 18, 39, 53, 58, 129, 216–17, 292,
294–95n30
Musselmann, Musselmänner, 142
myth, 60–61n76, 97, 97n13, 98–100,
105, 108–15, 212–13n67
mythic violence, 5, 106, 109, 115

negative political theology, 259, 268–69
new
creation, 2, 6, 30–33, 56, 165, 188,
199, 205, 210–14, 216, 218,
218n81, 219–22, 236, 240,
244n53, 248, 293
humanity, 139, 236, 248–51,
251n78, 252, 298n36.
faith as participation in, 238, 242,
244, 250
moral agent, 28–29, 31
New Perspective (on Paul), 136, 136n3,
148, 291
Nietzschean, 55, 71, 159, 209n53, 279,
279n65
nihilism, 5, 42, 45, 68, 73, 81, 88, 266,
269

now-time (*Jetztzeit*), 5, 50, 53, 59, 113,
191, 201, 201, 207, 301, 306,
306n59, 307, 308n64, 310

Onesimus, 261, 267
ontology, 46, 66, 72, 156, 169, 216, 220,
229n9, 231–32, 236, 240–41,
243, 250

parable, parabolic, 2, 51, 51n51, 52,
54–55, 61, 61–62n78, 62–63,
303–4
participation in Christ (God), the
divine, the incarnation, 8,
29–30, 166, 169, 169n45, 171,
229, 234–38, 238–39nn34–35,
239–40, 242, 244, 248–49,
249n73, 250–53, 308
Pauline
Christianity, 44–45, 221n88,
244n53, 253, 272
gospel, Paul's gospel, 4, 22–23, 28,
32, 39, 57, 122, 126, 136, 139,
151–52, 209, 220–21, 221n86,
235–37, 240–41, 245–47, 283,
283n3, 286, 288, 295, 299, 306,
311–12; *see also* gospel
language, 6, 107n23, 110, 126, 185,
189, 201, 213
theology, 155, 198–99, 233n17, 234,
238–39, 248, 253
peace, 5, 25, 28–31, 68, 72, 78, 83, 89,
137, 173, 222, 267–68, 298,
308n64
Peter, 22
Philemon, 267
Philippians, Letter to the, 30, 49, 126,
130–31, 145, 154, 171, 210,
219n82, 220, 235n23, 237n28,
267, 308n64
philosophical
curriculum, 13
logos, 123, 150–51, 158
readings (of Paul), 8, 13, 42, 55, 64,
67, 137n5, 198, 227–30, 232,
234, 236, 240–42, 245, 248–49,
253, 256, 268, 281, 304

philosophy, 1–4, 7–9, 14–15, 17, 19,
    21–22, 26, 28, 31–32, 37–39,
    42, 70n21, 73–75, 77, 90, 94,
    112n31, 119, 120n1, 155–56,
    174, 179, 199n2, 202, 203n28,
    209, 229–31, 231n10, 232–33,
    236, 242–43, 245, 250, 253, 305
    Continental, 8, 229–30, 232–33,
    242–43, 250
Pilate, 44
pneuma, -tikos, -tos, pneumatic, 26–27,
    42–43, 46–48, 270, 271n39
pneumatology, pneumatological, 239,
    239n37, 312
political
    interest, 7, 191–92, 194–96
    theology, 37, 39, 42, 47–48, 58,
    58n70, 59, 259, 268–69, 269n31
    unconscious, 152
politics, 5, 7–8, 38–40, 42, 52–53, 57–
    59, 65, 75, 90–92, 92n6, 93–96,
    99–100, 100n19, 101, 103, 106,
    108, 111, 114, 120–21, 127, 129,
    140–41, 143–44, 149, 151, 155,
    157n5, 160n20, 161–62n23,
    162, 166, 169, 172–74, 179–80,
    183, 189, 191, 195–96, 198–201,
    201–2n18, 204, 206–9, 213–14,
    215n73, 218–20, 222–23, 230,
    236, 243, 245n57, 248, 253, 257,
    258n11, 261n14, 267, 271, 273,
    276n63, 279n65, 282, 285, 289
progress, progressivism,
    progressivist, 5, 9, 17, 29,
    38–40, 51–53, 56–57n67, 60–61,
    60–61n76, 91–93, 126, 129n14,
    153, 203–4, 206–7, 207n46, 209,
    219, 256, 256n22, 289, 292–93,
    293–94n26, 295, 297, 300, 302,
    306, 312

quietism, 90, 154, 191, 191n12, 192–95,
    197, 269

Radical Orthodoxy, 5, 66, 66n9, 67–68,
    70n21, 73, 75, 82, 86–88
rationalism, 300

recapitulate, recapitulation, 63, 180,
    188, 207, 251, 254, 260, 263,
    290, 306, 308–10, 312
remnant, part/all, 59, 62, 91, 100n19,
    182, 191, 202–3, 206–8, 241,
    256, 260, 262–63, 262–63n17,
    264, 275, 279, 295, 301
repetition, 52, 71, 75–76, 86, 205n34,
    296n32
resurrection, 2, 4–7, 40, 42, 44–46,
    56–57, 65–67, 109, 122–23,
    125–27, 130–31, 133–35, 137,
    146–48, 147–48n37, 150–51,
    154–55, 158–60, 164–66, 168–
    75, 190, 212n63, 219, 236–41,
    244–45, 250, 264–65, 278–79,
    290, 293–94n26, 295, 299, 304,
    308n64, 312
revolution, revolutionary, 6, 60, 64,
    66, 91–92, 102–4, 104n22, 105,
    110–14, 139, 155, 166, 170, 179,
    181, 195, 203–4, 233n17, 236,
    243, 248, 259, 262n15, 269,
    270n35, 273–74, 274n52, 275–
    76, 279, 280n68, 296, 303–4
rhetorical theology, 5, 88–89
rights, 56–57n67, 60–61, 156, 181,
    189–90, 200, 217, 243n51, 254,
    259, 262, 266
Roman Empire, 6, 143–45, 150–52,
    167, 268, 287
Romans, Letter to the, 6–7, 9, 20, 22,
    32, 32n30, 43, 46–47, 52, 54,
    59, 63, 103, 107–8nn23–24,
    109–10, 115, 122n6, 124–26,
    130, 132, 136n1, 137n5, 152–53,
    154n58, 155, 158–59, 160n18,
    166–70, 171n52, 179–80, 184,
    201–2, 205–6, 209–10, 212n65,
    214, 218, 222, 237n28, 237n30,
    238, 238n34, 239n35, 250n74,
    258n10, 261, 263, 267–68,
    268n26, 269–70, 271–72n41,
    278, 282–83, 283n3, 284–93,
    294n30, 294–95n30, 295–97,
    299–301, 304, 304n51, 305–8,
    308n64, 309–12

ch. 6, 7, 155, 159, 166–70, 171n52,
214, 238, 261, 267
ch. 7, 6–7, 46–47, 54, 107–8nn23–
24, 155, 158, 160n18, 166–68,
170, 205–6, 210, 212n65

salvation history, historical, 9, 169n45,
170, 266, 271n41, 292, 295–97,
299–300, 302–3, 309, 311
secular reason, 66–68, 73, 75–76, 86–88
security, 5, 68, 74, 78–80, 83–87, 89,
281, 298
Self, the, 49, 80, 83, 87–88, 130, 159,
168, 215n74, 218, 231–32,
232n14, 233–34, 239n37, 243,
246, 250–51
servant/slave, 29, 47–48, 52, 57, 60–61,
124, 128, 132–34, 144–45, 147–
48, 150, 159, 168, 170–72, 175,
182, 184–86, 197, 210, 261, 267
sestina, 186, 186n7, 188, 207, 207nn45–
46, 305n52
sin, 2, 4, 27, 29, 46, 73, 109, 124,
131n17, 132–33, 159–60,
160n18, 166, 168, 170, 170n48,
171, 210–11, 217, 219, 233n17,
235, 252, 309
Sirach, two separate steps in, 18–20
sovereignty, 4–5, 37–39, 42, 45, 48, 53,
55–57, 143, 179, 181, 189, 191,
199–200, 215n73, 257, 266,
268–69, 271n41
Spirit, 2, 4, 6, 25–29, 31, 43, 46, 74, 79,
109, 126, 152, 168, 173, 175,
210–14, 214n72, 215, 217–18,
218n81, 219, 237n30, 238–
39nn34–35, 240–41, 244, 246,
248–49, 249n73, 252, 284, 299
fruit borne by, 25–27, 29
Holy, 1–2, 42–43, 78, 125, 134, 240,
247n64, 249, 274, 274n52
state of exception, 142, 181–83, 185,
189–90, 197, 201, 204, 206, 208,
219, 257, 263
subject, the (human), 1–2, 7–8, 39–40,
40n8, 41, 61, 65, 73, 92, 95–96,
98, 104, 106–9, 111, 113, 115,

121, 124, 126–27, 155–56, 158,
160, 160n20, 161–64, 170–73,
198, 200–201, 206–7, 230–31,
231n10, 233, 233n17, 236–37,
240–45, 245n57, 250, 258n10,
261, 274–75, 277–79, 300, 305,
308n64
subjectivity, 41, 56, 64, 120–21, 126–27,
129, 147, 155–56, 164–66, 170–
72, 174–75, 231n10, 234, 237,
243, 246, 256, 260, 274, 279, 281
sublime, the, 75–76, 83, 86, 88, 234, 300
supra-human powers, 26–28
symbolic law, *see* law, symbolic
symbolic order, 7, 161–65, 246

telos, telic, 51, 124, 187, 263–65, 280–
81, 294–95n30, 295
theological
event, 284, 288, 299, 303
exegesis/interpretation, 286–89
Thessalonian(s) (the people/
church), 76–81, 85, 87
Thessalonians, Letters to the, 5, 40n8,
47, 49, 64, 68, 76, 78nn50–51,
80, 80n59, 80n63, 81n65, 89,
89n86, 183, 214, 222, 267
time, 9, 32, 49–51, 51n51, 51n53, 52–
53, 56–57, 59, 62–63, 73–74, 76,
81–83, 87–88, 93, 95, 98, 99n18,
113, 132, 153–54, 185–87, 187–
88n9, 188, 198, 202–4, 204n30,
205–8, 211, 216n77, 220–21,
232n12, 260, 264–65, 276,
282–85, 287–90, 294–99, 303–5,
305n52, 305n54, 306–8, 308n64,
309–12; *see also* messianic time;
now-time
of the gospel, 282–85, 288, 299,
301–4, 310
of legibility, 254–55n3, 257, 306,
306n59, 310
torture, 142, 142n22
transcendence, 8, 42, 48–49, 67, 73,
103–4, 122, 159, 209, 212,
212nn66–67, 213, 213n69,
214–15, 215nn73–74, 217–18,

transcendence (*continued*)
229–31, 231n10, 232–34, 236,
239, 241–43, 245, 250
truth procedure, 41, 120, 123–24, 154,
157, 256, 276, 278
two ways
in pagan moral literature, 16–17
in the works of the Jewish
sages, 18–20
typology, typological, 8, 43n23, 62, 256,
290–91, 291n21, 292, 304, 307,
308n64, 309–10, 312

universal, universalism,
universality, 6–7, 9, 16, 19, 26,
30–31, 40, 40n8, 41, 58, 61,
63–67, 90–92, 102, 106, 119–21,
121n5, 122–25, 128–31, 132n18,
133, 136, 140–41, 143, 147–49,
151, 158, 161, 169, 172–73,
175, 183, 189, 207n26, 230,
232, 233n17, 234, 236–37, 239,
241, 245, 245n57, 246, 248–50,
252–53, 256, 262, 262–63n17,
264, 267, 270, 273nn47–48,
275–78, 281
relation of the particular with, 63–
64, 66–67, 122–25, 127, 132,
140, 161, 172, 175, 230–32, 237,
241, 245, 245n57, 246, 253, 277
union of the personal with, 239–41,
244–46, 251
univocity, 8, 125, 132, 208, 211–13,
213n69, 215–16, 216n78
Untergang/Untergangen, 49, 51–52
utopia, utopian, 151–52, 179, 195, 256–
57, 265, 272, 274, 274n52, 280

vanguard, vanguardism, 9, 155, 262,
262n15, 272–73, 275, 280–81
vice and virtue, 16–17, 19, 30
violence, 5, 46, 55, 56n66, 72, 101, 103–
7, 109–10, 110nn25–26, 111–12,
114–15, 165, 171, 208, 257, 275
vocation, re-vocation, calling, 9, 40, 60,
62, 115, 184–85, 187, 190–91,

197, 204–5, 205n34, 206–8,
257–61, 262n15, 263–64, 266–
67, 271–72n41, 274n52, 281

wager, 67, 71–72, 72n28, 87, 310

Zarathustra, 47, 49–50
zōē (nonpolitical life), 181–84, 189,
199–200